CARFREE DESIGN MANUAL

Salizzada San Rocco, Venice

CARFREE DESIGN MANUAL

J.H. CRAWFORD

FOREWORD
STAVROS DIMAS

UTRECHT

INTERNATIONAL BOOKS

2009

Dedicated to everyone working
to make carfree cities
a reality.

Also by J.H. Crawford
Carfree Cities (2000)

Colophon
Typeset by J.H. Crawford
Cover by Karel Oosting
Body text: Monotype Bembo
Marginalia: Helvetica Light
Printed in the Netherlands by
Drukkerij C. Haasbeek BV on
Symbol Freelife 100% recycled paper

J.H. Crawford
www.carfree.com
mailbox@carfree.com

Notices
Published by
International Books
Grifthoek 151
3514 JK Utrecht
The Netherlands
+31 30 273 1840
fax +31 30 273 3614
E-mail: i-books@antenna.nl
First hardcover edition May 2009
2009 2010 2011   ISBN 9789057270604   6 5 4 3 2 1

CONTENTS

PART I
THEORY

PART II
PREPARATION

PART III
ELEMENTS

PART IV
DESIGN

Appendices

FOREWORD BY STAVROS DIMAS

Imagine a city of a million, completely free of cars and trucks. The longest commute is 35 minutes door-to-door aboard an advanced metro. J.H. Crawford demonstrated the feasibility of this plan in his earlier book, *Carfree Cities,* and once urban design is no longer constrained by the need for cars, a new and better future becomes possible. In *Carfree Design Manual,* Crawford sets himself the task of designing a carfree neighbourhood so practical, satisfying, and attractive that "people will clamour for it."

It is clear from this book that we can learn much from ancient city design, starting with the Acropolis, the organic city of Erbil, and the fine design of early public spaces. People also love medieval cities because of their irregular pattern, enclosed spaces, cosy streets, and lively squares. Crawford shows that beneath the superficial disorder lies a deeper organization that people still recognize and value today.

After considering the special requirements of carfree infrastructure at the neighbourhood level, Crawford proposes a democratic process where residents can play a key role in the design of their own neighbourhood. This brings local knowledge to the job of designing urban areas that respect the character of the site and the needs of the people who will use it. This is the real innovation of the book: a design process that can deliver neighbourhoods finely tuned to the needs of their residents and which allows people to follow their own visions to sustainability.

Many visions of a sustainable future have people living in low density rural environments. But today's reality is that most Europeans and North Americans live in urban areas, so plans for sustainable cities are essential. Crawford's basic design for carfree cities foresees a sharp boundary between compact city districts with about 15,000 inhabitants and open spaces just beyond, giving city residents rapid access to natural areas. These areas are entirely suitable for local production of food, fibre, timber, and renewable energy, or they can be left in their natural state.

Crawford "thinks outside the box." He offers a new paradigm for the city, one that also opens new vistas for sustainable cities. The *Carfree Design Manual* sets out a vision but the book also suggests practical ways that today's cities can be rearranged. It is a book on which to build a sustainable future.

Stavros Dimas is the Member of the European Commission responsible for Environmental Protection.

USING THIS BOOK

Please begin with these brief notes and the INTRODUCTION.

SPECIAL TERMS

Squareness, undersquare, and *oversquare* refer to the ratio between building height and street width. The undersquare street is wider than the adjacent buildings are tall; the oversquare street is higher than wide, as in this EXAMPLE FROM BASEL.

Metro-freight is a term I coined in *Carfree Cities* to describe a modified metro system that delivers standard shipping containers within a city, providing most heavy freight service.

Auto-centric cities are those based on transport by private automobile. Occasional buses offer indifferent public transport.

A *Reference Design* is a benchmark, a point of departure. Normally, a reference design is not actually built, although it should in principle be employable in some real situation. The Reference Design presented in *Carfree Cities* could be built on a flat, featureless site.

The American and British usage of *gallery* and *arcade* conflict with one another. In this work, a GALLERY is a street covered by a glass canopy that keeps the weather out and allows plenty of light in, as seen in Valladolid. An ARCADE is a covered walkway along the edges of buildings, usually bordering on a street or square, as here in Bologna.

MEASUREMENTS

This work is bimetric. Dimensions are given first in metric and then in customary units, except where the source employed customary units. Conversions are approximate and reflect the imprecision of the source measurements, which are usually just estimates. Accurate conversion factors are given on page 108.

Chapter References

References to chapters within this book are given in small capitals without quotation marks, e.g., Design Constraints.

Notes

The "Harvard System" is used. Citations are given in the side notes in the form "author (year), page." The year is included only if necessary. The Bibliography includes full publication data.

Christopher Alexander's *A Pattern Language* is cited by Pattern, thus: "Four-Story Limit" (APL, Pattern 21). His *The Nature of Order* is cited in the form: TNO, IV:99, which is Book IV, page 99.

Notes are in the outer column as near as possible to the material to which they refer. Citations are aligned as near as possible to the end of the quoted or cited material. Notes are given in-line in a few places where the margin was already occupied.

Internet

In fact, the "www" can often be omitted as well. Even with the use of smaller type, not all URLs would fit on a single line. Overruns continue on the next line. If a source has disappeared, try the Way Back Machine: www.archive.org

I have dropped the leading "http://" from Internet URLs, to save space. In practice, this can almost always be omitted when typing a URL into a web browser's location bar.

Place Names & Spellings

Some original images did not identify the locale. Where I made educated guesses, these are qualified. Originals were sometimes mislabeled by the publishers, and these errors may have been carried into the text. I have identified my own images with care, but minor errors may have crept in. This is not a work of geography, and street names are given only to aid later investigators.

In the case of errors, the site is almost certainly in the vicinity of the location given.

Place names and their spellings change remarkably frequently. Place names on source images were followed, and the spellings may no longer be current. The modern spelling usually does not vary greatly. Venetian place names are found in a mixture of Italian and Venetian (which are similar). I have not attempted to use one form or the other consistently. I have favored spellings in the original language, but with cities like Cologne, Florence, and Venice, I have used the customary English names.

ILLUSTRATIONS

The locale of photographs is opportunistic. When a concept was to be illustrated, I simply chose the best image available at the time of writing. Nearly all the old images were scanned from my collection of postcards, which was assembled from what came readily to hand. Many people generously allowed me to use their photographs. A list of photographs, with copyright data, begins on page 574.

In the drawings, buildings are shown in light orange, streets in light gray, open space in light green, and water in blue. Many drawings are only schematic and are not to scale.

CAPTIONS

Photograph and drawing captions are given in the main text, next to some part of the illustration except as otherwise mentioned after the caption (parenthetically). The locale is in SMALL CAPITALS and the city is Capitalized. I wrote much of this book while living on the ALAMEDA DA GUIA in Cascais, Portugal.

Photographs that are not directly mentioned in the text carry their captions beneath, as in the example from Spain.

DATES

Dates for photographs are given starting on page 574. Those I took myself carry accurate dates; the original postcards rarely carry dates, so I have dated them "circa 1900" unless I have a clear indication that a later date applied. (None of the cards, so far as is known, predates 1896, and most predate World War I.)

BCE means *Before the Common Era; CE* means *Common Era,* i.e., the system of dating in general use in the Western nations. Where no possibility of confusion exists, this suffix has been omitted.

Madrid

St. Mark's Basilica, Venice

PREFACE

I believe that the carfree city offers the best means to improve the quality of urban life while at the same time making it more sustainable. I have single-mindedly pursued this goal since 1996. At the start of this quest, it seemed an almost absurd notion despite its great attractiveness. I published *Carfree Cities* in 2000, which gave the agenda a small but significant boost. Subsequent events have shown the practical advantages of this proposal. In this work I focus on designing carfree places so irresistibly beautiful that people will clamor for them. Unlike the first work, this one is less a matter of fact and more a matter of vision or opinion. I cannot prove much of what I say here, although I have made extensive recourse to other works that support my thesis. The ultimate proof—or refutation—of the philosophy and methods I present here can only come from the residents of completed projects.

My passion for carfree cities arises mainly from the great joy I have experienced when fortunate enough to spend time in one. Perhaps the strongest support I have for what I say here is simply that many other people have found Venice as enchanting as I do. I hope to share the source of this joy and to help others create places for themselves that they will find equally delightful.

This book is founded on thousands of years of urban design practice. The BIBLIOGRAPHY includes sources of any importance. Citations are not given in the running text where sources are in broad agreement. (Modernists, and the splinter groups that followed, broke so unsuccessfully with tradition that I have generally ignored their teachings.)

Carfree Cities outlined some design resources that are now widely known even if not yet so widely used. Principal among these was Christopher Alexander's seminal *A Pattern Language*. The 253 patterns developed by Alexander and his colleagues are brilliantly described and illustrated in their book. His work has

Via Diaz, Ravenna

been widely misunderstood and harshly criticized. Many of his critics would do well to attend to the title of this work. He never claimed to have developed a universal pattern language; he correctly titled the book *A Pattern Language,* not **The** *Pattern Language.* This notwithstanding, many of its patterns are indeed recognized and used around the world. Alexander recently published his four-volume *The Nature of Order,* which expands upon many of his earlier works but does not replace *A Pattern Language,* which I find to be the more useful work.

First published as *Der Städtebau nach seinen künstlerischen Grundsätzen*

Camillo Sitte's *City Planning According to Artistic Principles* was also highly influential in my thinking, as it was in Alexander's.

The carfree movement has gained momentum recently, with a large carfree project proposed for Abu Dhabi. Few details of this project are now known, but the early proposals do not differ greatly in their basic arrangement from what is proposed here. We are on our way.

I offer my thanks to the many who contributed to the making of this book during the tumultuous seven years of its gestation. The help of the following people was indispensable: Jan van Arkel, Robin Bassett, Ed Beale, Ann & Vance Crawford, Randy Ghent, Markus Heller, Piper Hollier, Jason Kirkpatrick, Robert S. Matthews, Christopher Miller, Dave Morris, the Morris/Goldsmith family, J. Gilbert Plantinga, Erik M. Rauch (1974-2005), Richard Risemberg, Nikos A. Salingaros, Doug Salzmann, Roberto Coronel Stucky, Arin Verner (lead graphics consultant), and Roel Zaal.

I wrote this book in Amsterdam, Cascais (near Lisbon), and upstate New York. I was fortunate to have been able to visit many cities in Europe and North Africa during this period. The beautiful medieval quarters found in many of these cities were a continuing source of encouragement and inspiration.

J.H. Crawford
New Paltz, New York
31 August 2008

INTRODUCTION

In my first book, *Carfree Cities,* I made the case against what I call
auto-centric cities, those based on intensive automobile use. I
proposed a carfree alternative that would maintain the high level
of access to goods and services that prevails in rich nations. Two
strategies were employed. The first was to bring destinations
closer together by building at moderately high density. The
second was to use public transport, bicycling, and walking for
personal mobility. That book only touched on what is the focus
of this one: designing carfree districts. I begin with the pre-
sumption that the site under design is vacant, although many of
the approaches may be useful to carfree redevelopment and infill
projects. The conversion of existing urban and suburban neighborhoods into carefree areas is not directly addressed.

This book is devoted to design, not planning, of which design
is a subset. We will take up regional planning, regulation,
finance, infrastructure, design methods, transport planning, and
project developer only as they affect design. Many of these issues
were treated at some length in *Carfree Cities.*

This work is in many respects more speculative than the
earlier one, much of which was founded on a review of existing
urban forms and a mathematical analysis of urban density and
transport systems. This book is more personal and reflects my
own long experience with cities on five continents. I have been
photographing for about fifty years now, and much of my
understanding of beauty is framed in photographic terms. I
attempt to share here my sensibilities with others on the perhaps
brash assumption that they may be of some value.

It is in any case true that I have found the greatest beauty in
city districts that are several centuries old, and it has been there
that I have found the most rewarding photographic subjects. I
have chosen almost 800 of my own photographs to share here;
thousands more are available at Carfree.com. I have found much

Via San Romano, Ferrara

www.carfree.com/library.html

Madrid

Ayamonte, Spain

beauty in thousands of postcards depicting urban scenes from about a century ago, and some 150 of these are included, mainly in Part III, Elements, which will serve as a palette from which to choose principal design elements.

Perhaps the most surprising and controversial conclusion I reach in this work is that medieval urban forms are superior to everything that came before or has come since. Once the needs of automobiles (and their forebears, carriages) can be neglected, a remarkable degree of design freedom arises, allowing us to return to quirky, fine-grained, human-scaled urban areas that reflect the demands of the site and the needs of its users.

The arrangement of medieval city quarters is similar everywhere. This book adopts medieval forms with the addition of public transport to support larger populations. Until the introduction of horse-drawn carriages about five centuries ago, city streets were seldom very wide, because there was no need for more street space, which was in any case costly to provide. Indeed, narrow streets minimized the city's extent and kept the whole of a city within walking distance. Modern rail systems allow us to transport people and goods while using very little land (almost none if underground). Huge populations can be forged into a single rail-based city, like Tokyo. Medieval cities usually have loosely radial street plans, with many streets converging on the most important squares and buildings at the center. Medieval city forms can still serve us well today, and the radial street plan is uniquely well suited to rail-based transit systems with a halt at the center of each district. Medieval forms are rich and yield places that will intrigue people for a lifetime.

The book is general in its approach. The methods proposed are not specific to a particular culture but are intended to be adapted to local circumstances. Project sponsors intending to design a carfree area in accordance with the precepts of this book will face some preparatory work. Many of the methods proposed must be refined before they can be applied.

THE CARFREE PREMISE

The arguments against intensive automobile use are better known today than when *Carfree Cities* was published. People have realized that it is time to rid ourselves of the "junkscapes" that accompany extreme reliance on cars: the ugliness, the noise, the stink, and the danger. Perhaps the most important objection is that cars rob the streets of their function as a common ground where the sense of community is nurtured.

People are also coming to understand the terrible burdens imposed on planetary ecosystems by extreme car use. Our current way of life is not sustainable over the long term and probably not even on a time scale of a few decades. We need to think in terms of greater economic *and resource* efficiency in every proposal for changing societies. We simply must do more with fewer natural resources, and we must reuse resources to an ever-increasing degree. These are not such great challenges as people assume.

The effects of heavy urban car use are now part of public discourse and will not soon be forgotten. Many people are seeking solutions. Carfree cities are not yet widely regarded as the best and most practical approach, one that also carries the bonus of a higher quality of urban life. I expect that as the seriousness of our plight dawns, and as the mirage of fuel cells and biodiesel fades, people will turn to carfree cities as the best alternative.

Although this book is written for a Western audience, carfree cities are likely to find first acceptance in China, India, and other nations with rapidly growing populations and economies. I believe that there is no other way to provide citizens of these nations with a better life while protecting the ecosystems that sustain us all. I challenge anyone to put forward a vision that would improve the quality of life in these nations at a lower cost in money, natural resources, and ecosystem damage. I think it is simply impossible, mainly because the car consumes so many resources and so much land.

These arguments are present in *Factor Four: Doubling Wealth, Halving Resource Use,* by Ernst U. von Weizsacker, 1997. I find that book rather flawed, but it does give many examples of ways to make dramatic cuts in resource consumption without adversely affecting standards of living.

Faro, Portugal

New Urbanism, Livingston NJ
The American preference for privacy, not community, finally seems to have crested. The New Urbanism is an expression of a deep longing for communities and places to care about. Although the movement is still young, the depth of the yearning for community is revealed by the higher prices people will pay to live in New Urbanist communities.

The "car-lite" New Urbanism is not considered at length, as the accommodation of even a few cars distorts design requirements and usurps too much land: good urban design is incompatible with car use. I am certain that proponents of the New Urbanism and Smart Growth mean well. I simply believe that the methods they propose do not provide a great enough improvement in the quality and sustainability of life. New Urbanists may find some useful ideas here and would, I think, agree with many of the design principles I espouse, even though they may be uncomfortable with the arrangements I propose.

The carfree city movement in general and the approaches proposed in this book in particular are fully compatible with the growing awareness of the need to refocus our activities more locally, owing in large part to the high energy costs of shipping goods over long distances. In an era of worsening energy shortages and rapidly emerging concerns about global climate change, localization is an almost self-evident approach that ameliorates our problems. Goods worth a great deal of money will undoubtedly still move in global trade, but I anticipate that the total mass of this trade and the average distance that it moves will begin to decline soon, as measures are implemented to reduce greenhouse gas emissions and in response to rising fuel costs.

At the same time, this should not be a fear-driven process. Rather, it should be a joy-driven quest for a more sustainable way of life that better meets fundamental human needs.

REFERENCE DESIGN FOR CARFREE CITIES

Carfree Cities presented an idealized design for a carfree city on a flat, empty site. I dubbed this the "Reference Design for Carfree Cities." It remains the best generalized design I have so far imagined. The Reference Design was based on several factors that I wanted to optimize. It was intended as a proof-of-concept, not as an actual plan for a real city. In practice, local

Guimarães

requirements will almost always dictate substantial deviations from that design. The first book has stood the test of time. No significant errors have been brought to light since its publication eight years ago. No serious objections have been raised to its assumptions or hypotheses, except to the basic assumption that people might be willing to give up their cars if a good alternative were offered. The growing popularity of carfree days and the increasing number and size of carfree urban areas is evidence that people are at least interested in the idea. I therefore believe that the Reference Design for carfree cities stands as first proposed and that it is time to take up the design of carfree places. My strategy is simple: make the carfree city such an attractive alternative to auto-centric life that people will clamor for it.

I intended the Reference Design to become the standard against which carfree designs would be measured. I have reproduced the important drawings here: the Reference Topology (page 30), the Reference District (page 128), and the Reference Block (page 248). A Reference Building (page 376) is added.

For a list of carfree places worldwide, see: en.wikipedia.org/wiki/List_of_carfree_places

Simple elements are employed: narrow streets, four-story buildings, interior courtyards, small squares, and excellent rail-based transport of passengers and freight. The Reference Design could have been built with only minor changes in 1900, by which time modern sanitation and electric rail vehicles had come into use, permitting the removal of pestilent horses from cities. These advances made possible urban environments in which high levels of public health could be maintained.

Guimarães

Major Changes to Urban Design Methods

This book does not pretend to be a balanced consideration of urban design in general, or even of carfree design in particular. The premise that people will accept carfree neighborhoods is not the only sweeping change I propose. My examination and experience of medieval city centers in Europe and Morocco has

Madrid

Salamanca

convinced me that their arrangement is superior to almost everything built after the start of the Renaissance. The downfall was the shift from on-site design to paper plans. This is not an article of faith but a matter of long deliberation. Many topics in this book will be cast in terms of the advantages and disadvantages of medieval patterns as compared to later practice. In virtually every respect, complex medieval designs are more interesting and better meet human needs than later designs. Streets from the automobile age are the worst in history.

The change in urban form through the centuries is a fascinating topic, but the treatment in ORDER & ORGANIZATION IN CITIES is necessarily brief and narrowly focused. It should be noted that I define order and organization differently, although they are commonly regarded as synonyms. In this work, order relates to superficial appearance whereas organization relates to underlying physical, economic, and social forces. The two are largely independent of one another, and a given urban area can have high or low levels of either, quite apart from the other. The principal question is: why do we shift back and forth at long intervals between rigid grids and organic forms?

The proposed change to medieval design will surely be controversial, nowhere more so than in schools of Modern architecture. Similarly controversial is the proposal that carfree districts be built using a radial street plan. The all-too-familiar grid form could be imposed, but, as already mentioned, radial patterns are well suited to transit-based districts because they minimize walking distances. Radial districts can be formal and regular if people wish, but the irregular forms of the medieval period are more flexible and interesting. They easily adapt to sites that are not entirely featureless, which is nearly all of them. They are more humane than arbitrary geometric patterns.

The proposal for design by users is equally fundamental. Ever since Renaissance methods were applied to city design, it has been assumed that the best designs arose when someone had a stroke of brilliance, got it down on paper, handed it to the leaders for approval, and built it, all in one go. The notion was that a single moment of inspiration was superior to centuries of accumulated design wisdom and the deliberations of thousands of people over time. This I believe to be a serious error.

Today, it is assumed that an architect or urban planner will design every new neighborhood. This approach also arose at the start of the Renaissance, and I believe that it was also a mistake. People should design their own neighborhoods, with experts serving in an advisory capacity. This book sets out to make city design accessible to everyone, in the hope that the resulting places will better fit the needs and desires of their inhabitants.

I propose not only to place design in the hands of users but also to conduct design on the site itself, not on paper. This allows people to respond to the physical constraints and opportunities of the site while designing their neighborhoods.

Finally, I propose to replace today's usual contracting methods, which are based on detailed plans and specifications, with a return to artisanship based on local vernacular styles that reflect the available materials, the local climate, and the culture of the region. Each building would be unique, which is nearly universal in medieval areas but rare in modern cities. Christopher Alexander pioneered some of these methods, which must still be regarded as experimental. These new methods also support a change to more local economies and particularly to reducing the energy costs of transporting building materials.

The simultaneous proposal of so many fundamental changes in city design and construction is a long reach indeed. However, these proposals, though compatible with one another, are also largely independent of one another. If one is shown to be an error, that need not imperil the others. I fear only that, if one proposition is invalidated, the others will be discarded without independent consideration. The methods I propose must be regarded as provisional until successfully demonstrated.

Valladolid

Madrid

URBAN DESIGN & QUALITY OF LIFE

Lisbon

This was Paris a few decades after Haussmann had done with it. As a model for a city, it is far better than the British industrial slums of the same era. Even so, people lived at far higher densities in the Paris of 1900 than they do today. The density of Paris today exceeds the density required for efficient carfree cities.

Humanity is urbanizing at a staggering rate. Not only is the population rising, but the proportion of people living in cities continues to increase. During the next 50 years, we will build more urban floor area than exists today. Given the huge investment of labor and materials, it is vital to get this work right the first time. This is especially true of the arrangement of streets; buildings come and go over the centuries, but streets endure.

The public street is one of the foundations of civilization. Until the death of the American City Beautiful movement around 1920, the need for attractive, livable streets had almost always been taken as a given, notwithstanding the use of streets as sewers and dumping grounds throughout most of history. Europe did not so quickly abandon beauty as a goal in city design, and even today European cities still value it.

During the past two centuries, technology has had huge effects on every aspect of life in the richer nations, and cities rank high on the list of things that have changed. Some technologies certainly benefited cities, such as sanitary sewers and safe drinking water. It was the sudden, rapid growth of cities in response to industrialization that had made them unhealthy and unpleasant places by the end of the 19th century. Terrible overcrowding, with large families living in a single room, had by 1900 led to extreme population densities in many large cities. This in turn gave rise to Ebenezer Howard's Garden Cities movement, which sought to disperse populations into semi-urban areas at much lower density. Industrial pollution is today a smaller problem than it once was in the richer nations, but the low-density suburban arrangements that have the Garden City as their origin are the cause of today's car crisis in metropolitan areas. I believe that good streets can only be built at human scale, which is only possible in spaces that need not accommodate automobiles or tall buildings. Today's densest urban areas, such as

Paris, are often regarded as among the best urban environments. However, even moderate density is a huge burden on residents *if there is significant car and truck traffic.* Today, far too many people suffer under the noise, pollution, and danger of heavy traffic, which is, in its own way, as debilitating as the industrial pollution of a century ago. The problems are in most respects even worse in the older areas of our cities, which often see very heavy traffic in narrow, congested streets. Residents of these areas suffer from these problems in many different ways. They deserve something much better, and carfree districts can provide it.

Mistakes in the form of cities are terribly costly, and the costs are not only economic but social and environmental. We are certain to make many minor errors when building cities, but we can ill afford irretrievable blunders. In the long history of cities, minor mistakes were recognized and corrected over the centuries. Today, we fail either to see or to correct them.

Madrid

Values

Values affect virtually every human activity, certainly including city design. The question then becomes: which values, whose values, and how should they be expressed? Since the beginning of the industrial revolution, the answer to that question has shifted increasingly towards values that favor the accumulation of private wealth, even if this comes at the expense of the commonweal. I believe that this set of values serves mankind poorly and that our very survival now hinges on a return to values that emphasize the common good. Certainly, the accumulation of vast private wealth has been coupled with a decline in the quality of the urban environment and in the health of the ecosystems upon which we ultimately depend for survival.

The design of cities has long been affected by the clash between Cartesian and humanist values, a clash that became more pronounced at the start of the industrial revolution.

Salamanca

Ferrara

Olsen, 24
Since Olsen wrote (1986), feverish privatization in the industrialized nations has led to housing becoming just another commodity and public space simply one more place to make money. When we limit our consideration to profit, we cripple the discussion. Merely because other values cannot be expressed in money terms is no reason to ignore them.

See *Carfree Cities,* 55-64.

Throughout history, prevailing values have swung back and forth between the precise order that characterizes Cartesian thought and the deeper, more complex but less tidy organization that characterizes Humanism. I postulate that humanist values are ultimately more satisfactory and will discuss this question at some length in VALUES & PHILOSOPHY. It may be that the greatest challenge of our time is to find a way through this clash without alienating anyone.

The deteriorating quality of design was treated tentatively by Jonathan Hale in *The Old Way of Seeing.* He traced the decline in the once-universal ability to design attractive objects to the start of the industrial revolution and the exchange of aesthetic values for acquisitive values. Hale's belief is supported by Donald J. Olsen, who says that the period between 1825 and 1837 saw the "growth in influence of a class that cared less about beauty than about economy and efficiency" and an "abrupt change in the standards by which people decided what was beautiful and what was not." This may be the most profound change brought about by industrialization. Certainly, innate design skills can still be found in contemporary pre-industrial societies like Bali. The origin of the decline probably has its roots in the Cartesian errors (or, more accurately, the errors of those who interpreted Descartes; see VALUES & PHILOSOPHY).

THE INFLUENCE OF TRANSPORT

Carfree Cities examined the influence of transport systems on city form. Even by Roman times, urban transport limited the growth of cities and had become a burden on their residents. A transport revolution occurred in the first half of the 19th century. Steam-powered railways and horse-drawn omnibuses and trams date from this period. They allowed a city's physical extent to grow beyond walking distance and enabled the rapid expansion of cities. The introduction of electric traction around

1890 was a great boost and led to the building of subway (metro) systems in the world's largest cities, allowing them to expand beyond two million inhabitants. Horse-drawn trams were rapidly converted to electric traction. Then, the acceptance of the private automobile reversed most of the gains of the previous century. Cities stopped becoming cleaner, healthier, more attractive places to live and instead became ugly, congested, dangerous, and unhealthy. Cars enabled the explosive growth of low-density suburbs and made cities so unpleasant that suburbs suddenly became an attractive alternative.

In some European cities, the bicycle was adopted as an inexpensive and practical means to triple the distance that a person could travel with a reasonable expenditure of time and effort. The bicycle transformed some cities, such as Amsterdam, where it remains the most widely used means of transport. Even in US cities, the bicycle rapidly took root once a safe and practical model was introduced. It was, alas, just as quickly abandoned.

We must bring bicycles back into cities. They are not a universal solution, as some climates are too harsh to permit their year-round use, but even in the heat of India they are popular. Heavy snow can stop a determined cyclist, but many climates will permit cycling throughout the year, at least by hardy souls. Hilly terrain is also difficult. We must accommodate bicycles in our cities while solving these minor problems.

Carfree cities, except for the very smallest, must rely on public transport that achieves levels of service and convenience seldom attained. The means are known and have been demonstrated, most often in SWITZERLAND. In large cities, underground rail systems serve best, despite their high cost. In smaller cities, the well-proven tram (streetcar, light-rail) serves nearly as well at much lower cost. The temptation to use buses as a quick, cheap solution should be resisted, despite successful implementations in South America, most of which should now be replaced by quiet, comfortable, clean tram systems. Unlike buses, rail

When I checked into my hotel here in Basel, I was handed a transit pass valid on all public transport in the city center, doubtless having paid something for it in the price of my room. The convenience must surely encourage those not accustomed to using public transport to give it a try. The quality of service is high.

systems cannot be moved from one day to the next, thereby allowing people to make location decisions with the assurance that good public transport will remain available into the future.

Changes Since 1945

Salamanca

The world has changed almost beyond recognition in my life-time. A number of causes can be identified: rapidly increasing prosperity, a doubling of world population, dramatic increases in urbanization, and demand for larger dwellings. Prosperity has come at the cost of rapid destruction of natural environments, depletion of natural resources, and now, apparently, climate change. Wealth has made it possible for many individuals to own an automobile, a change that had been expected to improve personal mobility. Instead, it decimated public transport systems and increased traffic at a rate that even intensive road building could not match. Greater wealth in Europe and North America has led to a large increase in the floor space of the average domicile at the same time that family sizes have plummeted. In North America in particular, this has led to the construction of huge houses inhabited by just a few people and situated at a great distance from urban centers, barely within commuting range, even by car. People in rich nations are now "enjoying" a standard of living their ancestors could never have imagined, at the same time that social systems are being damaged and the environment assaulted. The ironic result is a declining quality of life. We must choose a different direction.

The Spectre of Misunderstanding

Venice

It is the fate of many thinkers to be misunderstood, sometimes by those with devious ends. I fear that some of my thinking may suffer this fate, so I will address this risk. The trouble centers on the word "modern," which has two conflicting meanings.

When not capitalized, "modern" refers to the rational era, initiated by Descartes. Cartesian thinking supplanted the earlier humanism but did not provide better answers than humanism in the search for happiness, notwithstanding the great advances it fostered in science and technology. I plead for a return to the expression of humanist values in our public spaces. This plea may be labelled irrational, but humanism is only irrational within the most narrow interpretations of Cartesianism. Humanism seeks to understand the human condition and human needs and to find enlightened, decent solutions to the challenges of life. The most mechanistic understanding of Cartesian rationalism could be regarded as irrational in the realm of human affairs, as it is not rational to ignore the influences of unconscious, irrational forces and of genetically-determined pathways of perception. The influences of non-rational forces in human affairs are large, and account must be taken of them.

Valladolid

When capitalized, "Modern" refers to the movement closely associated with Walter Gropius and the Bauhaus in Weimar, Germany, following the First World War. It is not always understood that "Modern" is not just a design style. It encompasses an entire system of philosophy based on the exigencies of technology and mass production. Its goal was the complete rearrangement of culture and thought, "starting from zero." Traditional art, architecture, and literature were outdated and should be scrapped. The work of Frank Lloyd Wright, which had enjoyed brief eminence in the USA, was rapidly eclipsed by the Modernists. Traditional architectural forms, especially including the Beaux Arts, were reviled. This new world view required its adherents to accept that "new" equaled "better."

A good introduction to Modernism may be found at: en.wikipedia.org/wiki/Modernism
Tom Wolfe's *From Bauhaus to Our House* is excellent.

I am in this book intensely critical of Modernism. I believe that it owes much of its later influence to the "entrepreneurs" who adopted it in their quest for the riches to be gained by constructing the cheapest possible buildings. Modernism conveyed a shabby philosophical respectability and concealed the moral

Salamanca

bankruptcy of their design. I discuss Modernism and other systems of belief in the first chapter, VALUES & PHILOSOPHY.

I do not propose a return to mysticism; rather, I propose to correct some errors in the modern view of the world, errors that cause deep unhappiness in many Western people. The Modern movement was simply an error. This is the philosophical basis from which I proceed.

ORGANIZATION OF THE BOOK

Not every reader will be interested in Part I, Theory, but I do suggest reading two short chapters: DESIGN CONSTRAINTS and THE DENSITY QUESTION, as that material is central to design. The discussion of values and philosophy is included because of their great influence on what and how we build. A theoretical framework for analyzing the choices we face in city design is presented. About two dozen axes of analysis are presented. Order and organization are the most important axes and are closely related to one another. I believe that urban areas that exhibit deep organization function best. Relatively low levels of superficial order are sufficient, and many of the best-loved urban areas are not highly ordered, such as the VIA SAN ROMANO in Ferrara. Organization should never be sacrificed for order. High levels of superficial order can usually be attained if desired, without harm to the underlying organization. The matter is important enough that it merits a chapter of its own, ORDER & ORGANIZATION IN CITIES.

The discussion in Part II, Preparation, may not interest every reader but does warrant at least skimming. The matters taken up in this Part often constrain design, and designers must be aware of them if only to conduct informed discussions with regional planners and the engineers arranging district services. The use of urban villages to improve the quality of urban life and particularly in development of a sense of community leads to a

proposal to use urban villages as the primary instrument of on-site design. The proposed method brings the members of the newly-defined urban villages onto the site, where they would conduct design down to the level of siting individual buildings. The Part concludes with a discussion of the final site program. This must include the design of the most central areas in a district, where arrangements are constrained by rights-of-way for freight and passenger rail systems.

I intend for Part III, Elements, to be used as a palette from which to compare and choose alternative solutions to common city design problems. This Part is filled with illustrations that I hope will facilitate the discussion of alternatives and the effects that various choices would exert on a particular site.

The heart of the work is Part IV, Design. Everyone involved in a project should understand that the methods and techniques of design exert a large influence on the final design. I propose a major break with the methods of the past 500 years by returning design to users, with experts playing only an advisory role. The proposed method is based on the allocation of building sites through an auction-like process. Those willing to pay for expensive locations along major squares and main streets will take the first turn in on-site design, and the major elements they arrange will become the basic armature for the design of the remainder of the district. This will be based on the formation of urban villages whose members are compatible with one another. The villagers will assemble on the site to design the remaining small streets and squares, as well as their interior courtyards and building sites. When the process is complete, the district's streets and buildings will have been staked out in final form on the land. The is an untested approach, but I believe that it recovers the methods that were used in medieval times, which produced some of our finest urban areas. Case examples are given, and the Part concludes with some thoughts on poetic spaces. Each Part carries its own brief introduction.

Venice

Salamanca

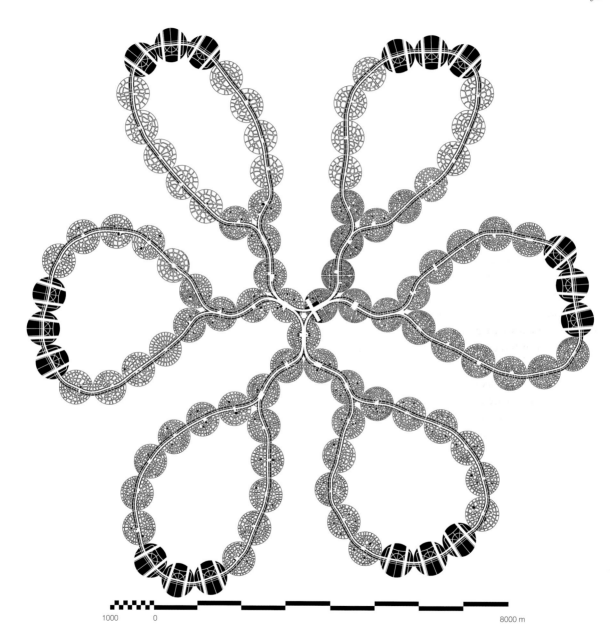

1000　　　0　　　　　　　　　　　　　　　　　　　　　　　　　　8000 m

PART I

THEORY

The first three chapters in this Part delve into the influence of values and philosophy on urban design, axes of analysis that can be applied to city design, and a brief history of urban design. I will plead for major changes in the underlying theory of design and its application in designing urban areas. The final two chapters consider design constraints and the issue of urban density.

VALUES & PHILOSOPHY

Examines the question of whether any activity can be value-free, asks whose values should prevail, considers the need for serviceable values, asks whether or not architecture is art, and reflects on the limitations the Cartesian ways of thinking about the world. Gives particular attention to Modern thought and the problems it has created in architecture and urban planning.

AXES OF ANALYSIS

Establishes that many axes can be used to analyze urban design and that the analysis can become too complex to comprehend. Specially considers the matter of order versus organization and the question of scale. Identifies and considers briefly a further two dozen axes.

ORDER & ORGANIZATION IN CITIES

Studies the influence of philosophy on city form, street geometry, advantages of curved streets, bias of planners towards grids, imperfect grids, crumbling grids, and changes in urban form from antiquity to the present day. Addresses the question of why street forms have alternated, at long intervals, between irregular radial patterns and rigid grids.

Coimbra

Madrid

Design Constraints

Takes up design constraints affecting cities, including walking, bicycling, freight, costs, safety, the site, and density of construction. Gives unit conversions and explains Plot Ratio and Floor Area Ratio, two important ways of measuring density.

The Density Question

Considers issues that affect both actual and perceived density, including the fear of density. Reflects on density as expressed by plot ratio, and floor area ratio. Compares gross and net density. Discusses the importance of scale. Presents the virtues of hollow, medium-rise blocks. Concludes with a comparison of the density of ten urban areas.

VALUES & PHILOSOPHY

Values underlie almost every decision in urban design and exert large influences on the organization of space. We are less aware of this than we should be, mainly because we rarely state our values explicitly even though they affect nearly everything we do. It has become difficult in some nations to discuss values. "Political correctness" may distort such discussions as do occur. As long as we cannot clearly state in public what our values are and the reasons we hold them, this vital discourse is hobbled.

One of the reasons this problem has become so acute in the USA is that there is little common ground, in the literal sense, where such discussions might occur. When values are discussed in private, the discussion has less impact than public intercourse. The retreat of many well-to-do Americans behind the walls of gated communities, where they are seldom exposed to people from a different social class (except service personnel) has had a pernicious effect on American society and the maintenance of the social glue that binds the nation together.

Disasters have a way of exposing weaknesses in a society, and the recent destruction of New Orleans revealed deep social divisions in this notionally egalitarian society. Even France suffers from major social divisions, as evidenced by widespread rioting in working-class suburbs in November 2005.

I can offer no quick solution to this problem, which seems to afflict most Western nations to an increasing degree. Ultimately, we must decide that we are all in this together, that no one group can dominate, and that social and economic justice are prerequisites for an egalitarian society. The foundations of democratic societies require continual maintenance, and good public spaces are essential to sustaining the necessary dialog. These must be places where people from all walks of life will encounter one another, even if only superficially. Places from which any member of the public may be excluded are not public spaces.

Trevi, Italy. This church says a great deal about the values of the society that built it.

Any admission fee, even if to a publicly-owned venue, removes the place from the realm of "public." This is even true of public transport when a fare is charged. A shopping mall is certainly not a public space, being privately owned and operated for profit. Any activity that is not directly profitable or that might threaten the genteel atmosphere is probably prohibited. Anyone deemed "undesirable" can be ejected without preliminaries.

The social isolation of people in North American suburbs is by now quite well known and understood, but even North America's cities are alienating. It is zoning, more than any other cause, that is at fault. With few exceptions, North American urban areas are single-use areas. Residential areas lack services and employment. No one lives in the downtown cores, where office towers are deserted by dinner time and the entertainment districts empty by early morning.

Dense construction does not make a city. The French riots in 2005 revealed that the dense but distant *banlieu* is somewhere to dwell but nowhere to live. Masses of poor people were relegated to these grim places, engulfed in ugly auto-centric landscapes. Revolt was expressed by symbolic burning of cars, the objects that robbed these districts of functioning public social spaces. The lack of jobs, entertainment, and shopping also played a role.

No Activity Is Value-Free

No activity is value-free, if only because the decision to undertake an activity (or not) is itself an expression of values. A pluralistic society requires considerable tolerance for the values of others, but a democratic society cannot survive without general agreement on some fundamental values. It is essential to maintain a dialog that nourishes and supports fundamental values, so that the reasons for their adoption are never forgotten.

Values are expressed in what we build and how we use the resulting places. Note that the *operative* values are not always the

Social housing, Venice

The notion of "value-free" education is absurd on its face: the decision to attempt value-free education is itself an expression of values.

Today in the USA, the once rock-solid agreement that the functions of church and state ought to be separate is under attack, threatening the very continuation of the Republic.

same as the *prevailing* values, and that this is expressed nowhere more clearly than in allocation of land to private transport. A substantial portion of the population continued to value non-motorized land uses long after the introduction of automobiles, but because the rich and powerful were the first to buy cars, the value they placed on convenient driving became the operative value long before it became the prevailing value.

Values change through the ages. Sometimes this simply brings values in line with prevailing behavior, as with the change in sexual mores during the 1960s, which was really only an acceptance of behavior that is as old as mankind. At other times, changes in values reflect real changes in people's deepest beliefs.

Public Values or Private Values?

It is only recently that this question would have had to be seriously entertained. Until 1800, religious or civic values, as expressed by the head of a church or state, would have been the only values with serious standing. In the 19th century, the corporation joined the ranks of organizations with enough power and wealth to affect values, and groups neither ecclesiastical nor aristocratic accumulated fabulous wealth and power. Today, the corporation competes with civic and religious authority on an even footing in the establishment and expression of values.

Corporate values tend to be stealth values. Society is often unaware that it has been manipulated in subtle but important ways by advertising. Today in the USA, corporate media have succeeded in convincing large sectors of the population that black is white and up is down. How long this will continue is impossible to guess, but the values that were established when the USA was founded have changed beyond recognition.

In architecture and urban design, the ascendancy of private values has corrupted what is proposed, accepted, and built. It allowed Modernist architects to contend that a building could

Another example of changes in prevailing and operative values is US public policy regarding broadcasting. The FCC once required a modicum of balance and accuracy by broadcasters, and extreme concentration in the ownership of broadcasting outlets was prohibited. These requirements were eviscerated during the past twenty years, and the result has been a strong rightward shift in the content of nearly all US broadcasting and a stunning concentration of outlets in the hands of a few large corporations. The airwaves are still notionally the property of the public at large, but the values that prevailed when these requirements were established are no longer operative.

To take a minor example, in the 1930s corporate media in the USA made people ashamed of their body odor, causing them to buy grooming products in the hope of not "giving offense." Until that time, body odor had simply been one of many personal traits, and not one to be ashamed of unless it was particularly unusual.

be designed without regard to its context. It permitted the erection of the junk landscapes that are so awful and depressing that James Howard Kunstler has said:

> I often joke that we are a wicked people who deserve to be punished. But the joke is, it's no joke. I believe it with all my heart. I also often remark in my public utterances that when we succeed in creating enough places that are not worth caring about, that we will succeed in becoming a nation that is not worth defending, and a way of life that is not worth carrying on. We are guilty of foreclosing our own future, and we are evil because we don't care.

James Howard Kunstler, "Where Evil Dwells: Reflections on the Columbine School Massacre," delivered at the Congress for the New Urbanism, Milwaukee, 6 June 1999

All of this has been done in service of the new god, private profit. Anyone who opposed this used to be tarred with the "Communist" brush. Today, the victory of corporate values is so complete that opposition is safely ignored.

SERVICEABLE VALUES

If, in the year 1 CE, you had invested US$0.01 (one cent) at just 2% real interest (i.e., nominal interest minus inflation) compounded annually, the annual interest on your investment would today roughly equal Gross World Product. The principal in 2003 would be $1,650,227,679,638,880, and the annual interest would be $33,004,553,592,778. Growth has limits!

Economic growth cannot continue indefinitely. Evidence of this mounts daily, as we see the toll our profligacy is exacting on the Earth. We must find ways of making a good life while halting the growth in consumption. We must find useful employment for people who would formerly have been part of the consumption economy. During the past century we have made such a mess of the physical world that many people can be kept busy for decades just cleaning up the mess. But what then? How will we find useful employment for everyone? Shorter work weeks and more vacations will help. Beyond that, we must find productive work outside the consumption economy. Would it not be a fine solution to train more people in the high crafts, and to build some fine buildings? This is expressive, deeply satisfying, and largely autonomous work.

We must put sustainability at the center of human affairs. We must ask: Is what we are doing today sustainable? How can it be made sustainable? Is the activity itself really necessary? Does it improve our lives? Sustainability must become a core value if our civilization is to survive.

None of this can occur without some degree of economic justice—the necessary changes are impossible as long as many people are still grindingly poor. The trickle-down theory cannot be maintained once it is admitted that economic growth must stop, or that, at a minimum, resource consumption must stabilize. I have lived among people who regarded a dollar as a good day's wage, and many of them were tolerably content. But how long can we go forward with one class that is rich beyond imagining and another class that never has enough to eat?

Our physical appetites are accompanied by a hunger for the sacred in our lives. That does not necessarily imply theism. We can express this urge through a reverence for nature and life, for the systems that sustain us both physically and emotionally. People have used the word "cathedral" when speaking of the great first-growth forests, expressing their reverence for the processes that created these life-giving places. We can do the same.

With these questions, I have perhaps strayed from my brief, but can we go forward without considering these questions? Can we achieve sustainability without adopting different values and making new arrangements? Mankind is at a critical juncture and must soon choose between a set of values that can sustain life and a set of values that enriches an elite at the cost of most of humanity and all of the planet. Cast in your lot with those who favor not only survival but truth and beauty. These things we can have in abundance. They have enduring value.

Carfree cities can improve the quality of life for rich and poor alike, while at the same time reducing material inputs. They offer a basis for a sustainable and just future. But what of their design? Who is to do it, and following what principles?

One school of thought holds that technological progress will permit economic growth to continue even in an era of resource limitations. If this proves to be true, which I doubt, then growth might continue for quite some time. Of course, more efficient use of resources helps generally.

Salamanca

Is Architecture Art?

We need to reach agreement that architecture and city design are *not* art forms, that they are extremely important and useful crafts whose conduct should be guided by artistic principles but not viewed as art. Agreement on this point cannot be left to the architects and designers; the built environment belongs to us all and is a foundation of our civilization.

Throughout history, architecture and city design have been inseparable. It is only since the birth of Modernism that it might occur to an architect to design a building without reference to its context, or to design an urban area without considering the buildings that would stand upon it. Today, technical requirements (especially transport) often dominate urban design, while architecture has elevated itself to an art form at liberty to ignore its context. This was a fateful turning.

I will concede that in the case of the ACROPOLIS, a work built as an expression of aesthetic and spiritual values, architecture did in fact reach the heights of art. In normal practice, however, architecture is not art. Consider what Stewart Brand has to say:

> Architect Peter Calthorpe maintains that many of the follies of his profession would vanish if architects simply decided that what they do is craft instead of art. The distinction is fundamental, according to folklorist Henry Glassie: "If a pleasure-giving function predominates, the artifact is called art; if a practical function predominates, it is called craft." Craft is something useful made *with* artfulness, with close attention to detail. So should buildings be.
>
> Art must be inherently radical, but buildings are inherently conservative. Art must experiment to do its job. Most experiments fail. Art costs extra. How much extra are you willing to pay to live in a failed experiment? Art flouts convention. Convention became conventional because it

The Acropolis in 5 BCE   ©2004 Gavin Zeno Watson

Lido congress hall, Venice

works. Aspiring to art means aspiring to a building that almost certainly cannot work, because the old good solutions are thrown away. The roof has a dramatic new look, and it leaks dramatically.

Brand, 54

However, agreement on this point is so distant that Spiro Kostof simply dismisses the question, having reached the opposite conclusion:

Urban design is of course an art, and like all design it does have to consider, or at least pay lip service to, human behavior.

Kostof (1992), 9

What is wrong with Kostof's statement is that art need *not* pay attention to human behavior. Art expresses the artist's insight into the human condition, or his own psyche, or whatever, but it enjoys the luxury of being allowed to ignore human behavior. I think it is impossible to reconcile the conflicting demands of artistic expression and human needs and behavior. Architecture simply cannot be *allowed* to be art, except perhaps in unusual circumstances, such as the Acropolis.

The word "art" has so many meanings that it can be taken to mean almost anything, and the meaning of the word has changed over time. I take art to be that which serves no utilitarian purpose and is intended to enrich our lives. Craft is the satisfaction of practical human needs in a pleasing fashion. It often reaches the height of art, almost incidentally, but the achievement of such high standards is not necessary to create attractive and useful urban areas. Indeed, in recent years, much of the architecture that has been foisted off on the public as "art" would have done well to have reached the more modest standard of "craft."

Another serious error afflicting Modern architects is the notion that their buildings can be designed in isolation from their neighbors. This is only possible when designing a house in the countryside. When a building will have neighbors, and especially when it will directly abut some of those neighbors, it is arrogant to imagine that it can be designed without considering what has already been built. I believe this faulty thinking has its roots in the misperception of architecture as an art form.

Fortunately, some architects are modest enough to understand that architecture is not a pure exercise in ego expression. Traditional/classical architects, probably best represented by INTBAU, often possess sufficient humility to be entrusted with urban design. New Urbanist architects, who have close ties to

www.intbau.org

Madrid

In 1868, Charles S. Peirce wrote as follows on Cartesianism:

Descartes is the father of modern philosophy, and the spirit of Cartesianism—that which principally distinguishes it from the scholasticism which it displaced—may be compendiously stated as follows:
1. It teaches that philosophy must begin with universal doubt; whereas scholasticism had never questioned fundamentals.
2. It teaches that the ultimate test of certainty is to be found in the individual consciousness; whereas scholasticism had rested on the testimony of sages and of the Catholic Church.
3. The multiform argumentation of the middle ages is replaced by a single thread of inference depending often upon inconspicuous premises.
4. Scholasticism had its mysteries of faith, but undertook to explain all created things. But there are many facts which Cartesianism not only does not explain but renders absolutely inexplicable, unless to say that 'God makes them so' is to be regarded as an explanation.
In some, or all of these respects, most modern philosophers have been, in effect, Cartesians.
"Some Consequences of Four Incapacities," Charles S. Peirce, *Journal of Speculative Philosophy* (1868) 2, 140-157. www.peirce.org/writings/p27.html

the traditional, are usually responsive to history, context, reality, and the need to integrate architecture and urban design.

Architecture is an honorable and essential craft, to be practiced by people with the gift of creating functional beauty in the everyday environment in which we pass most of our lives. Let us be done with the notion that architecture is art.

The Limitations of Cartesian Thought

Our methods of thinking affect what we do and the solutions we conceive for the challenges we face. This is as true of city design as of any other endeavor. The modern era began about four centuries ago and ushered in new ways of thinking that gradually displaced the humanism that had held sway for two centuries. The very faces of cities were altered by the change. New, more "rational" pathways of thinking brought an end to complex, irregular street networks and revived the grid form that had been widely used during classical times.

French philosopher René Descartes laid the foundations of modern Western thought and the scientific method. Rationalism displaced intuition; reason overtook passion. Much was lost in the process. Intuition, it can be argued, is a higher mode of thought, one that requires a deeper understanding and broader experience than reasoning. Intuition produces better results in less time. The displacement of passion by reason drained the blood from our culture, not least from the form of our cities. Even today, many believe this was an unqualified blessing.

Cartesian thinking is so universally enshrined in Europe and North America that we are scarcely aware of it. At the same time, however, irrational thought and behavior continue to govern much of life. This gives rise to the paradox that we consider ourselves "rational" while acting irrationally. Not every society has succumbed to this error, but all of the industrialized nations seem to suffer from it to a greater or lesser degree.

True rationalism must take account of not only the irrational elements of the human mind but also the mechanisms of perception and the pathways of thought. Fractals are one of the most commonly found mathematical structures in the natural world, and it is a reasonable hypothesis that our brains would have evolved to operate with fractals as the underlying basis for comprehension and even memory. (A fractal is a geometric pattern that is repeated at smaller and larger scales to produce self-similar shapes and surfaces.) "Beauty" may be nothing more than a preference for the mean in human features and for objects that echo the structures of the natural world.

Romanesco cabbage

The thrust of Alexander's argument in *The Nature of Order* is that well-structured human creations exhibit characteristics similar to natural objects. His arguments are long and elaborate, and it may be that a more accurate, or more useful, explanation is simply that our minds strongly prefer objects that echo the fractal objects that it knows how to process efficiently. It may be decades before we have any certainty on this point.

Whatever the case with fractals and mental processing may be, Alexander pleads for a rejection of the limitations of Cartesian thought and the mechanistic/rationalist view of the world. He calls instead for design based on human response. The enormously hopeful finding of his research is that we are all, basically, in agreement about what constitutes good design. He analyzes many examples of pairs of objects to determine which one is more a "mirror of the self" or "has more life." When these pairs are shown to other observers, they agree with Alexander by large majorities. Even architecture students, confronted with a choice between a Modernist object and an "old fashioned" object, made the same choices as everyone else. The students were disturbed by their own judgments, which ran contrary to their indoctrination, but they could not escape their own feelings.

Vernacular buildings, Alfama

TNO, I:73-75

Alexander says that Descartes presented only a *method,* and that Descartes himself understood this. Others have forgotten:

This business of isolating things, breaking them into fragments, and of making machinelike pictures (or models) of how things work, is not how reality actually *is*.... [Descartes] would have been horrified to find out that people in the 20th century began to think that reality *itself* is actually like this....

TNO, I:16

Alexander proposes a synthesis that reunifies the objective and the subjective. Good form has both feeling and substance:

This is, scientifically and artistically, a hopeful and amazing resolution. It means that the four-hundred-year-old split created between objective and subjective, and the separation of humanities and arts from science and technology can one day disappear as we learn to see the world in a new fashion which allows us simultaneously to be cold and hard where that is appropriate, and soft and warm where that is appropriate.

TNO, I:298

Alexander contends that the weaknesses of Cartesian thought cannot be allowed to limit our analysis of the built environment:

The factual character of modern science—what we call its objective nature—arises chiefly from the fact that its results can be shared. The method of Descartes—the observation of limited events that are tied to a limited and machine-like view of some phenomenon—creates a circumstance in which we all reach roughly the same results when we do the same experiments. It is this which allows us to reach a picture which is *shared,* and this in turn which then leads us to call the picture so created an "objective" picture.

What is vital, then, about any objective phenomenon is that the observation of its essential points lead to shared results....

But the methods described in this book—methods which I believe to be necessary if we are to arrive at an adequate view of life in the world—are not based on the Cartesian way of sharing results. To see the phenomenon of life as it really is, the methods used cannot be tied to the crutch of mechanism as the basis for the sharing of observations and results.

TNO, I:352

Alexander then proposes to extend the methods of scientific observation:

I want to emphasize that this method of observation, like the method of Descartes, still refers always to *experience. It is empirical in nature.* It dismisses fantasy and seeks constantly to avoid speculation. In this sense, it is as empirical as the method of Descartes. But where Descartes only allowed observation to focus on the outer reality of mechanisms in the world, my method requires that we focus on the inner reality of feeling *as well*.

TNO, I:353

Alexander's method of asking groups of people to compare two designs and choose one or the other as being a better "mirror of the self" or as "having more life" clearly fails the test of Cartesian logic. However, the remarkable consistency he has found in people's responses, even when the objects compared are quite similar, is probably a sufficient basis to claim that we are all basically alike in our perceptions and judgments of design. It means that a rational approach to designing objects for human use must be based on shared human responses to the object. So, to call upon people to make judgments about what is dead and what is lively in the built environment is not by any means irrational. In fact, *failing* to do so would be irrational.

Alexander uses "life" in the sense of "liveliness."

William Morris: "If you want a golden rule that will fit everybody, this is it: Have nothing in your houses that you do not know to be useful or believe to be beautiful."
"The Beauty of Life," address to the Birmingham Society of Arts and School of Design, 19 February 1880.
www.allthingswilliam.com/home.html

Praça 8 de Maio, Coimbra

AXES OF ANALYSIS

We can analyze cities using a wide variety of measures. Each measure is considered here to be an "axis." Not all axes are considered—only those I find useful. A pair of axes that work together form a "plane of analysis." The twin axes of order and organization are crucial. They form what I believe should be the basic plane of analysis in urban design. The scale axis is also of great importance. A further two dozen axes are considered.

Humans have difficulty conceiving of objects with more than three dimensions, but problems requiring analysis often have many more than three axes. The simultaneous analysis of more than three aspects of a problem is therefore difficult because the visualization of the relationships is so difficult. Beyond six dimensions, the problem becomes impossible for ordinary mortals, and the analysis can only be abstract. The focus of discussion in this chapter will be on the three principal axes of analysis; the others will receive only brief attention. The three critical axes are discussed first, starting with the plane of analysis formed by the first two axes, order and organization. This plane of analysis underlies much of the discussion in this book. Scale is taken up immediately after and is nearly as important. The question of order and organization is so important that it takes up the next chapter, ORDER & ORGANIZATION IN CITIES, in which this plane is used as the framework for a historical review of city form. The introductory discussion here serves to bring all of the axes together in one place. The remaining two dozen axes are considered in the most convenient order.

Designers should be aware of the secondary axes and may occasionally need to consider them explicitly, but I do not expect them to receive a great deal of attention. Still, designers ought to reflect briefly on all of them before commencing work on a given site. For convenience, they are tabulated on the next page in the order in which they are taken up.

Piazza Lupatelli, Perugia. This church illustrates many of the axes of analysis that will be discussed here. How did the ugly concrete block in the foreground come to disfigure this modest but pleasant square?

In this list, pairs separated by an ampersand are *planes* of analysis; those separated by "vs" are unidimensional axes. The plane "Order & Organization" might also be written "High Order vs Low Order & High Organization vs Low Organization."

It will be instructive for the student to reflect on the illustrations in this book in the context of order, organization, and scale.

Order & Organization
Human Scale vs Industrial Scale
Hierarchy vs Network
Individualism vs Communitarianism
Private Enterprise vs Public Enterprise
Random vs Patterned
Simple vs Complex
Geometric Shapes vs Natural Patterns
Repetitive vs Unique
Dispersed vs Enclosed
Straight Streets vs Curved Streets
Continuous Edges vs Broken Edges
Form & Function
Ingenuous vs Sophisticated
Dissonance vs Harmony
Symmetry & Balance
Classical vs Vernacular
Formal vs Informal
Intimate vs Impersonal
Mechanistic vs Humanistic
Efficient vs Effective
Unsustainable vs Sustainable
Sprawled vs Concentrated

"No building (and no part of any building) has real life unless it is deeply and robustly functional. What I mean by this, is that the beauty and force of any building arises always, *and in its entirety,* from the deep functional nature of the centers that have been created." (TNO, I:404) Or, order springs from organization.

One warning: Great design is not analytical. It is the unified expression of underlying organizational forces using available means in ways that reflect local geography, materials, and culture. It is not a purely analytical process—it must reflect the hopes and dreams of the host culture.

Order & Organization

I believe that the relationship between order and organization is fundamental to all thought on urban design, even though this is seldom discussed. My dictionary actually gives order and organization as synonyms of each other, but I take them to have quite different meanings. Order has to do with superficial appearance, whereas organization has to do with the underlying physical, economic, and social forces. The two phenomena are independent of one another; an urban area can have high or low levels of either, quite apart from the other.

Consider an example: an orderly bookcase is one in which the books are all arranged by their height and set into shelves that are just high enough for the books. This looks neat and tidy, and it does minimize the volume of space occupied. An organized bookcase is one in which the books are arranged by author or subject. In this case, a high level of organization actually induces a lower level of order. An organized bookshelf takes more space, but it is more useful in practice than an orderly bookshelf. That is why libraries are organized, not ordered.

Another example is nicely illustrated by typefaces. The main text of this book is set in Bembo, first cut in Venice by Francesco Griffo in 1495. It was designed at a time when printing was still comparatively primitive, and, to maximize legibility, a highly non-geometric design was adopted. The lowercase "a" is distinguished from the "e" by having the middle stroke quite low in the "a" and unusually high in the "e." The lowercase "n" has a slight curve to the right leg. The lowercase "r" has an unusual tail. Contrast this with Helvetica Light, a simple geometric typeface used here in the side notes. It omits the grace notes of Bembo. It is very pure and exceptionally orderly, but it is not particularly attractive and is comparatively difficult to read. (I chose it because it allows the secondary text to lie quietly beside the main text, without drawing the reader's eye.)

Venice

Think, for instance, of San Francisco's rigid street grids, which simply ignore the hills in all but the steepest terrain.

Pirsig (61) has stated this differently:
"A classical understanding sees the world primarily as underlying form itself. A romantic understanding sees it primarily in terms of immediate appearance. If you were to show an engine or a mechanical drawing or electronic schematic to a romantic it is unlikely he would see much of interest in it. It has no appeal because the reality he sees is its surface. Dull, complex lists of names, lines and numbers. Nothing interesting. But if you were to show the same blueprint or schematic or give the same description to a classical person he might look at it and then become fascinated by it because he sees that within the lines and shapes and symbols is a tremendous richness of underlying form."

Faro, Portugal

Organization in urban design stems from the inherent demands of the site and the needs of the society that uses it. Any given form of order can be imposed on almost any site. A high level of order often makes a place more immediately comprehensible to strangers, but it is no substitute for organization.

I think it self-evident that we should strive for highly organized urban spaces. This, of course, begs the question as to which organizing principles will rank highest. I believe that the most important considerations are social and topographic. Transport requirements are heavily influenced by topography and nearly as important.

What of order? Is a high level of order necessarily good, even if it does not come at any cost to organization? Is the absence of order necessarily disorder? I admit to some uncertainty on these points. In practice, however, I find that I relate more readily to urban spaces that are not particularly orderly but are very well organized. As in so many things in urban design, there is probably no single best choice; variety may be the best approach. With organization, however, I think that we will nearly always want to seek the highest possible levels.

We must consider Alexander's recent *The Nature of Order*. I had at first thought that Alexander had used "order" in the way that I use "organization," but we are, in fact, using order in a similar way. The order he discusses has most to do with the appearance of things, not the underlying organization, but the underlying organization is rarely far removed and usually drives the ultimate expression of order.

We must also remember that, in Alexander's view, order is a way of creating life in things, that ordered things are perforce more lively. However, for Alexander, order need not be of the rigid classical Greek kind. He gives many examples of lively objects that are not geometrically orderly, but that are ordered according to deeper principles. These could be, but are not necessarily, organizational principles.

High order usually facilitates a quick grasp of the arrangement of an urban area. This is helpful to strangers supplied only with a map. However, if strangers receive, on their arrival, some hints as to the organizational principles of an area, the lack of superficial order perhaps becomes less important. Suppose, for instance, that upon arriving in a town, one passed beneath an arch on which was incised, "Main streets follow the ridges" (as they do in Siena). This message gives a street map new meaning.

Do we really want all of our cities to resemble one another in the interest of saving visitors the trouble of asking directions? How much of the character of a city is worth sacrificing on the altar of convenience? Perhaps, in some cases, the answer will be that it's worth a lot. I think that in most cases, other goals should predominate. Let us argue the case of Venice. To anyone who does not know that Venice is organized into 70 parishes, each with its central square and church, the city when viewed on a map appears to be a maze designed to thwart the movement of the uninitiated. Once the nature of the parish organization is understood, the whole city makes more sense. This same organization fosters tight-knit communities, so we must ask if this deep but subtle organization is worth sacrificing for more order.

There exist urban forms that permit very high levels of both order and organization, such as this CITY ON A HILLTOP based on a highly-regular design by Francesco di Giorgio Martini. The spiral street allows the hill to be ascended at a moderate grade. The demands of a site can often be met while providing both high order and deep organization. There is no reason not to offer this arrangement for those who prefer it.

Nevertheless, order for order's sake must be avoided. While I will admit to picking the worst example, this HOUSING BLOCK in Amsterdam's GWL carfree development seems to be order for its own sake. That order comes, I think, at the cost of any apparent deeper level of organization. This building says only that it is the product of a regimented mind.

Fes-al-Bali, Morocco

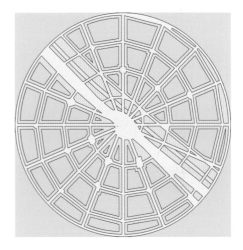

Human Scale vs Industrial Scale

The scale of an environment greatly affects our reaction to it. Most of us are more comfortable in rooms and public spaces that are not too much larger than they need to be to serve their purpose. The CAMPO SAN ZULIAN in Venice certainly obeys this dictum, especially given that at other times many more people are present. (This view shows nearly the entire square.) This is a very human space, one whose comfort encourages people to linger for a chat even though there is nowhere to sit.

Scale is a complex matter. It is possible to get many things right and still fail. The MAIN SQUARE in Houten, the Netherlands, is not so very large, much smaller than Piazza San Marco. The buildings are also comparable in scale. Alas, while San Marco bustles for 16 hours a day, nobody passes through the square in Houten for minutes at a time. Thus, scale is not simply a matter of physical dimensions but also degree of use. Houten is a small town and should have had a square small enough to make it feel somewhat busy during lunch hour.

I believe that spaces and buildings with overly-large scale are uncomfortable for most people. This WORM'S-EYE VIEW OF AN INTERSECTION in Manhattan shows a space at gargantuan scale, one in which almost nobody could feel significant, although it may be that some people do not object to this. What is odd here is that while the buildings are truly enormous, the streets are of moderate width. When this street had buildings of normal size, not so very many years ago, it would have been a place in which people were fairly comfortable. Five-story buildings would be reasonably proportioned to the side streets, and along the much wider avenues, ten or even twelve stories would not have been out of place. When, however, we have ranks of 60-story behemoths towering over everything, there is nothing that can bring balance to the scale; the dominant elements are much too large to make people comfortable.

The clash of scales is further illustrated here on WEST 57TH STREET in Manhattan. Once, this street was lined with townhouses much like the one in the middle. Today, this lone holdout is totally overwhelmed by its huge neighbors. It can be argued that Manhattan requires skyscrapers to accommodate all the necessary activities on one comparatively small island, but the urgency of this need does not ameliorate the clash.

HIERARCHY VS NETWORK

Hierarchy and network are the two basic arrangements used to manage complex human organizations. Traditionally, hierarchy was used because it accommodated the limitations imposed by the means of communications then available. However, modern communication technology makes network organization feasible for large organizations. (Indeed, today's communication systems are themselves networks.) Today we can choose either method. In principle, networks can respond faster to challenges than hierarchies with their long chains of command and centralized decision making. Networks are more responsive and permit low-level cooperation to arise, which characterizes the kind of human relations that develop naturally in small groups.

Not only human systems but also the web of streets can be organized along either of these principles. The most common tool of city planners has been the street grid, which is intrinsically a network. I argue, though, that a street system based on hierarchical principles is more efficient for collective transport, as it concentrates flows into a few high-capacity channels where frequent tram and metro service can be provided. However, when concentric streets are added to the intrinsic hierarchy of a radial pattern, the system again takes on the attributes of a network. On a larger scale, the joining of either hierarchical or networked sub-centers into a single city results in a hierarchy, with transport lines branching out from the center.

Hierarchical Street Grid

Individualism vs Communitarianism

No society that does not hold community values above raw individualism is likely to develop such fine public spaces as the campo san rocco in Venice. Societies based on individualism are generally not capable, or desirous, of working together in the way that produces such exceptional results as this.

In the arc of history, individual and communitarian values have swung back and forth, from the Greek city-state with its emphasis on the public realm, to contemporary American society, in which any reference to the common good is likely to be labeled "socialism." This brings on the kind of corporate mayhem characterized by this strip mall in Los Angeles; private profit is somehow conflated with the public good. This is a fateful error in logic.

A sustainable society cannot be based on greed; some sense of the public good is essential. Those who engage in building truly junky environments must be brought to heel. First, however, the broader society must decide that this behavior is, indeed, contemptible, not meritorious.

Private vs Public Enterprise

Closely related to the individualism vs communitarianism conundrum is the private-public balance. Societies arrange for human needs to be met by some combination of public systems, owned and controlled by everyone, and private systems not under direct public control. The private systems include the family, which is important even in socialistic societies. In most societies, private, for-profit organizations fill major roles in satisfying human needs. In capitalist societies such as the USA, for-profit organizations are expected to bear the brunt of the work. They provide many services, such as child care and cooking, once the sole province of the family.

The balance between public and private undertakings affects how cities are developed. It is clear to me that this balance has long been highly unfavorable for the public welfare in the USA. Take, for example, this BIG-BOX STORE in Los Angeles. This building shows virtually no respect for the commonweal and denies even the possibility of any social life on the street.

On the other hand, central government control, such as in the USSR and its client states, led to results that were at least as bad as in the USA. Nearly as bad was the top-down planning applied by the Dutch government and the housing associations that built these HIGH-RISE FLATS in Amsterdam Southeast. They were such a social disaster that many of them were torn down only 30 years after their construction.

The historical failures of centralized planning have led me to recommend local control of local development, regardless of whether the enterprise is public or private. The question does arise as to whether or not local groups are truly capable of designing environments that meet local needs. Early evidence suggests they are. This question is taken up in DESIGN TECHNIQUES, DISTRICT LAYOUT, and NEIGHBORHOOD DESIGN. Strong local control does carry a risk: a locality might decide not to permit any development at all. This may run counter to the interests of the larger society, so some limitation on local power is clearly required. In the end, it comes down to politics.

In societies where public enterprise holds more sway than private enterprise, such as the Netherlands during the 1970s and 1980s, the interests of corporations are held subservient to the common good. The American notion that a land owner has the right to do anything he wants with a parcel of land would be found laughable in the Netherlands even today. To be sure, American municipalities do exert some influence on development within their jurisdictions, but attempting to stop a land owner from any construction on a given site would run the risk of a costly legal settlement.

See Kushner's *Comparative Urban Planning Law,* "The Taking of Property Through Regulation"

Random vs Patterned

Urban areas can be arranged in ways that vary from the kind of chaos seen in this strip mall on HOLLYWOOD BOULEVARD in Los Angeles through the patterned but irregular arrangements seen in the ROOFS OF THE ALFAMA DISTRICT in Lisbon (middle), to the numbingly regular repetition of modern projects such as these DREADFUL OFFICE BUILDINGS in Porto (bottom).

We must not confuse chaos and irregularity. Although the leaves of trees are irregular, in that no two are precisely alike, they are hardly chaotic, as all unfold according to genetic rules that are fractal in their effect. We will want to avoid the appearance of randomness, just as we will usually want to avoid perfectly regular arrangements. I believe that Alexander's patterns lead us to where we want to be. His *Pattern Language* was the first serious attempt to identify patterns in the built environment, and I believe that his work convincingly demonstrates their existence in historical practice all around the world.

It is clear that the patterns are in no way random, even though they are often irregular. Whether or not the Lisbon roofs are truly fractal is almost irrelevant; their variation within a common pattern is the thing that commends them to our eye. Further analysis may eventually reveal that these roofs are described by fractals, but this is not yet clear. The mathematics may only be of purely academic interest. Even if the design of buildings and cities by informal processes turns out to be described by mathematical fractals, what actually matters is that successful towns and buildings are most likely to arise when we understand certain proven patterns and apply them during design.

This question is worthy of the continuing attention given to it by Nikos Salingaros, a colleague of Alexander. Whatever results this investigation may yield, we certainly want to avoid chaotic environments like Los Angeles. Such places are not good for people.

SIMPLE VS COMPLEX

In a time when most people lived and died within a day's walk of their birthplace, they had little reason to demand simple architecture that could be rapidly comprehended by anyone passing through. Nearly everyone seeing a given building would have seen it many, many times before. Surely it made sense to build complex buildings with detailed ornament and enduring subtlety. When Cologne built its CATHEDRAL, it chose sophisticated complexity. (See also the illustration on page 362.) Even among religious buildings, however, there are exceptions. Some Dutch churches exhibit spare detail, although their basic form is complex and similar to their more detailed brethren.

Zuiderkerk, Amsterdam

When Post-Modernism supplanted the purist geometry of Modernism, we began to see slightly more complex designs. The AT&T building in New York, with its Chippendale pediment, is a clear example. This building is instantly recognizable, but is this parody of beautiful furniture any more enduring than parody ever is?

Should we not build complex buildings that engage us for a lifetime? Does the casual passerby suffer from the incredible complexity of the cathedral (see page 363) at Strasbourg? My one brief encounter with it was memorable, and I cannot imagine plumbing its depths even in a lifetime. Yet I do not feel abused by its designers because it is not simple enough to take in during a single sitting. Let us be done with simplistic architecture and again build with complexity, subtlety, and depth.

At the same time, comparatively simple design is suitable for minor buildings. It is, in fact, too expensive (in the near term, at least) to include complex detailing in every building. We will have to make do with, at best, simple, unique buildings, such as these OLD BUILDINGS in Lisbon's Alfama district. This is an easy compromise to accept. The arrangement of groups of simple buildings can itself be complex, as indeed it is here.

"Yet it is, I believe, only when these two [engineering and architecture] work together, that deep feeling or life can be attained in a building."
TNO, III:140

GEOMETRIC SHAPES VS NATURAL PATTERNS

Designed shapes always have one motif or another. The human body, animals, and plants have all been used as a source of inspiration at one time or another. From the Arab world we have a rich dictionary of patterns based entirely on geometry, as seen in these beaten copper DOORS OF THE ROYAL PALACE in Fes, Morocco. These complex tessellations are difficult to comprehend even after prolonged study.

Although the West might do well to study Islamic patterns more closely, Western cultures will probably continue to prefer patterns that are derived from nature or from their Judeo-Christian heritage and not from abstract geometry. Art Nouveau drew its inspiration from natural forms. I consider it to have been the last successful decorative style before the dreadful Modern usurped everything from typography to tea sets. This STORE ENTRANCE in Lisbon is a simple example. Art Nouveau, like most later forms, can sometimes be criticized on the grounds that it does not integrate structural requirements with artistic expression, but the natural forms often *are* efficient—here, the scalloping provides local stiffening.

The Hindu religion has given us arts and crafts derived from the two great Indian epics, the Ramayana and the Mahabharata. I came to know these traditions during my time in Bali and was always impressed by how widely they were known and understood among the Balinese. The many personae are a fount of inspiration for all arts there, although their significance will be lost to anyone not steeped in this tradition.

This brings us to an important point: patterns ought to derive from something that has relevance for the local population. This need not mean that the patterns will be static, even dead, but only that the source be familiar; how the variations are rung on the theme is for the artisan to develop. As for myself, I prefer natural patterns to those based on religious teachings.

Repetitive vs Unique

One of the boring things about modern life is that we see the same object over and over again. Identical cars, telephones, books, and of course repeated building elements (and entire buildings). The RUA DO ASTROLÁBIO in Cascais gives us a relatively benign example. Here, at least, the repeated elements are in themselves somewhat complex, but many examples lack even this small grace.

Consider by way of comparison Amsterdam's famous BEGIJNHOF. This lovely courtyard (so often used as an example in this book) is composed of individual houses; I believe no design is repeated. Some houses have repeated elements within them (mainly windows), but many do not. Even the handmade bricks differ subtly from one another. Yet this place is certainly not chaotic even despite the presence of two different and somewhat conflicting roof arrangements. The commonality of materials (brick, sometimes stuccoed, and roof tiles), the relatively narrow range of scales, and the universal application of divided lights (multi-pane windows) all come together to give the place excellent coherence despite the individuality of the elements from which it is assembled.

This approach to developing urban landscapes, of individual elements in a common set of patterns, strikes me as the ideal balance. Many will claim that this practice has somehow become too expensive to use today. (Aren't we supposed to be richer than ever?) Alexander contends in *The Production of Houses* that craftsmen can produce individual results at costs comparable to mass produced elements. Certainly, I once watched a young woman at Arcosanti decorating tiles. Each tile was unique, although all followed a common style. She was able, while conversing with me, to decorate a unique tile in about one minute, each one a masterpiece. Truly competent artisans are capable of remarkable feats, and we should patronize their work.

Dave Morris gives the example of a friend who commissioned a local craftsman to make and fit a new oak front door. The final cost was no more than what a contractor would have charged for installing an ugly mass-produced plastic door. Short supply chains, local materials, and low overheads made it possible.

Dispersed vs Enclosed

The development of a sense of enclosure is a major theme in Part III, Elements. Here we consider it only as an axis of analysis.

For years I had seen photographs of the HÉMICYCLE DE LA CARRIÈRE in Nancy, and one day I stumbled into it, exclaiming, "I didn't know that this was *here.*" This is enclosure for enclosure's sake: the oval arcade serves no other function. This one example shows how powerful enclosure can be.

Not everyone likes cozy, enclosed spaces. A few people react strongly against them; I think most of them might be uncomfortable in any urban environment. They are natural candidates for rural living. Alexander admits that "The fact that people feel more comfortable in a space which is at least partly enclosed is hard to explain." ("Positive Outdoor Space," APL, Pattern 106) He admits that this is not always true, as in the case of a beach, but believes that small, enclosed outdoor spaces give a sense of security. The carfree city gives us a good balance: we can have small, enclosed outdoor spaces, similar to the STRADA CAVOUR in Parma, while preserving open natural lands immediately adjacent to the built-up area. I believe that this can meet the needs of nearly everyone who can tolerate urban life at all.

For an example of a fully-developed urban space completely devoid of any sense of enclosure, consider the HOLLYWOOD FREEWAY in Los Angeles. Only the motorists on the freeway below have any sense of enclosure, and they would, given the choice, prefer to look at something other than concrete walls. Although it is not impossible to develop enclosure even under these adverse conditions, it becomes far more difficult. Developing large urban areas with tight enclosure is impossible unless broad circulation arteries are underground. If courtyard blocks were built above the highway, at least the courtyards would exhibit full enclosure. The cost would be great, and the courtyards could not have deep-rooted trees.

STRAIGHT VS CURVED STREETS

I have come to believe that the straight street is the enemy of good urban design. (I must admit that many experts disagree with me on this.) Although there is no reason not to apply both approaches, in different districts, I hope city designers will consider anew the virtues of the curved street. Moderate curvature is sufficient to introduce a sense of enclosure in a street. Narrow streets need less curvature than wide ones, as on the PETERS-GASSE in Basel, a street perhaps 10m (30') wide. The rate of curvature is not high, but the vista down the street is closed off in less than a hundred meters (yards).

I believe that it is essentially impossible to develop a good sense of enclosure in a street that runs straight to the horizon, even if that street is comparatively narrow and the buildings considerably taller than the street is wide. This is illustrated by a STRAIGHT STREET in the recently developed Holendrecht area of Amsterdam Southeast. No matter how far the street extends, if it stays perfectly straight, there remains above the street a notch in the enclosure. In this case, the repetition of identical houses makes the street even less interesting and comfortable. Only the trees at the end of the street draw our attention through the scene, while also serving to enclose it somewhat.

Trees, in fact, can and should be used by those called upon to repair dull, straight streets. In many cases, it will prove too expensive to raze enough buildings to repair the damage, but trees are reasonably cheap to plant and maintain. They can soften the harsh character of straight streets. Even planting trees in straight lines can have this effect, as the trees are themselves unique and do help a sense of enclosure to arise, as long as the branches of the mature trees form a full canopy. Even when the leaves are off the trees, a distance of 100m (yards) or so is enough for the bare branches to create a sense of enclosure. When the trees are in leaf, the sense of enclosure becomes strong.

Braga, Portugal

CONTINUOUS VS BROKEN EDGES

There is no agreement among architects and designers working in the traditional manner on the question of the corner between building façades and the street. The general advice is often, "wrinkle the edges." (See "Building Edge," APL, Pattern 160.) This gives rise to an interesting complexity, and I tend to favor it myself. The pure case, in which the building line is unbroken, for the length of the street, as here along the SALIZZADA SAN SAMUELE in Venice, is clean and uncluttered. The street can be taken in at a glance and the architectural intent is clearly apparent. To my eye, this purity imparts a faintly unfriendly air to the street, mainly because there's absolutely nowhere to linger.

Those obsessed with personal safety will claim that this is the ideal approach, as a mugger has no place to hide. I would argue, however, that in a properly functioning, fairly dense neighborhood, this is not really necessary, as there are so many people around at all times of day that someone is sure to see and react to any cries for help. This only applies, of course, in mixed-use areas, where there are always substantial numbers of people nearby, and in the case of communities with good cohesion.

This RESIDENTIAL STREET in Óbidos exhibits broken edges. The form is in part imposed by the hillside, which necessitated the branching ramp to the right. The jogs in the façades on the right make this street interesting into the distance. Óbidos is a small, self-contained community that stands on a sharp ridge, and most of its streets are interesting, although jogs like these are uncommon on level streets. The buildings have windows on all faces, so the overlook of the street is nearly continuous and street crime is doubtless rare in this close-knit village.

When we examine streets in areas where no buildings touch their neighbors, the edges are broken at each building. Breaks of this kind, however, greatly increase the dispersion of the enclosure, which bleeds away between each building.

FORM VS FUNCTION

Architects have long debated the relationship between form and function. Some believe that form is everything, some that function is all, some that form is part of function, others that function determines form. I will not attempt an answer.

Form is often dictated by passing aesthetic whims, which may be dysfunctional. The ABN BANK BUILDING on Amsterdam's Vijzelstraat is by no means an extreme example. It was built to augment the fortress-like 1930s headquarters building in the next block and designed by an architect under the influence of the International School. Although I would suppose the building to function tolerably well from the perspective of the owner, its form is appalling. Worst is the deep arcade supported by thick, square columns in dark colors and paved with cheap, dull concrete tiles. The arcade is a few steps above street level, which isolates it, thereby savaging the principal reason for building an arcade in the first place. The resulting dark arcade is a bit threatening and in no way attractive. The building is also completely at odds with its surroundings.

Form can also be governed by function with little regard to aesthetics, as in these SOLAR HOUSES in Groningen, the Netherlands. The design was largely dictated by engineering considerations, including the roof overhang to shade the buildings from the summer sun, large glass areas to help heat it in the winter, and the massive earthen berms to reduce energy loss. It doubtless functions fairly well, but function has been allowed to dictate form, unsuccessfully and unnecessarily.

In some designs, no conflict arises. Consider the PALAZZO DELLA PILOTTA in Parma. At the time of its construction, spanning any great distance required the use of the masonry arch or vault, and so the function of the masonry largely dictated its form. With only moderate room for further elaboration, simple but attractive ornamentation was chosen.

Ingenuous vs Sophisticated

The CATHEDRAL in San Marco is the antithesis of sophistication. It was pieced together in a variety of styles over the centuries by many hands, some more artful than others. It is as close to being a garish building as Venice has to offer, a rich, complex building that is at the same time ingenuous and unaffected. From its onion-topped domes to its gilt mosaics to the ranks of multi-colored marble columns, no expense was spared to make this building unique in the world and memorable to everyone who sees it. Compare it to the Parthenon in Greece, also a religious building, which, while very simple, is extremely sophisticated. I am glad that there is room enough in the world for both types.

At the end of the CALLE DELLA PASSIONE in Venice rises this quite plain building at the junction of two canals. It is not made more attractive by the rather ugly color of yellow it is painted or by the accumulated gray dirt. It is, however a more sophisticated building that it first seems, and a building one might come to like better on long acquaintance. The plainness is relieved by the arched water entrances, the boxy bay window, the simple artic-ulation of the eaves, and the opening and closing of the shutters during the course of the day. The stone framing of the windows, common throughout Venice, adds just enough complexity to allow the building to succeed.

The need to create something "sophisticated" afflicts many contemporary architects. Indeed, some buildings are held to be so subtle that only architects can understand and appreciate them. I would submit that, in most cases, this sophistication exists mainly in the mind of the architect. This MONSTROSITY in Los Angeles is the height of sophistication—and bad architec-ture. Its "strong regulating lines" are praised by Jonathan Hale (see his page 125), an author whose opinions I usually respect. In this case, both he and the architect got it wrong. This build-ing is a blight on the neighborhood.

DISSONANCE VS HARMONY

The ear may be truer than the eye, for it is not often that we fail to hear a sour note. The eye, however, often fails to notice a discordant element in a scene.

The AMSTELPLEIN in Amsterdam is as clear a case of dissonance as I have come across. When this area was redeveloped during the 1990s, one small building from a bygone era was preserved at the center of the small square around which three skyscrapers are arranged (the third is behind the camera). The old building is perfectly inoffensive, a fairly good example of Dutch architecture from around the turn of the last century. The skyscrapers are no worse than usual (nor any better) for these megaliths. Together, they're a train wreck. The small building in the middle of the square breaks it up and kills the last chance that this square ever had of succeeding. In cases like this, everyone should find the courage to demolish (or, better, relocate) this now misplaced symbol of a bygone era.

Léon Krier has argued more clearly than anyone I know for the preservation of good areas, which includes forbidding the intrusion of clashing contemporary buildings. Let them, he says, build their modernist buildings where they clash with nothing worse than their own kind. I agree.

The RUE DU BAIN AUX PLANTES in Strasbourg is a beautifully harmonious space. The buildings were very likely the product of different hands, but probably built at around the same time. The materials available and suitable to use in this climate were applied in similar, but not identical ways. We don't actually need to spend more than a moment looking at places like this to know that we're in the presence of a cohesive, harmonious whole. The area is worthy of careful study, but doesn't demand anything of us. We can study it at our leisure and take in the harmonious relationship among the parts whenever we have time. It will be waiting patiently for us.

L. Krier, 16

Symmetry vs Balance

The meaning of symmetry has changed from Greek times, when it basically meant good proportion and balance, to today's usual meaning of mirror symmetry. To avoid confusion, I will use "balance" to denote the original meaning and preserve today's "symmetry" unmolested. To claim that symmetry is natural to us because the human body is symmetrical is false. To prove this to yourself, find a series of frontal portraits and place a mirror vertically so that first one side of each face and then the other are reflected. You will see two quite different people emerge from each portrait, even though the actual differences are small in most faces. A truly symmetrical face is very rare.

The ROYAL PALACE in Fes exhibits perfect symmetry, right down to the twin flag poles. Although this composition is harmonic in its relationships, the whole is a trifle static. This is appropriate in a palace, which has as one of its functions the implied assurance of enduring stability. This is a building to admire and respect, but not one to love.

The Palais de Fontainebleau exhibits fine balance in its COUR DES ADIEUX. The symmetry, however, is quite imperfect. The eye does not immediately perceive the absence of mirror symmetry but does notice the balanced composition. Even quick examination reveals the absence of mirror symmetry, but who would complain?

If we go farther afield in search of asymmetric balance, we cannot fail to notice that most Gothic cathedrals exhibit it; their two towers are usually different, sometimes very different. I think that we will want to reserve mirror symmetry for a few very formal buildings and strive for good balance in the rest.

Symmetry may be more desirable in small objects than in large. Alexander notes that the Alhambra exhibits a high degree of local symmetry but has no symmetry overall. Maybe we expect symmetry in human-sized objects but not in larger ones.

Sitte, 51

TNO, I:187

Classical vs Vernacular

Comparing classical architecture and the vernacular can arouse intense debate. I begin with Oscar Wilde's indictment:

> To me one of the things in history the most to be regretted is that the Christ's own renaissance which has produced the Cathedral at Chartres, the Arthurian cycle of legends, the life of St. Francis of Assisi, the art of Giotto, and Dante's *Divine Comedy,* was not allowed to develop on its own lines, but was interrupted and spoiled by the dreary classical Renaissance that gave us Petrarch, and Raphael's frescoes, and Palladian architecture, and formal French tragedy, and St Paul's Cathedral, and Pope's poetry, and everything that is made from without and by dead rules, and does not spring from within through some spirit informing it.

Well. A consideration of Palladio's buildings, such as his famous IL REDENTORE in Venice, reveals works that are exquisitely precise, exceptionally formal, rather stiff, and ultimately chilly.

Computers can write music in the classical style. The results may follow the rules of counterpoint, but there is no depth to the compositions. A computer cannot write Bach's Goldberg Variations. Equally doomed is any attempt to design entrancing buildings by the application of algorithms. The result will lack Wilde's "spirit informing it," whether that be religious fervor, delirious transport, or love. So, the problem with "dreary" classical architecture lies not in the rules themselves but rather in the absence of real inspiration guiding their application.

Were these simple VERNACULAR HOUSES in Amersfoort "informed" by some strong feeling? The point can be argued, but are these buildings not ultimately more responsive to human needs and aspirations than the sort of mechanistic design seen in the building at the top of page 68? Is this not a sufficient answer?

"'Vernacular' is a term borrowed since the 1850s by architectural historians from linguists, who used it to mean 'the native language of a region.'... 'Vernacular' means 'vulgar' sometimes and 'the bearer of folk wisdom' sometimes. It means 'common' in all three senses of the word—'widespread,' 'ordinary,' and 'beneath notice.'" Brand, 132

De Profundis, Oscar Wilde (Penguin, p.172)

Formal vs Informal

Some spaces are more formal than others. It is appropriate for important locales to be more formal than quiet neighborhoods. Formality generally comes at a higher price than informality because more elaborate ornamentation and more expensive materials are usually associated with more formal spaces.

The PLACE STANISLAS in Nancy is a highly formal space. The square itself is rectilinear, and the buildings surrounding it are in a nice but stiff style that is consistent around the square. Entrance to the square is through elaborate iron gates. Even the lamp standards are complex and expensive. (How ever did those cheap-looking planters land there?)

By comparison, the CAMPO SAN GIACOMO DELL'ORIO in Venice is very informal. The architecture is mainly in vernacular style, saving aside the more complex architecture of the church on the left, which is still comparatively informal. The paving is high-grade stone, but it is simple and devoid of ornamentation.

Neither space is necessarily better than the other; each is well suited to the uses to which it is put.

Intimate vs Impersonal

Fairly closely related to the degree of formality is the degree of intimacy. Formal spaces are rarely intimate, as can be seen in Place Stanislas. Informal spaces are not invariably intimate, but they are usually of smaller scale and tend towards intimacy.

This NARROW STREET AND CAFÉ in Leiden exemplifies the intimate public space. The street is hardly 4m (13') wide and the blocks are very short. A street any narrower could scarcely support even a small café. I believe that small, intimate, informal spaces like this one are the reason that people fall in love with particular neighborhoods. We ought to do everything in our power to make more places like this.

Impersonal spaces are not without their uses. The PRAÇA DO COMÉRCIO in Lisbon is surrounded by the offices of various government ministries. This is probably the stiffest and most formal space in all of Portugal. It is a highly impersonal space, and I have rarely seen anyone linger here, even though large numbers of people pass through on their way between the ferry terminal and the Baixa district that lies just beyond the arch. Since nobody lives in this vicinity, the impersonality of the space does relatively little harm to its utility. This is, really, a space that belongs to all of Portugal, not just a small urban neighborhood. The wide street carrying heavy traffic along one side of the square certainly adds nothing to its intimacy.

MECHANISTIC VS HUMANISTIC

Design can be mechanistic, governed by formal and sometimes complex rules, or it can be humanistic, governed by nothing more than what people agree feels right. Although I normally associate mechanistic design with Modernism, mechanistic effects can actually be found throughout history.

The BASILICA COURTYARD in Assisi is an interesting example. The pavement was striped in endlessly repeating straight lines at great cost in time and materials. The monotonous arches march the full length. While this is an interesting and fine space, it is nonetheless rather mechanistic, which is arguably out of place given the personage in whose honor it was built. It has been said that Francis of Assisi would have objected to the lavishing of a fortune on a church in his honor. His objection would probably have extended to this courtyard.

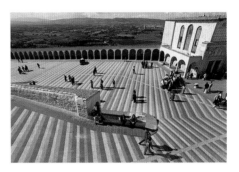

This TINY SQUARE in Lisbon's Alfama district is diametrically opposed to any form of mechanistic design; it is a fine humanist space that doubtless developed into its present form over a long period, in a way that local people found to satisfy their needs. Is there really any better way to design a space?

Efficient vs Effective

Great danger lies in confusing efficiency with effectiveness. The former has to do with costs, the latter with how well the needs of people are met. One vicious aspect of privatization is that it is done in the name of efficiency, with little regard for how well the resultant system meets the needs of those who use it. All that matters is efficiency and profitability.

The GWL CARFREE PROJECT in Amsterdam was afflicted by the efficiency disease. Strolling through this project makes clear that construction costs dominated the design, leading to the architectural poverty we see here. The space probably works reasonably well, and it *is* carfree, but what a dull place to grow up!

On the other hand, this charming SMALL SQUARE in Leiden would be condemned by building contractors as highly inefficient because they would be unable to duplicate it cheaply.

Unsustainable vs Sustainable

No discussion of urban development can ignore sustainability issues. Although we cannot yet forecast what the ultimate sustainable carrying capacity of the Earth may be, we have clearly exceeded it, temporarily. Any design project must strive to reduce energy consumption and rely on renewable materials. Those that can be reused when a building is dismantled are preferable to those that must be landfilled. In this respect, wood is good, as it is renewable and its fuel value can be captured. Stone and brick are excellent, as they can be reused. We tend to think of stonework as expensive, but SIMPLE STONEWORK is still widely used in Portugal. It is more expensive than wood, of course, but is extremely durable, highly attractive, and never requires paint, which avoids the need for a continuous production of toxic materials in order to supply fresh coats of paint. In a nation of rock, stone is an excellent material.

The life-cycle analysis of building materials and techniques is highly complex and not yet very far advanced. When assessing the sustainability of various construction methods, we must consider the matter of energy embedded in the building itself, its longevity, and the reusability and recyclability of the building materials. In most cases, probably the larger factor is the energy that will be consumed every year to operate the building. In this respect, modern glass skyscrapers, like the PHILIPS BUILDING in Amsterdam, generally fare poorly.

SPRAWLED VS CONCENTRATED

The degree of concentration in our urban areas exerts a great influence on their sustainability, quality of life, transport arrangements, and costs, both capital and operating. In most respects, these considerations are all favorably affected by increasing density. Higher density not only leaves more land available for natural and agricultural use, it also reduces water, energy, and materials consumption. The real reason, though, for building densely on as little land as possible is that it allows us to bring many people together for economic and social purposes. Dense cities also permit the arrangement of good public transport.

Many people feel that scattered rural settlements are an ideal form of habitation, but they offer little choice in social life and require long travel to reach all but a few stores, services, and employment. Because of the travel required, they are not particularly sustainable despite the use of firewood for heating.

We will do much better to emulate the dense but low-rise ALFAMA in Lisbon, which offers a large variety of social contacts, a wide field of employment, and nearly any goods or services that may be required, all within easy walking, cycling, or public transport distance. Areas like this can be built of simple materials from local sources and are highly sustainable because they make efficient use of energy.

Dorsoduro, Venice

ORDER & ORGANIZATION IN CITIES

This chapter lays the foundation for what is perhaps the most radical of the changes in city design that I propose. I believe that city design, as it has evolved during the past 500 years, has brought us poorer, not richer environments. This evolution reflects a shift in the balance between order and organization, favoring order at the expense of organization. We will first consider some basic issues that affect urban form as seen through the frame of order and organization. We then review the history of city design in this context.

What I propose in Part IV, Design, is largely a return to urban patterns that were the norm a thousand years ago and that have since been all but abandoned. I must support this proposal by dissecting what I believe to be the errors of the past five centuries. We will begin with the influence of philosophy, the geometry of street networks, and the significance of the grid form. We then consider the design of cities from ancient times, through the classical era, and then, in more detail, the changes that occurred starting with the Renaissance. This discussion is almost entirely in the Western context (taken to include the ancient civilizations of Mesopotamia), but oriental cities are briefly mentioned near the close of the chapter.

For whatever reason, city design seems to alternate, at long intervals, between gridirons and irregular patterns variously called "organic," "medieval," "unplanned," or "chaotic," depending on the viewpoint of the author. Even the gridirons vary quite a good deal. Sometimes, as in Manhattan above 14th Street, they are strictly regular, with perfectly straight streets and intersections at exactly right angles. Blocks are sometimes rectangular, sometimes square. In some cases, street layouts are topological grids, but the streets neither intersect at right angles nor run perfectly straight. This is common in the *bastide* towns, such as Naarden, pictured on page 85. These were new towns

Narrow medieval street, Siena

The radial form came to be favored by Renaissance military strategists, and their concerns often overwhelmed other design issues. The late 15th-century idealized radial plan of Francesco di Giorgio Martini was the first workable scheme, with a large public space in the center and radial streets leading alternately to bastions and gates. Kostof (1991), 189-190

Campiello Centani, Venice

See the chapter "Cities & Transport"

established across Europe near the end of the medieval period. The *bastides* show an interesting transitional form. Most of them have grid-like aspects but only a handful are pure grids.

The perfect gridiron is, of course, highly ordered; the complex arrangement of medieval areas is clearly less ordered. I will argue that, correctly executed, the more complex and less orderly forms exhibit a higher level of organization and are thus to be preferred. The fundamental organizing principle is the arrangement of roughly radial street plans that converge on the main squares and transport halts. Of course, as shown on page 49, this arrangement can be achieved in a form that is also highly ordered. I believe, however, that there is no reason to don the straightjacket of geometric purity, in which all streets are the same width and all blocks in a given sector follow the same progression in size (or are even the same size). Greater flexibility allows us to accommodate differing needs while also designing with, not against, the existing development and topography. This leads to richer, more complex arrangements.

At the same time, it should be evident that irregularity is not per se good; it is only good if the irregularity arises from deeper organizational principles applied to the site and the needs it must serve. Consider the organizational forces that have always underlain city form. Transport is one of those root forces, and transport concerns have worried city designers and planners since at least Roman times. Decisions regarding the mode and volume of transport have enormous effects on city form. The prevailing transport technologies also exert a huge influence on city planning, a matter taken up in *Carfree Cities* at some length. In an era of large cities, it is only high-capacity rail systems that permit the use of medieval city forms—without rail, streets must be much wider to accommodate passenger and freight transport, and this quickly destroys the sense of enclosure that usually arises with narrow streets and small squares. The modern era in city planning and design appears to begin with the

Hungarian invention of the coach in the 15th century, which demanded broad, straight streets. The invention of the elevator in the late 19th century also had major effects.

Construction methods also greatly influence the organization of cities. In earlier times, when materials were cut to size on the site, buildings with irregular shapes posed no particular challenge to the craftsmen who built them. In the modern era, the use of prefabricated parts coupled with modern framing and forming techniques have made the adoption of non-rectilinear shapes somewhat problematic (although still not uncommon). From a cost-driven perspective, the rectangular box is hard to beat, but it is poorly adapted to use in a city whose streets are neither straight nor at right angles to one another.

Energy sources and methods of space heating have also exerted a large influence. Electricity and natural gas permit the supply of energy to buildings without the need to transport fuel over the streets. This yields a quite significant reduction in the total bulk of material moving over the streets. The choice of fuel affects the volume and character of combustion products, which in turn affects the space that must be reserved for chimneys and the like.

Design methods exert, I believe, a large influence on the final design. When designing on paper, the use of straight lines and right angles is so simple and quick that they tend to displace less regular geometries, even when there may be compelling reasons for more complex arrangements. This is a question taken up at some length in DESIGN TECHNIQUES. In fact, the shift to paper-based design seems to occur at the same time that streets stopped being designed by the people who used them and started being designed by experts of one sort or another. That change appears to coincide with the start of the Renaissance. This, as we shall see, was a fateful change. It marks the end of the ability of users to adjust spaces to fit their needs and yields spaces with lower underlying levels of organization.

Alexander's *The Production of Houses* offers some ways out of the quandary. This challenge is considered in the current work on page 491; see also page 303 for a sub-optimal way to circumvent the problem.

Plaza Mayor, Salamanca

INFLUENCE OF PHILOSOPHY ON CITY FORM

Yet not so rational as all that. Zucker (page 43) says, "[The scheme of Pergamum], from the then prevailing Hellenistic viewpoint extremely irrational, was actually dictated by its location on steep and irregular slopes." There is, of course, nothing irrational about adapting the design of a city to its site!

See: "Environmental Complexity: Information for Human-Environment Well-Being" [of the elderly], Alice Ware Davidson and Yaneer Bar-Yam. PDF at: www.necsi.org/projects/yaneer/envcomp.html

Kostof (1991), 99-100

The Cartesian grid is the "rational" way to lay out a city. It's quick, simple, and cheap. The Greeks and Romans used it when laying down colonial cities and military camps. It has been used very widely since the Renaissance. It *does* yield paper plans that are immediately comprehensible. However, even within the context of Cartesian thinking, the grid is irrational. Unlike the irregular branching radial patterns of the medieval era, the grid does not exhibit hierarchy. An orthogonal grid of streets offers few orienting clues and does not lead visitors to the important places—these they would find only by chance or by asking a local resident.

On the other hand, medieval arrangements are full of subtle clues regarding the organization of a town. This point is difficult to illustrate, but the RUA JOÃO DE DEUS in Évora hints at it. This street runs out of the left side of the square and is one of a dozen major streets in this walled medieval town. Although narrow, this street is, like the other major streets, appreciably wider than the secondary streets. Somewhat more imposing buildings are located along it, and it exhibits a high concentration of ground-floor shops and offices. Anyone in search of the large squares of this town would, upon stumbling into this street, be inclined to follow it, and soon be rewarded. However, the Cartesian grid offers little more than a shallow (if satisfactory) order. Grids lack good organization and take no account of the human longing for deep, organized complexity in our environments. We are not simple creatures, nor do we seek extreme simplification in the things we make.

It is claimed that the grid is somehow democratic, that it provides an egalitarian form. However, given the extensive application of the grid form by absolute rulers, Spiro Kostof found little merit in this argument and cites numerous examples of absolute rulers establishing towns on a grid plan.

STREET GEOMETRY

It is my belief that informal, irregular streets often arose when paths turned into streets as people erected buildings along them. In hilly country, paths that have been beaten by humans and animals tend to hold the maximum grade to its lowest practical value. In flat terrain, drainage features and soft soils constrain the location of paths and favor drier sites and firmer soils.

Beaten paths usually take interesting, agreeable shapes. The course of a beaten path is almost never straight but is by no means random. Many needs are expressed by mechanisms that are mainly unconscious. Take this FOOTPATH ACROSS A VACANT LOT. A Cartesian would draw a straight line across this nearly flat lot as being obviously the shortest distance. Those who beat this path, however, chose to take it over the flat stone in the foreground (which will be less muddy) and not directly to the corner, but rather to a point near it, the corner being approached more obliquely than the mean course of the path. This helps to avoid bumping into someone rounding the corner at the same moment and also opens up the view ahead sooner than a direct approach. Gentle curves avoid any sudden change in direction. This is a sensible arrangement from the perspective of human needs. Path formation normally seems to follow these kinds of subtle rules. A conflict arises when designers lay out a network of "sensible" paths that do not take account of human preferences. The result is the familiar beating of paths across the grass.

Hierarchical patterns provide short pathways between most locations and the centers, because this form of street network radiates from the centers. Nearby centers are connected by quite direct routes, deviating only as topography demands. Minor streets provide short routes between any two points in the area, as long as block sizes are not excessive.

A great failing of the grid is that it is actually inefficient, at least in districts with clearly-defined centers (such as transport halts).

"Pave where the path is. An oft-told story (perhaps apocryphal) tells how a brilliantly lazy college planner built a new campus with no paths built in at all. She waited for the first winter and photographed where people made paths in the snow between the buildings. Next spring, that's where the paving went." Brand, 187

Compare a square district (divided into square blocks by streets of zero width) with a circular district (having radial streets infinitely close together). If the circle is drawn through the corners of the square, then the longest path length to the center of the circle is 0.707 of the distance in the grid plan. However, a circle encompassing the same area as a square has a diameter only 0.798 of the diagonal of the square. In theory, the longest trip in the radial layout is $0.707 \times 0.798 = 0.564$ of the longest trip in the grid layout. In practice, the number is around 0.7.

See especially Pattern 106, Positive Outdoor Space

Coimbra

Consider an arbitrary grid of square blocks with the district center in the middle. This arrangement actually *maximizes* the average path length from random origins to the center (for any reasonable layout; see note). Since the most common trip is to the center, this argues strongly for a radial plan. Thus, while a grid is perfectly orderly, it is quite poorly organized.

ADVANTAGES OF CURVED STREETS

For the purposes of this discussion, I will lump together curved streets and articulated streets, as the results are almost the same. Both arrangements yield enclosed spaces, as long as the street is narrow in relation to the rate of curvature. (See the discussion in ENCLOSING STREETS.) Camillo Sitte considered the development of enclosure at great length, a cause later taken up by Christopher Alexander and which is reflected in quite a few of his Patterns.

The curved street is often seen as chaotic and as evidence of the lack of planning. Cartesians favored straight streets, but, in 1889, J.J. Stevenson cogently summarized the issue:

The present infatuation for making streets straight is really curious. No trouble or expense is thought too great to effect this object.... There seems to be an idea that a straight line is the perfection of art. But it is not a beautiful thing. Nature abhors it. In Greek temples there is not a single straight line; when statues are placed beside them their pedestals are often a little out of square....

The designer seems often to think he has achieved a work of art when he has made an arrangement which looks pretty on his paper plan. What is wanted is that the streets should look well as we walk along them, and all experience proves that this is best attained by some departure from the absolute straight line. This is characteristic of all the streets most celebrated for their beauty…. As such streets wind, even if it be but gently, the buildings lining them are placed at an angle of perspective in which they are better seen, each building stands out better in its own individuality, and the change of angle gives varying effects of light and shade….

The actual increase in length of a gently curved street compared to a perfectly straight street is almost negligible. When the curve is introduced by following natural contours, the design is both economical and inspired.

BIAS OF PLANNERS TOWARDS GRIDS

The earliest known street grid was at Kahun in 2670 BCE, although this was clearly a measure of expedience, and the site was soon abandoned. From that time forward, gridirons have been widely applied to cities, much more so in some epochs than in others. Many thinkers on city design seem to have an almost unconscious bias in favor of gridirons. This prejudice seems to be held for a wide range of reasons, including military necessity, capitalist expediency, religious symbolism, aesthetic preference, and simple efficiency.

For A.E.J. Morris, the grid is synonymous with urban planning—the absence of a grid is presumptive evidence of unplanned development. He says, "A gridiron layout cannot just happen—in direct contrast to organic growth it must be consciously determined and applied to the chosen site." Why this is intrinsically better is not made clear, nor is it a given that organic forms are accidental.

Some writers firmly believe in an innate human desire for grids. Paul Zucker says:

In India, as in Egypt, Asia Minor, Hippodamic Greece, and later on in Rome and Central American civilizations, the

J.J. Stevenson, "On Laying-Out Streets For Convenience Of Traffic And Architectural Effect," Royal Institute of British Architects, Transactions 5, new series (1889):89-104. Available on line at: www.library.cornell.edu/Reps/DOCS/stevensn.htm

Morris, 13

Morris, 15

Zucker, 20

Stedman's Medical Dictionary, Houghton Mifflin Co.

Alexander, TNO:II, Part Two

appearance of the gridiron may be explained by mankind's generic urge for order and regularity in contrast to the chaotic growth of nature.

Notice how natural growth is disparaged as "chaotic," a serious logical error. Consider "morphogenesis" as Alexander uses the term, which he borrowed from biology. Morphogenesis is the "differentiation of cells and tissues in the early embryo which results in establishing the form and structure of the various organs and parts of the body." It is anything *but* chaotic. Alexander believes that the best city design and architecture arise when the correct sequence of unfolding occurs, thus mimicking gestation. I believe that a similar process was at work in the design of medieval city districts. The method would have been informal, and the process based more on feeling than thought. The pace was slow enough that the design rationale would have been lost from one generation to the next. Good designs were preserved; mistakes were corrected over the years. The results, as they have come down to us, were often supremely humane.

Both grids and irregular forms can be seen in San Francisco. Where a grid was imposed on steep hills, we find precipitous streets, such as DUNCAN STREET on the flanks of Diamond Heights. It is insane to build vehicular streets so steep. In the steepest areas of San Francisco, vehicular streets sensibly make use of switchbacks to mount the slope at a reasonable grade. When very steep streets are required, they can be built with stairs, foreclosing their use by vehicles but offering pedestrians a shortcut, as here at the BECO DO LOUREIRO in Lisbon's Alfama.

Notwithstanding the association of grids with planning, not all planned areas are gridded. In fact, contemporary US sprawl development is rarely gridded. The tracts are laid out in a cul-de-sac maze, which eliminates through traffic on most streets. The streets are usually curved and sometimes respect topography. In all other respects, they are a disaster. They presume that all travel is by car and often omit sidewalks entirely, even though there is always ample room for them. People walking or cycling must make long detours to reach many nearby destinations, as the web of connections is weak, and no rights-of-way were left for a connecting network of paths. Aside from this important exception, most city design since the Renaissance adopted the grid. During the 19th-century US westward expansion, hundreds of gridded towns were platted beside the railroads. This was a matter of expedience, but these towns almost all still have their original grid.

Sometimes the same exact street plan was stamped on dozens of towns.

It is, alas, uncomfortable to rely on the accuracy of street plans as given in many texts. Minor irregularities in the line of a street may greatly affect its appearance from the street, and errors that appear slight in plan may have important effects in reality. Many town plans depict the streets both straighter and wider than they are. Morris gives an example of a plan of Monpazier "based on over-regularised versions of the actual layout," but should a plan be regularized *at all?* I would argue: certainly not.

Morris, 87

IMPERFECT GRIDS

Many grids, especially old ones, are inexact. This bears thinking about, since it has been known at least since Greek times how to lay out a perfect grid. Irregular grids are sometimes found where the original gridiron crumbled, as discussed in the next section. In other cases, the grids never were perfect. Why do we often find these close approaches to perfect grids in old cities?

Kostof (1991), 48-51

The Harappan cities of the Indus Valley, founded from 2150 BCE onward, had streets at approximately right angles, what Morris calls "more or less regular gridiron layouts." His plans, however, show rather less than more regularity. He gives a plan of Pompeii that is only a rough grid. The streets are not exactly parallel. Intersections are sometimes jogged. Two forks are shown in a plan covering just a dozen blocks. Morris's map

Morris, 15

Morris, 53

Morris, 84, 85

of Aigues-Mortes can be checked against his vertical aerial photograph of it. When his map is superimposed on the photograph, we discover large errors, with some streets far out of position. This town is built on a grid topology, but the streets are not parallel nor even perfectly straight. Some streets are articulated or offset at intersections. Morris claims that grids were used in laying out *bastides* at the end of the medieval era, yet his own plans of eight *bastides* show not a single one with a fully regular grid, and in two cases the deviations are very large. I find it strange that he persists in seeing grids where they do not exist.

Crumbling Grids

Morris, 86, bottom

Once established, a street layout resists short-term change, but changes over a span of centuries are common. Many Roman colonial towns saw their original street layouts altered over long periods of time, sometimes when the towns were reoccupied after long abandonment. Principal streets were often retained in roughly their original form, but other streets became irregular. Unwin gives the example of Aosta, a gridded Roman colonial town. By medieval times it had entirely lost its regularity while retaining some of its original topology.

Venice

Why do people dislike grids sufficiently that they go to the trouble of altering them? Regarding the breakdown of grids in once-regular towns, specifically including Aosta, Kostof finds that three processes were at work. First, the "grid is inflexible in terms of human movement" and people dislike sharp turns, so shortcuts were created through the partially-occupied grid. Second, cultural changes of the occupants led variously to the consolidation or splitting of blocks, along with reoccupation of once-public spaces. "Third, *the impact of new public foci on the urban fabric.* Traffic flow, like running water, will forge its own course: a castle, a cathedral, a bishop's place… will tend to pull the circulation net toward themselves."

Unwin, 49-51

"The background for the urban retrenchment and readjustment in post-Roman Europe is well known—depopulation, reduced circumstances, and a social revolution that consigned towns built for a pagan culture of multiple cults to the monotheistic religions of Christianity and, later on in some regions of the Empire, of Islam. There was no place in the new social structure for theaters, amphitheaters, temples, or (in the Christian case) baths. The civic institutions of the Classical city were also defunct, and as one consequence of this, the defense of public space was weak or non-existent." Kostof (1991), 48

Kostof (1991), 48-51, emphasis in the original

These forces led to the breakdown of many ancient grids. The new city of Dura Europos was given a regular layout when established in Alexandrian times, but the grid soon broke down. Morris, in a note accompanying a plan of medieval Chichester, says, "As re-established however, the main axial crossings of the *cardo* and *decumanus* formed the basis of the layout; other minor streets have also followed the original gridiron to varying extents." However, the plan shown is anything but a grid. The main streets approximate the Roman plan, but there are no unbroken straight streets and many are frankly curved.

Kostof gives two plans of ancient and medieval Rome, as REDRAWN AND SUPERIMPOSED by me. Rome in Imperial times is shown in light green; in 1748, the street plan is as shown in red. The breakdown of the regular plan is dramatic. Is the process more than opportunism or the theft of materials? As summarized by Kostof (1991, p.16), Joseph Rykwert holds that the form of ancient towns was symbolic of myth and ritual, not an expression of rational or practical considerations. Yet can practical considerations really be so far removed? The gridded Roman colonies and military camps may have symbolized Roman authoritarian government, but is it not more likely that the expedience of a grid layout is the most probable explanation for its use? Yet the visions people hold of themselves and their cultures must surely be important. And what about the breakdown of grids? Is it simply a rejection of arbitrary central authority, or is aesthetic awareness or spiritual belief also in play? Do the crooked streets of medieval towns, converging on the principal church, express a notion that each man must find his own, stumbling way to his god? I am not sure.

Having considered some issues that affect city design in every era, we turn now to a history of city form in the West. We will be seeking enlightenment regarding the geometry of street layouts and the design methods that were applied through the ages. This will be studied in the context of order and organization.

Kostof (1991), 105
Dura Europos lies in southeastern modern-day Syria.

Morris, 75

Changes in Rome (Pantheon at right)
As adapted from Kostof (1991),13; medieval Rome is from the Nolli plan of 1748. The source material is difficult to interpret and the drawing should be treated as schematic only.

CHANGES IN URBAN FORM THROUGH HISTORY

www.carfree.com/papers/huf.html

The discussion that follows is a condensation of a paper I wrote in 2005. I concluded that there is a limited range of urban forms and that they are found throughout history. However, scholarly opinion is widely divided on many points, foremost among them the suitability of the grid form and its relationship to conscious planning. I found a contest between the high order of grid plans and the better organization of radial plans.

From the start of the Renaissance, a strong bias appears in favor of grids. Because I believe this to be a critical error, I studied this issue at length and recommend the original paper to those with an interest in the historical and philosophical aspects of this question. For our purposes, however, it will serve to review the changes through history and to pay less attention to the conflicting viewpoints of scholars, attempting always to frame the discussion in terms of order and organization.

Valladolid

ANTIQUITY

We know more about this period than the medieval period that follows it. As in all periods, religious beliefs often influenced city design, and city form expressed a civilization's values.

Kostof (1991), 183

Early in this period, round cities reflected a despot's claims of a cosmic alliance that was the source of his power. Later, in Greek times, a new urban element was introduced: the agora, which expressed growing democracy. It contrasted with axial design, which, according to Zucker, "always represents the architecturally crystallized form of a dictatorial concept of society." Amazingly, Zucker later lavishes praise on the axial designs of the Renaissance and Baroque, the age of nation-states and absolute monarchs.

Zucker, 31

Although gridirons were commonplace in antiquity, neither Athens nor Rome were built on a gridiron. Grids were applied to many of their colonial cities. Morris says that Priene was "… a clear example of the form of a small Greek city of the period. The close-knit but ordered urban grain can be contrasted with that of Erbil—an organic growth counterpart…." Gridded Priene was arranged with the major streets running approximately parallel to the contours of the site and the minor streets running fairly steeply up hill. This led, however, to a low corner of the site having rather steep streets in both directions. On the other hand, ERBIL (Irbil, Arbela, etc.) is a walled town atop a huge earth mound, thought to be the world's oldest continuously occupied urban site. The map shows a complex street pattern, with many streets converging on the Big Gate.

R.E. Wycherley, writing on the relationship of architecture and town planning to everyday life, says of the gridiron plans applied to Greek colonial towns that "No great genius was needed to think out this method." It was quick and simple to apply, and "They made no pretence of aiming at grandiose or picturesque effects, splendid vistas and the like…." However, the new plan for Miletus arranged three separate gridirons, with space left between them for the great public spaces. Edmund N. Bacon says, "Miletus … is one of the most splendid city plans ever made. It shows how it is possible to develop forms of tremendously dynamic quality as counterpoint to the rigid discipline of the gridiron plan." However, Bacon concerns himself chiefly with the main public spaces and considers the gridded residential areas only as a foil for the public spaces. This focus on the public realm is typically Greek and yielded some fine urban spaces, but the areas where people actually lived would have been dull.

In ancient times, a variety of city forms was to be found. The ordered grids variously expressed expedience, convenience, and regimentation. The irregular forms, many of which were no doubt inherited from periods from which we have no records, appear to show excellent organization. The composite forms emphasize some aspect of the society, as at Miletus.

Morris, 24, 39

Morris, 29, 9. He illustrates Priene on his page 29.

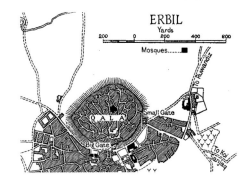

Wycherley, 16-19

Bacon, 75

Madrid

MEDIEVAL TIMES

Regarding epochs, "medieval" encompasses both the dark and middle ages. Morris (82) and Zucker (63) take this period as the 9th to 15th centuries. Henri Pirenne thinks that Roman ways only disappeared when Mediterranean shipping ceased at the time of the Moorish invasion, in the 7th & 8th centuries. (See his Chapter I.) Many take the period to begin with the fall of Rome.

I take the Renaissance to begin in Florence in 1420. Morris (104) says that architectural history divides the Renaissance into four phases: Early Renaissance (1420-1500); Late Renaissance (1500-1600); Baroque (1600-1750); Rococo or Neoclassical (1750-1900). Zucker (144) has the Baroque beginning with Michelangelo's death in 1564.

Valladolid

Kostof (1991), 110, 126

Zucker, 67-74

Kostof (1991), 126

We know comparatively little about what befell cities during the long medieval age. Disasters such as the bubonic plague that repeatedly decimated Europe's population are tolerably well recorded, but written records for the period from 410 CE (the fall of Rome) to 1300 are generally sparse. From the start of the Renaissance, plot and building plans began to be filed in city halls, but it is difficult to obtain much insight into changes in the urban fabric during the course of this earlier period. The Italian Renaissance began around 1420 but affected the form of just a few cities during its first century; medieval city design continued for a long time, particularly in England.

Few new towns were founded in Europe until late in this era, and comparatively little expansion of existing towns occurred. That is not to say, however, that cities and towns did not change. Some towns were abandoned for centuries and eventually rebuilt. Most cities would have burned at least once. It seems that for most of this period local people made minor changes as the need arose; cities evolved slowly. Streets were arranged by those who used them, to suit their needs and desires. These places have very few streets that are straight for any great distance, as is true of informal settlements in all times. In most cases, the widths of the streets change over quite short distances.

In the 13th and 14th centuries, hundreds of new towns were built, the *bastides,* nearly all exhibiting at least partial gridirons, but most of them quite irregular. The form of a *bastide* is thought often to have been influenced by local circumstances. Expansions of existing fortifications, churches, or villages tended to be less regular; towns that were newly founded or based on earlier Roman towns tended to be more regular. But Kostof says, "Among hundreds of *bastides,* uncompromised grids like Monpazier and Aigues-Mortes in France, and Flint in Wales are extremely rare." Yet even Aigues-Mortes lacks a truly regular grid form. (It does seem that Monpazier really is a perfect grid: photographs show a fully-rectilinear street pattern.)

The Dutch town of NAARDEN is one of the few *bastides* I have been able to visit. This was clearly a planned, not organic, town, but its *appearance* owes more to organic arrangement than to the gridiron. The streets are slightly curved, as can be seen here.

Kostof (1991), 54-55

Until late in the period, the more important streets tended to converge on the central square(s), where the city hall, principal church, and market may still be found today. It is often said that medieval street arrangement was haphazard, but I believe this view is incorrect. Kostof cites the Italian hill town as proof that a good fit was arranged between human needs and existing topography. Even those who disparage medieval cities agree that the development of medieval spaces involved something more than random acts. Morris says that the layout of the medieval towns offered informality, romance, and visual surprise. He admits that it only *appears* to be accidental. He laments that "there are only a few recorded instances of aesthetic awareness." However, the lack of records is no reason to presuppose the absence of awareness and intention. There was nothing wrong with the artistic sensibilities of these people, as witnessed by the cathedrals they left us. Why imagine that they brought no thought or skill to the arrangement of their cities?

Morris, 71, 73

Camillo Sitte has a very different view from Morris and has no doubt as to the purposeful nature of medieval city design: "[T]he pattern of their streets was in no way arbitrary; it was the result of events or of orientation, and it complied with the con-figurations of the terrain." We may never know for certain, but I think that there was a great deal of informal collective action; this might have been as simple as neighbors chatting about their street through the years. It is otherwise difficult to account for the stunning results; they could not have arisen by chance. Speaking of the strong defense by Brussels mayor Charles Buls of his city's irregular streets, Kostof says:

Sitte, 60-61

Kostof (1991), 84

Zucker, 91

Zucker, 97

What accounted for the geometries of modern urban design was the professional's habit of arranging on the flat surface of the drawing paper symmetries which will never be experienced on the ground by the pedestrian once the scheme has been realized. At any rate, it is not a question of straight *or* crooked streets, Buls argued. Classical buildings demand an extended point of view, a vista, that would make clear the symmetry of their design; Gothic buildings need to have a closed perspective and a picturesque context.

Zucker seems almost obsessed with symmetry; he can hardly imagine a design that is not based on the symmetrical location of a fountain in a square. However, in medieval space, everything is fluid, and the law of symmetry is not in play. This in no way makes the medieval spaces random or incoherent. In fact, medieval squares show an exquisite sensitivity to the creation of good space. Zucker eventually admits that "Medieval squares owe their beauty to the growth through centuries, each epoch adding its specific architectural values, but never to the intent of conscious planning." I hope to revive this mechanism and mean for it to be conscious, which I believe it was in medieval times.

Except for the hastily-arranged *bastides,* city design during this period reached a level of organization and aesthetic sensibility that I believe has never been rivalled. Even the more ordered, partially-gridded towns from late in the period seem to show great aesthetic awareness.

RENAISSANCE

Comparatively few new towns were established during the Renaissance, but existing towns grew rapidly. Many expansions were based on a rigid grid. Some new towns were founded, however, especially in Sicily, Scandinavia, and the New World. Most of them were fully gridded, many with a square near the

Valladolid

center. Important exceptions include the original Dutch settlement south of Wall Street on Manhattan, which remains a web of irregular streets to this day. Geometrically-regular schemes other than grids have sometimes been proposed, and several of them were actually built during the Renaissance—some of the Scandinavian towns took a radial form. Renaissance thinking was actually quite slow to affect city design, with Genoa's Via Nuova (1470) being the first important example.

A pronounced authoritarian thread runs through this era of increasingly powerful monarchs, to which we owe the application of formal design principles by an all-powerful designer. The results are often stunning at first glance, but these spaces usually lack any sense of evolution. (We must exclude Michelangelo's work on the Capitoline Hill, where he improved on what he found.) These spaces are stiff and cool. Consider the city of Ferrara, which has a large intact MEDIEVAL QUARTER adjoining a similarly-sized RENAISSANCE QUARTER. People still prefer the older part of town, with its curving, narrow streets.

What consequences did Renaissance ideas have for the design of urban spaces? Symmetry and the creation of balanced axial compositions were central motifs. This was sometimes carried to extremes, as in the Piazza del Popolo, with its matching churches flanking the start of the Via del Corso. (Notwithstanding the twin churches, this space is not rectilinear nor even fully symmetrical.) Also of great importance was the placement of monumental buildings, obelisks, and statues at the ends of long, straight streets. Buildings were wrought into coherent ensembles by repeating basic features. Morris says that the "primary straight street" was the basis of Renaissance urbanism and that new, direct routes to facilitate carriage travel were laid. Thus, it can be seen that even 500 years ago, vehicular traffic had already become a major influence on the design of cities.

Renaissance aesthetics and ideas were expressed in the design of streets. Zucker observes that "Definite laws and rules directed

Kostof (1991), 111

Morris, 107

Zucker, 141

Zucker, 99
In most cases, I find it erroneous to say that Gothic spaces exhibit "dispersion." Usually, in fact, they show good enclosure, and the spaces are not overly large.

Morris, 108, quoting Patrick Abercrombie, *Town and Country Planning,* no page cited.

Morris, 108

Zucker, 110
For Oscar Wilde's "dead rules," see page 65.

In fact, these spaces had long *been* the city centers.

Sic, northeast

Zucker, 113-115

the limits of space and volume. Purity of stereometric form was in itself considered 'beautiful.'" He also says, "From the fifteenth century on, architectural design, aesthetic theory, and the principles of city planning are directed by identical ideas, foremost among them the desire for discipline and order in contrast to the relative irregularity and dispersion of Gothic space."

Patrick Abercrombie says of the straight streets and their terminal monuments, "The monument at the end is recompense, as it were, for walking along a straight road (devoid of the surprises and romantic charm of the twisting streets) and economies are met by keeping the fronting buildings plain so as to enhance the climax...." Morris adds, "[T]he gridiron also conformed to the Renaissance ideal of aesthetic uniformity, even if the resulting townscape all too frequently reveals this to be mere monotony...." Even Zucker, who prefers regularity, ultimately concedes that the "continuous repetition of a stereotyped pattern of a square bespeaks the mechanization of an idea" and that "some important three-dimensional creations of the Renaissance developed more or less independently of theoretical thinking; intuition rather than systematization inspired these crystallizations of the human spirit in space." Zucker then goes on to say:

> Strangely enough, the most famous Renaissance squares in Italy do not follow the scheme of the typical closed squares of this period.... They owe their final shape rather to a gradual development from the Middle Ages to the Renaissance, when they took on the characteristics which made them the heart of their cities.
> ... And yet, the combination of Piazza [San Marco], Piazzetta, and the third smaller square at the northwest corner of St. Mark's fuse into one of the greatest space impressions of all time, comparable in their symphonic effect only to the Imperial Fora in Rome.

This is a remarkable admission, coming from someone who is so disparaging of medieval city design. The great works of the Renaissance are thus more than the simple application of rules. The spaces that work best draw at least some of their inspiration from their earlier, less ordered medieval designs.

During the Renaissance, the relative value placed on order increased and, in many cases, the value placed on organization declined. When this was done sympathetically and with a respect for earlier work, some very fine spaces arose. It may be that the Renaissance was one of the rare times when both ways of knowing operated together: the intuitive and the rational. That this led to some of the best art in history is more than chance.

Plaza Mayor, Valladolid

Baroque

We turn now to the Baroque, sometimes considered a part of the Renaissance, but actually a distinct era of its own. Baroque notions remained influential into the 20th century. The ideas of René Descartes (1596-1650) influenced thinking during the Baroque and later periods (see Values & Philosophy). Paper plans and straight lines continued to dominate, now as a reflection of Cartesian logic. Transport concerns became ever more important as cities grew. Kostof says that "It can be demonstrated that a principal motive for the widening and straightening of streets in the Age of Absolutism was to ease the passage and parking of coaches in the old urban cores."

Kostof (1991), 231

The steadily increasing power of nation-states and their absolute rulers finds expression in Baroque design. Nancy's 18th-century expansion had two axes, one a major new east-west route passing through today's Place Stanislas and the other running, at a right angle, north into the old medieval city. This latter axis includes three formal, related spaces, the Place de la Carrière; the short Rue Héré; and the terminal HEMICYCLE, in front of the Provincial Government Palace.

The Baroque is the era when plans began to be *imposed* on a site. No longer would topography stand in the way. Local features were to be accurately ascertained and dramatized or suppressed according to the will of the designer. This marks the start of man's willful imposition on nature. Kostof says this willfulness was even "cherished."

Kostof (1991), 218-219

The avenue is the principal feature of the Baroque city. By adding a few straight avenues to a city, its character could be changed. The rigid geometry also expressed "the dominant sense of life." The City Museum in Lisbon exhibits several plans of Lisbon's Baixa, a flat area sloping gently up from the Rio Tejo (Tagus River) that had always been the heart of the city. The Baixa was flattened by the 1755 earthquake and tsunami. Plans of the area (see my adaptation at the end of this chapter) prior to its destruction show a web of streets. Reconstruction plans developed for the Marquis de Pombal show a steady evolution towards rectilinearity, until a perfect grid is attained. Pombal, driven by exigencies, chose this version, which can still be seen in much the same form today, as here on the RUA AUGUSTA. The rigidity of the plan is relieved by the varying distance between parallel streets and the differing widths of those streets. It is interesting to note, however, that Pombal elected to retain the old street plans in the hills on either side of the Baixa, where the destruction was only partial, and these, too, are still visible today.

Morris, 107

Straight lines also dominated Renaissance design, so what distinguishes the Baroque period from that earlier era? Morris quotes Heinrich Wölfflin: "In contrast to Renaissance art, which sought permanence and repose in everything, the baroque had from the first a definite *sense of direction.*" Morris then quotes Wölfflin at length:

Morris (106), quoting Wölfflin (58)

> Renaissance art is the art of calm and beauty ... its creations are perfect: they reveal nothing forced or inhibited, uneasy or agitated ... we are surely not mistaken in seeing in this

heavenly calm and content the highest expression of the
artistic spirit of that age.

Baroque aims at a different effect. It wants to carry us
away with the force of its impact, immediate and overwhelming…. Its impact on us is intended to be only momentary, while that of the Renaissance is slower and quieter, but more enduring, making us want to linger for ever in
its presence. This momentary impact of baroque is powerful, but soon leaves us with a certain sense of desolation.

Morris (106) quoting Wölfflin (38), ellipsis in Morris.
Zucker (143) also cites Wölfflin.

So, in this view, the Baroque represents a transition from quiet
reflection and enduring interest to, if you will, glittery designs
calculated to impress. But perhaps the situation is not quite so
simple. Indeed, Zucker found two distinct Baroques:

Alexander speaks of "the fallacy of baroque architecture which piles on detail, but which never reaches a
very intense kind of life." Alexander, TNO, I: 128

What is historically called baroque is divided aesthetically
into two tendencies. On the one hand, there is the baroque
derived from Michelangelo, exaggerating and contorting
the more placid forms of the High Renaissance, accentu-
ating individual parts within a whole, dramatizing and
emphasizing volumes and masses. On the other hand, during the same centuries there was manifested the classicistic
approach, based on Palladio and the Vitruvian Academy,
leaning heavily on ancient examples, regular, reticent in
expression, sometimes of a certain dryness which often
leads to the reproach of "academicism." These opposing
tendencies, Michelangelo's emotional, individualistic concept and Palladio's rational, classicistic attitude, become so
outspoken in the works of their successors that it seems
almost impossible … to cover both trends by one heading:
"baroque," referring merely to chronology.

See, for example, Palladio's Redentore, page 65.

Zucker, 144

So it was not all Palladio and his "dead rules" after all. Some of
this work has real heart in it.

Vila Real de Santo António, Portugal
This city in the extreme southeast of the country is also
the product of Pombal. The plan is almost perfectly
regular, and this large square is actually square.

The Old Way of Seeing

Grid in Vila Real de Santo António

Much of the Baroque can be seen as order for order's sake. The wealth and power of the ruler were to be extravagantly expressed by rich and expensive detail, most of which lacks deep underlying organization. In fact, organizational considerations were limited mainly to ensuring the smooth movement of coaches, to which end the straight street was admirably suited.

INDUSTRIAL ERA

Industrialization jolted urban planning and design. High-grade, standardized materials became widely available at low prices. Unfortunately, the effect on city life and urban design was quite negative. Belching smokestacks darkened the skies. Mass production replaced craft. British tenant farmers were forced off the land, driven to work in the mills and live in mean housing nearby. So began an era in which anything that could not be bought and sold was held to be of little real value. Jonathan Hale traces the steady decline in the design skills of ordinary people to the beginning of this period, although he can give no specific cause. It may be nothing more than materialism.

The impact of industrialization on cities was not wholly negative, however. Inventions such as the railroad, water treatment, gas lighting, and electricity made larger cities possible, which fed the phenomenal growth in knowledge that continues to this day. Nor is it true that all urban design of the period had the depressing character of mill-workers' housing; some fine urban areas were also built in 19th century.

Zucker criticizes the design that characterized the period:

… the straight line became predominant in architecture and hence rectangularity in city planning—in other words, the gridiron scheme. Thus, quite naturally, the *street,* conceived of as a continuous perspective, mostly of similar units, became more important than the square. In the opinion of this period, utmost clarity suggests to the mind structural truth and creates automatically therewith aesthetic pleasure, which now actually became identical with mere intellectual satisfaction.

Zucker, 189-190

For Sitte the problems were not only this rarefied intellectualism. Like Zucker, he finds that the importance and quality of squares declined sharply and that the feeling of space deteriorated. Streets became so broad that a square could only be defined if its dimensions were huge, hence the shift of emphasis from the design of squares to the design of streets: it had become nearly impossible to make squares. Sitte complained:

Sitte, 87

An undeviating boulevard, miles long, seems boring even in the most beautiful surroundings. It is unnatural, it does not adapt itself to irregular terrain, and it remains uninteresting in effect, so that, mentally fatigued, one can hardly await its termination.... But as the more frequent shorter streets of modern planning also produce an unfortunate effect, there must be some other cause for it. It is the same as in the plazas, namely *faulty closure of the sides of the street.* The continual breaching by wide cross streets, so that on both sides nothing is left but a row of separated blocks of buildings, is the main reason why no unified impression can be attained.

Rue de Rivoli, Paris

Sitte, 86

Sitte uses the example of an arcade to explain why the creation of enclosure had become impossible. The streets are so wide that each block stands out distinctly; the repeating arches of the arcade can no longer create enclosure because they are broken by such wide streets. The continuity needed to create enclosure can no longer be achieved. Medieval comfort has been sacrificed to transport requirements. The best that can be had is monumentality. Order has become an end in its own right.

Sitte, 86-87

GARDEN CITIES

The movement begins with Howard's 1898 publication of *To-morrow: a Peaceful Path to Real Reform*. Howard's ideas continue to influence the form of suburban sprawl, although probably in ways he would not have desired.

A reaction to the 19th-century poverty came with the Garden Cities movement, which responded to both deteriorating living conditions and the excessive width of streets. Ebenezer Howard is the figure most closely associated with this movement, which arose when tuberculosis was burning through the overworked and overcrowded masses of poor people in industrial cities. Howard wanted to spread cities out across the countryside and provide each household with a decent house on its own plot.

This spoke to the British soul, which had remained stubbornly pastoral—the aristocracy had its estates and mansions, and the working class deserved its own miniature versions. In English-speaking lands, echoes of this urge still prevail, and the suburban house standing free on its own plot is still widely considered the most desirable form of housing in these countries.

About 30 to the hectare

The Garden Cities movement also gave us the work of Raymond Unwin, whose deep appreciation of medieval forms is eloquently reflected in his *Town Planning in Practice*. But he then strangely concluded that 12-to-the-acre single-family housing was the best contemporary solution. His views on cities contrast sharply with Renaissance thinking. He found that the beauty of the Gothic town was "due in no small degree to its irregular plan, combined with a style of architecture which displays great freedom in the proportion and outline of its masses, and a richness and picturesqueness in its details" in contrast to classical forms consisting "mainly of groups of cubes." Speaking of the irregular design of medieval Rothenburg, he says:

Unwin, 62

[W]e see how, especially in the original old town, the scale of the principal *places* and streets is sufficiently large for them to dominate the town, and to provide for it a frame and centre points which render the whole really simple and easily comprehensible to the stranger....

Unwin, 112

Unwin held that the irregular arrangement of streets must not be determined by whimsy but informed by all of the site's physical and cultural design constraints. It would be all too easy to sketch an irregular plan that was superficially pleasing but that lacked some underlying organization. Referring to his German contemporaries, he says, "Some of the irregularity in their work appears to be introduced for its own sake, and if not aimlessly, at least without adequate reason...."

Unwin, 112

MODERNISM & OTHER VIRUSES

In the 20th century, the accumulated wisdom of architecture and city design was not simply abandoned, it was reviled. Modernism took a perverse pride in breaking with thought and design from all prior epochs. It was based on a presumed need to completely reinvent culture to suit the dawning new age. The end of Modernism is placed by some at the demolition of the failed Modernist Pruitt-Igoe housing project in 1972, but it can reasonably be argued that Modernism is with us still.

Modernism was a response to industrialization, to the era in which mass-produced, standardized products really began to affect the world. This was a time of great optimism, a time when technology was expected to end hunger, clean up squalor, and eliminate ugliness. Architecture would lead the charge: the Bauhaus, "starting from zero," would reinvent architecture.

Modernism relied upon designs that used large numbers of cheap, mass-produced parts. Given the imperative of standardized parts, it was necessary to seek an uplifting style based on endlessly repeated elements. Some early efforts were modestly successful in this regard, and even a few recent buildings have some merit, such as this MISPLACED HOUSE in Amsterdam.

Modernism adopted the automobile as an icon, and Modern architecture and city design are wedded to the automobile, which was to bring freedom to all. This led to Corbusier's

"Modernism began in the 1890s with the arrival of whole new *kinds* of buildings...." Brand, 55

towers–in–a–park scheme, with broad highways connecting the districts. Corbusier proposed demolishing vast swathes of central Paris to impose this scheme, and his alienating concept was widely adopted, with disastrous results, in the postwar era.

Corbusier never really understood just how much space was required by cars, or how inadequate his proposed highways would be. Of Corbusier's Chandigarh, Peter Hall says, "There was a grid of fast traffic roads, already used in plans for Marseilles and Bogotá, to cater for a level of car ownership even lower than the Paris of 1925, which was low enough." Ultimately, of course, the demand for road space in large auto-centric cities proved insatiable. The view of the car as an ideal mode of urban transport was disconnected from reality in ways that became increasingly familiar as Modernism became ever more threadbare.

Hitler gave Modernism a providential boost when he kicked the Bauhaus out of Germany. His pet architect, Albert Speer, promoted a brutal German classicism. And so, in a fateful turn of history, classical architecture came to be associated with fascism, and the Modernists, many of whom were equally absolutist, were seen as the defenders of democracy. Once Hitler had been crushed, they knew no bounds. The arrogance characteristic of so many Modern architects is probably most evident in Corbusier and Philip Johnson. What is most ironic is that the Bauhaus had its roots in socialism, in the concern for the welfare of the worker. But the fatal flaw was *elitist* socialism: all-knowing architects would design perfect buildings for the grateful masses.

Modernism slowly developed into a purely intellectual exercise: the buildings were great because the thoughts behind them were great. As Modernism devolved into Post-Modernism and Deconstructivism, this reached absurd proportions. Mathematical concepts, such as fractals, were seized upon by architects, who had no idea what a fractal actually was. They took it to mean "broken-edged," and a rash of buildings, like the Guggenheim Museum in Bilbao, appeared with rough edges.

Hall, 214

Zeppelin Field by Albert Speer

Johnson was himself a one-time Nazi supporter

For an explanation of what a fractal actually is, see: Nikos A. Salingaros, "Fractals in the New Architecture." www.math.utsa.edu/sphere/salingar/fractals.html

So far were they from understanding fractals that the Deconstructivists eliminated real fractals, which had always underlain architecture and city design. Nikos Salingaros considers this loss:

> People actually have to be psychologically conditioned before they can create non-fractal objects. Unfortunately, that is just what our education and media have been doing to us throughout the past several decades. The "image of modernity" is one of sleek, abrupt geometric shapes, and this is perhaps the most powerful force in shaping our cities.

Salingaros, "Connecting the Fractal City"
applied.math.utsa.edu/~salingar/connecting.html

The number of buildings designed according to the principles of Modernism and its followers is actually fairly small. Most of what was built after WW II is not really Modern at all, even though auto-centric design came to hold nearly universal sway. The vast majority of postwar houses built in the USA were caricatures of early-American styles. Most commercial buildings since 1970 are engineered structures, in the sense that cost and profitable function determine everything. The trend culminates in the "big-box" store—a giant box standing in a sea of black asphalt parking lots. "Architecture" cannot be used in the same breath. These stores are sited on cheap land at highway intersections. The highway has thus become the American icon, symbolizing a total, if temporary, victory of auto-centric city design. Cars organized everything; even order was lost.

Big-box store, Los Angeles

THE NEW URBANISM

The New Urbanism is a reaction to the increasingly bizarre swerves of contemporary architecture and urban planning. It chiefly revisits early 20th-century urban forms, typified by the US streetcar suburbs built in the 1920s. These were comparatively dense, close-in residential suburbs built on a grid plan and connected to downtown by light rail. The automobile was

Livingston, NJ

already a presence but had not yet dominated cities, and city dwellers had not yet arranged their lives around them. There is really nothing much wrong with the streetcar suburb as a residential form if located near a small city, and quite a lot that's right. It is, however, distinctly suburban. I believe that the New Urbanism might more honestly call itself the Old Suburbanism. However, some New Urbanist architects and city designers are true urbanists and understand and love the urban context.

Léon Krier and Peter Calthorpe, for example

Like the 1920s suburbs that it emulates, New Urbanism adopts the grid as the basis for city design. I think this arises not from any particular love of straight streets but from a recognition of the need for a fully-interconnected web of streets, such as the grid topology provides. (This is a reaction to the cul-de-sac that typifies contemporary sprawl development.) In fact, a review of New Urbanist plans shows many that are topological grids but make little use of unbroken straight streets.

See Léon Krier's *Architecture: Choice or Fate.*
See also Lucien Steil's "Tradition and Modernity in Contemporary Practice":
www.periferia.org/3000/tradition_mod.html

Allied with the New Urbanist movement are contemporary forms of architecture such as the New Classicism or Traditional Architecture. Their exponents understand the worth of historical urban forms, including the curved street.

Non-Western Cultures

Ville Nouvelle, Fes

We will touch only briefly on the history of urban form in a non-Western context, but the subject is fully as complex as in the West. We see in cities from Beijing to Mexico City that powerful figures have throughout history preferred to arrange their cities using axial and gridded forms that express their status, power, and wealth. In freer times and places, from Asian *kampongs* to Brazilian *favelas,* groups of ordinary citizens seem always to arrange their communities in irregular shapes. Even taking the camps of the Palestinian refugees, we find that the original rectilinear arrangement of tents morphs into a complex web of streets in a single generation. We make a serious error if we assume that this rejection of the grid is a random or anarchic act. It expresses a yearning for freedom and independence. It is a stout rejection of regimentation.

A Conundrum?

Zucker draws a harrowing conclusion to his chapter on 17th- to 19th-century streets and squares:

> Quite generally the meaning of the square as a spatial experience can be grasped only by those who are aware of the phenomenon that the human reaction toward the form and dimensions of shaped and molded space changes continuously. This change happens not only from century to century, from country to country, but even within one period and one nation; and it means more than a mere alteration of "taste." It is not dependent on contemporary abstract doctrines and philosophies, although it is certainly influenced by them. It is elemental. It grows from a specific and characteristic mode of human behavior and attitude, articulated in specific forms by the creative process....

Venice

Zucker, 236

If he is right, then there is little hope that the design solutions of one generation will suit the next. Fortunately, this does not appear to be true. Some people live in urban areas that have not changed appreciably in a millennium, and they seem to enjoy and take pride in their patrimony. I think we need not be concerned that good solutions reached today will be cast aside in a few decades. Good urban fabric endures.

We will take with us the lessons of this chapter and attempt to apply them to the design of new urban areas. The methods I will propose emphasize underlying organization. Superficial order can be had at whatever level people prefer.

Cava de San Miguel, Madrid

Baixa, Lisbon, before and after the 1755 earthquake
The pre-earthquake condition is shown in red. Pombal's plan is shown in light green. The source material is exceptionally difficult to interpret and the drawing should be treated as schematic only. Some minor streets may be missing from the pre-earthquake plan.

DESIGN CONSTRAINTS

Virtually every design problem is constrained to some degree by external circumstances, and urban design is no exception. The development of the Reference Design for carfree cities was tightly constrained even despite the assumed absence of geographic and climatic constraints. The design was constrained by the need for quick and efficient transport, low energy consumption, and rich social life.

In this chapter we consider the principal design constraints that will affect all real-world carfree projects. These constraints should be established and formally stated at the start of the design process. Local practices, including the legal, political, and economic systems, exert a large influence on most projects. Location and climate also greatly influence design. Intimate knowledge of local circumstances must be acquired before design begins; if this knowledge is not directly available, design work must be postponed until it is assembled. Of course, local knowledge is usually available from local experts who can and should be brought into any project.

WALKING

The walking speed of an adult is commonly given as 250 ft/min (76 m/min), which is a reasonable estimate for most purposes. In reality, of course, walking speed varies both from individual to individual and from time to time. There is also general agreement that public transport and basic daily needs must be within a five-minute walk if people are to find carfree life an attractive choice. In the development of the Reference District, this led directly to a district radius of 380m (1250'), the radial street pattern, and metro entrances at several points along the platforms.

I do not regard 5 minutes as an absolute limit but rather as best practice. By increasing the limit to 7 or even 10 minutes, a great

Arezzo, Italy. This town was much affected by its hilltop site. A radial street plan was chosen, with the cathedral at the top and streets falling down the hillside. Other streets, with lower grades, run concentrically around the hillside. The constraints imposed by the site were integrated into a fine design.

The possible extent of the pre-industrial walking city is reached in Fes-al-Bali, where a walk from one end of that city quarter to the other takes an hour, too long for most people to make regularly. Thus, the pedestrian city cannot expand much beyond the population of Fes-al-Bali, which was 156,000 in 2002. Venice, with a permanent population of about 70,000 today, also takes about an hour to cross on foot. Larger pedestrian cities require a public transport system that makes it quick and easy to travel the longer distances between districts. This is indeed one of the design constraints that shaped the Reference Design.

deal of flexibility is gained, including the possibility of large reductions in construction density. The actual limit adopted for a given project will depend on many circumstances, including culture and climate, but careful consideration should be given before deviating far from the five-minute standard. I can say that, in my own experience, a walk of more than ten minutes to a transport halt feels like a long way.

BICYCLING

Local conditions greatly affect bicycling. In cultures like the USA, nearly everyone regards the bike as a child's toy or a way to exercise, not as serious transportation. In the Netherlands, the bicycle is regarded as just one of several normal means of getting about. Virtually everyone can ride a bike and nearly everyone has a bike at his disposal. In the newer parts of Amsterdam, such as here in GAASPERPLAS, excellent bike infrastructure was built, but the older parts of the city generally lack the wide bike paths and freedom from car traffic found here.

The effects of climate are important, but even in very hot places, people prefer biking to walking, although the normal speed of cycling is slow due to the need to avoid becoming overheated. Even in frigid Canada, some people bike all winter.

When designing a carfree area, the local bicycle culture must be considered from the start, because biking is the ready substitute for driving. In Ferrara, cycling is common and accepted (despite the large Fiat assembly plant), as witnessed by the bike racks here on the VIA GARIBALDI. One could safely assume that the bicycle could be relied upon for much local transport when designing a project in that city.

This matter has important implications for design, including the capacity of the public transport system, the distance from transport halts to the most distant doorways, capacity of bike paths, and the volume of bicycle storage that must be provided.

FREIGHT

The transport of freight is the most difficult constraint and must be addressed from the outset. The economic position of any city is much affected by its connections to the global freight network and the efficiency of local delivery. When laborious freight handling is required, as here on RIO DI SANTA MARIA FORMOSA in Venice, the increased direct costs reduce the competitiveness of the local economy in the global market. However, the real costs of freight delivery are increased by externalized costs, and on this measure, freight delivery in Venice may be more effective and less burdensome than the high price implies.

Global competition is ruthless, and businesses will do anything to cut their direct costs, including externalizing costs to other businesses, the government, and the public at large. Global trade may decline in the face of energy and climate constraints, but I doubt the decline will be as great as some people may hope. The key challenge here, I believe, is to end the externalization of costs and to greatly reduce the energy expended in freight transport. This will probably require reductions in total ton-miles. However, large improvements in energy efficiency can be achieved simply by shifting to rail systems.

The major constraint in designing freight systems for carfree cities is the need to accommodate standard shipping containers, which are rapidly displacing most other means of shipping. Although commodities are often handled in bulk, it is possible to load virtually any cargo into one or another specialized container. The day is fast approaching when most goods moving any great distance will be containerized by the shipper, and so we must ensure that containers can be delivered directly to commercial and industrial locations throughout the city.

Carfree Cities proposed a means to deliver containers using an automated rail system. As discussed on page 169 of the present work, such a system must serve at least 50,000 people to be

Externalized costs of freight delivery include danger to third parties, noise, air pollution, greenhouse gas emissions, damage to rights of way and abutters, and congestion. Of course, freight delivery in Venice also involves many of these costs, but at a level that may be appreciably less than for delivery by truck.

Standard shipping containers

Freight delivery, Murano

This can be achieved through a combination of taxation, government regulation, and fundamental revision of the structure of limited-liability corporations.

Sprawl development in the USA is consuming land at a frightening rate as people move ever farther from cities and demand ever larger building plots. The highways that support this are themselves significant consumers of land.

economically viable, but the right-of-way can be reserved at the start of planning and used for truck deliveries until it becomes practical to install a dedicated rail system. A region's economy and its freight needs must be clearly understood. Good estimates of freight volume, origins and destinations, types of freight, capacity of existing long-haul freight systems, and planned additions to the freight infrastructure are essential.

COSTS

The world must assess the costs of all human activities in more than monetary terms alone. "Costs" must include both internal and external costs, whether monetary or non-monetary. We currently lack a system for the assessment of non-monetary costs but will soon be forced either to monetize them (e.g., a carbon tax) or to enact limits (e.g., energy rationing). I do not believe that advanced civilization stands much chance of surviving the 21st century intact unless the need for this approach is widely accepted and rather promptly implemented; we are today destroying the very ecosystems on which we depend.

What costs are of concern? Clearly, of course, direct expenses will continue to be important. We must build efficiently and durably in order to hold down the cost of decent housing and comfortable workplaces. Efficient investments in public infrastructure are essential, with a critical eye towards maintenance costs. Barriers to the externalization of costs must be erected.

We must minimize all material inputs, including energy and water, so that we never run short of these crucial supplies. We must protect the purity of both surface water and groundwater. We must not pollute the air and must limit greenhouse gas emissions to a level that halts climate change. We must conserve land for productive use and species preservation. In short, we must return to the thriftiness that once characterized virtually all human endeavor. This need not lead to meanness, but it does signal an end to profligacy, which, after all, does not seem to have made us any happier. Finally, we must minimize the human costs of all that we do. Noise must be limited, danger from all sources minimized, and the public health protected.

We urgently need better tools to assess these circumstances: economics alone is no longer a sufficiently capable tool. While such simple measures as the "ecological footprint" are useful and help to raise public awareness, they fail to provide a deep understanding of the processes involved. We need sophisticated computer models to answer these questions. For now, however, we can simply strive to reduce all inputs as much as possible and to minimize externalized costs of all kinds.

In this regard, the Reference Design for carfree cities is the best model I have been able to develop that stands some chance of public acceptance. Its widespread adoption would give us a century in which to develop new energy supplies.

SAFETY

Public safety considerations are taken up briefly in URBAN PLANNING (page 139). Personal safety is not considered there, but the environments we build must foster it. This is achieved in two ways. First, we must build places that tend to discourage criminal activity. Relatively dense urban areas have fairly high resistance to crime, as long as economic disparities are not too great. Narrow streets overlooked by many windows ought to be safe enough in any society in which people feel some responsibility for the welfare of their neighbors. This, in fact, leads to the second condition: we must build environments that encourage people to get to know one another. It ought to be an explicit design constraint that our built spaces must foster positive social contact. Given that we are by nature a gregarious species, this is not such a difficult condition to achieve, although suburban sprawl fails here, too.

If the Bicycle-Centric Carfree City as proposed in an appendix of *Carfree Cities* is accepted as a viable model, even greater reductions would be possible than provided by the Reference Design. I did not advance that model because I believe that too many people in Western nations would reject such dramatic changes in their way of life.

I think that the transition to carfree cities will be an easier proposition if we offer convenient public transport, instead of the bike, as a replacement for driving. Good public transport is sufficiently energy-efficient that I think it reasonable to hope for a sustainable energy infrastructure capable of supplying its requirements. Certainly, this is a much more reasonable proposition than to assume that sustainable energy can be found to power suburban sprawl, even if cars do become very much more efficient.

Mixed uses are essential to provide good security around the clock. This is the only practical way to assure the presence of eyes and ears on the street throughout the day, as here in the CASTELLO DISTRICT of Venice.

SITE CONSTRAINTS

The nature of the site itself imposes physical design constraints. The Modernists chose largely to ignore site constraints, and their engineers found ways to carry the burdens this imposes on, for instance, heating and cooling systems. In an era of cheap energy, this approach did work and led to office towers that could have been built in any city without exciting notice. Local climate was not allowed to influence the "purity" of design, but rather only the tonnage of air conditioning capacity provided. Today, it is folly to ignore climate in design.

When building a skyscraper, one can largely ignore conditions on or in the ground. Sloping sites and mushy soils can all be overcome with enough concrete. The cost of this remains a fairly small part of total costs. In the construction of minor buildings, we are forced to take local site conditions into account, and this is no bad thing. Any sensitive designer can find opportunities in nearly any site, although a steep north-facing hillside in a cold climate is a difficult proposition. By paying attention to local soil conditions, we can build to an efficient height, perhaps a story lower than we might otherwise desire, and in so doing keep foundation costs under control.

Local culture and history are routinely ignored but must also be taken as site constraints. Buildings that respect local traditions are more likely to be viewed as good neighbors than buildings based on abstract theories of architecture that pay no heed to what has gone before. Buildings considerate of their neighbors are likely to be valued, and so maintained for longer periods. Site assessment is considered starting on page 135.

A friend once gave me a paper by James P. Collins, "Foundations and Substructures." Alas, it seems never to have been published. The author, obviously the embodiment of the practical engineer, proposes many ways to save money on a foundation without impairing the safety of the building. Make sure your engineers are practical people who will speak up if you are about to do something stupid or expensive.

Density Required for Carfree Districts

One of the constraints that must be defined at the start of design is the question of density. How many people are to be accommodated? On how much land? How much of that land will be built upon? There has been what amounts to a revulsion on the part of many citizens in English-speaking nations against dense cities. In some US cities, the cheapest dwellings (often derelict) are found in the oldest inner-city neighborhoods. This aversion to density is not shared by much of the rest of the world. Evidence of this can be found in the relationship between housing prices and distance from the city center. In many European cities, the most expensive dwellings are in the city center, as here along the HERENGRACHT in Amsterdam.

Dense neighborhoods can offer a very high quality of life and a rich social environment. Think of central Paris or Amsterdam. It is very difficult to buy or rent a house in these places due to the very high demand. Dense city centers remain popular in many cultures around the world, but English-speakers seem aversive to these places. The only advantage of low density that residents of a carfree city must forego is big green spaces next to their houses; one of the specific goals of the Reference Design is to provide very large green areas immediately adjacent to every district, plus green courtyards behind every house. When carefully arranged and tended, these are highly satisfactory.

We must achieve sufficient density to support good public transport. Single-story construction cannot satisfy this requirement, and two-story buildings are a difficult proposition.

People seem to have a very poor sense of just how dense an area is or what various levels of density look like on the ground. The following chapter considers the question of density and illustrates various sites with differing densities. Those who are not familiar with Plot Ratio, Floor Area Ratio, and Human Density should first study the explanation on the next page.

Courtyard, Ca' d'Oro, Venice
For more examples of just how much can be done with *small* green areas, see other examples from Venice in *Carfree Times* #42:
www.carfree.com/cft/i042.html

Units & Density Measurements

Throughout this work, measurements are given in the original units, usually metric, followed by rough conversions to the other units (in parentheses). Errors usually do not exceed the low precision of the source data. Accurate conversion factors are given below.

Length

$$1 \text{ centimeter (cm)} = 0.3937 \text{ inches (")}$$
$$1 \text{ meter (m)} = 3.281 \text{ feet (ft } or \text{ ')}$$
$$1 \text{ kilometer (km)} = 0.6214 \text{ miles (mi)}$$

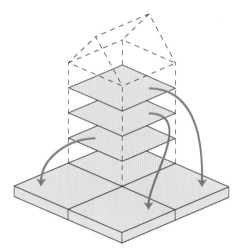

Floor Area Ratio (FAR)

This book makes frequent reference to FAR, which is simply a measure of the building density of a given site. To calculate FAR, first determine the site's Plot Ratio (PR). In the example above, the building covers 25% of the site, so PR = 0.25. The FAR equals PR times the number of stories. The building shown above has 4 stories, so FAR = 0.25×4 = 1 for this site.

Human density is simply the number of residents and employees living and working on one hectare.

Urban forms are compared below, using data from Fouchier (1996), page 10. (Venice and carfree city by author).

Area

$$1 \text{ m}^2 = 10.76 \text{ ft}^2$$
$$1 \text{ hectare (ha)} = 2.471 \text{ acres}$$
$$1 \text{ km}^2 = 0.3861 \text{ mi}^2$$

Weight

$$1 \text{ kilogram (kg)} = 2.205 \text{ pounds (lb)}$$
$$1 \text{ tonne (t)} = 1.102 \text{ short tons}$$

Power

$$746 \text{ watts (w)} = 1 \text{ US horsepower}$$

Adult Walking Speed

$$76 \text{ m/min} = 250 \text{ ft/min}$$

The US system of counting floors is used: the ground floor is the first floor (most Europeans count the ground floor as floor zero). The US number system is used: 10,000.00 is ten thousand. Currency is expressed in 2007 US dollars.

District	FAR	PR	Avg Stories	Human Density
Hong Kong	3.73	.33	11.2	2205
Paris-Montholon (IX)	3.20	.55	5.9	753
Central Venice	2.69	.67	4.0	unk.
Carfree design	1.50	.38	4.0	440
French public housing	0.63	.15	4.3	186
Single-family housing	0.23	.19	1.2	39

THE DENSITY QUESTION

When cities required encircling walls to protect them against attack, the cost of the wall imposed great discipline in the use of urban land. High density brought the cost of strong walls within reach and made available many defenders in relation to the length of wall. There are still quite a few intact medieval cities available for study. Fes-al-Bali (Morocco) and Évora (Portugal) are especially noteworthy. Despite their different cultural heritages, these two cities are quite similar in their densities. In both, streets are quite narrow (especially in Fes-al-Bali) and buildings are typically two or three stories tall. I do not have accurate FARs (see previous page) for these cities but 1.5 is a reasonable estimate for both, or about the same as the Reference Design, which has much more open space but is four stories tall.

These are by no means the extremes of density in old cities, however. The FAR of the San Marco district of Venice exceeds 2.5. Venice was built on artificial islands protected by the lagoon and its treacherous sand banks. The huge labor involved made this land about as valuable as walled sites. San Marco is the densest old urban district of which I am aware. The high-rise quarters of Manhattan are only about twice as dense.

It seems that the high density of cities was rarely considered; it simply went along with the benefits of urban life and good protection against marauders. As long as these high-density cities escaped the ravages of industrialization, they remained satisfactory places to live. When industrial pollution was added to the filth and disease caused by extreme overcrowding, early industrial cities became the dreadful places memorialized by Charles Dickens. Escape was thought the only option, and from this arose the low-density, quasi-urban proposals of Ebenezer Howard and the Garden Cities movement.

Dense medieval cities such as Perugia and Siena remain to this day excellent and much sought-after places to live, except

Perugia, Italy. The walls are no longer as complete as those of Évora or Fes-al-Bali, but the arrangement and width of the streets is quite similar in all three cities. The density in Perugia is higher than in the other two cities.

High density in Venice

where conditions have deteriorated because of industrial pollution or the admission of automobiles. However, we must note that, although the building density of these areas has changed little or not at all for centuries, the population density has declined appreciably during the past 50 years, as family sizes have declined. This trend is further affected by the practice of fusing two old dwelling units into a single, larger dwelling. Thus, the population of Venice has declined by about 65% in 60 years, with very little change in the urbanized area or the density of construction. (This figure does not consider the conversion of dwelling units into hotel rooms, and the number of beds has declined much less than the size of the permanent population.)

FEAR OF DENSITY

Why do people, especially those in English-speaking nations, so fear density? Why does it carry such negative connotations? Part of the answer is culture. On the Continent, rich people always had houses in the city, even if they also had country estates. Power and wealth were less directly associated with the landed aristocracy than in Britain. In the UK, planners had come to associate high density with the back-to-back industrial slums of the 19th century, which they had struggled to demolish and replace between about 1920 and 1970. The high-rise projects that were built in the latter part of this period maintained about the same overall density as the slums they replaced, but with considerably more open space. Virtually all of these projects were social disasters. This seems to have led to a conclusion that density itself is the culprit, and British planners have been afraid of density ever since, as have most Britons.

Pruitt-Igoe block demolished

At the core of the desire to live in sparsely-populated areas is the apparent increase in the difficulty of getting along with the neighbors. The fantasy is that living in the country simply eliminates this problem, even though the reality is rarely so simple.

It is certainly true that radio, television, and amplified music make it more difficult for neighbors to get along. The problem became even more acute when musical tastes began to fragment after about 1965; there is no longer even agreement as to what "good" music is.

When social bonds are strong and there is broad agreement on culture, these problems are easier to manage. One of the failures of modern cities is the loss of the public spaces where agreement on these matters is sustained, as discussed starting on page 33. Multi-ethnic society has many advantages, but the easy-going agreement on societal norms is often lost, which strains people's ability to get along. The proposals in URBAN VILLAGES are intended to reduce the friction in daily life by helping people to establish communities with clusters of shared values.

It is interesting that most vacation destinations in Europe are actually quite dense, even those built in recent years. People seem to have no fear of these dense urban areas, nor of the cheek-by-jowl accommodation, and they seem to enjoy the excellent people-watching that characterizes high density. Yet they seem reluctant to take this arrangement home with them.

It may be that, for many people, the absence of large open spaces is a marker for "too dense." Even if houses are spaced fairly far apart, people may perceive an area as too crowded unless there are open fields or good-sized parks. One of the advantages of building densely is that it permits adjacent lands to be left open. This pattern is often found in Italian hill towns, where construction ends abruptly at the CITY WALL, with open land beginning right on the other side, as here in Perugia. I myself greatly prefer areas arranged in this manner.

So, what is density? How is it measured, What does it look like? What implications do various levels of density have for the organization of a city? There are two principal measures that describe density and one adjunct that greatly affects the perception of density. We consider these matters next.

Venice

See also "City-Country Fingers," APL, Pattern 3

Plot Ratio

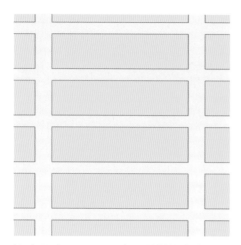

Manhattan's avenues are about 100' (30m) wide and the cross-town streets about 65' (20m) wide.

See *Visualizing Density* by Campoli and MacLean for many US examples of density. Unfortunately, they give density only as "dwelling units per acre," which is less useful than plot ratio and FAR (see next page), which are independent of unit-size effects.

GIS=Geographic Information Systems

The first and perhaps more obvious component of density is plot ratio. This is simply the proportion of a given site that is built upon. Values above 0.7 are unusual. Suburban patterns of development can be said to exist on most sites with a plot ratio below 0.25. Only if buildings are very tall (as in the example of the Amstel Station area in Amsterdam, page 120), can urban densities be achieved with such low plot ratios. Plot ratio is not always easy to assess from the street, as it is greatly affected by the size of interior courtyards, which are usually hidden from view. It can safely be assumed, however, that plot ratio cannot exceed about 0.6 in any city with fairly broad streets (MANHATTAN BLOCKS reach about 0.63, but the cross-town streets really cannot be considered "broad.") So, we will generally find plot ratios in urban areas varying between about 0.3 and 0.6.

It is nearly impossible to accurately determine the plot ratio of an urban area without recourse to detailed maps. Even then, the value may be difficult to compute, as many plot maps do not show what part of the site is built upon. Of those maps that do depict buildings, many are outdated, and the buildings may have encroached upon both the street and the interior courtyard. A really accurate assessment requires both detailed vertical aerial photography and ground inspection of any areas whose use may not be evident. This is almost never done, so plot ratio is only known with any certainty in the case of projects that have recently been completed and can be assumed to have been built in accordance with detailed plans that are available for measurement. This situation is changing rapidly in many localities as highly accurate GIS data becomes available. Unfortunately, GIS data still does not usually indicate the height of buildings in stories. However, exact figures are not actually required. If plot ratio is known to within 10%, this will generally suffice for our purposes.

Nothing affects plot ratio as much as the width of streets. Although block length and courtyard size will have a considerable effect, comparatively minor changes in the widths of streets have a large effect on plot ratio. This can be understood by considering a CHESS BOARD. If the streets are taken to be the outer rows and columns and the remainder of the board to be solid buildings, the plot ratio is $(6{\times}6){\div}(8{\times}8){=}0.5625$. Just the single outer box of squares is nearly equal in area to the rest of the board. (Of course, streets are shared by adjacent blocks, so the numbers are not actually as bad as it first appears.)

The tremendous efficiency of narrow streets is not widely appreciated but is a central issue in planning. This is the Achilles heel of the auto-centric city, which requires extremely broad streets. In US cities, 60% of the land in downtown areas is routinely given over to circulation. Buildings and green space are thus left to share only 40% of the land. One of the ironies of auto-centric transport is that it works against itself, by forcing destinations to spread out, to provide room for circulation.

FLOOR AREA RATIO

The Floor Area Ratio (FAR) of an urban area is the most telling single expression of its density. It is nothing more than a comparison of the floor area to the land area of a given site. FAR is simply the product of plot ratio and the average number of floors (including the ground floor). See page 108 for an explanation and an example. The amount of space allocated per bed and per workplace may vary quite widely between societies, but FAR is transportable across societies as an expression of floor area per unit land. Areas with similar FARs will often have somewhat similar appearance from the street, although the examples that follow make clear that this is not always the case.

Since, for a given culture, the average amount of floor area per resident and per worker will be relatively constant, FAR is a useful expression of how densely populated a given urban area will be when completed. This in turn provides important data points such as the amount of water required, the demand for transport, and the number of children who must be educated.

It will thus be seen that, from the standpoint of urbanism, the higher the FAR, the more efficient the use that is being made of the site. If a given number of people must find housing and employment on a given site, a high FAR allows more land to be left undisturbed as parks, forests, fields, or open water.

One caution: since the average number of stories is so important in this calculation, a comparatively small error in estimating this value causes an appreciable error in the result. Floor counts cannot be determined from vertical aerial photographs. In my practice, it is obtained simply by walking through an area and counting floors in individual buildings. The practice is far more difficult and appreciably less accurate in areas that are not relatively homogeneous, which was an important consideration in selecting the examples that follow.

Erratic story counts, Venice

GROSS VS NET DENSITY

I have chosen in all cases to work with gross rather than net density. The difference is simply that gross density neglects the loss of usable space to walls, utility spaces, stairs, etc. The calculation of net usable floor area is nearly impossible except on a small scale and is further complicated by variations in standards. In some cases, floor area includes a percentage of the measured area of porches, unfinished attics, garages, etc. It must be remembered that in nearly all cases, net usable floor area will be at least 20% less than gross area. In the case of some skyscrapers, net area may be less than 50% of gross area, due mainly to the large amount of space lost to elevators and thick supporting columns. Hallways consume a surprising amount of space except in the very smallest buildings, which may lack them entirely.

The Matter of Scale

One consideration that does not directly affect plot ratio or FAR but does greatly affect *perceived* density is the question of scale. The sense of scale created by an area is affected by two main factors: street width and building height. (The question of scale is also taken up in AXES OF ANALYSIS.) The width of buildings also affects scale, to a lesser degree. The depth of buildings has even less effect (from the street; from within the building the effect is large). However, if buildings are so shallow that people in the street can see right through them and on into the courtyard, the apparent scale is considerably reduced.

Amsterdam

If a given plan is stretched or shrunk uniformly in three dimensions, both FAR and plot ratio are unaffected, assuming that ceiling heights are changed rather than the number of floors. In practice, this is not how changes of scale occur. Principally, what happens as block lengths become shorter and streets become narrower is that buildings remain fairly constant in depth from front to back. As the scale gets smaller, the height of buildings is reduced, with a consequent reduction in the number of floors. The result is that the amount of green space declines sharply but that the FAR declines rather slowly. This is illustrated by the island of BURANO in the Venetian lagoon. This dense community is built mainly of two- and three-story houses on streets that are not terribly narrow in comparison to the height of the adjoining buildings. There is, however, very little green space. (Open space is available around the shores of the island, which are nowhere more than a few minutes walk away.) I have estimated the FAR at 1.5.

Woven through the remainder of this book is a plea for small-scale environments. They are intrinsically human-scaled, and the importance of this is greater than normally admitted. In the most extreme cases, such as in the southeast of Amsterdam, over-scaled buildings were demolished after a short life.

People seem to be alienated by large-scale urban areas and to feel comfortable in small-scale neighborhoods. Of course, not every urban area can be arranged at very small scale, and the contrast between a few large-scale squares and buildings on the one hand and the large body of narrow streets and small buildings on the other hand may actually enhance the sense of comfort in the small-scale areas. Even Venice has the large Piazza San Marco with its three large buildings (St. Marks, Palace, Campanile), which is certainly the largest-scale area in the city. Although grand, this is not an intimate space, nor was it intended to be. Most of the rest of Venice is much smaller-scaled, even including the parish squares, many of which have quite large churches. These, however, are balanced by the other buildings around the square, which are nearly always at fairly small scale. You may wish to carry with you an image of a VERY SMALL-SCALE AREA, such as this one in Amsterdam. The center building is approximately the size of the Reference Building.

HOLLOW, MEDIUM-RISE BLOCKS

Budens, Portugal

An interior courtyard surrounded by four-story buildings offers many advantages, including a great deal of street frontage, excellent light, useful amounts of green space, and moderate construction costs. The courtyard pattern yields blocks short enough to provide many streets, which, because of their large number, can be fairly narrow and still provide ample capacity for foot and bicycle traffic. Free-standing buildings can only provide these advantages at low densities or by resorting to high buildings. The courtyard arrangement avoids the need for alienating, expensive high-rise buildings. It yields an arrangement that is comfortable to most people and requires a minimum of energy for heating and lighting. These buildings do not usually require elevators and are economical to construct. Operating and maintenance costs are reasonable.

FAR Illustrated

The following pages illustrate the Floor Area Ratio ("FAR"; see explanation and example on page 108) of nine relatively homogeneous neighborhoods. Each includes a plan at 1:5385 scale (the page-edge scale divisions are 10m and 100m). Amsterdam was chosen for most cases because homogeneous examples of many city forms can be found there.

The selection of the precise area to be mapped and measured is somewhat arbitrary. Clearly, shifting the area of measurement would yield different statistics, and in some cases the changes would be fairly large. However, the area included is reasonably representative of the neighborhood and a reflection of its density. North is at the top, within about five degrees.

Maps were compiled from site inspections and a variety of sources. The maps and the resultant statistics are fairly accurate, but minor systematic errors (such as tracing the inside or the outside of building outlines) will have noticeable effects on the statistics. The same method was applied consistently, and the statistics are accurate enough to give a good understanding of the relative efficiency of different urban forms in providing floor space per unit land.

Statistics apply to the full area of each plan, which is in all cases a square 360m (1181') on a side. The FAR is given first and then the average number of floors. This is followed by the percentage of the site devoted to each of the following uses. "Buildings" are shown in light orange and depict the bases of the buildings, irrespective of setbacks, overhangs, or canopies. (This figure is Plot Ratio × 100.) "Paving" is shown in light gray and includes open pavers with grass growing between. "Green" is shown in green and is any earthen surface. "Water" is shown in light blue.

Following the statistical summary is a description of the area and its uses. Nearly all the photographs were taken fairly close to the center of the mapped area, and all with my 20mm lens.

The neighborhood around the Rua 5 de Outubro in Évora is homogeneous. Most buildings are three stories tall, and none less than two or more than four. The side streets are somewhat narrower than this main street, and the architecture is less grand than here, but the density is fairly consistent.

These same examples are available on line at:
www.carfree.com/design/far/index.html
I hope to add to the on-line collection over the years.

Piazza San Marco

Campo San Zulian

Back street

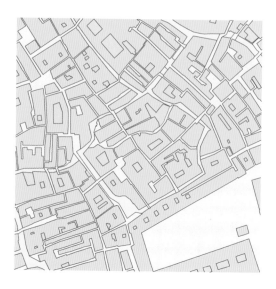

SAN MARCO, VENICE

FAR	Floors	Built	Paved	Green	Water
2.85	4.5	63	26	5	5

This is the oldest part of Venice. Streets and buildings have been in substantially their current form for half a millennium. The dense construction and narrow streets are broken only by the occasional square. Piazza San Marco, shown here, is by far the largest of these. Most streets are very narrow, with no street more than 10m (33') wide. Many, like the alley shown in the bottom photograph, are not even 3m (10') wide. This part of Venice has the tallest buildings, many up to five stories, and very few less than three. Most of the scarce green space is private.

The waterways are the area's principal transport network, with virtually all goods being delivered by water to a point as close as possible to the final destination. The area sees very heavy tourism, which is now the primary industry.

Nieuwendijk

Sint Jacobsdwarsstraat

Medieval Heart, Amsterdam

FAR	Floors	Built	Paved	Green	Water
2.40	4	60	36	0	4

This district in central Amsterdam is near the site of the original dam from which the city takes its name. The area typifies medieval city districts. The broad street to the west marks a former city wall; the broad street to the east is the Damrak, Amsterdam's main street. Other streets in the area are rarely more than 10m (33') wide, and some of the *steegjes* (alleys) running roughly east-west are only 2m (6.5') wide. Much of this area is carfree, simply because the streets were not wide enough to permit significant traffic. Buildings are 3-5 stories high. There is no green space.

The blocks are built nearly solid, without interior courtyards. However, there are often setbacks and light wells in the interiors of blocks, so that many spaces have some light from the back. This is both a mixed-use area and a major commercial center.

Kolksteeg

Rembrandt Tower

Philips Building

Base of the third tower, left

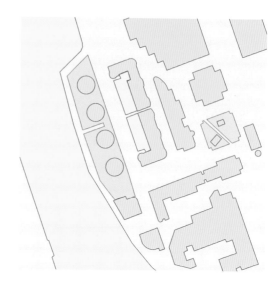

AMSTEL STATION AREA, AMSTERDAM

FAR	Floors	Built	Paved	Green	Water
2.31	9.1	25	41	6	27

The soft soils of Amsterdam delayed the appearance of skyscrapers for decades. In the past 15 years, three of them were built on this site along the Amstel River and adjacent to a major rail station, in the northeast corner. The skyscrapers cluster around a small open space in which one old building was retained; the other buildings on the site are 4-12 story office blocks and apartments; two of these lower buildings are visible on the left side of the middle photograph. To the east of the site is a large transport corridor. Most open space is paved; none is private.

Setback is the critical design parameter in skyscraper districts, and the average story count here is held down by setbacks. When combined with the 25% plot ratio, this yields a FAR that is actually appreciably lower than that of San Marco.

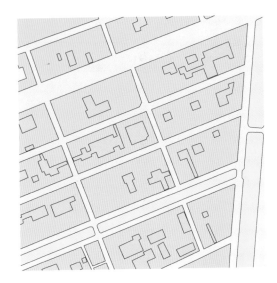

Tweede Laurierdwarsstraat

JORDAAN, AMSTERDAM

FAR	Floors	Built	Paved	Green	Water
1.90	3.5	54	26	10	9

This area was built at the same time as the famous and more lavish Canal District. The neighborhood was first home to the artisans who built both areas, and later of cottage industry. The area was laid out on a regular plan that once included more water. (The broad street in the north was a canal like the one to the south until it was filled in to provide more parking.) Many of the private interior courtyards have been encroached upon over the years, and some have nearly disappeared, which gives rise in part to the rather high FAR.

Cars are permitted throughout this area, but many streets are too narrow to allow parking, so some streets often appear to be carfree. This mixed-use area has enjoyed sharply increased popularity and urban renewal since about 1990.

Laurierstraat

Courtyard from Tweede Laurierdwarsstraat

Corner Utrechtsestraat & Kerkstraat

Keizersgracht

Courtyard behind the Utrechtsestraat

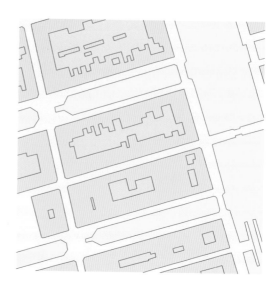

Canal District, Amsterdam

FAR	Floors	Built	Paved	Green	Water
1.65	4.5	37	23	13	27

The Canal District contains many of the sights by which Amsterdam is known. This area makes rather inefficient use of space. Canal streets, such as the Keizersgracht, are about 40m (130') wide, including roadways on both sides. If the map were shifted to the west, dropping the Amstel River, the FAR would rise some. The scale of the area is quite large, and the blocks are among the largest in the whole city, which gives rise to the large interior courtyards, accessible only to abutters.

The Utrechtsestraat (to the west) is a major artery running into the city center. It is only 12m (40') wide. Side streets, such as the Kerkstraat, are about 10m (33') wide. Some use is made of rooftops and balconies. This is a mixed use area with many shops, especially boutiques. Bikes are widely used.

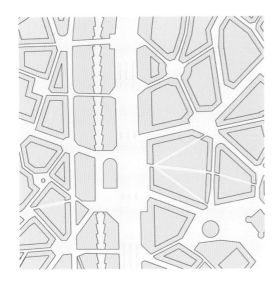

Bahnhofstrasse, Zürich

REFERENCE DISTRICT

FAR	Floors	Built	Paved	Green	Freight
1.53	4.0	38	35	25	2

This is a portion of the Reference District as presented in *Carfree Cities*. The design was inspired by the medieval city, but I have devoted more space to interior courtyards than was usual during that period, because I think people need more green space. Energy-efficient rail systems provide quick and easy movement across cities, which leaves more room for green space.

All buildings are assumed to be four stories tall. The buildings abutting the central boulevard are much larger than the others, and it was envisioned that these would be mainly for office and commercial occupancies. There is no water, but the metro-freight line occupies 2% of the area and is colored as for as water. It could, in fact, be replaced by a canal and boats used to move freight, although this practice is expensive and inefficient.

Calle del Pistor, Venice

Salizzada di San Lio, Venice

Eeftink

Egeldonk

Gravestein

HIGH-RISE, AMSTERDAM SOUTHEAST

FAR	Floors	Built	Paved	Green	Water
1.12	8.4	13	28	51	7

Starting in the 1960s, Amsterdam expanded to the southeast. This area had previously been uninhabited, so planners began with a blank canvas. Many of these hexagonal high-rises were built, and some were torn down after just 30 years due to severe social problems. The buildings themselves were adjudged part of the problem. New mid-rise units, seen in the southeast corner of the map, replaced the high-rise buildings. A large parking garage in the northwest was counted as providing no usable floor area. The large green areas are public.

This area was once entirely carfree and much of it remains so today, but some surface-level roads have been allowed to encroach upon the district. Despite the high-rise buildings, the achieved FAR is quite low. It is almost entirely residential.

MID-RISE, AMSTERDAM SOUTHEAST

FAR	Floors	Built	Paved	Green	Water
0.93	3.75	25	28	46	1

When the 1960s high-rise projects failed, planners turned to more practical and effective arrangements, such as these mid-rise units, which were built on most of the remaining land in the Southeast district. Unlike the nearby high-rise areas, this area was never carfree (despite good metro service), and large areas are devoted to car parking. The interior courtyards are not fully enclosed and so are open to anyone.

The area is entirely residential, although shops and services are available just to the south. The cubes at ground level, visible in the top photograph, provide storage, particularly of bicycles. The entire area is very well supplied with bike paths, and cycling is an important mode of transport, as it is almost everywhere in the Netherlands.

Maarsenhof

Interior courtyard

Maarsenhof parking

Maldenhof

Maldenhof

Maldenhof parking

ROW HOUSES, AMSTERDAM SOUTHEAST

FAR	Floors	Built	Paved	Green	Water
0.51	2.5	20	36	42	2

It was felt necessary to include some traditional Dutch row housing in the Southeast district; houses like this can be found in almost any Dutch city or town. This level of density is barely enough to support good public transport, but the area enjoys fine metro service, in part due to higher densities along other sections of the line.

The area is difficult to illustrate. The top photo is quite characteristic of the streets onto which the houses face. The middle photo shows what could best be considered the back yards, but these vary somewhat, with this one wider than most. One of the large parking lots can be seen in the bottom photograph. All houses are two-stories-plus-usable-attic; the area is entirely residential. Much of the surface is paved.

Minervalaan

MINERVALAAN, AMSTERDAM

FAR	Floors	Built	Paved	Green	Water
0.22	1.50	14	30	47	8

NB: Only the single-family area was included in the statistics.

Minervalaan

This section of the Minervalaan is included only as an example of suburban density to which true urban density can be compared. (This is a small area of single-family detached houses not typical of Amsterdam; the row houses to the east and west are appreciably denser and not included in the calculations.)

These are among the most expensive houses in the city. This area is located within a short walk of Amsterdam's World Trade Center and its excellent metro and rail connections. It will probably be redeveloped in the coming years, as the land is too valuable to be devoted to such low-intensity use. No city can be developed at this density if it is to rely on public transport instead of cars; the costs and distances are too great.

Minervapad

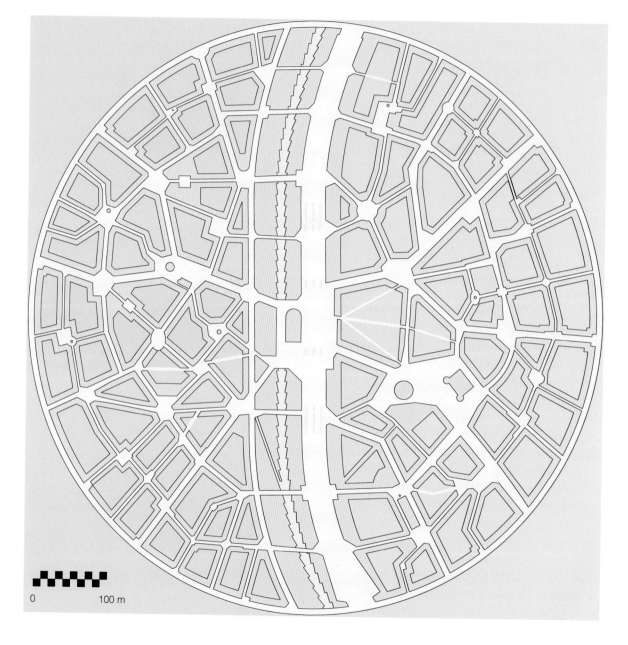

0   100 m

PART II

PREPARATION

The eight chapters in this Part consider the preparations that must be made in order to support the design process described in Part IV, which presumes that the design of most areas will be conducted on the site and by the future residents. Most of this preparatory work is the responsibility of urban planners.

Urban planning decisions and choices regarding essential services and infrastructure must be made before design can begin, as these decisions affect the design of the districts and neighborhoods. Decisions regarding passenger and freight transport, street engineering, and energy supply all exert an influence on the final design of an area. The choice of a developer has many implications for the nature of the completed project. The establishment of urban villages is proposed as the basic unit of organization and design. Only once the basic urban planning tasks are substantially complete and a final site program adopted can the design method suggested in Part IV be brought into play.

Woonerf, Delft

URBAN PLANNING
Considers design goals, planning studies, site information, open space & ecology, hazard management (including fire, earthquake, landslide, siting of emergency facilities & evacuation), solar access, the site in the region, citizen planners & designers, and the transition from planning to design

PASSENGER TRANSPORT
Examines transit route structure, transit modes, convenient service, handicapped access, carriage of wheeled vehicles, pedestrians, bicycle infrastructure, local transit service, taxis, nuisance modes, and external transport.

Venice

Freight

Considers wholesale distribution, container-based freight, metro-freight, intermodal yards, district depots, alternatives to metro-freight, special cases, light freight, the concierge system, local services & shopping, personal freight, and waste handling.

Paving, Grading & Drainage

Discusses the civil works and engineering that affect street layout, paving, drainage & street profiles, grading & drainage, and mixed carfree/auto-centric cases.

Energy & Utilities

Examines sources of sustainable energy and considers energy strategy, overhead utilities, street lighting, underground utilities, junctions & cabinets, data pipes, electricity, gas, and water & sewer installations.

Developer

Considers the fear of chaotic development, types of project initiators, influence of the developer, project owner, funding, construction, project type, and project management.

Urban Villages

Examines urban village size, village formation, shared values & values clusters, subculture boundary, interior courtyards, social life, children, the elderly, walkable communities, local economies, concierge service, mixed uses, and nuisances.

Site Program

Discusses the final site program, which can be considered a design specification. Includes economic basis, mixed uses, population density & distribution, parameters of the Reference Design, baseline floor and land allowances, the final site program, and the design of the central boulevard area.

URBAN PLANNING

This is a book about city design, not urban planning. However, planning directly affects design, and we must consider its influences. Urban planners must ensure that we build in the right places at densities that can be sustained on the site. Planning must include public transport arrangements and the designation of areas that are suitable for development. In this chapter, we consider how planning decisions affect design. The principal end product of planning is a "site program" that defines the neighborhood to come in fairly specific terms that do not yet foresee the actual streets and buildings (see SITE PROGRAM).

Planning is by its nature an intensely political process. The interests of citizens who live in the area and those who are expected to move there should be represented by one means or another. Public hearings are usual in Western democracies, and the final recommendations often require legislative approval.

The kind of developer, if not the specific organization, is often identified before the start of planning, as each kind of organization has certain types of projects that it knows how to execute and will accept (see DEVELOPER).

The final design of neighborhoods should begin only after urban planning is essentially complete. It is otherwise likely that the work will have to be done again once final planning decisions are known. However, some preliminary design exercises may be useful during the planning phase, as these studies can influence planning. The two tasks do overlap somewhat.

Today, nearly any site can be turned into a city, but this was not always so. When energy was scarce and expensive, more frugal choices were made than today, especially with respect to earth moving. Ironically, the sparing use of resources yielded results that were better than most present-day projects.

We begin by considering the goals that should guide urban planners in their thinking about a project.

Venice. The most difficult design constraint here was the conversion of a tidal mud flat into a city. The work had to be accomplished with muscle power, so great economy was sought in earth moving, and an effort was made to work with nature rather than against it.

Design Goals

Planners and designers must satisfy a range of conflicting goals. The costs of land, site development, construction, and operation stand opposed to other needs, and a satisfactory compromise may be difficult to reach. Fortunately, mid-rise buildings that abut one another offer a satisfactory and comparatively economical solution. We must set fundamental goals for planners and designers, which should include the following:

Assure a high quality of life for those who will use the area. This requires the arrangement of:
- Opportunities for informal social contact
- Safe, early independence for children
- Continued self-reliance of the elderly
- Ease in meeting life's daily needs
- Mixed uses in every neighborhood
- Routine destinations located within the district
- Ample pedestrian traffic to assure safe, lively streets
- Low noise levels
- Small gardens behind most buildings
- Accessible natural areas

Beauty is not optional: good human functioning and successful societies require it. Beautiful urban areas are characterized by:
- Carfree streets
- Human scale
- Well-proportioned streets & squares
- Richly-textured buildings

No city functions well without good passenger transport, and in carfree cities we must ensure its provision by arranging for:
- Short walks to halts
- High utilization

"Site Repair" (APL, Pattern 104) is one of Alexander's most important patterns. Although Alexander developed this pattern in the context of siting individual buildings, it applies equally well to entire projects. The principle is simple: build on the most damaged parts of the site and preserve undisturbed, to the extent possible, the best parts of the site. This pattern often complements the decisions that will be taken in designating open space.

Venice

- Frequent service
- Single-transfer journeys
- Minimal land occupation
- Low capital & operating costs
- Low externalized costs
- High energy efficiency

A diverse, vigorous economy is essential to a successful society. Achieve this by providing:
- Ample space for businesses
- Workable sites for heavy industry
- Diverse infrastructure to support innovation

An efficient freight network that does not unreasonably burden residents of the city is essential. Provide:
- Truck-free city streets
- Inexpensive delivery of standard shipping containers
- Fast & economical rail-based freight
- Full interchange with the global freight network
- Low capital & operating costs
- Low externalized costs
- Minimal land occupation
- Energy efficiency

Venice

PLANNING STUDIES

In order to achieve these goals, planners conduct many studies of the region, and the results of these studies ought normally to have overriding effects on the decisions that are made regarding development. Some of the principal topics of study are:
- Hazards assessment
- Critical species habitats
- Human carrying capacity of the site, including water sources
- Energy demand & supply

Regional Sketch Plan for EuroCity
This proposal amounts to the construction of a second
Venice. Like the original, it would be surrounded by
water. The Markerwaard was to be the fourth and last
of the great polders in the IJsselmeer (created when
the Afsluitdijk turned the Zuider Zee into a lake). The
first three polders were diked, drained, and inhabited
long ago. The Markerwaard was cancelled because of
objections to draining so much of the remaining area
of the IJsselmeer. The proposal for EuroCity involves a
different land reclamation technique, one that was
used to build the IJburg district in the IJmeer, near
Amsterdam. EuroCity would preserve most of the
lake's surface area while lengthening its shoreline and
creating new habitats. It would house 250,000 people.
It is consistent with current proposals to fuse Amsterdam, to the west, with Almere, to the east, into a single
metropolis. However, the proposal is no longer feasible given the lack of timely action on global warming
and sea level rise.

See Topology, Passenger Transport & Freight Delivery

- Demand for residential & commercial space
- Transport infrastructure

On the basis of these studies, a regional plan is established that guides development for 20 or 30 years. It will usually project transport requirements into the future and propose methods to meet demand. Areas that are too hazardous for habitation require protection against development, as do critical species habitats. Open space reservations for productive and recreational use will also have been identified. The study of hydrology is critical, as it is the basis for flood-risk assessment and the supply of potable water.

As city designers prepare for their work, they can expect to receive urban planning documentation and mapping that show:
- What areas are excluded from development
- What areas are to be developed
- The anticipated basis of the local economy
- Projected income levels
- How many people will live or work on the site
- How much floor area will be required
- Which major public facilities must be built on a site
- The route alignment of public transport
- Any transport arteries that will cross the site
- The contours of the site, including its watercourses
- Soil conditions & existing vegetation

Designers will need to know who their actual client is (if not themselves), how the project will be financed, and what price and form of ownership are intended. They also need to know what kind of organization will undertake the development.

The arrangement of the transport system is a complex matter that was considered at length in *Carfree Cities* and greatly affects city design, especially the width of the streets that will be needed to carry the anticipated traffic. In this one choice alone, urban planning determines much about the form of the urban area that will follow. Cars always require streets that are too wide.

SITE INFORMATION

A vast store of information is required by the urban planning process. Most of this information is also needed by urban designers, who often must gather additional information that the planners do not require. This section considers the site information needed to design attractive, practical city districts.

The physical features of the site are critical. In most cases, even the most detailed available mapping of an area is inadequate to the needs of designers, and contour lines on existing topographic maps may be quite approximate. A detailed survey of the site is essential. Contours should be at intervals of no more than one meter, and one foot is much better. It is useful to convert contour maps into physical models of the site, and this is becoming cheaper to do. (Vertical scales are sometimes exaggerated to reveal slight grades.) The ability to view such a model from any perspective gives a clarity about the site that can otherwise only be obtained from a helicopter. It is not just the hills and valleys that interest us but the slopes themselves. Very flat areas are most likely subject to flooding and may be difficult to drain. Steep areas may be subject to landslides and subsidence; these areas may be entirely unsuitable for building or may require expensive stabilization.

Watercourses and wet ground must be identified and a decision made as to the treatment of these features. Watercourses are frequently put into culverts, but some people (Richard Register in particular) have called for creeks to be restored to their open condition. If a creek is treated in this way, important design consequences stem from the decision. Another approach is to build a canal, keeping the water in the open but maintaining it at a constant level. This is a more urban treatment, one that often improves a city, as here in AMERSFOORT in the Netherlands.

Although entire cities, such as Amsterdam and New Orleans, have been built on saturated ground, this is a poor choice if

Porto

The risk of building below sea level was thrown into sharp relief by the recent destruction of most of New Orleans when the storm surge from hurricane Katrina overwhelmed levees and flooded the city.

alternative sites exist. Foundations are expensive and may be troublesome. Subsidence of the ground will often occur if the soil is allowed to dry out, and wooden pilings will start to rot as soon as the water level falls below their tops. Most of these sites are subject to flooding. Still, a great many otherwise-promising urban sites are located in lowland areas with wet soils.

It will generally be easiest if storm drains follow the existing water flows on the site. This will influence the course of some streets, because drainage piping is nearly always laid beneath the street owing to difficulties of maintaining piping that runs underneath buildings.

Foundation engineering is both an art and a science. The art lies in knowing what kinds of foundation will be economical to construct on a given site and what the economical building height is for that site. Sometimes the addition of one story to a building can drive up the foundation costs considerably. The depth of frost also has a major impact on foundation costs. Economical building heights should be determined early in the process. Foundations are also considered on page 507.

Designers must have a thorough knowledge of existing uses on the site, especially when some of these are to be retained. When assessing existing uses, begin with the inhabitants of the site. How many people live there? What is the distribution of ages? Will these people remain on the site after it is developed? What are their transport requirements? Is it necessary to house them somewhere else during reconstruction? These are always politically sensitive matters. Remember that the elderly fare badly when their neighborhood is demolished, so a great effort should be made to preserve functioning neighborhoods.

Decisions must be taken regarding which uses will be retained and which buildings will be preserved, possibly after renovation and a change in use. The temptation is often to demolish everything on the site and start over, but it is wise to resist this impulse and attempt instead to incorporate old buildings into the new

New construction, Cascais

design for the site. This is not usually a pinching design constraint and will permit fine results, but it is also true that some existing buildings have neither the quality of design and construction nor the location and orientation to make it possible or worthwhile to save them.

The planning process ought to include the identification of traditional skylines and natural vistas that should be protected. Designers will have to accommodate these requirements, but an existing skyline can even be enhanced by building in the local vernacular style.

Kostof reminds us that the ownership of land exerts a large influence on decisions regarding how streets are arranged. In the USA, planners often enjoy the luxury of working on a site that is in the hands of a single owner. When a site is in many hands, it may be possible to design around existing divisions, but this is a daunting task. The most desirable plan may be so at odds with the existing land division that the project cannot move forward unless the parcel can be reassembled and divided anew. The legal and financial obstacles to this vary from nation to nation but are usually great. Centralized authority was essential to many large Baroque projects that required reassembly of land. Irrigation works are always important and usually reflected in existing land ownership patterns and topography. I will not address these issues directly, but anyone planning an urban project must be aware of land ownership patterns, laws affecting the assembly of parcels, and irrigation works that will be retained.

OPEN SPACE & ECOLOGY

The designation of green space merits close study. The Reference Topology preserves more than 80% of the site as open space, but real-world projects are unlikely to reach this standard. Tiny parks, like this pocket park off the VERONESESTRAAT in Amsterdam, are a great boon, but larger open areas are essential.

I lived for several years in this former car factory that had been redeveloped as artists' lofts. It was a sturdy old building with abundant light.

E.g., Haussmann's Parisian boulevards

Kostof (1991), 57, 59

Open space is the point on which Venice is most subject to criticism. The vistas over open water help, but it is rare to be alone while outdoors.

At least 10% of the land should be devoted to parks and similar, highly-managed green spaces, such as playing fields.

Parks must be provided within easy walking distance of all, or nearly all, urban areas. Always include open water in green spaces, even if nothing more than fountains and wading pools. A natural watercourse is best. A river of some size, with a SMALL ADJACENT PARK, such as here in medieval Strasbourg, is ideal. Watercourses should be suitable for swimming and able to maintain their water quality without chemical treatment.

Small parks are generally more useful than large ones because more of them can be established, which brings them within easy reach of most people; see the discussion on page 348. The restful LIZZA PARK in Siena is just a few steps away from a main street. By carefully shielding the park from the city, the illusion of a natural setting can be created adjacent to dense neighborhoods.

Consider the manner of the transition between built areas and open space. The boundary may be wrinkled, often to pleasing effect, but the demarcation should be abrupt: the city ends and open space begins, as seen here near SAN GIUSEPPE in Siena.

When large amounts of open space will be preserved on a site, much flexibility arises. It makes sense to allocate the areas closest to the inhabited zones to parks and playing fields. Other, more distant areas can be put to various uses, including farmland, forest, and even wilderness. The productive use of open space may influence the design of adjacent inhabited areas. In many cases, these areas can be kept in farmland, but intensive rearing of livestock is incompatible with nearby urban areas due to odor and disease problems. Forests should be kept back a safe distance from built-up areas to reduce fire danger. Insects may breed in wetlands and forests, although the problem can sometimes be kept in check by bird or bat populations.

Urban planning requires a survey of the local ecology. The awkward question arises as to the extent that development will be governed by ecological issues, but do remember that a dense city in the right place burdens the natural environment less than sprawling suburbs. A low level of ecological damage to an ideal urban site is preferable to the widespread damage of sprawl. The decisions are usually governed by laws, regulations, and politics.

Some areas are likely to be placed off-limits to development because of adverse effects on endangered species. Fortunately, as often as not, the sensitive habitats are wetlands that are less than ideal for urbanization. Adjustments may be required to avoid splitting a species habitat. In the case of districts strung out along rail lines, a narrow gap may be introduced between two adjacent districts, with but a slight increase in travel times.

HAZARD MANAGEMENT

Most regions of the world face serious hazards, whether natural or man-made. A few risks, such as the volcano that obliterated Pompeii, are so serious that cities simply must be kept out of the affected area. Other risks can be mitigated, but some level of risk is intrinsic to most sites. Hazards assessment and management belong more to urban planning than urban design, but some issues directly affect urban design.

Comprehensive hazard identification is required when planning a new urban area. More accurate assessments of a particular risk may be required, but most hazards have long been known.

FIRE

Throughout history, entire cities have burned. The risk can never be entirely eliminated, and even "fireproof" buildings can burn because their contents are flammable. Automatic fire sprinklers greatly reduce the risk of a fire getting out of control.

No urban building should be constructed of flammable materials, except for trim and furnishings. The structure should be fireproof. In practice, this requires either reinforced concrete

The Rembrandt Tower in Amsterdam is undoubtedly as fireproof as possible and has multiple exit stairs, but the World Trade Center disaster showed that skyscrapers are vulnerable to fires. A broader discussion of hazards is available at:

www.carfree.com/papers/hazards.html

or steel members treated with thick fireproofing. Flammable roofing materials are a special danger. Fireproof buildings make conflagrations nearly impossible.

Fire protection in Venice is provided by boat, but the Fenice opera house burned in 1995, in part because the adjacent canals had been drained for repair, and the boats could not reach the scene of what began as a minor fire. One of the tasks of city managers is to ensure that fire brigades can reach the scene of any fire, notwithstanding maintenance work in progress.

Considering the Reference Topology, I think that each district should have its own small fire company, which provides the rapid response so critical to lifesaving efforts. Crews from adjacent districts would be called for all but the smallest fires.

Access requirements for fire equipment are affected by the height of buildings, which determines the length of ladders and booms. That in turn determines the street widths and corner radii required for fire vehicle access. SMALL FIRE VEHICLES, such as this one in Tokyo, can negotiate narrow streets. (In this case, the mother vehicle even carries a small daughter vehicle that can move through the narrowest alleys.)

The width of emergency-access streets must be established in conformance with local ordinances. The initial demands of regulators should not be blindly accepted, but they will ultimately establish minimum street widths, which probably cannot be less than 3m (10') in most jurisdictions. Reductions to the widths currently required in the USA would reflect the absence of cars on the street and the consequent large reductions in required street width. The New Urbanists have usually obtained reasonable regulation on the basis of field demonstrations. Actual tests with fire trucks have shown that considerably narrower roadways than standard are entirely acceptable. Corners must be eased to permit larger vehicles to turn, and emergency clearways should be paved in a contrasting color or style. Taller buildings require longer ladders and correspondingly wide radii.

Also subject to negotiation is the distance between adjacent emergency-access routes. Not every street requires fire truck access, but no street that is too narrow to permit such access can be very far removed from wider streets. Access standards vary between jurisdictions, but 90m (300') is a reasonable point of departure. In a fine-grained district, this allows intermediate streets to be very narrow, as long as the access standard is met.

The provision of force-main hydrants at every intersection will shorten hose runs and allow water to be quickly put on a fire. If building heights are limited and pressure is high enough, then it is possible that no pumper is needed, only enough hose to reach the scene of the fire.

Hydrant, Venice

Most American cities once required EXTERIOR FIRE ESCAPES from upper floors. This led to the addition of ugly exterior steel fire stairs to many buildings. Exterior fire escapes were advisable before the advent of sprinklers and smoke alarms, but modern fireproof buildings probably do not require them. European practice has not generally required them, although casualties do sometimes arise from this omission. Fire escapes are themselves a cause of death from collapse, falls, and intruders. The local code will govern, but they are no longer widely required.

EARTHQUAKE & LANDSLIDE

Having experienced the 1989 San Francisco earthquake, I am thoroughly impressed with the destructive power of violent earth movements. This quake, measuring 7.1 on the Richter scale, caused a viaduct some 100 km (60 miles) from the epicenter to collapse with heavy loss of life. The damage from stronger quakes can be extreme; San Francisco was all but destroyed by the 1906 magnitude 8.6 quake.

In fact, most regions face some risk from earthquakes, even though serious events may be very rare. All that can be done is to obtain the best seismic assessment available and to build well enough to survive the anticipated shaking. Earthquakes often collapse buildings on soft soil, and extreme caution must be exercised when building on these sites. Landfills, mud flats, and alluvial fans are better devoted to open space.

Buildings must be designed to protect their occupants, even if the building subsequently requires demolition. Catastrophic failures must be prevented at all costs.

Unstable soils are well understood by soils engineers, who can solve most problems. The greatest risk is landslide, and an engineer can give a definitive assessment of the risk. Subsidence and expansive soils are also troublesome but rarely cause deaths.

EMERGENCY FACILITIES & EVACUATION

The recent flood in New Orleans following Hurricane Katrina put that city's hospitals out of action. This occurred in part because emergency generators had been installed below the level of the flood.

Countless bitter lessons have shown the importance of correctly siting hospitals and other vital facilities. Too often, hospitals are damaged or destroyed in a disaster, just when their services are most needed. Hospitals and fire stations must be sited where they are as immune from disaster as possible, while still maintaining access to all areas of the city. No hospital should be sited in a flood zone if an alternative exists. Keep in mind that the collapse of buildings in an earthquake may block access routes.

Patients who see trees from their hospital windows recover more quickly. See: R.S. Ulrich, "View Through a Window May Influence Recovery From Surgery," *Science*, 224:420-421 (1984).

Hospitals should be in quiet locations, preferably surrounded by green areas. With respect to the Reference Topology, six hospitals would be built, one in the center of each lobe, surrounded by green space, and connected to the city by bus.

In the event of a calamity, a city's entire population may require evacuation. In the case of the Reference Topology, most of the population could simply cycle into the surrounding countryside. Every family should have a tent and sleeping bags, which can be transported by bike. In hurricane country, public transport may be the only means to evacuate people to a safe distance, a need that may affect design requirements.

SOLAR ACCESS

Solar access is a subject in its own right and includes the management of sun and shade on buildings and rooftop collectors. The arrangements required vary so much from climate to climate and are so greatly affected by latitude that I can give no specific advice. See Watson et al. for a good introduction.

Their sections 4.6 through 4.9

In the middle latitudes, the effect of slope on local temperatures is large. Lynch & Hack say that a 10% south-facing slope has the same effect as moving the site 6° of latitude to the south.

This assumes a site in the Northern Hemisphere. Lynch & Hack, 51-53; see also their Appendix E, "Sun Angles," for the method of constructing a table of altitudes and an illustration of annual sun movements.

Solar access concerns should not be limited to current needs; increasing energy costs are likely to raise demand for solar collectors in the years ahead. It may not be possible to ensure an ideal situation for every building, but any limitations should be known to the affected families. I think that solar hot water heating will soon become normal in sunnier climates. Photovoltaic roofing could become cost-effective fairly soon.

The Site in the Region

We must consider how a project will fit into the larger region. The development and maintenance of regional character have been studied at length; the work of Kevin Lynch is especially important. We will consider just a few issues in passing.

See in particular: *Managing the Sense of a Region* (1976) and *The Image of the City* (1960).

Development never occurs in a vacuum. Designers must always be aware of what has already been done in the areas outside the project site as well as what is likely to come in the future. Try to work towards a harmonious whole that strengthens regional character. Green space can be used to separate incompatible areas and uses, but a better approach is to integrate with what has gone before, not to hide it. Suburban sprawl will be difficult to bring into harmony with dense carfree development. Carfree areas harmonize best with dense urban fabric, but sprawling suburbs are likely to redevelop using a denser, more urban model as energy becomes scarce and expensive.

Rural areas are another matter entirely. The character of rural land normally differs greatly from that of cities in the same region. Rural character is best accommodated by making an abrupt transition from urban to rural. The resulting contrast is interesting and poses no real conflict.

The size and scale of the site will affect its relationship to the

Siena

Burano

Vila Real de Santo António

surrounding region. Development of a small, infill site may pass almost unnoticed if it conforms to the character of the district. A large site can impose its own character on an area, although it is best to respect existing nearby areas.

I advocate design that uses dense, small-scale elements. The character of such places is in keeping with European city centers but fits poorly with most city-building in the last half-century. Pay particular attention to managing the transition between the large-scale streets and buildings of recent years and the narrow streets and smaller buildings that suit carfree areas. The use of entrance features (such as gates) can help the transition.

CITIZEN PLANNERS & DESIGNERS

Central to the success of any development project is, I believe, a good understanding of the needs and aspirations of the people who are to use it. Although it is not absolutely essential to have those people directly involved in planning and design, this is the simplest way to assure a good outcome. It is possible, and has frequently occurred, that a single individual with a clear vision has designed a large development and carried it to successful completion. The problem with this approach is that it relies on the wisdom of one person and completely lacks any before-the-fact corrective mechanism. The success or failure of the project only becomes apparent when people buy houses at the anticipated price, or do not. Certain geniuses, such as the Levitts, who built enormous suburban developments in the USA in the early postwar years, got the formula right and delivered exactly what the GIs and their young families were looking for. While in many ways these projects were public-policy disasters and caused the disappearance of the middle classes from entire urban neighborhoods, there can be no doubt that the developers accurately anticipated what the prospective buyers wanted. What is also interesting is that the thousands of identical houses have metamorphosed until there are scarcely any two still alike.

Most of the greatest planning disasters were the work of centralized authorities trying to do the right thing. It is possible for such an authority to build well, but it must be sensitive and flexible, and successes are comparatively rare in practice. One instructive example is the redevelopment of two districts in Copenhagen, discussed briefly on page 397. This was a clear case of a local authority becoming sensitive to the wishes of its citizens in the wake of an earlier failed attempt. Current practice increasingly stresses the rehabilitation of existing areas in preference to demolition and rebuilding. This approach has the advantage that it does not destroy functioning neighborhoods.

In the early 1970s, Rod Hackney involved local citizens directly in the design of, and sometimes even in the execution of, urban redevelopment. He renovated a district in Macclesfield, England, for a third of the cost and in a third of the time required by the usual practice of demolition and replacement. Hackney believed in the abilities of citizens to guide their own futures. In his vision, experts do not make the important decisions but work under the direction of the users:

Valladolid

> Community architecture means attempting to understand the needs of a small group of residents and then working with them and under their instructions and guidance, in order to articulate their case and represent it to the various powers....

Hackney, cited by Hall, 271, ellipsis in Hall

Various techniques have been developed to help experts explain to citizens what their choices are, how to visualize the consequences, and the methods they might use in making their decisions. The Neighborhood Initiatives Foundation has promoted its "Planning for Real" method, which has been in use since the late 1970s. It gives local people a voice in the planning and design of their community while helping professionals to

"Planning for Real is distributed in the form of a 'kit', a small box which contains basic instructions on how to conduct sessions, a sample model, cutout masters for physical items—for example, houses—and non-physical attributes—for example, problems and opportunities: play areas, high crime areas, etc. Instruction is provided through four 'packs': publicity, suggestions menu, priorities, and follow-up. Each provides props and suggestions with techniques in managing the sessions. The style of the kit is simple and deliberately crude, which makes it accessible and unforbidding to communities. Much is hand-lettered, and only in recent versions have more typewritten materials been produced."
"Interactive Community Planning: Planning for Real"
http://web.mit.edu/urbanupgrading/upgrading/issues-tools/tools/Planning-for-Real.html
The referenced "A Practical Handbook for 'Planning for Real' Consultation Exercise" (1995) is out of print.

"To my great surprise, two of them were openly weeping while they did it. I asked them why they were crying and received this answer: 'We are people who have been living in mass housing in Nagoya. It was almost unthinkable, almost unimaginable to us that our ordinary necessities could be put into a building in such a direct way. Therefore we are upset, because it is so beautiful, the possibility of real life, such a freedom, for our children, is almost too much to bear!'"
TNO, III:382-384

understand the needs and desires of the local people and assist them in meeting their needs.

The Planning for Real kit guides people in the building of a simple model of their community and then uses that model as a stage for the discussion of problems and solutions. One goal of the process is to strengthen the commitment to plans developed from shared knowledge and common purpose. The process begins with the assembly of a simple model at a scale of 1:200. At public meetings, people express their ideas by placing pictorial "option cards" on the model. As community concerns are identified, ad hoc work groups negotiate between conflicting interests and develop detailed proposals. Priorities are set using a simple "Now, Soon, Later" scheme. Most of the participants are from the local community, but government officials, local representatives, and professionals are available to answer questions. Participants agree that these "outsiders" are essential to the process, but they are seen as resources, not stakeholders.

One of the questions that arises early in any citizen design exercise is the selection of the citizens who will do the design. I believe that the best results can be expected when all of the citizens who will use the final space are represented. The process does require that the size of the group be limited to a manageable number, and this in turn requires that the geographic extent of the project be constrained.

Citizen-design is also a tremendously empowering process, one that many people can scarcely even imagine. Alexander recounts an experience in Japan in which families were allowed to arrange the interiors of their new apartments. Each family was given a floor envelope of 6×12m (20×40') and allowed to arrange it to fit their own needs. The plans that different families devised for themselves were as varied as can be imagined, and the families were overjoyed to have real control over their space.

The carfree movement has had more experience with citizen planning than citizen design. A number of the projects that have been built have involved future residents in many aspects of the planning and development, but so far the direct involvement of residents in the actual design appears to be limited.

The 600-unit GWL PROJECT in Amsterdam involved residents as advisors to the architects, but it seems that standard design methods were employed. The results were not, to my eye, attractive, but it does seem that the residents are satisfied. One unusual aspect of this project was the provision of small gardens for most apartments, not always directly abutting the apartment.

The Saarlandstrasse project in Hamburg was organized by a group of future residents led by an architect. From its inception, the planning involved most of the future residents. Design was a protracted, collaborative process, with a great deal of feedback. Jan Scheurer, my source for this, says that it "is immediately obvious from wandering around the development that the residents designed and landscaped the open spaces themselves."

Citizen planning is no easy thing. It is raw democracy, and the process can become embroiled in petty disputes, inflated egos, and loud-mouthed contrarians. However, Alexander has reported consistent success with methods, based on an effective decision-making sequence, that help residents to reach surprisingly quick agreement on some of the most important decisions, such as where the center of the community should be situated. In addition, the self-selecting nature of the process proposed in URBAN VILLAGES should tend to reduce conflicts within a group, although this still leaves conflicts between groups to be resolved. Alexander has often achieved success in working with small groups of people right on the site. I think this is the best and most direct approach and can be expanded to much larger groups. I have little direct experience with this method in the real world, but the maquette trial that was undertaken in Budapest in July 2005 was instructive, as was the on-site design exercise in Prague in May 2006. (See CASE EXAMPLES for a description of these exercises and their results.)

See: www.gwl-terrein.nl
and
www.omslag.nl/wonen/ecodorpen.html#GWL

Jan Scheurer, personal communication, and
wwwistp.murdoch.edu.au/publications/projects/jan/pdf/ch16-5.pdf

Venice

Transition from Planning to Design

Elements that probably require some level of definition during the planning phase are: freight access, siting of small-scale industry, and noise. There may turn out to be quite a few other elements that must be predefined; only experience can tell.

Depending on circumstances, it is possible that some flexibility regarding the exact route alignment and location of the halts can be retained until final engineering of the system is started. Tram systems will have more flexibility than metros. The precise location of metro entrances may be flexible within small limits.

It should be possible to shift the alignment of the freight track several meters (yards) closer to or farther from the route of the passenger metro, thus giving some flexibility in the depth of the buildings sandwiched between the boulevard and the freight line.

The transition from planning by experts to design by users with expert assistance must be made at the correct level of scope and at the right moment. I believe the transition should occur at the district level—the area that will be served by a single transport halt. I believe that the right moment is when urban planning is substantially complete. This means that the alignment of the transport system (and thus the central boulevard) has been fixed. The minimum dimensions of the major squares and streets will probably have been established during the planning phase, but those who will live nearby should determine the final arrangement, working on the site as described in Part IV. At the even smaller scale of minor streets and buildings, only some guidelines need be established during the planning phase.

Prior to the start of neighborhood design, the number, size, location, and character of the main squares should be determined. Will there be only one central square, or will subdistrict squares (i.e., squares in the two areas created by the division of the central boulevard) be established? Will there be both a central square and subdistrict squares? These questions are at the uneasy junction of planning and design.

The character of each large square should be decided: will it be a formal and regular square in the Renaissance style, like the PLAZA MAYOR in Salamanca, or an informal and irregular square with a medieval character, like CAMPO DI SANTA MARGHERITA in Venice? (Small squares are less suitable for formal arrangement.) Because of their inflexibility, formal squares must be carefully and accurately defined at this time, as they are difficult to adjust during subsequent neighborhood design work.

The type and purpose of each of these squares will exert a considerable influence on the surface area that will be required. These matters are taken up starting on page 327. The most important point to be watched is not to make the squares too big. The total surface area of major squares is little affected by their number—the more there are, the smaller each must be.

The rest of the design work can be accomplished by groups of future users guided by professionals. Other design methods are not only possible, they are actually the norm today. I think we already have ample evidence that these methods yield generally poor results and therefore propose to abandon them. I do not expect this to occur on a large scale for several decades, although I hope to see trials of community-based design of carfree areas in the near future. I will not specifically discuss the mechanics of design by experts, but the process and methods presented in DESIGN TECHNIQUES are well known to planners and architects.

Amsterdam

Venice

PASSENGER TRANSPORT

For nearly a century we have had the tools we need to provide good passenger transport in our cities without resorting to private motor vehicles. Any relatively large carfree development will require public transport for internal circulation, and every project requires connections to the rest of the city. An entire chapter of *Carfree Cities* was devoted to the provision of passenger transport within cities. That book proposed some comparatively minor improvements to existing practice, but none of these is difficult or even essential. Of course, walking and bicycling will account for most trips, if not the majority of passenger-miles travelled.

This chapter considers passenger transport requirements as they affect the design of carfree areas; the complex task of developing route structures for heavy transport systems belongs to urban planning and is taken up only briefly. TRAM SYSTEMS like this one in Freiburg will be the means of choice for improving public transport in most existing medium-sized cities that now rely on buses. Trams are somewhat invasive and not as safe as metros, but they are comparatively inexpensive to build and have a long history of fast, reliable service, at least where cars are kept off the tracks, as in Freiburg and Zürich. Larger cities will rely on metro systems. We begin with a brief consideration of the effects of public transport systems on urban development.

TRANSIT ROUTE STRUCTURE

Transit route structures are inextricably linked to the arrangement of cities: development follows transport. No choice made in the planning of a city has a greater effect on its subsequent development than the choice of a route for rail-based transit. People hesitate to base location decisions on bus lines because they may be changed at any time. However, the construction of

Freiburg im Breisgau, Germany. Narrow-gauge tram tracks and overhead power.

a rail line clearly states that service will be available indefinitely. People will rely on that when making location decisions.

Carfree projects need direct rail service to downtown. If the project is far from the city center, bus service to peripheral areas may be needed to complement rail service to central locations. A carfree district can only succeed if residents can reach routine destinations without a car, but some people will still want a car for travel outside the area served by transit. Transit service to outlying parking garages that serve car owners is also required if these garages lie beyond reasonable walking distance.

Rail systems can be located below grade, at grade, or above grade. Above-grade systems do provide the grade separation that ensures safe, on-time operation, but I do not believe that transit systems should be constructed overhead. Their impact on adjacent areas is unacceptably high, as with an ELEVATED LINE in New York. This is not only a question of noise but of visual clutter and privacy. We have had enough bad experience with overhead systems never to build another one.

TRANSIT MODES

The underground metro is the best choice for large cities, but smaller cities will probably install less expensive surface-running trams (possibly TUNNELING UNDER DOWNTOWN, as here in Newark, New Jersey). We should be clear, however, that street running is a compromise with best practice. A further important point regarding trams, and one frequently overlooked, is that small trams can operate in streets that are too narrow for buses. Lisbon's tiny ELÉCTRICO still plies the steep streets and sharp corners of the oldest quarters of the city. These trams carry comparatively few passengers and are thus expensive to operate (on a per-passenger basis), but they provide transport on routes that could otherwise be served only by minibuses with even higher operating costs.

Aside from the threat to pedestrians and cyclists, the biggest problem with street-running trams is that they must be supplied with electricity. The usual practice is to install overhead wires, but Washington, D.C., required that trams collect their power from an underground source, simply because the wires are so ugly. Overhead power is indeed one of the strongest arguments against conventional trams.

Bordeaux recently built a tram line that uses a third rail to which power is supplied only as a tram passes. I have proposed a tram system that dispenses with overhead wires except within stations and on hills. Fuel-cell power has been demonstrated in buses and would presumably work on trams, which require less power per unit mass and volume. However, cost and durability problems are unresolved after 30 years of effort.

Other possibilities include flywheels charged while the vehicle is in a station, batteries charged in stations or exchanged at end halts, and hybrid forms (engine plus flywheel or battery). Eventually, wireless trams should become commonplace. These vehicles are already under development.

The newest trams, such as these EUROTRAMS in Strasbourg, are 100% low-floor, which makes the vehicles less intrusive and allows low-height platforms for level-loading. The trams are fully accessible to wheelchair users, and the impact of the boarding platforms on the street is minor, although the curb is rather high. This is a huge advance in tram technology.

The bus is a clumsy, inefficient, uncomfortable mode of public transport. It must be admitted, however, that bus systems can be implemented rapidly and at comparatively low capital costs. A good bus system was implemented years ago in Curitiba, Brazil. This system permits level loading, and passengers pay their fare on entering the platform, so loading is much faster than in normal bus operations. This method is being widely implemented in Bogotá and other South American cities and has the political advantage of yielding short-term improvements.

Another approach is mixed light- and heavy-rail, with trams running over conventional rail lines for part of the trip. This method is all but impossible in the USA due to Federal regulations, but it is being implemented in some European cities. Safety is a concern. www.lightrail.nl/TramTrain/tramtrain.htm

Regarding Bordeaux, see: www.verkeerskunde.nl/nieuws2004/bordeaux.htm For the wireless tram proposals, see: www.carfree.com/short-wire_tram.html Regarding the fuel-cell tram, see: www.carfree.com/fuel-cell_tram.html

See, for example, www.parrypeoplemovers.com

"Urban Planning in Curitiba," *Scientific American*, March 1996.

CNG = compressed natural gas
LPG = liquefied petroleum gas

The trolley bus is an interesting variant that resembles an ordinary bus but has two trolley poles connecting its electric propulsion system to an overhead power supply. Unfortunately, this involves two conductors in place of the single conductor used in tram systems. These buses emit no local pollutants and are very quiet. Their excellent hill-climbing ability has led to their adoption in San Francisco. In my opinion, trolley bus systems should only be constructed if very steep hills must be climbed; otherwise, trams are better.

Vehicle capacity ranges from 2 to 40 passengers. Systems based on larger vehicles are usually called "Automated Group Transport" (AGT). See the PRT discussion in *Carfree Cities*, pages 101-104 and 187. PRT will apparently be applied in the Masdar carfree project now being designed in Abu Dhabi. The extreme heat in the region made very short walks to transit halts highly desirable, and PRT was chosen because of its ability to provide many, closely-spaced halts.

The newest buses burn either CNG or LPG and are cleaner but remain quite noisy. The poor ride quality of buses seems to be intrinsic. If buses must be used initially, they should eventually be replaced by trams, as is under consideration in Curitiba.

In any discussion of urban transport, someone is sure to raise the supposed advantages of "monorails" or "Personal Rapid Transit" (PRT). Monorails have been heralded as the wave of the future for more than a century. Their greatest disadvantage is their above-grade location. They offer no operating advantages over conventional rail, except perhaps that they are quieter because they run on inefficient rubber tires. (Metros can also run on rubber tires, but they then suffer from the same poor efficiency.) The automated system installed at NEWARK AIRPORT, near New York, required major repairs within a few years. Average speeds are low. Switches (points) are complex, cumbersome, and expensive. A monorail might be useful if a moderate-capacity, short haul system is needed to serve a carfree project and the only available route is overhead.

PRT encompasses dozens of somewhat similar systems and was briefly mentioned in *Carfree Cities.* It is a complex, expensive technology that offers few advantages (except that some systems provide private vehicles, if this is seen as a benefit). Its capacity is less than that of a conventional tram or metro. Like monorails, PRT may find useful application in an isolated carfree development that requires a connection to the main public transport system. The smaller vehicles do permit higher service frequency on lightly-used lines.

FREQUENT, NEARBY SERVICE

The largest component of many journeys by public transport is waiting for a vehicle to come along. This can take an hour or more, and only in dense areas does service operate every few minutes, and often then only at peak times. If public transport is to succeed as the primary replacement for cars, we must limit waiting times to a few minutes. This requires serving a large number of riders, so that vehicles can operate on short headways while still carrying good loads. Any given line must serve a population of at least 50,000 if frequent service is to be practical.

Public transport service should be available within a five minute walk of every doorstep. This cannot always be achieved, but walking distances of more than ten minutes (760m, 2500') are simply not admissible. Even ten minutes may seem like a long walk, but remember that the walk will not be encumbered by car traffic and should be quiet, pretty, and certainly healthful.

Budapest

HANDICAPPED ACCESS

The entire public transport system must be fully accessible to those in wheelchairs, and carfree districts should become the most accessible urban areas we have yet seen. Accessibility helps everyone, because it means that low-slope ramps will be installed, which permits handcarts and other small wheeled conveyances to be brought aboard vehicles (see page 158.)

That is not the end of the accessibility question, however. Even if all public transport is accessible and no street has curbs, the mobility of people in wheelchairs is still restricted by steps leading into buildings and by internal stairways. Conflicting requirements affect the design of building entrances. On the one hand, the ground floor should be a bit above street level, so that any minor ponding of water on the pavement does not run into the building. On the other hand, we want wheeled appliances and wheelchairs to enter without hindrance. The solution is simple: keep ground floors 1-2cm (half an inch) above the street. Good storm drainage should keep the water out.

Some systems approach accessibility without actually attaining it, as here at the CAIS DO SODRÉ station in Lisbon. How this might ever have occurred is difficult to imagine. Most railroads

Scootmobile
If your city's infrastructure permits unrestricted scootmobile use, true accessibility has been achieved.

in Europe suffer from this defect, with the floors of rail cars being a single step higher than the platforms.

Access to upper floors in small buildings is troublesome. We will not generally install elevators in these buildings due to the cost and space required. Stair lifts can be installed on an ad-hoc basis, to provide a disabled resident access to his apartment. Another solution is to give the elderly and mobility-impaired priority when renting ground-floor apartments. Amsterdam has successfully applied this approach for years. As long as civic and commercial functions are located on ground floors, then elevator access to upper floors of most buildings is not required. Large buildings will be equipped with elevators, if only to handle freight. Local regulation may require elevator access to all floors in all new buildings, which would necessitate the use of apartment buildings rather than narrow houses. Elevators are expensive, and their cost must be divided among a dozen or more apartments. If buildings are limited to four stories, then the most obvious design approach is apartment buildings with center hallways. This does not permit apartments with through ventilation or light from more than one side. These are grave limitations and should not be accepted unless there is simply no other choice.

An alternative solution is to build a loggia around an interior courtyard, with an elevator serving the loggia. This provides access to all quarters in all buildings, as long as the floors in all buildings are at the same height. Good light and ventilation are provided to all apartments. The ARCADE-CUM-LOGGIA FORM can be very attractive, as here in a courtyard in Perugia.

Even making all buildings accessible to wheelchairs does not provide mobility for all. Some people are so debilitated that they cannot move even a short distance in a wheelchair. Battery-powered wheelchairs do not solve the problem for those who cannot tolerate cold. Really frail people need ambulances or cars for their transport. Non-emergency transport for these

Lisbon

people can be provided by low, narrow, slow, battery-powered ambulances.

I noticed in Spain that many PEDESTRIAN OVERPASSES have been built across rail lines. These structures are arranged with low slopes. (Others I have seen in the Czech Republic have even lower slopes plus frequent landings.) They cross electrified rail lines, and the required vertical clearance is about 8m (25'), so the total rise is large. These structures are costly and ugly. D.K. Ching (1975, page 9.3) gives ramp slopes variously as 1:8, 1:10, and 1:12, the latter carrying the note "for the handicapped," but whatever the slope of ramp, the rise is so great that many people in wheelchairs lack the strength to climb it. We should build relatively steep ramps with few landings. Motorized wheelchairs should be provided for those who lack the strength to climb ramps (or hills) under their own power. Local politics and regulation will, of course, govern. Whatever we do, we must not build obstacles like this STEPPED BRIDGE in Venice, which also complicates life for those who make deliveries using heavy carts or bicycles.

This INVALID CAR in Amsterdam raises an issue that must be considered in designing carfree areas. These miniature cars have a top speed of about 45 km/hr (28 mi/hr), so they are fast enough to degrade the safety and quality of life on the street. All of them that I have ever seen use filthy two-stroke engines. My suspicion is that they are increasingly being used by people who do not really need them but like the convenience of being allowed to park anywhere they "need" to. The speeds of these vehicles should be physically limited to 20 km/hr (12 mi/hr) in carfree areas. This would reduce their attractiveness, as they would then be no faster than battery-assisted bicycles. This may conflict with laws in some countries, but they cannot be allowed to run at full speed in carfree areas, as they would soon come to be as common and noxious as regular cars. The legal foundation of a carfree development must address this issue.

Carriage of Wheeled Vehicles

Residents of carfree areas will benefit greatly if the transport of small, low-powered passenger and freight vehicles is possible aboard metros. These vehicles may lack the battery (or muscle) power to travel long distances and would otherwise clutter the streets. I propose that metro trains be adapted to permit rapid loading of these small vehicles into special areas of the train, so that they can be transported as readily as passengers and without delaying service. The EUROTRAM, seen here in Strasbourg, has huge doors, which would permit the loading of relatively large wheeled vehicles. If this provision proves unworkable, small vehicles can be transported by metro-freight (see page 172).

The bicycle lobby wants to allow bicycles aboard public transit vehicles. When this can be accomplished without impeding operations, it is highly desirable. I would argue, however, that this can only be achieved when bicycles can be loaded directly from a platform level with the vehicle floor. The use of external racks or the presence of even a single step means either that other users will be encumbered by the bicycles or that service will be delayed while the bikes are loaded and unloaded.

Local Transport

Transport within a carfree district, as distinct from transport between districts, is critical to that district's success. All routine destinations must be quickly accessible and the time spent in local transport must compare favorably with auto-centric cities. This is not so difficult to achieve.

A ten-minute walk is a fairly long way to go for something. Longer walks will be too much for many people. (I do not count myself among them and routinely walk to destinations half-an-hour away, but not everyone shares my enthusiasm for this healthful mode of transport.) We must keep as many routine destinations within a five-minute walk as possible. In practice, this requires a number of vendors and services in every district (see listing on page 228). Each district will require its own primary school, although secondary schools may have to serve several districts.

Local destinations can be reached on foot, but if there is much to carry, some help is needed, which may be nothing more than a FOLDING SHOPPING CART. Until the last century, urban areas were always arranged with local shops selling daily necessities. Routemen delivered many goods to the doorstep, including milk, fruit and vegetables, baked goods, and ice. A return to these arrangements would reduce the need for local travel.

Bicycles will be a critical local transport component in most carfree cities. The Freight chapter proposes the use of freight bikes for most local deliveries. Passenger transport must accommodate "fair-weather cyclists" (like myself) who prefer other modes in bad weather. Some cyclists delight in riding whatever the weather, but carfree areas cannot presume such enthusiasm.

Our task would be simpler if we could decide either to use bikes for all urban transport or not to use them at all. As it is, we must develop a complete bicycle infrastructure, with the assumption that, as in the Netherlands, most people will bike during part of the year (if only to enjoy the health benefits). Unfortunately, bicycle infrastructure is moderately expensive and space-consuming, but I see no real alternative to providing it at a high level of comfort, safety, and capacity. For example, to accommodate all of the cyclists using Centraal Station in Amsterdam, a GIGANTIC BICYCLE PARKING GARAGE was built. At the same time, the public transport system must have sufficient capacity to move everyone who travels during the morning rush hour when the weather is foul. The public transport system has to be there anyway, and rail systems can accommodate very heavy demand if the trains and platforms are long enough and the signalling system allows closely-spaced trains.

I have proposed that metros should be sized so that everyone can find a seat even during rush hour, but it is not unreasonable to expect people to stand on rainy or snowy mornings. This is a modest compromise.

Pedestrians

The pedestrian was, until two centuries ago, the mainstay of urban transport. Few people could afford horses, much less carriages, and absent any form of public transport, most people simply walked everywhere they went. Cities were compact, to enable people to get where they needed to go in a reasonable length of time. This led to high density, narrow streets, and small or absent interior courtyards, an arrangement that is remarkably consistent throughout medieval districts in Europe.

Arezzo

The pedestrian is today the most neglected participant in traffic. Many traffic studies simply omit pedestrians, who also have the lowest status of any traffic participant. In carfree cities, we turn this paradigm on its head: the pedestrian is king, and all other traffic is subservient to him.

The pedestrian's requirements are easy to meet. Pavement must be smooth enough not to catch the toe of a shoe but rough enough to provide good traction when wet. Traffic needs to be kept out of the way, and there should be few or no traffic signals. Direct routes between destinations are needed to minimize distances. The streets should be safe, attractive, and interesting to pass through. That's about all.

Bicycle Infrastructure

Bicycles require two significant infrastructure items: road space and parking. Streets in modern carfree areas will be wider than most streets in Venice, where even major streets are just a few meters (yards) wide. The densest parts of a city might be bike-free, with bicycle parking on the periphery. However, the requirements for emergency access will generally dictate that many streets be wide enough that cyclists can also use them. If the radial streets are made wide enough for bikes and emergency vehicles, then the concentric streets can be very narrow. Nearby

Ravenna

emergency access can still be provided. Cyclists would be expected to dismount in these very narrow streets.

Bikes are cumbersome to store, and when many are concentrated in one place, as here at Amsterdam's CENTRAL STATION before the new, multi-story bike garage (see page 159), chaos can result. Storage is most convenient at ground level, although ramps leading down into basement garages are common in the Netherlands. Bikes can be stored in two tiers, but some strength is needed to heft a bike into the upper tier, and the handlebars and cables of adjacent bikes often become entangled.

Cyclists often prefer to lean their bikes against a building, but this is not always tolerated in the Netherlands, due mainly to damage to the façade and glazing. Off-street bike parking is routinely provided in new Dutch construction, and bike racks are situated where space allows and demand requires. Enough off-street parking should be provided that each resident or employee has a space. (Shopping districts will need more.) Bike parking can be provided in the concierge facilities proposed on page 180. This gets the bikes off the street, out of the weather, and away from thieves. The concierge would also rent bikes, including specialty bikes like tandems and freight bikes.

Bikes permit early and wide-ranging mobility for quite young children, as here at the PIAZZA DEL POPOLO in Ravenna. Bikes allow kids to explore their neighborhood and even places some distance from home. Older children are more choosy in their friendships, and bikes allow them to pick their friends from a much wider circle. Even in Venice, where bike riding is effectively impossible due to the stepped bridges, children still LEARN TO RIDE in a nearby square. Parents must think that this skill is sufficiently important that all children should learn it.

A seeming limitation of bikes is the inability to use them to move children around. This is a myth. Even before the recent advent of specialized bikes for carrying kids, many Dutch children travelled much more by bike than by car. It is still common

Ravenna

to see ordinary bikes fitted with two child seats, one fore and one aft. This works for children as old as six, by which time most Dutch kids can ride on their own (they learn much earlier, but generally begin serious biking around school age). There are also recent innovations, such as a trailer that allows the child to pedal but leaves the steering and most of the pedaling to a parent, and a TWO-WHEEL TRAILER WITH A SEAT that has secondary uses. Specialty bikes from Denmark have a large cockpit that can accommodate a wheelchair or a gaggle of small children.

As to the matter of defining where bikes may ride and where they may not, the obvious solution is the use of sidewalks and curbs. I think, however, that the obvious solution is wrong in most cases. Riding and walking areas can be distinguished by a change in pavement, as here on the VIA CAVOUR in Ravenna. This is both safer, as a brush with a curb will often cause a cyclist to fall, and more attractive, as the street is more unified. This arrangement also invites a rather casual approach. Cyclists belong on their part of the paving and pedestrians on theirs, but there will be some mixing. As long as people endeavor to stay out of the way of other traffic when they are where they "don't belong," the system will work fine, as it seems to in Ravenna.

Corners must be laid out wide enough to allow them to be taken at moderate speed. (Just as with cars, it is probably wise not to make them too gentle, as this encourages excessive speed; infrastructure should encourage responsible behavior.) Don't forget clearance for the handlebars! As noted on page 186, paving for bicycles should be as smooth as possible, consistent with providing good traction when wet. On the other hand, rough paving will keep speeds low on streets where this is desired; nothing moderates the speed of a cyclist like cobblestones!

Conflicts between cyclists and pedestrians require consideration. *Carfree Cities* proposed that cyclists be required to proceed rather slowly in most streets, but be able to ride fast on the "bicycle freeway" that runs along the central boulevard.

We must consider two kinds of traffic conflicts. The first, between cyclists and pedestrians at corners, can be handled by pavement markings, signs, and traffic signals where conflicts cannot be handled by simpler means. The second, among cyclists, can be treated in various ways that will be considerably affected by local traditions and laws. To the extent possible, signs and signals should be avoided. The principle of through-routes with presumptive right-of-way would probably work fine in the case of the Reference Topology, in which no through route crosses another. If major routes must cross, it may be necessary to install traffic lights. The basic rule that "traffic from the right has right-of-way" (in nations where traffic keeps to the right) can govern in most intersections. This minimizes the amount of visual clutter from pavement markings, signs, and signals.

The "drag and drop" bike is an idea whose time has come. In fact, it came a long time ago, but various problems have delayed its widespread adoption. In Copenhagen, the city furnished many distinctively-painted bikes that anyone can use by inserting a coin in the storage rack. When the bike is locked back into a storage rack, the coin is returned. The scheme is financed by ads on the bikes.

Amsterdam has recently attempted a similar approach, so far without success. Bikes are released from racks by inserting a smart-card, which identifies who took the bike. When the bike is returned to another rack and locked, the user again inserts the card. The return of the bike is credited and a small charge for its use is debited. Two problems have beset the Amsterdam effort. First, despite heroic efforts, the innovators have not been able to build a bike rack that is actually theft-proof, although they have not yet given up hope. Second, the bother of fussing with a smart card and the question of whether or not there is rack space for the bike at the destination make the system inconvenient. The innovators have designed a bike that needs almost no maintenance. The tires are solid rubber, making flats impossible.

Salzburg

German Rail (DB) has a similar system that unlocks one of their bikes using codes supplied by telephone and paid for by credit card. The system is just complex enough to be a deterrent to casual use, as you also have to phone in when you're finished with the bike. www.callabike.de/i_english.html

Salamanca

Quad bike

I favor a simpler system. Large numbers of cheap bikes indelibly marked with the city's name would be set on the street. They would have the solid tires of the Amsterdam bikes but no limits on their use. Grab a bike, ride it, and drop anywhere—the drag and drop bicycle. The convenience of simply being able to use a bike when needed is a wonderful inducement to cycling, and every effort should be expended to make this system work. Bought in large quantities, these bikes would cost as little as $30, and thefts could simply be tolerated. Advertising on the bike could, if necessary, be used to fund the system.

A recent development is the electric bike. Some are powered only by the battery and motor, but most allow or require the rider to pedal. The one example I have tried was much too heavy and had far more power than I would have liked. Simple, light-weight bikes with modest boost are highly suitable for those who lack the strength to cycle long distances without some kind of assistance.

Many people think that the elderly are unable to cycle, but in the Netherlands, even very old people often do, and this is an ideal form of exercise at any age. However, some people have lost their sense of balance and need a three- or four-wheeler, and a few are no longer fit enough to pedal. Those who need special bikes should be able to find them; a wide range of specialty bikes are already in at least limited production.

The latest "bright idea" is the Segway, a battery-powered two-wheel scooter with artificial balance. The promoters have deep pockets and have managed to convince many state legislatures in the USA that Segways should be permitted to operate on sidewalks. I am absolutely opposed to their being treated as pedestrians, as their speed is quite high (about 20 km/hr or 12 mi/hr), and their mass is great enough to do real injury. Despite claims for ease of use, they seem to be more difficult to control accurately than a bike. They are extremely expensive, and I see no reason to encourage their use.

LOCAL TRANSIT SERVICE

The Reference Design for carfree cities provides public transport service only to a limited number of halts, always located at the center of a district and within a five-minute walk of anywhere in the district. In practice, however, we may not always be able to achieve this standard. Consider the case of a long, thin site with a transit halt in the center. Walking times to the ends of the site could considerably exceed five minutes. Inexpensive, convenient service between the transit halt and the far reaches of the district is desirable. We consider here some approaches.

We almost certainly need a system that runs on the street. A tunnel-based system would have to be deep enough to pass beneath the metro tunnel, which makes it expensive to build and inconvenient to use. An overhead system might be cheaper but is still inconvenient to use. A street-running system must be slow, safe, and attractive. Speeds can be very low; a 15-minute walk can be replaced by a 5-minute ride, as long as the wait is short. If a single vehicle runs in a loop from the central transport halt out to the edge of the district, service can be provided every 10 minutes, which is a rather longer wait but may be consistent with the relatively small number of passengers. If a system is provided to advise passengers when the next vehicle will arrive, some of the objection to waiting is removed and use can be made of the time to run errands. Such systems are already in use in quite a few cities.

Narrow-gauge trams can negotiate remarkably tight curves, but even this is not always adequate, and so-called GAUNTLET TRACK has been resorted to in some places, as here in Lisbon. This poses a small operational risk that is within the normal "see and avoid" operating practice of many tram systems. (See page 152 for a photo of the small trams that run on these tracks.)

Small buses can also provide this service. These vehicles are now in use and can be battery-powered, like the 20-passenger

Funicular, Budapest

See, for example, the work of my friends at NextBus: www.nextbus.com

See *Carfree Cities*, p.189

Gulliver bus found in many European cities. A variety of light vehicles can also be put into this service, ideally one of the doorless types that permits rapid boarding, such as this JITNEY in Salamanca. If at all possible, they should not charge a fare, as this delays service and makes usage inconvenient.

In very hilly terrain, a modern-day version of San Francisco's cable cars could be used. If vehicles are small and speeds limited to that of a San Francisco cable car (9.5 mi/hr, 15 km/hr), it is even possible for a fit adult to hop on or off between stops.

It is critical to hold station dwell times to just a few seconds, in order to permit the service to stop every 100-200 meters (yards), which is essential if it is to offer a significant improvement on walking. Speeds must be low because the vehicle will operate in a fairly narrow street with foot and bicycle traffic.

Economic feasibility of these local systems is much improved if no driver is required. This AUTOMATED BUS from Frog Systems ("Free Ranging On Grid") is self-guiding and has obstruction detection. It may be some time yet before collision-avoidance really is sophisticated enough to rely on it for unrestricted street running, but the technology is already advanced. Slow vehicles have been in use for some time in a number of locations with similar distances and traffic flows to those we are discussing. These systems are not particularly cheap to install, but the fully-automated operation holds down operating costs.

TAXIS

I had always wanted to eliminate taxis from the urban scene, in part because taxi drivers are some of the most aggressive and dangerous drivers on the road. I finally admitted that some form of taxi is nearly essential in a city and turned my attention to minimizing their impact. In the first place, special-purpose vehicles must be used; ordinary automobiles are totally unsuited to a carfree area. Top speeds must be mechanically limited to about 20 km/hr (12 mi/hr). Propulsion must be nearly silent and non-polluting, which probably limits it to muscle power or batteries. Cruising for passengers would be prohibited; taxis would be called by the methods in wide use today. Taxis would be small and need carry no more than two passengers plus driver. (A portion of the fleet must be wheelchair-accessible.) Taxis should be as small as possible; the conventional golf cart is rather large (due to the wide tires) and, like the ELECTRIC TAXIS used in Zermatt, too fast. Full enclosure may not be required, and a canvas top may suffice. Fares should be very high to discourage their use, with a tax of about $2.50/km ($4.00/mi) to recover external costs. Their operation would be limited to streets wider than 5m (16'). Of course, pedal rickshaws provide exactly this kind of service in cities throughout Asia, and their speed is well below that of a bicycle due to their much higher resistance. In Amsterdam and London, pedal rickshaws are available for hire. They are heavily subsidized by advertisers by virtue of their novelty and scarcity. If the rickshaw were used in significant numbers, the price would be quite high, probably roughly in line with the tax proposed just above.

Some of them have battery-assist for hill-climbing.

NUISANCE MODES

What I regard as "nuisance modes" have proliferated in recent decades. These include mopeds (by far the worst of the lot, given their high speed, pollution, and noise), skateboards, inline skates, and PUSH SCOOTERS (barely objectionable due to their low speed). I assume that any form of motor scooter will be prohibited in carfree cities, unless it takes the form of a battery-assisted bicycle that cannot exceed about 20 km/hr (12 mi/hr), when it is functionally indistinguishable from a conventional bike. A few people do use nuisance modes other than motor scooters as serious transportation, but most use is recreational. In principle, the slow modes ought to coexist with bikes, but

most are slower than bicycles, which may cause some conflict. If people can behave reasonably, these conflicts should be minor.

EXTERNAL TRANSPORT

Passenger transport to destinations outside the city must be to a high standard if carfree residents are not to be restricted in their travel. Residents will need rail, bus, and probably air service to distant cities. In truly rural parts of the world, private cars will probably continue to be used for external transport, as public transport can never provide decent service in these areas. Car-sharing can help meet these needs.

Car-sharing schemes, typified by this SITE IN AMSTERDAM, have been used in Europe for some time and reduce the amount of parking required. Multi-level parking garages are expensive and the cost per space is high, but if the cost is spread among many users, it becomes reasonable. Only rich people or those who use a car frequently will be likely to own one.

Small carfree projects may have their parking within walking distance, but all parking should be provided in multi-story garages, in order to conserve land. This ABOVE-GROUND GARAGE in Amsterdam blights the entire vicinity, and it is not as ugly as most of its kind. Ideally, these garages would be built underground. Most new garages in Amsterdam are indeed built below grade, sometimes even beneath the canals. The cost is very high but their visual impact is minimized. They should be sited farther from downtown, at the ends of public transport lines.

FREIGHT

The delivery of freight is probably the most difficult problem to solve in any carfree project, and hence this entire chapter devoted to such a troublesome matter. Freight falls into two classes, heavy and light. For our purposes, heavy freight can be taken as sea-container-sized shipments destined to a single address. Light freight is that which is easily carried by a light-duty delivery van. We take up heavy freight first.

A full-scale implementation of metro-freight as proposed in *Carfree Cities* would normally require a project with 50,000 inhabitants. Smaller projects will have to contend with truck deliveries, but these projects should be designed so that metro-freight can be implemented later if growth eventually requires it. Therefore, a freight route through the project should be identified and protected against encroachment. In the interim, this route can be used for truck deliveries, and the necessary distribution patterns will already have been developed, since large freight customers will choose to locate along the route. The development of metro-freight technology is in itself a fairly substantial task that must wait until several projects are calling for it.

WHOLESALE DISTRIBUTION

Each region develops its own distribution patterns. These patterns are affected by tradition, geography, economics, national borders, local laws, international treaties, and local transport modes. Sophisticated technology and cheap energy fostered the development of large-scale, high-speed freight systems that encouraged the shipment of large quantities over great distances to a few destinations. Once goods arrive at regional distribution centers, they are consolidated into truckloads and delivered to the point of sale or consumption. During the past two decades, retail stores in the USA assumed gargantuan proportions. These

Venice. Small local freighter

These stores can usefully be regarded as warehouse retail stores, as the quantity of goods in storage is very large, and in some stores, goods are stored in bulk above the shelves accessible to shoppers. Sometimes, the goods are never shelved; the consumer takes them from the original shipping pallets.

Computerized commerce could allow the make-up of mini-container shipments destined to a single small store. Containers can be shipped by rail, minimizing energy consumption, and can be handled automatically at all points between shipment and receipt, which holds down the cost. Transport distances are reduced and warehousing costs avoided.

retailers buy goods from suppliers around the globe on intensely competitive terms and sell them at extremely low prices, which encourages rampant consumption. This has led to huge consumption of raw materials for the production of goods and their transport over vast distances. Food is no longer grown near where it is consumed, and much of it moves long distances at high speed, with especially high energy consumption. Local retailers largely failed to adopt more efficient purchasing and distribution mechanisms that might have saved them.

The entire system relies on cheap petroleum. Since this is unlikely to be available for much longer, we can expect major adjustments in global trade patterns fairly soon. Transport by ship will be less affected, but transport by truck and especially by air will become expensive. More costly petroleum will also increase the price of many materials, as petroleum is the primary feedstock in the production of plastics and artificial fibers.

As energy becomes more expensive (especially if a carbon tax is added to limit greenhouse gas emissions), I think manufacturing will return to locations closer to the ultimate consumer. The energy cost of transport will also affect the willingness and ability of consumers to travel long distances to big-box stores, which can only exist if they can sell enormous volumes of very cheap products from huge, cheaply-built stores located on sites where cheap land is to be had for VAST PARKING LOTS. The upshot is that if drivers must pay for the costs they now externalize, the big-box business model may collapse. We may see a return to older patterns of retail distribution, with goods being brought to smaller stores closer to customers.

Although the price of goods will probably rise as a result, there are ecological and social advantages to a smaller-scale system. The externalized costs of the big-box model are a heavy drain on economies and ecosystems. Unfortunately, early carfree developments will be too small to affect regional distribution patterns and must adapt to the prevailing arrangements.

Container-Based Systems

Standardized shipping containers were first developed in the USA during the 1950s and have played a steadily more important role in freight transport, especially sea freight. They come in a fairly small variety of sizes, mainly 8' wide and 8.5' or 9.5' high. Principal lengths are 10', 20', 40', and 45', but other sizes exist. Oversize containers 8.5' wide are coming into use, and they have given rise to some compatibility problems. Containers are increasingly used for storage, temporary offices, and even dwelling units.

The advantages of lower costs, reduced handling and breakage, and less pilferage are so great that containerization seems sure to continue. "Break-bulk" ships have nearly disappeared, along with the long delays that resulted from the laborious loading and stowage of loose cargo. This work is now performed only once, by the original shipper, who seals the container.

Note that the flimsy aluminum containers used for air freight are not interchangeable with the heavy, rugged steel containers used elsewhere. Air containers come in many sizes, to fit the holds of different airliners. Standard containers can be moved by almost any mode, including truck, rail, and ship, but they are too large and heavy for routine air shipment.

A drawback of standardized shipping containers is that they are too large for many shipments. Standardized mini-containers are needed. They would be sized to pack tightly in larger, purpose-built containers compatible with standard sea containers. About seven mini-containers would fit in a half-height standardized tub. Two such tubs would be stacked and locked together for transport, at which time they would become the same size as a standard 40-foot container and could be handled as such. I propose mini-containers that would be approximately 7' long, 5' wide, and 4' high. They would drop into slots in the tub to prevent their shifting during transport. They could be

Containers have always been dimensioned in feet; the approximate equivalents in meters are:
Width 2.44 (2.59 extra-wide)
Height 2.59, 2.90
Length 3.05, 6.10, 12.19, 13.72

"Break-bulk" is loose cargo in individual cartons or crates that is stowed directly in the ship's hold. Such cargo must be secured against shifting in a seaway.

The Dutch Stadsbox was proposed, after long study, to improve the efficiency of city deliveries. The outside dimensions of a Stadsbox are 2.15×2.55m by 2.25m high (8.37'×7.05'×7.38'). Six boxes fit on a conventional heavy truck. One, two, or three boxes can be loaded on urban delivery trucks. The low-strength containers cannot be stacked but could be loaded into sea containers for long-haul transport.
www.stadsbox.nl/Stadsbox-hoofdrapport.pdf
See also "Just-In-Time by Rail: Enabling Railfreight To Return to the City," Peter Foyer, paper, BESTUFS 2001.

individually sealed for small shipments, and if the doors are at the end, they cannot be opened once packed inside a tub. A tub would be filled with mini-containers all destined for the same city where, upon arrival, they would be removed from the tub and routed to their final destinations by whatever means is in local use. Automated handling is possible.

METRO-FREIGHT

Metro-freight is the best way to deliver heavy freight in a carfree city. We will not delve here into the technical details of metro-freight, which were discussed in *Carfree Cities*. Suffice it to say that this automated, container-based system delivers loaded containers to the rear of basements located along the route. Containers open directly into the basement for unloading. The metro-freight line is built below grade; streets are carried across the fairly narrow right-of-way on bridges. Containers are mounted on "roller-frames" that allow them to move under automated control within the metro-freight system and to move over the streets at slow speed under human control. Containers with attached roller frames are loaded automatically onto metro-freighters at depots in the outlying utility areas.

Shipments not destined for addresses directly served by metro-freight are first delivered to the local freight depot (see page 173) in each district, from whence they are moved over the streets to their final destinations. Most shipments moving over the street will be small, as the larger freight users will locate along the metro-freight line. The proposed mini-containers should eventually comprise the bulk of these smaller shipments.

If a metro-freight system is installed, it can be used to move almost anything that must enter the city, with the few exceptions mentioned on page 176. It is possible to back a SMALL VEHICLE into a container for shipment within the city, although this requires that the vehicle have a front exit door to allow the driver

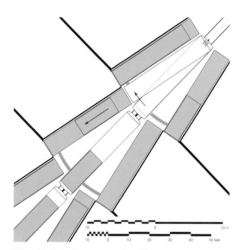

Metro-Freight System, *Carfree Cities*, pp. 194-203

to leave the vehicle. This eliminates nearly all driving except from the district freight depot to the final destination in the district. Most heavy vehicles are too large to fit into a shipping container, which limits the application of this approach.

Intermodal Yards

Incoming heavy freight is handled at an INTERMODAL YARD in one of the utility areas. These yards are equipped with cranes to load and unload containers from trucks and trains, and, in port cities, also from ships. Most of this can be partially or fully automated, and the cost of handling a container at one of these facilities is quite low. The yards must include storage space for containers awaiting routing or loading. The automated metro-freight loaders can interface directly with automated overhead gantry cranes operating in the storage yards.

The intermodal yards are connected to external rail and road systems, thereby integrating the city into the global freight network. Cargos arriving in conventional trailer trucks must be trans-shipped into containers, but virtually any supplier can arrange for a containerized shipment, so there should in practice be very little of this tedious work.

The District Depot

The district depot is located along the main freight route and near the center of the district. It handles all freight destined for addresses not served directly by the freight line. The facility is fairly large and must have several metro-freight bays where small freight can be shipped and received by the district.

Containers can be received into the district depot for further delivery over the streets to the final destination. The proposed roller frame allows towing of the container up a ramp from the metro-freight dock, onto the streets, and thence to a location

Coimbra, Portugal

See examples at:
www.trainweb.org/utahrails/drgw/plate.html

close to the consignee, from which point the shipment must be broken down for final delivery.

Loose freight from various origins with destinations within a single district is delivered in a single container to the district depot. There it is routed for delivery throughout the district, using the means described on page 178.

ALTERNATIVES TO METRO-FREIGHT

Given that the construction of a dedicated metro-freight system is unlikely in smaller projects, we must consider alternatives for handling freight in these projects. As already mentioned, the right-of way of a future metro-freight line can be used initially as a truck delivery route. Because the metro-freight line runs in a cut, trucks moving over this right of way impinge on the public only by their air pollution and noise. The route is free of other traffic, so trucks would travel at a steady, moderate speed, which minimizes both noise and pollution.

A so-called "clearance plate" must be adopted before any construction begins on either a full-fledged metro-freight installation or an interim truck route. The maximum height of vehicles passing below street-level bridges must be defined, as well as the width, lateral clearances, bed height, maximum length, and minimum turning radius of the vehicles. This will require field tests. In practice, the clearance required for tractor-trailer combinations will exceed those of containers-on-roller-frames aboard metro-freighters, possibly excepting height. The use of self-guiding vehicles would reduce the required width of the right-of-way; this technology is already in use on busways.

Freight trams were abandoned following some use early in the 20th century, and MODERN FREIGHT TRAMS like this one in Dresden are just now appearing. The Dresden installation has inspired other cities to explore freight tram installations, and Amsterdam recently conducted a successful test. The new trams are considerably larger than the old ones (which were the same size as the small passenger trams then in use), and trams of this general type should be capable of carrying 20' standardized containers (40' containers may also be possible). The use of freight trams may require greater horizontal and vertical clearances, although some existing systems already provide adequate clearance. Off-line unloading sidings must also be built. Passenger and freight service can probably be mixed, except perhaps at rush hour, when passengers may need full system capacity. Final delivery of goods from the trams would be made using the various arrangements described starting on page 178.

Any system using freight trams should accommodate mini-containers (see page 171), which can be rolled off freight trams onto modified golf cars and delivered to nearby addresses.

Conventional trucks will be used in most early carfree projects. It may be feasible to arrange the district so that stores can have a freight alley behind them, with the trucks following a route that does not impinge too seriously on the otherwise carfree nature of the area. This approach is already widely used in Europe, particularly in downtown carfree shopping areas where streets are narrow and often full of pedestrians. Trucks are only allowed during certain periods, typically in the morning.

The disadvantage of this approach is that it brings with it all the disadvantages of CONVENTIONAL TRUCKS, as here in a carfree street in Basel. These vehicles are obtrusive, noisy, smelly, and dangerous, as the driver's visibility is restricted. Backing up without a flagger is dangerous, as a small child may dart into the path of a reversing truck. For all of these reasons, the number of trucks entering a carfree area should be kept as low as possible.

The Dutch city of Groningen built a freight consolidation facility on its outskirts, where trucks with partial loads deliver their cargos. Full truckloads destined to the center city are then assembled, reducing the number of trucks entering the city. A simple and effective means to ensure that loads are consolidated

www.apta.com/services/intnatl/intfocus/cargo.cfm
www.lrta.org/dd023.html
www.dvbag.de/untnehm/gbahn.htm
www.proaktiva.ch/tram/zurich/cargotram.html

A tram with off-rail capability has been proposed but not, so far as I am aware, developed. It would have rubber tires in addition to steel wheels, plus battery power for off-route operation. This system should be feasible, but the cost may be high.

is to charge a hefty fee for every vehicle entering the area, irrespective of the size of its load.

In the 1920s in the USA, battery-powered delivery trucks were widely used, and this practice continues on a small scale in Europe today. The British "milk float" is a simple, small, quiet vehicle that delivers dairy products to small grocery stores and households. Some municipalities in Europe use BATTERY-POWERED SERVICE VEHICLES. Little stands in the way of extensive use of battery-powered local delivery trucks, especially given the recent strides in battery technology. These vehicles can be quite simple if their required radius of action is short and top speeds are held to 50 km/hr (30 mi/hr) or less. Deliveries from load consolidation centers could readily be accomplished using this prototype BATTERY-POWERED TRUCK from 2004.

The drivers of delivery vans and taxis are among the most aggressive and dangerous on the road. If trucks are to be allowed in a carfree area at all, speed-limiting governors should be installed, set to 30 km/hr (20 mi/hr) or preferably less.

One of the difficult problems in designing a carfree area is that the stores want to be in the center, and the roads should stop at the edge. If metro-freight is not installed, a single-lane tunnel to the center of the district might be built. This permits truck traffic to reach building basements, keeping the surface streets clear. Traffic signals can regulate the alternating flow.

SPECIAL CASES

The following types of heavy vehicles will probably have to be permitted to use the streets (possibly only the major streets):

- Moving vans
- Construction equipment
- Ready-mix concrete trucks
- Maintenance vehicles
- Emergency services

Their admission to city streets should be stringently regulated, and drivers specially licensed. Speeds must be kept very low, and battery-powered tugs used whenever possible. Ideally, these vehicles would travel as far as possible on a network of slow, narrow roads near the city before actually entering it. These roads would be shared by cyclists and special vehicles.

Alternatives may exist for some of these special vehicles. Cement mortar is now routinely mixed on-site in container-sized silo plants. An on-site concrete batch plant that can be delivered using metro-freight may be feasible. Concrete is routinely PUMPED SHORT DISTANCES, so if there is no room on the street where the system is needed, it can be erected nearby.

Those moving to a new house could use containers, which can be moved by metro-freight. Conventional moving vans arriving at the edge of the city could be required to transship their loads to containers for final delivery. Eventually, container service from door-to-door will actually be cheaper, as the shipment can travel mainly by rail, with automated intermodal handling. In fact, container-based movers are already doing business in the Netherlands. Local moves within the city can be handled by various means, including freight bikes, a practice that is still quite common in Amsterdam (see page 178).

To avoid the entry of over-the-road self-erecting cranes now widely used in Europe, I have considered the possibility of permanently installing in each block a self-erecting, self-housing crane. Alas, this approach seems infeasible, but it might warrant further consideration. The problem is that the required reach is too great unless the blocks are quite small.

Alternatives should be explored before granting vehicle permits. I must emphasize this point: any motorized traffic whatsoever compromises the benefits that accrue from a truly carfree approach. Accept it only if there really is no alternative. Creativity can be encouraged by levying very high fees on the few conventional vehicles that are allowed into the city.

Fes-al-Bali

LIGHT FREIGHT

I define LIGHT FREIGHT as that which weighs appreciably less than a tonne (ton) and can be man-handled. Its footprint is no larger than about one square meter (yard), and it is no more than man-high. If necessary, one or two men can wrestle it aboard a cart, freight bike, or pallet mover for further transport. Mini-containers fall at the heavy end of the light-freight category, but if fabricated from aluminum and lightly loaded, they could be delivered by the simple means proposed here. Some problems will have to be solved on an ad hoc basis, but we can sketch out the main approaches here.

Light freight comprises the large majority of shipments, but a much smaller percentage of global ton-miles. Many of these are shipments with local origins and destinations; the majority of them are small, often very small. Freight coming from outside the city usually reaches its final destination by one of two means. Goods may be delivered to retail stores, from which they make their way to individual householders. Alternatively, shipments from afar are broken down and reassembled at a consolidation center for final delivery within a given locale.

The mainstay of local delivery worldwide is some form of bicycle, often a rickshaw. Even in the USA, bicycle couriers are still an important link in the local delivery chain. I envision that pedal-powered vehicles would be used for the bulk of this work. There is some debate about the upper limit of loads for pedal-powered delivery vehicles. I think that about 200 kg (450 lb) is a practical upper limit. Much heavier loads can be moved, but the amount of work for the driver is large, and speeds are correspondingly low. Above this limit, some form of battery power makes economic sense, owing to the increased productivity of the drivers.

After decades of stagnation, the TRADITIONAL FREIGHT BIKE is being supplanted following a minor revolution in Denmark and the Netherlands. The NEW FREIGHT BIKE is lighter, has flexible gearing, a lower load platform, and higher capacity. Some of these bikes have an open cargo hold that can contain almost anything that fits, including several children. These bikes are comparatively expensive to purchase but cost hardly anything to use. Their total cost of operation is far less than that of a car or van.

Local freight that is too heavy or bulky for transport by freight bicycle will require some form of battery-assisted delivery (unless we revert to draft animals, which I cannot recommend). These can be quite simple devices, like this BATTERY-POWERED POSTAL VEHICLE in Brig, Switzerland. It is equipped with a small motor and a couple of ordinary car batteries. The postman controls direction with the tow arm, which also has simple controls for starting and stopping. No suspension beyond the pneumatic tires is provided. It appears to have been assembled mainly from STANDARD CAR PARTS (photo just below). As always, any battery-powered vehicle must be speed-limited and pose no threat to other street users. The Brig-style follow-me-along cart obviously cannot exceed the pace of the operator.

Battery-powered pallet movers, already in common use, can move quite heavy loads over the streets, provided the paving is very smooth. They can easily move a tonne (ton) and are also follow-me-along vehicles.

A variety of handcarts is required to accommodate any shipments that are not too big for manual handling. In practice, this means developing LIGHT-WEIGHT HANDCARTS that can accommodate bulky loads. Good bearings, large-diameter wheels, and proper balance all ease the chore. Supermarket carts are only useful inside stores. Their small wheels require very smooth surfaces, they are noisy on rough pavement, and the cargo is high above the wheels, making them prone to upsetting. Safer carts with similar capacities need to be readily available to residents of carfree areas, and I envision that the concierge system, described just below, would rent or lend these carts out.

The Concierge System

Good hotels and apartment buildings offer concierge service, which is simply the presence of someone who helps guests and residents with their logistics. The attitude of a good concierge is, "The difficult we do immediately; the impossible may take a bit longer." The concierge system proposed for carfree cities is intended to make life easier for people with busy schedules.

Each concierge service would serve one block (or perhaps two adjacent blocks) and would be operated by a few people, possibly a family. It would open early in the morning and close late in the evening. The service would be supported by several hundred residents, so the cost to each family would be fairly reasonable.

The concierge would operate a local utility area, where bikes are stored. The concierge would send and receive packages, including groceries, store them (in refrigerators or freezers as needed), and hand them over to the resident when he is ready to receive them. The concierge would lend or rent ladders, tools, and specialized carts and bikes. Short- and long-term storage would be offered. Mailboxes would be located there, so that every resident would visit the area at least daily. It should include a small area where people can chat and sip a cup of tea. It would become an informal hearth for the community and ought to have a wood stove where people can warm their hands after a cold trudge through the sleet and snow.

Freight carts, Venice

I have never made a detailed accounting of the space requirements for the concierge service. The requirements will vary between cultures and climates and will surely require some experience to estimate correctly.

One of the great conveniences that cars offer is a place to store things while one is out and about. This function cannot entirely be replaced, but there is no reason that each concierge should not offer short-term storage for anyone who needs it. This would allow people to arrive in a carfree area with a cartful of baggage and store it temporarily with a concierge. The popularity of left-luggage facilities in bus and train stations attests to the importance of this function to people on the move.

LOCAL SERVICES & SHOPPING

Big-box retail stores are really wholesale-to-the-consumer operations. The customer receives little service. He picks his own order, pays for it, and lugs it home. Many corner stores are SMALL FAMILY-RUN BUSINESSES. They offer good service closer to home. Prices are higher, but the quality of service and convenience partly make up the difference, and the great savings in time and transport costs make up for much of the rest. People use simple handcarts to bring home the groceries, a practice that is still widespread in Manhattan, where few supermarkets have parking. In Europe, many people still shop daily and carry their groceries home. Small groceries usually offer home delivery. Many goods and services should be available locally, in order to maximize access and minimize travel. See the list on page 228.

The carfree city assumes a return to local stores. If big-box stores are thought essential, they might be located in the utility areas, where they would have the necessary direct access to the global freight network. Customers would either bring the carts aboard the metro or pay for metro-freight delivery.

Family businesses have not yet devised effective strategies to compete against large retailers, and their distribution patterns are often highly inefficient. For instance, corner groceries in Portugal are supplied by hundreds of small operators, each of whom makes regular deliveries to dozens of stores. I have watched van after van pull up to the small grocery near me, each one carrying just a few kinds of goods and calling at many stores in the course of a day. Clearly, some sort of centralized purchasing and delivery system would dramatically improve the energy and economic efficiency of these small stores.

PERSONAL FREIGHT

When people travel by car, they often take along everything that comes to mind, just pitching it in the trunk (boot). Americans have become so used to traveling in this manner that they often stagger through European airports with a hundred kg (200 lb) of baggage in enormous suitcases. I have never understood how they manage this, or why they would ever want to.

However, we will always need to take things with us, whether for pleasure, business, or sport. Small hand carts and knapsacks can answer for much of this need, as can bicycles with panniers. A different approach is needed for the times when this does not serve. When people leave the city for vacation, they may wish

Shopping carts, Venice

Heavy cart

See page 201

Évora

to rent a car and fill it with camping gear. Sailors may need to move a pile of gear from home to the boat. Someone may want to bring home a new piece of furniture immediately. These needs must be catered for, perhaps with a lower level of convenience than we now take for granted. The approach is simple. A HEAVY CART is obtained from the concierge and loaded. The cart can be moved to the car in either of two ways. If the load is moderate, the user can simply take it aboard the metro and on to the garage. If the load is large, or the person does not wish to handle it, then the concierge would arrange for a pick-up by the freight depot, which would in turn deliver the cart to the utility area. There the goods would be packed into the car at a special loading zone. This is slower and more cumbersome than loading in front of the house but is a workable approach. It would be useful to add storage facilities near the garages for those goods that are not needed at home or in the office but which need not be kept in the car at all times.

Waste Handling

Finally, we must remove a considerable mass of waste from the city every day. Conventional sewage systems will handle most liquid wastes (unless composting toilets are selected), but other waste requires different handling. We will soon be reusing and recycling a higher proportion of our wastes than today. All that is necessary is to keep waste streams separated and to move the waste to reprocessing facilities. Waste could be collected at the district depot, which would deliver containers filled with various kinds of waste to centralized processing facilities located in the utility areas. Alternatively, wastes can be separated into bins at the concierge service, from whence it would be delivered to the depot for consolidation and transfer to processing facilities. Even conventional trash trucks can be used. They can be made quiet, as was done years ago in San Francisco, but are a hazard.

PAVING, GRADING & DRAINAGE

The civil works that are required to develop new sites are generally known in the USA under the rubric "paving, grading, and drainage." In fact, it includes all the utilities and civil works required to make a site buildable, often including flood control and stabilization of hillsides that might slide. The work is expensive and occurs early in the development process, before lots can be sold, so it is a serious cash-flow problem for most projects. The quality of the work greatly affects the final appearance of an area, as seen here on the SCHOFERSTRASSE in Freiburg.

This work is especially expensive in US sprawl development because the area of paving per house is large and the utility runs are long. Developers are required to build streets that are 30'-32' (9-10m) wide, yet these streets often connect to country roads that are themselves barely 20' (6m) wide. The total cost of infrastructure for each single-family dwelling is more than four times as high as it is for moderately dense condominium developments (Zuckermann, 231).

One consequence of sprawl is that communication and power lines must be strung from cheap poles. This ugly practice is also common in Asia. In most European cities, utilities are buried in trenches, which protects them from storm damage and greatly improves the appearance of the street.

Practices vary from place to place and are affected by local conditions. Hire an experienced local civil engineering firm that knows the local regulators and how to make the process work. This is especially important if significant variations from standard practice will be sought, as they must be for carfree projects. A local firm known and trusted by the authorities will be more effective in obtaining the needed variances than an interloper. Local firms also know the capabilities of the contractors that engage in this work and can design projects that these firms can undertake with their existing resources.

Schoferstrasse, Freiburg im Breisgau, Germany

STREET LAYOUT

The actual design of the web of streets is taken up in STREET NETWORK. Many examples of streets are included in Part III. This section considers engineering questions that the project leader must address and that cannot simply be entrusted to the engineers. In fact, the carfree nature of the project has major implications for civil engineering. In particular, streets will be much narrower than usual practice dictates. Little or no car parking will be provided, and far more bicycle parking is needed. The following matters deviate from conventional practice.

Most of the streets proposed for a carfree city are less than half as wide as their counterparts in auto-centric development, and most will be narrower than would usually be allowed. The New Urbanists have successfully demonstrated to regulatory authorities that the appreciably narrower streets they propose are adequate, but it seems that the matter must be proven anew each time. Carfree streets will be even narrower and more difficult.

Corners need careful attention to ensure that emergency vehicles will be able to negotiate them without reversing. Many streets will intersect at angles other than 90°, and a single minimum radius will not suffice. Vertical radii must also be checked if long vehicles are not to ground on abrupt changes in slope. Also be alert to difficulties that may arise where turns are combined with cross-slopes. The best practice is to test the actual corner-negotiating abilities of the equipment. Be sure to document this so that specifications for new equipment will include minimum turning radius and swept area.

These arrangements are further complicated if some streets will not allow direct emergency access. Lynch & Hack give 250' (75m) as the maximum "distance from supply or emergency vehicle to door." I think we should argue for 90m (300') in areas where buildings are small and long hallways do not add to the distance that must be covered by emergency personnel. Various

I have repeatedly found serious errors in the work of registered engineers, and their work should always be closely supervised by a knowledgeable person with a sound technical and scientific background. Such supervision should, of course, be provided by the engineering firm itself but cannot be relied upon. Firms engaged in surveying work seem to be especially prone to huge errors; I have seen locations reported *miles* out of position, geographic north reported tens of degrees in error, etc. I was always stunned to find errors of such magnitude, but my experiences convince me that it must be quite routine. Be wary!

Braga, Portugal

Lynch & Hack, 458

jurisdictions will have adopted their own standards, and they may be reluctant to allow streets too narrow for direct access, even when such streets already exist in their jurisdiction.

Streets usually include curbs to separate sidewalks from roadways. Although there is nothing seriously wrong with the use of curbs in carfree streets, there are reasons to omit them: costs, aesthetics, and access for the infirm. Curbs are useful for channeling storm water to a drain, but other street cross-sections will serve in narrow streets, as here in AMERSFOORT, where a low lip channels water into a small drain. It is possible to eliminate curbs entirely, but it is then essential to ensure that all surfaces slope towards drains, as curbs no longer channel the water. Slopes can be quite shallow, especially in carfree areas where it is less critical to prevent minor puddles from forming during heavy rain, as cars will not be splashing water everywhere or hydroplaning out of control. In practice, I think that the widest streets, carrying heavy bicycle traffic, may want curbs, in order to reduce the conflicts between pedestrians and cyclists, although, as discussed on page 162, the contrasting paving used on the VIA CAVOUR in Ravenna clearly delineates the bikeway.

Normally, paving structures are designed to accommodate moderately heavy traffic at the maximum permitted axle loading. In the case of carfree streets, peak loadings (from emergency vehicles or loaded shipping containers) will only rarely be experienced. The engineers can be asked to design a structure that will bear this load only infrequently, which may reduce costs.

The petal-shaped lobes of the Reference Topology are separated by wide swathes of open space. I always assumed that these lobes would be connected by lanes that cyclists will use as shortcuts when riding from one lobe to another. These lanes may also be used by emergency vehicles, especially ambulances, assuming that hospitals are located in the green areas, as proposed on page 142. Heavy vehicles such as concrete trucks and cranes will also use them occasionally.

PAVING

Paths and light-duty roads outside built-up areas do not always require hard paving; firm soil covered by GRADED GRAVEL, with fine grit at the top, may be adequate. In the Netherlands, even rural bike paths and light-duty roads are often paved with brick, as are most city streets. Brick is easy to repair and can be taken up if access to utility runs beneath is required. Brick has the serious disadvantage that, even when in good repair, it is rather rough to cycle over. Engineered gravel paving offers more resistance but a smoother ride. There are significant ecological advantages to permeable paving, so it makes sense to choose something other than asphalt or concrete if possible. The cost is lower and puddles caused by surface irregularities will drain away. The local need for ground water renourishment should also be considered.

City streets should ideally be smoothly paved for their full width, which will normally be from building front to building front. In areas with soft soil, such as Amsterdam, BRICK PAVING adapts itself to the inevitable subsidence without too much trouble, although tree roots will cause surface irregularities. Smooth stone paving of the kind used on the CALLE DEI FABBRI in Venice is ideal. Its cost per unit area is high, but the amount required in dense carfree areas is quite small per inhabitant, and the cost may be tolerable. Asphalt is normally the cheapest of the homogeneous paving materials, but concrete is preferred in the tropics because it does not deform under intense sunlight and heat. In regions subject to freeze-thaw cycles, concrete may soon spall if salt is spread to melt ice and snow. Much depends upon the quality of the cement binder and the finish work.

The beautiful patterned sidewalks found throughout Portugal are, alas, impractical if heavy vehicles ever traverse them, which quickly breaks up the paving. Even when subjected only to foot traffic, they still occasionally break up. However, when well maintained, as here at the LARGO DA OLIVEIRINHA in Lisbon, they are beautiful indeed. They can be surprisingly slippery in the first rain following a long, dusty dry spell.

When using brick, a choice must be made between setting it in a bed of concrete with cement between the bricks, as is done in Boston, and setting it in sand, as is done in Amsterdam. Bricks bedded in cement are essentially impermeable, and the Boston practice would tend to prevent frost heaves. A sand bed serves well in Amsterdam, which is seldom subject to hard frosts, and helps to maintain the water table at the constant level needed to protect the wooden pilings upon which the city is built.

When choosing a paving material, always consider the need to take up the paving to reach utility runs located beneath it, unless the system of utility chases proposed in the next chapter is adopted. Concrete usually requires heavy jack-hammering, whereas asphalt can be sawn and taken out in blocks, so the work is both cheaper and less disruptive. If utility chases are installed, the paving in a carfree area might remain intact for centuries. Both concrete and asphalt are fairly easy to patch when they are taken up, but patched asphalt looks slipshod and is usually rough to cycle over. Brick can be taken up and replaced almost invisibly, as can the large-block stone paving used in Venice. I would be very reluctant to install either concrete or asphalt paving in a carfree city unless utility chases were first installed. I must confess to a strong dislike for the dark color and general appearance of asphalt, but in some cases the cost advantages may be too compelling to ignore. In dry regions, earth or graded gravel paving might be considered for city streets, especially if a stabilized earth mixture is used (see note).

Whatever paving material is selected, it must be as smooth as possible if it is to be used by wheeled vehicles, especially hand carts and bicycles. The increase in resistance from rough paving is large and discourages cycling. Brick paving must be laid by artisans or it will settle unevenly.

Wood does not rot when dry or when continuously immersed, only when alternately wet and dry. The foundation pilings in Venice and Amsterdam must be kept below the water table and thus always saturated.

Patched asphalt, Lido

"To make a light road surface, the sands and gravels show marked hardening if stabilized by adding 3 to 5% of cement, by dry weight, in the upper 150 mm (6 in). The nonplastic silts can also be stabilized with 4 to 10% cement, and so can the plastic silts and nonplastic clays, but they will perform less well. Four to 10% of hydrated lime is the best additive for the clays and for the clayey sands and gravels." Lynch & Hack, 384

The addition of bitumen is also known to stabilize certain soil types and may be worth investigating for soil-paved streets.

DRAINAGE & STREET PROFILES

Lynch & Hack, 456

Lynch & Hack, 456

Lynch & Hack give the minimum slope of paved surfaces as 1% on broad areas and 0.5% when paving is laid to exact elevation or where temporary ponding is acceptable. From the standpoint of drainage, the slope can be in either direction, as long as the water is LED AWAY TO DRAINS. If the paving is permeable and the soil beneath is not usually saturated, we can accept temporary ponds while the water drains through the paving. If some streets run along the contour lines of the site, then a slight gradient can be obtained by crossing the contour lines at regular but long intervals. The centerline is thereby sufficiently sloped even if the cross-section is nearly flat and level. Occasional transverse drains can collect water sheeting down the street.

Flat sites impose level streets. Drainage is provided by install-ing curbs with storm drains at regular intervals. The point to be watched here is that the paving near building façades must slope at 2% away from the building. A slight pitch between curbside drains will prevent ponding except during torrential rains.

In regions where snowfall accumulates until the spring thaw, pay attention to disposing of snow. If heavy falls (50cm, 20") occur periodically, there will be no choice but to scoop up the snow and dump it outside the district. Usually, though, the snow can be shovelled into two lengthwise rows, with a passage for vehicles in the center and walkways at the edges.

GRADING & DRAINAGE

Freiburg

Depending on the porosity of the soil, the normal height of the water table, and the intensity of rainy spells, it may be necessary to provide artificial drainage for part or all of the site. Account must be taken of precipitation that falls on building roofs (which might in dry areas profitably be stored for later use) and into courtyards. This water must be led away so that it does not flood the surrounding buildings. This problem is particularly acute when the rear entrances of buildings are only slightly above the level of the ground, which is desirable for several reasons, including aesthetics (see page 497).

If the interior courtyards are given a slight slope towards the center, then a single storm drain can be installed there to drain the whole courtyard. If this drain is unable to cope with a downpour, water will pond in the center of the courtyard, where it will do little harm. Downspouts, if not arranged to flow into cisterns or storm drains, are best arranged at the rear of buildings. In areas not subject to heavy rainfalls, they may simply be led onto the surface of the courtyard if the soil is permeable. Otherwise, downspouts should be conducted to the storm sewer system, which will normally be easier if they run down building fronts. Local custom is often a useful guide.

Mosquitos breed in standing water. Brief ponding does not pose a serious risk, but standing water in the tropics provides a breeding ground for disease-bearing mosquitos. If gutters do not drain dry, pools will remain until they evaporate, which may take weeks. Amsterdam has attempted to provide nesting places for swallows, in the hopes that their population will recover and the birds will keep the mosquitos in check. In some parts of the world other insects are also troublesome, and good design seeks to deprive them of their habitat.

MIXED CASES

We may have to accept some compromise with purely carfree arrangements, especially in the early implementations. This should be resisted, but car-lite is better than auto-centric. Even in mixed-traffic cases, we should strive to keep most streets and all important public spaces truly carfree.

It is possible to run streets through the basements of buildings. This would permit one row of diagonal parking plus a one-way

Buildings constructed with the ground floor well above grade never really look as if they belong to the site. Building codes require a large separation between ground level and the top of the foundation if wood construction is used, which explains why most US tract houses suffer from this defect.

Downspout

When London removed traffic from just one side of Trafalgar Square, the quality of that space improved dramatically, despite continuing heavy traffic on the other sides.

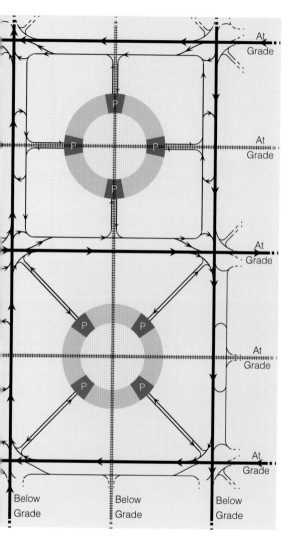

Lyon Protocol: www.carfree.com/lyon.html

traffic lane. If these basements are connected by short tunnels beneath cross streets, the streets can be arranged to loop into the district from a road at the edge. This keeps cars off the streets, but the arrangement is expensive and deprives residents in the buildings above of any other use of the space. Even with sprinklers and fireproof ceilings, the arrangement creates a fire risk that probably cannot be entirely eliminated. Ventilation must prevent exhaust fumes from entering the living spaces above. In parking garages, the sides are left open to provide natural ventilation, but underground roads and parking structures require mechanical ventilation, including a back-up power supply. The actual amount of parking and road capacity is small in comparison to its cost. I do not recommend this approach but do expect that it will see some application, especially until the carfree approach starts to enjoy widespread application and for as long as cars remain nearly essential in an auto-centric society.

In *Carfree Cities* (page 295), I mooted the AUTO-CENTRIC CARFREE CITY. (Only half of the original drawing is reproduced here.) I abhor this design, but it does suggest an approach that may find early, widespread acceptance. Cars are most obnoxious and difficult to manage at the center of a city, and we can be more permissive towards less congenial modes at greater distances from the city center. In the very center, only pedestrians might be allowed. A short ways out, cycling would be allowed. Still farther out, truck deliveries would be permitted. In the more distant areas, the cars of residents would be allowed entry. When converting an existing city to the carfree model, this is probably the most practical approach, and the bands of restriction can be enlarged as people become accustomed to the change and as new public transport infrastructure is built. Indeed, this is basically the approach recommended in the Lyon Protocol. We must be practical and politically sensitive if we are to advance the carfree cause in existing cities but should be less ready to accept compromises in new city districts.

ENERGY & UTILITIES

The shape of future energy supplies cannot today be predicted with any certainty. About half of the petroleum has been consumed, and we can expect its rate of extraction to decline slowly over the next decade or two, before a more rapid decline sets in. Natural gas reserves are large but inconveniently far from the points of consumption. Gas can be transported as a liquid in tankers, but liquefaction of the gas consumes a large amount of energy. Coal exists in huge quantities, but climate change concerns dictate reductions in its use unless underground sequestration of carbon dioxide proves economical and effective. Use of fossil fuels must ultimately be brought to zero, as they will either be exhausted or found too dangerous to climate stability.

Direct conversion of sunlight and wind to electricity is only moderately developed and comparatively little applied. The price of photo-voltaic cells has declined significantly, but other problems, particularly the difficulty of storing electricity, have limited their application. Wind power also suffers from the storage problem. Most hydropower sites were exploited years ago, and there is pressure to remove some dams for ecological reasons. Wave energy and the heat of the oceans might eventually be tapped, but these energy sources are difficult to harness. A few regions can rely on geothermal energy. Biomass yields little or no net energy gain in the case of liquid fuels. Solid fuels, mainly firewood, remain an important source of energy, but they must be consumed near the point of production, due to the energy cost of transporting them.

Perhaps the greatest challenge facing humanity is feeding the 6.5 billion people now living on Earth. Modern agriculture must be regarded as a system that converts petroleum energy into food energy, with very large losses. Intensive, mechanized agriculture in Western nations consumes huge amounts of energy for fertilizer production, herbicide and pesticide manu-

Perugia, Italy. Utility access plates and splice cabinet.

There is vigorous debate about most aspects of nuclear power. I'll summarize a few main issues.

The supply of U^{235} fuel is limited. However, thorium fuel and the breeding of U^{238} into Pu^{239} would greatly extend the supply. These resources will ultimately be exhausted but would probably last a century or more.

Circulating plutonium poses a grave risk of nuclear weapons proliferation. Some fuel cycles are claimed to reduce the risk to acceptable levels.

Construction of a nuclear power plant takes a decade from conception to commissioning. However, some of the "package plants" now proposed could be mass-produced and installed much more quickly, especially given that governments are likely to ease regulatory restrictions.

Nuclear power depends on centralized political and economic power, and is inherently undemocratic. This is true, but centralized electric power generation is nearly universal in any case.

Nuclear power is expensive compared to other solutions. This is true, but large corporations stand to make huge profits, so this option is likely to be chosen.

facture, cultivation, drying, processing, and transport. We will need to reserve petroleum for these uses during the transition to sustainable agriculture, which must occur just as the world's population reaches its peak and at a time of climate challenges.

I now expect that nuclear energy will enjoy a resurgence, popular objection notwithstanding. The risks may have been overplayed (given the large and known risks of coal-fired power generation), and new reactor designs may be safer. I generally oppose the use of nuclear energy and believe that we should reduce energy consumption and develop renewable sources. Alas, I see this as an unlikely outcome; too little is being done, and it may already be too late. The nuclear option is convenient, well developed, supported by big industry, and sufficiently economical that leaders will choose it in the face of looming shortages of fossil fuels and concerns about climate change. The problem of radioactive wastes will simply be ignored. The promise of nuclear fusion, long held to be the ultimate solution to the world's energy problems, now appears to be a mirage, and it seems unlikely that fusion power will play any role even 50 years from now, if ever.

Very little need be said about the "hydrogen economy" except that it is no solution to the coming energy shortages. Like electricity, hydrogen is merely an energy carrier (and an expensive and inefficient one at that). Hydrogen does not exist in useful quantities as a free element on Earth; all of it must be manufactured using processes that always consume more energy than is embodied in the hydrogen produced.

The uncertainty regarding energy sources complicates the design of carfree areas, because we cannot know how much energy will be available, or in what form. Any form of energy can be converted to electricity (usually with large losses), so basing transport systems on electric power is safe. We must design energy-efficient cities and arrange to supply energy from any likely source to the point of use. This is not difficult to arrange.

ENERGY STRATEGY

When building new carfree districts we should support the use of renewable energy. All that is really necessary in this regard is to make provisions for the installation of rooftop solar collectors, both thermal and electrical. Rooftop heat collectors are already widely used in tropical regions to provide economical hot water. Although the technique can be used to heat buildings in colder climates, it is less effective the farther away from the equator that the installation is located. At any given latitude there is an optimum angle for the collector face, and we will often be able to arrange roof slopes to coincide with this angle, which simplifies the installation and may do away with the need for ugly, expensive brackets prone to cause roof leaks. Similar considerations affect the installation of photo-voltaic collectors.

Near Groningen, the Netherlands

Wind turbines should probably not be installed in inhabited areas because they are quite noisy. They can instead be situated on a windy ridge near the city.

The biggest improvement in the efficient use of fuel is district heating, which requires the siting of combustion-powered electricity generation plants near inhabited areas, so that their low-grade reject heat can be piped to nearby buildings for water and space heating. The energy cost is limited to the energy used to pump water between the plant and the city; the heat would otherwise have been wasted. This practice is widely applied in Europe and well understood.

There have been some recent concerns that large-scale installation of wind turbines could disrupt winds on a global scale and thereby cause climate change. There is as yet no consensus on this point.

A variation on this approach is the use of cogeneration plants available from several manufacturers. They can achieve combined thermodynamic efficiencies as high as 92%, assuming a demand for all of the low-grade heat collected. Such plants could be located in and maintained by the concierge service.

The basic design for the carfree city includes the reliance on four-story buildings that touch each other on two sides. This minimizes the exterior wall surface (assuming that underground

Perugia

Fireplaces are notoriously inefficient, but some Scandinavian wood stoves recover most of the energy in the wood and burn relatively cleanly. However, absent catalytic converters or other emissions controls, the burning of firewood in cities is problematic.

Some work is under way, but the reduction in electricity consumption seems to be modest. See for example: www.solarserver.de/solarmagazin/artikeljuni2002-e.html
Right at press time I had word that solar-powered adsorption-cycle air conditioning has been developed. I do not know about costs, practicality, or electricity consumption.

In any case, an end to air conditioning need not mean suffering. Good cross-ventilation and the use of slow-turning, low-power ceiling fans go a long way towards making high temperatures bearable, without creating much noise.

In the USA, the adoption of urban growth boundaries by a few cities is a step in the right direction.

houses are not an acceptable option). Any of the usual methods of space heating can be employed, but reliance on firewood should be avoided unless emissions controls are installed on the flue. In most cases, some form of circulating hot water will be used. In-floor radiant heat should be considered, because lower air temperatures still feel comfortable when the whole body is directly warmed by infrared radiation. This saves energy and also reduces draftiness. Very good insulation of walls, windows, and doors is, of course, essential.

So far as I am aware, a practical solar-powered cooling system has yet to be developed. In principle, this ought to be possible, as sun energy is normally plentiful in places and seasons where cooling is desired. Such a system might use the same collectors as for heat and hot water, which would be a great simplification. Absent some practical means to cool buildings with sunlight, I expect that we will have to abandon routine use of air conditioning in homes and offices. We may be able to reserve it for use during life-threatening heat waves, but I doubt that we will be able to afford a renewable energy system with sufficient capacity to power air conditioning to the degree that Americans now expect. Vernacular architecture always includes simple methods to minimize discomfort from heat and cold. These methods can be discovered simply by looking at local buildings in the traditional style. One point is worth emphasizing: nothing cools a hot room on the top floor of a building so effectively as an open skylight. This has to be experienced to be believed.

The proposed transport system, based as it is on conventional metro technology, is extremely energy efficient and is powered by electricity. Steps should be taken to ensure that the carfree area does not become unduly dependent on cars for transport to areas outside the city. The long-term strategy is to recentralize our cities and arrange for public transport service to the city center from outlying areas. When energy was expensive, cities were always arranged in this way. We should encourage our leaders to inhibit the development of outlying areas, especially of commercial projects, which invariably increase demand for transport. Offices and stores should be located downtown, not at the periphery. This is the only approach that can dramatically reduce the number of auto miles driven, and will be necessary even if order-of-magnitude improvements in automotive fuel efficiency are implemented. (Volkswagen has road-tested a car that gets 235 MPG or 100 km/liter.)

The only reasonable energy strategy for a new carfree city is to provide for the distribution of all forms of energy in use today. Whatever the future may hold, this ought to be adequate, but we should nevertheless allocate space for the installation of new cabling or piping, should that ever be needed.

www.carfree.com/cft/i032.html

OVERHEAD UTILITIES

Only those utilities that absolutely must be overhead should be permitted in that location. Careful examination of Venice reveals that, despite an effort to minimize the visual impact of telephone and power cables, they do sometimes cross above streets, and are commonly attached (neatly) to the façades of buildings. There are a few UGLY INSTALLATIONS, but most work is not objectionable. We should avoid these practices in new districts. The placement of power and telephone lines on long rows of poles should not even be considered.

Antennas have blighted cities around the world since the advent of television. Television cables have reduced the need for rooftop antennas. Early satellite dishes were enormous and ugly. The current generation is smaller but still always an ugly addition to a building. Broadband cable TV should essentially eliminate the need for consumer SATELLITE DISHES.

Antennas for mobile telephone networks can be concealed inside bell towers and the like. A few specialized antennas may be essential, but their installation should be tightly regulated.

STREET LIGHTING

Manufactured gas was employed for street lighting early in the 19th century. The practice expanded rapidly until the advent of electricity. Gas light and standard tungsten incandescent lamps have many advantages over the gas-discharge lamps that are now ubiquitous. Mantle-type gas lamps gave a bright, full-spectrum white light. Incandescent lamps are similar to gas mantels except that the spectrum is shifted towards red and is quite deficient in blue. The resultant warm light might even be regarded as an improvement over the harsh white of the gas mantle.

Over the past 50 years, the quality of city illumination declined sharply, first with the shift to the mercury-vapor lamp (which has a discontinuous spectrum lacking red) and then to the sodium lamp with its characteristic yellow-orange light. Its spectrum is so poor that many colors cannot even be recognized under its light, and people always look terrible under its glare.

Venice elected, in most places, to retain its dim but attractive incandescent street lighting, since the high level of illumination needed by car drivers is not required. Even where brighter and more efficient gas-discharge lamps have been installed, as here at PIAZZA SAN MARCO, the ugly sodium lamps have been avoided. In carfree cities we do not require high levels of illumination. Even if a carfree area is illuminated with incandescent lamps, the per-capita energy consumption should compare favorably with suburban street lighting.

It is often claimed that bright street lighting deters crime, but this does not appear to be true. In fact, illumination with a monochromatic spectrum may actually be associated with increased crime, possibly due to the poor quality of the light.

The bad quality of the light is not the only problem with modern street lighting. The old cast iron lamp poles were always made with an eye to beauty and many of them are remarkably intricate in their design. These have been replaced by cheap

On-going advances in LED technology are yielding efficient illumination with a good spectrum.

See: "Outdoor Lighting and Crime," B.A.J. Clark at:
amper.ped.muni.cz/light/crime/html_tree/
and
amper.ped.muni.cz/light/crime/OLCpt2.htm

aluminum tubes topped with the standard "cobra head" fixture. This system has nothing to recommend it except very bright illumination at irreducible cost. Their intense light obscures all but the brightest stars.

In some cities, street lights are suspended from cables attached to buildings on either side of the street. This is economical, but these lamps oscillate in strong winds and the swaying pattern of light disturbs adjacent residents. Bracket-mount lamps like those attached to many buildings in Venice are preferable. These LAMPPOSTS ALONG THE ZATTERE are the usual solution in parts of Venice where lamps on brackets hung from buildings are, for one reason or another, impractical or unwanted.

UNDERGROUND UTILITIES

In Europe today, most urban utilities are in the ground. (Rural areas still often use pole-hung cabling.) The initial expense is higher, but maintenance costs are reputed to be lower, and widespread damage from an ice storm cannot put the utility network out of operation for weeks, as happened in parts of southern Quebec in 1998. The cost of upgrading underground systems can be high if the street must be taken up to perform the work, which is the usual case.

I think the ideal approach was taken by some US universities in the 1930s: tunnels were dug to all buildings on the campus, and a central plant was used to provide heat and power, with pipes and cables all running safely out of sight in the tunnels. (An added benefit is that heat escaping from the tunnels melts snow on paths running atop the tunnels.) The capital cost of this approach is the highest of all, but the tunnels should last for a century, and maintenance work can be performed with ease. When large-diameter piping must be renewed, it is only necessary to dig relatively small access pits. These utility tunnels, or chases, can be located just below the street, and it is even possible

Lisbon

for their covers to form the surface of the street, so that the chase can be opened with little disturbance when necessary.

If this method is used, then most, or perhaps all, streets would have a chase installed. These chases are, ideally, high enough for a man to walk upright, and wide enough to permit the installation of all known and likely utilities, with space left over to accommodate fairly large additional piping for which no need is yet known. Each house will need a conduit connecting the basement (or utility pit) to the chase. These conduits must be sealed against vapor intrusion. Shutoffs must remain accessible. I would strongly recommend this approach, unless the option discussed just below is shown to be practical for a given project.

When a single developer builds a large project and has control over all elements of design and construction, there exists the possibility to run utilities through the basements of the buildings, rather than in the street. This involves some risks, in particular gas explosions from leaks. If these utility runs are combined with the basement car access lanes mooted on page 190, the ventilation required for the cars also largely eliminates the already-small risk of explosion. This approach should be quite economical, and maintenance is easy.

JUNCTIONS & CABINETS

Splicing boxes and transformer huts are a blot on the city. They occupy more space than one might suspect, and they are rarely attractive installations, saving aside nice examples such as the one that begins this chapter. The ROUND TRANSFORMER KIOSKS (above) found throughout Europe are less objectionable and obtrusive than TRANSFORMER HUTS. Utility operators require regular access to their CABLE SPLICING BOXES (next page). If these were located in basements or utility chases, the ugly boxes could be removed from the street and given better weather protection in the bargain. The demands of utility companies for metering and junction boxes should not be accepted without question. I remember a project in which the utility company wanted to install large distribution and meter cabinets right on the waterfront of an expensive marina. I was able to get them to approve an alternative approach that was cheaper and much more attractive. This kind of inventiveness is not often to be found in utility companies, but many will work with a reasonable developer as long as nothing difficult or dangerous is asked.

Cable splicing boxes

Cabling

Like other utilities, electric power should be underground, possibly with the high-voltage transmission lines being concealed along the metro-freight right-of-way. Today's practice provides excessive capacity, given the need to reduce power consumption.

It might be useful to include on every block (perhaps in the concierge space) a high-capacity connection that can be used by film crews, maintenance workers, and other temporary users. It is not difficult to include such a connection with the transformer installation, and this averts the need to bring in heavy diesel generators, with their attendant smoke and noise.

Something on the order of 480-volt, 500-amp 3-phase power is probably adequate for most needs of this kind, and the possibility exists of pulling together power from several blocks if more is required.

I use the term "data pipes" to include all forms of telecommunication cabling. Any new urban quarter should be supplied with a single form of data pipe to which all customers and all suppliers would have access. This would take the form of fiberoptic cables routed into each building (ideally, one fiber to each apartment). These cables have ample capacity for all conceivable telecommunications requirements and save the cost of installing separate data, television, and telephone cables. The cables would be brought to central facilities where they would be linked to the various data carriers. One concern arises regarding this arrangement for telephones, which must work under emergency conditions. Telephones are powered by a small current

Underground utilities, Venice

Mobile phones are not yet sufficiently reliable to depend upon in emergencies; the battery will be discharged just when most needed. Land-line services inform emergency call centers of the exact origin of the call; cell phones give only an approximation. Conventional land lines have provided remarkably reliable service, which cannot be said of other phone systems.

supplied from a bank of batteries at the central exchange. The same twisted-copper-pair carries both voice and power. If no other solution can be found, then it may be necessary to provide traditional twisted-pair service into each building. Most telephone traffic would move over the fiber-optic system, with its nearly perfect voice quality. The twisted pair can be connected to a simple telephone for use during power failures.

GAS

Gas fuels require a pipeline into each building. These fuels include manufactured gas (now little used), natural gas (methane plus other light hydrocarbons), liquid petroleum gas (LPG, propane and/or butane) and, in the future, possibly hydrogen. The same pipes can be used for any of these fuels except hydrogen, which is astoundingly fugitive and leaks from nearly any container. House-to-house distribution of hydrogen would probably require replacement of the existing gas piping.

The gasometers of the past have been replaced by high-pressure mains that serve as reservoirs. I object to this practice in earthquake zones, as it dramatically increases the risk of catastrophic fire following an earthquake. (Recall that the disastrous fires following the 1906 San Francisco earthquake were fuelled by *low-pressure* gas mains.) A return to the use of low-pressure gas mains requires the huge and ugly GASOMETER. A system that vents the high-pressure network during a major earthquake could make the use of high-pressure distribution safer.

LPG is widely used in many urban areas, especially in the developing regions of the world. The familiar steel cylinders must be transported to the point of use, which is somewhat risky and quite expensive. When gas mains are installed, the transport and use of large LPG cylinders should banned. Only small bottles, such as for camping stoves and plumber's torches, should be permitted.

WATER & SEWER

It goes without saying that any city must have a reliable source of drinking water. This is a complex matter that belongs to urban planning, so we will consider it only briefly.

Standpipes are no longer routinely installed in many areas, but if they are standard practice, some location must be found for them, and the possibilities are often limited. A real effort should be made to avoid the ugly silver-sphere-on-legs design.

Little specific advice on the matter of sewage can be given, except that organic solids probably need to be reclaimed and eventually returned to the land, in order to maintain its fertility. Dry toilets like the Clivus Multrum should be considered, but they are not simple to build into multi-story buildings, as the large treatment tank must be situated directly below the toilet. Foam flush toilets from the same company allow the tank to be slightly offset from the toilet but still fairly directly beneath it.

Storm sewers must be kept separate from sanitary sewers, as the treatment requirements differ. It may also be useful to separate household sewage into "black water" and "gray water." Black water, from toilets, requires intensive treatment before release. The requirements for gray water treatment are not yet uniformly agreed upon, although it seems clear that less intensive treatment is required. Gray water contains detergent as a contaminant. Toilet cleaning chemicals can be troublesome in black water. The design for the sewage systems may require the provision of as many as three separate networks. Sufficient room for this should be provided in utility chases.

There are strict limitations on the pitch of sewers; they may not be too shallow, or sediment will accumulate, nor may they be too steep, lest scouring occur. Sufficient flow must be maintained to prevent sedimentation, a problem that may become troublesome as household water usage is reduced. All of these issues should be entirely familiar to civil engineers.

www.clivus.com

www.clivusmultrum.com/clivus_new.html

Gubbio

Coimbra

DEVELOPER

The organization that founds and develops a carfree project will exert a powerful influence on the unfolding of the project. The matter turns to a considerable degree on whether or not the project initiator remains in substantive control of the project. If, for instance, a green organization initiates a project that is later funded by, say, an insurance company, the unfolding of the project may change in ways that the initiators did not anticipate and do not support. We consider here the pure cases, but in reality hybrid arrangements will probably dominate.

In *Carfree Cities,* several projects were proposed, more by way of illustration than as practical suggestions. These examples do give some idea of the range of variation in potential developers.

EuroCity, a new town in what was to have been the fourth of the great polders in the former Zuider Zee, would have housed EU environment, transportation, and development functions. The EU itself would have been the primary developer.

Another proposal was for carfree retirement cities in the southern USA. These cities would have been built by existing large developers, some of which have actually undertaken projects of similar scope. Some of these projects did attempt to reduce car traffic by allowing the use of golf carts, so the developers are already familiar with traffic issues and the elderly.

I also proposed that the US government donate some of its vast land holdings for land-grant cities, to provide inexpensive housing for low-income families. One of the terms of the land grant would have been that speculative gains on their free land would have been prohibited. The application of community land trusts was proposed to maintain land values at zero in perpetuity. In keeping with the land-grant character of the proposal, the developer would most likely have been the state in which the new city was to be located. Ultimately, politics and economics affect project ownership, financing, and profit.

Bologna, Italy. Arcaded street.

CHAOTIC DEVELOPMENT?

Strip mall, Los Angeles

GIS = Geographic Information System

Wolfe, 80-82; see also page 110 of this work.

There has long been a fear of chaotic, unplanned development, which continues even today in the shanty towns of Asia, Africa, and South America. Girdirons are an effective countermeasure. It is quick and easy for the city to establish the streets, and development can be controlled by registering and selling surveyed lots. The lots determine the location of buildings and infrastructure, and the registered ownership simplifies regulation. This system has often yielded reasonable results over the years.

There is, however, nothing intrinsic in the grid as a guarantor of order and public safety. Streets can be laid out on any pattern that may be desired, with building sites identified and registered as the streets are arranged. The simplification of rectilinear surveying is now minor, given the powerful tools available and the ease with which irregular shapes can be reduced to vectors in GIS software. Only curves remain difficult to manage, and they are in any case usually better handled as a series of straight lines.

Although the fear of chaotic development is not unfounded, "informal settlements," as they are often called, are not always so bad. Slipshod utilities and unreliable emergency access often characterize these neighborhoods, but in other respects their arrangement is often reasonable. They are, so far as I am aware, invariably based on irregular streets. The buildings are occupied by their owners, who make continual improvements. The evolution of some Palestinian refugee camps is typical. They went from tents to multi-story buildings in a generation. Along the way, they shed their regular street patterns.

On the other hand, formal government planning has often failed, as with the Pruitt-Igoe housing project and Amsterdam's concrete towers in the 1960s. These projects have two common traits: the failure to involve future occupants in design, and the doctrinaire acceptance of Modernism. Informal sites have often had better outcomes than large, centrally-planned projects.

Project Initiator & Developer

Every project begins when someone decides that a project is needed, often with a potential site in mind. The person who initiates the process may have little involvement with it after the beginning—the project initiator may not be the developer. For example, the mayor conceives of a project. The political process decides that this is the right kind of project in the right place at the right time. The city establishes project goals and assembles a parcel of land in a blighted area. Bids are sought from developers and the project is awarded to the winner. In one form or another, this process has worked in US and European cities.

Some types of project initiators are:
- Governments
- Community boards
- Insurance companies
- Private developers
- Community land trusts
- Cooperative associations

The type of developer is usually known by the time planning begins, even if a specific developer is not yet identified. I favor community-based, public-sector development but concede that most projects will not be organized in this manner.

Real estate development projects can be managed and constructed by any one of a number of agencies, including:
- Government
- Non-governmental organization (NGO)
- Community land trust
- Cooperative association
- Private, for-profit developer

The nature of the agency that designs and builds a large project greatly affects the range of options available to the planners and designers, which in turn depends on the legal reach of the developer. To establish a CITY OF ARCADES like Bologna, the

Valladolid

See James A. Kushner's books for legal strategies.

See the Institute for Community Economics handbook.

ability to impose the arcade form must reside in the planning or development agency. The power arises almost automatically if a government is the planning agency. A developer who owns an entire tract can appropriate this power simply by establishing arcades as a term in the deeds of the individual parcels.

Project Owner

The largest hammer in any construction project is wielded by the fellow who pays the bills. This is simply inevitable. Ideally, the one paying the bills is the ultimate occupant, but this is not the usual case.

There are two classes of owners: pre-sales and post-sales. In the case of rental units, the initial and ultimate owner are often the same entity, but in most projects the ownership changes when the project is completed and occupied. There are usually many more post-sales owners than pre-sales owners. Residences are most likely to be built by a single owner and sold upon completion to hundreds or thousands of owner-occupants.

Each type of project owner employs a habitual set of methods. These are often not written down, simply carried in people's heads. They have a huge influence on the conceptualization of a project and the means by which it is executed. It is usually very difficult to make any change in these working methods.

Take one example. In the 1930s, the US government put into place a body of regulation that was intended to foster private ownership of houses by their occupants. This policy has remained substantially intact for 70 years and has had a profound influence on the patterns of suburban development (which it encouraged). Everyone involved understands the rules and how the game is played. Any approach that deviates even slightly from the standard path is fraught with the risk of rejection. Institutional funders usually refuse to play any other game. This system is so ingrained that the New Urbanists saw decades of

"By comparison, let us look again at a typical development of the late 20th century. Look at this public housing project in Florida. You see the problem. With the parking spaces, very little space is actually usable. You may think this is a problem of density, that as density increases you just cannot handle that urban space in a fashion that can become useful. Historically that was never true. It does not have to do with density. It has to do with whether there is a general understanding by the people who build, and who pay for buildings, that the public space needs to be made usable, every fifty feet a useful and beautiful place to be, and actually to be the living room of your society.

"In a living structure for society, the vital importance of the public room is fundamental. The street is not a thing to drive through, but a series of spaces which are the places where you most want to be. But to get it in meaningful fashion…, people need to be in control—in control of their individual space, and in control of the public space. Design alone cannot accomplish this. It needs a change in the way we make it possible for people to control the world around them."
Alexander, TNO, III:36

resistance to their projects, despite clear evidence of strong demand for them and higher prices in the market.

Once the project is complete, the initial owners will usually transfer ownership to one or another of several ultimate ownership schemes (not every scheme is suitable to a given project):

- Public
- Cooperative
- Condominium
- Community land trust
- Privately-owned rental property
- Fee-simple ownership by occupants

The USA essentially stopped building public housing around 1975 due to the failure of many projects as a result of ill-advised policies affecting their design. In the Netherlands, "public" housing is actually built by housing associations, which are non-profit groups, established with government support, for building affordable housing. (These groups have certainly known their failures, but the results have generally been reasonable.)

Projects are seldom built under condominium ownership. Rather, projects are built by private developers which establish the condominium association and its by-laws. The completed dwelling units are then sold to private individuals, with the public areas falling under the common ownership of the condominium association.

The cooperative housing associations that are so common in New York City are not well known elsewhere. They resemble condominiums in many respects, but the legal construction is very different. A cooperative association might have some success in securing funding through traditional channels.

Other project owners, such as cohousing groups and community land trusts, are rare enough that these groups may have difficulty securing construction funding for their projects. Since these are highly promising ownership structures for carfree projects, the funding issues are a significant obstacle.

A land-grant city initiative was proposed in *Carfree Cities*. A community land trust would be used to hold land values at zero in perpetuity. (pp. 282-284)

Social housing, Amsterdam

Auto-centric "snout" house

FUNDING

TNO, II. See chapter 19, Massive Process Difficulties, for a long discussion not only of the pernicious influence of contemporary funding mechanisms but many other aspects of the contemporary US development system. Alexander has decades of bad experiences and much wisdom to impart.

I will not address the question of funding at length, as practices vary from place to place. It is, however, worth noting that funding mechanisms exert a great influence on development and that the methods used in many Western countries are highly restrictive and ultimately unsatisfactory. Alexander has complained at length about the problems imposed by conventional funding practices (as well as regulatory systems).

The current US system is not widely understood. The first thing that must be grasped is the huge influence of front-end costs on profitability, especially during times of high interest rates. Many projects don't "pencil out." This means that the chief number-cruncher could find no scenario that yielded an ultimate profit. The usual culprits are land costs, site difficulties, and regulatory delays. These costs are incurred early in the project, and when interest rates are high, few projects are attractive. The other end of the process, sales, may not yield enough income or may yield it only over too long a span of time. These calculations are highly complex and require an understanding of the mechanisms of compound interest and "present value," which are mathematically quite simple. However, achieving an accurate projection is fraught with difficulties.

The developer is usually the one who puts up the seed money, acquires the land (or at least options to buy it), writes the preliminary design proposal, applies for permits, develops financial projections, and applies for construction funding. This is considered the riskiest phase of a project, and those who invest at the concept stage may lose everything or make a fortune. Interest rates on construction loans are much higher than for mortgages on the completed buildings, because this is also seen as a risky phase of development (and at this point a lot of money is at stake). Once the first loans are made, there is a great rush to complete the project, so that financing can be converted from

Washington Mews, Manhattan

construction-loan rates to long-term mortgage rates. During construction, time is money. The "net liquidated damages" clause in most contracts does not cover the costs of delays and is always the subject of dispute, as any delay can be claimed to be someone else's fault. Contracting in the USA thus often ends with legal battering that bruises all players.

Before undertaking any kind of project, and especially before putting money on the line, it is essential to understand how the game is played locally and what the formal and informal rules are. The inexperienced will be led into many pitfalls, each one more expensive than the last. Local experience is the only protection, and even that is by no means total.

It is important to know what the major sources of funding are. Surprisingly, banks are not always the best chance. Life insurance companies have huge sums of cash they must invest, and many have turned to real estate projects over the years. Insurance companies understand risks, and many of them are seeing the results of climate change in rising claims due to extreme weather. I think insurance companies are a promising source of funds for carfree projects, as insurers will understand the benefits of the approach in reducing risks. Pension funds also look for long-term investments that are secure against inflation, and real estate is attractive to them. It is not out of the question that a very rich individual can be induced to come up with the billion or so dollars needed to build a large carfree project. I myself think that this would be a safe investment, but the absence of "comparables" (used in projecting sales revenues) requires a lender who really believes in the promise of carfree districts.

Until the profitability of carfree development projects has been clearly demonstrated, we may have to look to other funding sources. If the European Commission can be convinced that new, energy-efficient urban forms are essential, it might provide money for demonstration projects. It is also possible that local governments would sell bonds to finance a carfree district.

A building society or progressive bank or credit union might see the light and take the plunge. Randy Ghent suggests that, in the UK, the Ecological Building Society, the Triodos Bank, or the Co-operative Bank might be successfully approached with a sound project. In the USA, the UK, and quite a few other nations, Real Estate Investment Trusts (REIT) are often used to fund real estate development projects, although the tax treatment is not always as favorable as it was several decades ago.

To judge by the New Urbanist experience, this takes at least 15 years.

See, for example, the proposals for the One Planet Living project on the Sesimbra peninsula: www.bioregional.com/programme_projects/ opl_prog/portugal/portugal_hmpge.htm

Some resort developers have found promise in "green" destinations and have sought partnerships with NGOs whose cachet is hoped to provide both speedy government approval and great demand from guests eager to take a green vacation. NGOs themselves lack the cash to invest in large projects.

Cooperatively-financed projects can be envisioned in which each of the future residents would put up a share of the cost of site acquisition, permitting, site work, and building construction. However, comparatively few people actually have enough cash available, and loans on reasonable terms will not be available until the project is complete.

CONSTRUCTION

One of the results of the North American system is that mass production is seen as the only path to success. It is difficult enough to get everything approved and reasonable contracts signed without having to worry about unique designs for each building. Instead, a floor plan is developed that will sell to the "demographic" and to the financiers. This plan is then endlessly repeated and built as fast as possible. Plans that are complete to the last nail become a legal agreement between contractors and the owner. Every tiny change to these plans is billed, at extravagant rates, as a "change order" by the contractor. This is, in fact, where they make most of their money. (Brand has said that the claims department is often the largest one in a contracting organization.)

Brand, 62

Alexander has rightly pointed out that good design is nearly impossible under these conditions and that any attempt to make on-the-fly adjustments is prohibitively expensive. The resulting projects are almost invariably numbingly monotonous. The older approach, which was simple agreement between a local builder and the owner, was more flexible and yielded better results. It is difficult to apply except to single buildings.

PROJECT TYPE

The type of carfree project under consideration affects the range of possibilities available to the designers. There are three fundamental types of carfree projects.

Rehabilitation of existing urban areas is the first type. The USA has many degraded, even abandoned, city neighborhoods. (Such sites are less common in Europe.) Paradoxically, some contemporary cities continue to expand even as their populations decline, a situation that occurs in midwestern American cities such as Cleveland and Detroit. Large areas of the old center city are abandoned and new suburbs built ever farther from downtown. The old, largely abandoned city centers are ideal sites for carfree redevelopment. Urban infrastructure is already present and buildings are often of sound brick construction. These areas are usually located close to the city center and thus better served by public transport than most of the city. These sites offer a way to improve the quality of life for people who do not have a lot of money and who often do not own cars. The cost of redevelopment should be much less than the cost of new development at the edge of the city, and the cost of living in these central areas should be lower, as families are not burdened by the expense of owning an automobile.

So-called "brownfield" sites are the second type. They are abandoned industrial sites, found in many parts of Europe and the USA. Many of them are fouled by some level of industrial pollution. It seems unfair that those redeveloping these sites should have to bear the financial burden of cleaning them up, but this is often the case. Large-scale demolition work may be required, but it is always worth considering whether the existing buildings can be salvaged. Just as with derelict residential neighborhoods, city administrators are usually anxious to find something useful to do with these areas, which cost the city for upkeep but yield little or no revenue. The practice of brownfield

Redevelopment, Alfama

Dayton, Ohio

redevelopment is actually quite advanced in much of the industrialized world, and the problem of cleaning contaminated soil is usually not too daunting. Like rehabilitation projects, many of these sites are favorably situated and close to public transport.

Greenfield sites, the third type, are at once the easiest to develop, since no account need be taken of previous uses, and the least desirable, since they are often prime farmland and quite distant from the city center. Public transport is rarely available at the start of the project, and most of the destinations to which residents might need to travel are distant and most easily reached by car. Only in the case of a project large enough to become a city in its own right will these areas escape the need for a tight connection to existing urban areas. Developing these sites without their residents becoming habituated to car use is difficult, and it will be necessary to provide plenty of parking at the edge of the project. When it is decided to build on such a site, rail service to downtown (and possibly to other important destinations) should be in operation when the first neighborhoods are occupied. Otherwise, people may get in the habit of driving to destinations outside of the district, even if it requires some time and effort to get from home to the parking garage. This negates many of the benefits of carfree development.

Even in the case of cities with growing populations, efforts should be made to build central carfree projects before turning to greenfield sites on the periphery. The most serious objection that will be raised to carfree infill projects is by neighbors who fear that the residents of the carfree areas will "of course" own cars, which they will then try to park in nearby areas, causing parking chaos. This fear is not entirely unfounded and should be addressed at the outset. Many projects of this type will be relatively small and will be surrounded by conventional auto-centric development. Quite a number of them have already been built. It is not reasonable to expect residents of these projects to deny themselves access to goods and services that are

San Bento Station, Porto

Listed at: www.carfree.com/carfree_places.html

readily available only by car. Most of the pilot projects have provided parking for private cars as well as car-sharing for those who choose not to own a car. Parking can thus become a significant consideration even in "carfree" projects. Only when the host cities themselves begin the shift to carfree arrangements (and the much better public transport that this demands) will the clamor for parking subside.

Project Management

I will touch here only briefly on the complex task of project management. Larger projects are usually managed by the field office of the general contractor. The work is done by someone who is on-site most of the working day. Good project managers have a nose for trouble and can identify and fix problems long before others are even aware of them. A good head for figures is essential.

Salamanca

In principle, the function of project manager can be filled by a team, but in my experience there is always one person who takes the lead role and coordinates the work. When the project is large, other people will take responsibility for various aspects of the project, with the project manager coordinating all efforts. The project manager must have a solid understanding of how all the tasks relate to each other and the order in which the tasks must be completed. There is no substitute for experience in this work, and even an experienced project manager can get into trouble when managing a project that is appreciably different in its scope or methods from projects with which he has prior direct experience.

Évora, Portugal
This is one of the largest intact medieval cities in the
world. Its radial street plan nicely illustrates many of
the principles of street arrangement discussed here.

URBAN VILLAGES

What is an urban village? Why might people prefer to live in one? A village could be defined as a circumscribed, integrated area with a population small enough that most people know most other people, at least on sight if not by name. Villages are characterized by relaxed social relationships and easy mutual assistance that larger urban areas often lack. Villages are places that people call home. I myself grew up in one and never recognized that fact until quite recently—it struck me one day that I had grown up in a small place, a valley hedged by hills on all sides, with a population of a few hundred people, most of whom knew each other. To a child, a village is like a warm bath—you don't necessarily realize that you are in one until you get out. When I left this place, I suddenly didn't know anyone and saw many people I would never set eyes on again. The safety, security, and comfort of the village were gone, replaced by suburban sprawl in which I was to come to know only a few of the neighbors. There were no community fixtures, no common ground, and little community social life. Adults drove almost everywhere. Children rode bikes, only to abandon them as soon as they could get a driver's license.

Christopher Alexander feels as deeply as I do about the role of villages in arranging places that are worth living in:

> But I would like, if I can, in this chapter first to shock you into a recognition of the truly dreadful meaning of my pleasant-sounding words about belonging—and persuade you that much of the emotional misery of the 20th century was caused by the terrible loss of belonging our contemporary process inflicted on society.
>
> The loss has been inflicted on us and on our fellow human beings. Belonging, although it was common in traditional towns and villages, is missing in far too much of

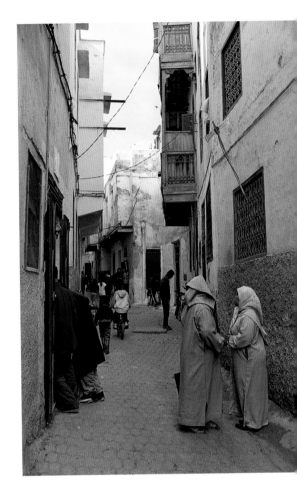

Fes-al-Jdid, Morocco. A functioning urban village.

modern society. The forms of the environment we have learned to create in modern times have caused us to lose the sense of true connection to ourselves and our society. That has happened, in large part, because of the nature of the space we have created. It has happened because the public space of our present-day cities, both legally and metaphorically, no longer belongs to us to any deep extent."

TNO, III:31

Alexander thus shares my view that the places we build for ourselves have a profound effect on the quality of our lives and that we have failed in the critical task of building neighborhoods that can support community. Just a little farther on, he says:

> All of my life I have been inspired by what happened in traditional society and marveled how much people all over the world knew about essential things. In traditional society, up until the onset of this century, the space that existed between buildings was like the living room of society. It was the place where people did things, got together, felt comfortable.

TNO, III:34

Villages are not confined to rural areas and may in fact exist quite comfortably within a city. Balinese society is organized by village, and even Bali's one real city, Denpasar, is organized into villages along the rural model. The medieval Italian town of Siena comprises 17 urban villages (*contrade*). Village distinctions are fortified twice a year by the intense competition of the Palio horse races held in the city's main square, during which each *contrada* vies against the others.

There are aspects of village life that not everyone likes or enjoys. There is less privacy, and people think they have a right to know what their neighbors are doing. Gossip is a staple of village life, and not all of it is nice. Villagers are often intolerant of people different from themselves.

If, in a given culture, there are some people who prefer the more anonymous life that now characterizes most Western societies, they might choose to settle along the central boulevard in neighborhoods that are not organized as urban villages; the rest of the district will be composed of villages whether people intend it or not. This may even be true of the central boulevard, but if those who prefer a more anonymous life gather in that location, it will be less likely to develop into an urban village.

Given the social advantages of villages, I think it is useful to help future residents to group into urban villages prior to the design of carfree neighborhods and then to use these urban villages as the primary instrument of design. Not everyone need belong to one, but I think most families, given the chance, will choose to join one.

Each village has unique attributes that define the community and differentiate it from nearby villages. Even cosmopolitan Amsterdam has strong neighborhood affinities. I lived for 14 years in a CENTRAL NEIGHBORHOOD in that city, and by the end of that time felt that I knew, at least by sight, quite a large proportion of the residents. I knew the shops and the shopkeepers. I had learned that only one of the drunks was likely to be troublesome. One day, when a new family was playing their music loud with the windows open, I heard another resident yell across the courtyard, "This is not the Kinkerstraat" (referring to another neighborhood where noise was the rule rather than the exception). The stereo was turned down, for good.

This block was not truly a village, probably because the interior courtyard was inaccessible to most residents and was thus never a place where residents of the block could congregate, but they nonetheless enjoyed some of the advantages of village life. Indeed, one hallmark of a village is that it has at least one place where almost everyone goes on a regular basis. In rural communities, it may be the general store, the pub, the church, or the meeting hall. (The village in which I grew up lost both its meet-

Donald Appleyard showed that the real barrier to the development of local communities was car traffic. His research showed an inverse correlation between community connections and car traffic in a San Francisco neighborhood. So, even along a large but carfree boulevard, people may get to know the neighbors.

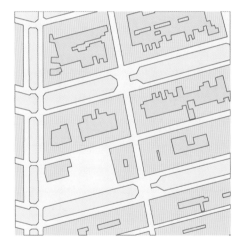

One of the reasons that this neighborhood was not really an urban village was that it lacked clear boundaries except for the Amstel River to the east, just off the edge of the plan.

Water supply was problematic in the saline Venetian lagoon. The ingenious solution was to use the squares as catchment basins, beneath which was a thick sand layer that absorbed rainfall for later withdrawal.

ing hall and general store during the time I lived there. The village was divided along sectarian lines, the one church serving only one sect, thereby eliminating it as a universally shared element. The village was thus left without a gathering place.)

In a city, you know you are in an urban village when people speak of "our street" or "our block." A village that functions well is a reasonable place to pass an entire lifetime, which has probably been the case for these residents of CERTALDO ALTO in Tuscany. These folks grew up together, have known each other all their lives, have certain pastimes in common, know each other's foibles, and have built a life that works for them. Villages may take generations to come to their full flower, but even the first residents will soon enjoy some of the fruits of village life.

Venice was organized into about 70 parishes, each essentially an urban village, the social functioning of which is described on page 312. Each parish has its church square, which doubles as a rainwater catchment and has a well. Fes-al-Bali in Morocco was organized into about 140 village-sized units, each with certain basic necessities: mosque, school, grain mill, bakery, fountain, toilet, bath house, and stables. In fact, urban villages seem only to disappear starting with the industrial revolution.

I think that small-scale elements tend to foster a sense of community. Narrow streets, small buildings, and intimate spaces all help to make a place that feels comfortable and can evolve into a village. Villages are possible in modern cities, as long as there are no cars. If cars are accommodated, the street space they require, their danger, and their noise preclude real villages.

URBAN VILLAGE SIZE

Urban villages can be as small as a few families and as large as 500, although the range of ideal sizes is about 20 to 150 families. A single household could establish itself as a block and so as an urban village, although this is rather artificial. Families would do better to gather into urban villages of a dozen families in as many tiny blocks. It is also possible for an urban village to comprise several very small blocks, as in the case of Arab-style walled housing compounds (see pages 245 and 514). In this case, very narrow streets are required if their land requirements are to be kept to reasonable values; streets about two meters (yards) wide are required if truly urban densities are to be achieved, and the resultant courtyards will be just a few paces on a side.

The scope of an urban village need not be limited to a single block. It is possible to form two urban villages in the same block, although the influence of the two villages upon one another is great enough that this arrangement is not very sensible. It is also possible for an urban village to span two or even more adjacent blocks, although "subvillages" will tend to arise in the blocks.

It is not even essential that courtyards be provided at all. In Europe, it is not unusual to see rows of houses (UK: "terraces") with streets at the fronts and backs of the houses. This arrangement provides no green space unless it is worked into shafts within the buildings, an arrangement that can actually provide pleasant, private courtyard spaces. Still, these strips of houses form identifiable blocks, since they will be pierced at intervals by cross streets, and each of these blocks is a suitable candidate for becoming an urban village.

Faro

It is likely that in many civilizations, speculative housing will be built either for rent or for sale. This is a product of the money economy and essentially precludes the direct involvement of future residents in the planning of an area. While the owner may attempt good design, if only to increase the value of the houses, the results will be less satisfactory. Most such housing will be arranged as flats in buildings considerably larger than the single-family townhouses that I prefer. Speculators building flats would be well advised, for simple financial reasons, to consider the methods proposed here, but it is, alas, not to be expected that they will.

Basel

Campo Santa Margherita, Venice

SHARED VALUES & VALUES CLUSTERS

The development of shared values in a given culture or subculture affects virtually every aspect of life and is really too large a question for this book. The lack of a widely-shared system of culture and values afflicts many nations to some degree. It is easy to forget that civilization requires general agreement about some fundamental values: the rule of law, public order, the right of free expression, the need to count every vote. Each of these values was adopted only after it became apparent that life was better when that value prevailed than when it did not. When life is good and strife is distant, these values may come to be taken for granted. But woe betide the society that loses sight of its root values. The great challenge of the age is the protection of the natural environment that sustains us all and which must, therefore, come to be valued by us all as a shared, vital interest.

We must achieve and sustain agreement on bedrock values. Regular, shared reinforcement of their worth is an essential activity of an enduring civilization, one that is expressed in pastimes and rituals. These activities sustain fundamental values, often in ways of which we are not fully aware. They embody the cultural heritage of the society. Public spaces provide the stage for their continuing expression and the reaffirmation of their worth. The lack of literal common ground endangers the maintenance of the values upon which a society is built. Never allow the need for public social space to go unmet.

The establishment of urban villages in new city districts can be facilitated by helping people to organize into what I will call "values clusters." These are simply groups of people who share some common traits and goals and who are reasonably likely to get along with one another. (Political parties are values clusters: citizens who share values and goals that are similar enough that they can work together as a political entity.) I grant that this method is somewhat artificial. In the past, people in a given region were a lot like one another. They shared a common ancestry and history, spoke a common language, practiced the same religion, and subsisted from similar and interwoven activities. Their villages evolved over the centuries, in ways dictated by their common interests. Modern societies are rarely so homogeneous, but even within them there are many groups large enough to have a common character, like the villagers of yore. These commonalities help to reduce conflict within the group and ease the way towards a harmonious community.

The concierge service proposed on page 180 is likely to become the warmest hearth for the community, as nearly everyone will pass through at least once a day. If a small, pleasant social space is provided there—some chairs, a table, a deck of cards, a water cooler—I expect that community will arise almost by itself, as long as there are some common ties.

Local governance facilitates the establishment and sustenance of urban villages. It is unrealistic to expect that regional governance will soon be altered to accommodate this need, but awareness is growing that small governmental units are often more responsive than large ones; jurisdictions should be no larger than needed to efficiently perform their functions.

Ideally, conflicts over mundane but important matters like flapping laundry, barking dogs, and late-evening ball playing should be managed by neighbors working with one another, not through recourse to the slow, cumbersome, and expensive mechanisms of government or the law. When people know and respect one another and have a degree of interdependence, simple and humane methods of conflict resolution can prevail.

Villages will come in many different flavors, depending mainly on the principal basis for the bonding of a group of people into a village. Some will be based on shared commercial interests, some perhaps along religious lines, some on common social, political, or artistic interests. The groups will be self-identified and self-organized, and as long as the aims of a group

For a discussion of shared values and the importance of community, see John Taylor Gatto's *Dumbing Us Down: The Hidden Curriculum of Compulsory Schooling,* especially pages 81-104, "The Congregational Principle." This is an odd source for this material, but Gatto's argumentation is strong.

Drying laundry, Burano

Stone masons, Fes

"Subculture Boundary," APL, Pattern 13
"Identifiable Neighborhood," APL, Pattern 14
"Neighborhood Boundary," APL, Pattern 15

Alexander's term for what I call an "urban village" is an "Identifiable Neighborhood" that contains "no more than 400 or 500 inhabitants." APL, Pattern 14

are not at odds with the larger society, any grouping should be acceptable.

There is some reason to worry that urban villages may isolate themselves. However, city life routinely takes people away from their immediate vicinity and into the wider city, and shared activities in the larger city should be sufficient to prevent any unhealthy fragmentation of society, especially given the increased chances for social interaction in carfree cities. Urban villages will remain open systems; unlike the gated communities in the USA, no one will be excluded from their streets (although interior courtyards may be reserved for residents only).

SUBCULTURE BOUNDARY

Villages need clearly defined boundaries. Alexander calls for large districts to be distinguished from one another by a "Subculture Boundary," which allows different cultures to "live at full intensity, unhampered by their neighbors." Smaller neighborhoods must also be distinct and identifiable; he believes that neighborhoods cannot otherwise truly exist. The major boundaries delineate groups with quite different cultures, and they separate larger differences than those between neighborhoods, which are often similar to one another.

In the relatively dense cities that I foresee, neighborhood boundaries can simply be the streets that separate the blocks from one another; each block, with its interior courtyard, becomes an urban village, separated from the next by the street. The population of a block is about right for an urban village—about 150 residents, with an additional 100 or so workplaces. Many people would be able to work in their own businesses on the ground floors of their houses. This greatly strengthens the community and provides lunch-time social opportunities if a nearby café is established or if tables and chairs are set out in the courtyard, as here in Certaldo Alto, in Tuscany.

Watercourses are perhaps the strongest divisions and also among the most attractive. Their principal disadvantages are that they are expensive to construct and normally consume quite a lot of space, although a NARROW CANAL, such as this one in Burano, is quite good in this respect; the building-to-building distance is only that of the main radial streets in a carfree district.

Alexander has mentioned the importance of allowing for mixing along subculture boundaries. Two subcultures will meet along a boundary that itself contains facilities shared by both subcultures. He calls for boundaries at least 200' (60m) thick, but notice that these boundaries are not dead spaces at all but are the locus of the most important facilities, those that serve fairly large populations. The boundaries, in fact, function best when they are densely-built, heavily-used spaces.

There is also reason to consider which kinds of villages will get along well when situated adjacent to one another. If a group of intellectuals wants a block of its own, they probably should not land beside a group that likes its music really loud and parties until dawn. There is some art to placing urban villages with respect to one another, and prospective villages should have a strong voice in the process.

Divisions among groups that are not very compatible with one another should be made along wider streets and should be signified by stronger elements than the streets alone. A SIMPLE GATEWAY, such as this one in Amsterdam, can mark the distinction. This one is actually locked at the end of the working day, but most such gateways will never be closed, and few will even be fitted with operating gates. The demarcation introduced by such a gateway is no less effective for its being entirely symbolic.

The cohousing movement has been building intentional communities for about three decades now. Groups of families, numbering up to a few hundred people, join together to build a physical and social community in which each family has its own quarters. The community has shared facilities including a

See McCamant & Durrett, *Cohousing: A Contemporary Approach to Housing Ourselves.*

Venice

Parma

large kitchen and dining hall where meals are taken together several evenings a week. Cohousing developments can readily be accommodated in a carfree city. Each cohousing group can simply take one block for itself. Project organizers should encourage the formation of cohousing groups.

SOCIAL LIFE

In modern Western societies, many people have become rootless during the past 50 years. Families no longer live, generation after generation, in the same house or even in the same city. A sense of place is no longer a touchstone for many people. Their commitment to the place they happen to live is often weak. They lack broad and deep local support networks developed over the course of a lifetime. Although I do not suppose that this sense of place and belonging will return as quickly as it ebbed, it does seem that people are finally noticing that its absence leaves a hole in their lives that is not easily filled. We must provide ample and easy opportunities for social interaction in both our urban villages and the districts that contain them.

The most difficult part in establishing any social relationship is the beginning. It is easiest to bridge the gap in the context of some shared activity, no matter how mundane. In years of sailing, I have always noticed how easy it is to strike up a conversation with someone on the dock. There is always a ready remark about a nearby boat or tomorrow's wind to break the ice. In a market, people can start a conversation with no more basis than "the tomatoes are unusually juicy this summer." In most cases, this does not lead much further, but sometimes it leads to lifelong friendships and marriage. Suburban living lacks these constant daily opportunities to start a conversation with a stranger. We must build these opportunities into our cities. Small squares, like the CAMPO SANTA MARIA NOVA in Venice, provide places to sit and cafés to get a cup of espresso. Locations like this create rich and abundant social opportunities. They not only lead to the making of new acquaintances, they also nurture existing friendships.

Small, LOCAL PARKS such as this one in Leiden are nearly as effective as small, local squares in fostering community social networks. It is here that young parents will meet each other when out for a stroll with the baby. Teenagers will meet others who are not from their immediate social and geographic circle. Parks are also places that can strengthen family bonds if they entice a family to pass an afternoon there. Although parks are difficult to build into dense urban areas, they most assuredly can and should be built at the edge of the inhabited areas. Don't forget to include places for people to sit. Low walls with flat tops are nearly as effective as benches for this purpose. In dry weather, people will bring blankets and picnic on the grass.

Local stores selling daily necessities, such as this one in Lisbon's BAIRRO ALTO DISTRICT, are also helpful. They tend to serve a small group of customers who first get to know the proprietors and then gradually the other customers. The social role of these small businesses is not reflected in any financial balance sheet, but it is no less important for all that.

The Needs of Children

Pay attention to the children. When they all know each other and are playing together, you are in an urban village, as here in a BACK STREET in Marrakech. The social lives of children differ from those of adults. Friendship groups among children divide along age lines, with a difference of just one year being significant. Young children are less particular in their choice of friends than they will later become, which helps to balance the limited pool of agemates. Teenagers find their peer group especially important but are already more flexible regarding the ages of their friends although more particular in their choices.

Amsterdam

"Children in the City," APL, Pattern 57

Salamanca

Children need gathering places, and, much as their parents worry about it, they seem to need private spaces—witness the popularity of tree houses, attics, and sheds. Urban areas often lack these places, and we should arrange the interior courtyards so that children can find isolated spaces that give them a sense of privacy. The green areas just outside the built-up areas can also provide spaces where children can feel like they are alone.

Younger children will often be content to orbit around their parents. As long as there is no danger from cars, parents can relax as the children burn off their excess energy.

Alexander calls for the graduated safe exposure of children to the real world, but in modern-day Western societies, children are severely limited in their ability to get around without adult assistance. (Small children in Venice are still allowed considerable freedom, as here on the SALIZZADA CARMINATI.) The independent mobility of children has declined steadily for decades. Today the number of children who get to school on their own is at a low ebb. This arises in part from a nearly hysterical dread of danger from strangers, which danger is in fact much less than the chance of a child being killed in or by a car. Certainly, in a carfree city with good public transport and safe cycling, even quite young children ought to be able to go almost anywhere. In the absence of car noise and with hundreds of adults within earshot, any danger from strangers will be kept more tightly in check than in sparsely-occupied suburban environments or city streets obscured by parked cars and awash in the roar of traffic.

Schools must be easy for children to reach on their own. This requires that primary schools be located within a few minutes' walk of every house and that secondary schools be easily accessible by public transport or bicycle. Given that small schools seem to do better at meeting children's needs and ensuring that no child is overlooked, it makes sense to locate a primary school in every district, and perhaps more than one in some districts. This makes it possible for younger children to go home for lunch, which adds a great deal of life to the neighborhood as children come and go. Schools can be arranged as their own villages, with classrooms on the ground floor and teachers living with their families in the floors above. The interior courtyard would serve as a playground during the school day.

The Needs of the Elderly

In the pattern "Old People Everywhere," Alexander cites the need of old and young people for contact with each other. Old people also need contact with one another. This latter is easy to arrange; nothing more is needed than a few benches where old folks can gather, as here in the LIZZA PARK in Siena.

APL, Pattern 40

The elderly need special consideration, not only with respect to their social needs but also their declining ability to manage life's daily challenges. In cultures such as the Netherlands, where adults remain active and fit, many elderly people still think nothing of hopping on a bike to run errands. In cities without cars, we can expect this to become the norm in a generation or two. The carfree city must be designed to ease the use of all kinds of carts and human-powered vehicles, which ensures the mobility of the wheelchair-bound and physically impaired.

The special needs of the elderly include the stability of the environment they have come to know; change becomes more and more difficult for people to accommodate as they age. We must help old people to continue living in their neighborhood for as long as possible. By sustaining old people in the places and routines they know, their independence is maintained as long as possible. If it eventually becomes impossible for them to remain at home, every effort should be made to keep the person in the community. This can be accomplished by establishing some housing in every district at the ground level and fairly close to the district center, where most of life's needs can be met. Home-care services can allow people to live independently

Venice

until very late in life. One of the real dividends of urban villages is that the necessary support can be obtained from within the village by a care-giver long known to the person who needs help. By these means, the problems faced by elderly people can be accommodated with a minimum of stress for everyone.

WALKABLE COMMUNITIES

These functions should be located in every district but cannot be supported by a single urban village:

- Automated teller machine
- Bike repair/rental/parking
- News agent/stationer/tobacconist
- Post office
- Baker
- Butcher
- Grocer/green grocer/mini-mart
- Beverage/wine/liquor store
- Pub/café/restaurant
- Inn/hotel
- Clinic
- Pharmacy/drug store
- Hair dresser/barber
- Dry goods store
- Shoe repair
- Laundry, including self-service
- Dry cleaning
- Video rental (until everything is downloadable)

One of the characteristics of a functioning village is that it is not necessary to leave it every day—people can meet many of their needs right in the village. As a practical matter, in most cities, urban villages will share common facilities, particularly those that require a broader base of support than is provided by a community of a few hundred people. However, some of the most important services ought to be within the village itself. I believe that chief among these is child care, which need be nothing more than a family who takes in children (see "Children's Home," APL, Pattern 86). Within a few blocks' walk, there should be a grocery and a news agent. The services listed in the side note are required within walking distance, so every district requires all of these services, and those that are represented by a single provider should be near the center and thus within easy walking distance of all parts of the district. District-level services have the effect of weakening the village somewhat, but this is counterbalanced by the strengthening of the district, itself a community of great importance.

MIXED-USE NEIGHBORHOODS

I do not believe that functioning urban villages can be established in the kinds of single-use areas that have predominated in new development during the past 60 years. I think mixed uses are essential to bring real life to an urban area. Jane Jacobs put the issue in the spotlight more than 40 years ago when she argued passionately for mixed-use neighborhoods, such as GREENWICH VILLAGE in New York, where she was living at the time she wrote *The Death and Life of Great American Cities.* Similar mixed-use areas are still found today near the center of most European cities. These neighborhoods are not for everyone, but having lived for years in one myself, I can attest to their practicality and convenience. The siting of businesses, residences, and shops in the same locale brings local people into more frequent contact during the course of the day and strengthens the community.

It must be admitted that mixed-use areas are more complicated to manage than single-use areas. It is necessary to make sure that the uses are compatible with one another and that people's needs for peace and quiet are not intruded upon by commercial activities. People have different tolerance for these intrusions, and one of the tasks in forming urban villages is to ensure that realistic choices are made. People who like to stay up late and enjoy spending time in bars, cafés, and restaurants are more likely to enjoy living in a neighborhood filled with these establishments than people who go to bed early and are easily disturbed by street noise. Some people are less tolerant of noise from shops and manufacturing operations than others. These issues must be considered at length when establishing urban villages.

Valladolid

Of course, uses that are incompatible with residences must be kept out entirely. The utility areas proposed in the Reference Design are there to accommodate these kinds of noxious uses.

The concierge service (see page 180) should be arranged in the least desirable location of the block. In temperate climates, this will be a dark location shaded by buildings across the street. In the Northern Hemisphere, this will be the north side of a narrow east-west street. The concierge service is essential to the proper functioning of carfree blocks, and measures are required to ensure that space for it is provided at a price that the operators can afford. (Apartments can be built on the brighter upper floors of the concierge building, but the basement, ground floor, and the floor above should be reserved for the concierge service.) It is probably not necessary to reserve the entire length of that side of the block for this use.

Villages are strengthened to the extent that they are self-reliant and have economies that do not depend upon a single industry that might suddenly collapse. Family businesses serving local needs are the core of local economies. Although small businesses have, in many cases, been undermined by the trend towards large-scale enterprises, I expect this trend to reverse as energy becomes more expensive, simply because the competitive position of local suppliers will be improved. Local businesses can simply be mixed in with residences in the age-old pattern.

Family shops, Coimbra

INTERIOR COURTYARDS & URBAN VILLAGES

The interior courtyard and its arrangement are critical to the development of urban villages. I would hope that agreement will be reached in most cases that the courtyard should be shared space, as here in Amsterdam's BEGIJNHOF, not divided up into private back gardens. The backs of houses should be accessible from one another through shared space. Children will benefit the most from this arrangement, but adults will profit from it too. If individual garden plots are desired, these can be arranged in a narrow strip adjacent to the houses, with common space in the center. Agreement on this point is, of course, required within any one urban village group, and some groups may elect to divide the land entirely into private holdings. So be it.

Courtyards can be very small, serving as few as a dozen houses, such as in the CORTE MORETTA in Venice. Here, it is the courtyard, not the street, that provides access to the surrounding houses, as is also the case with the Begijnhof, above. These examples of "inverted" courtyards can be replicated in similar form, which is likely in Islamic cultures. Most courtyards would be quite large, as discussed in Part III, INTERIOR COURTYARDS.

REGULATION OF NUISANCES

If people are to live in fairly close proximity to one another, it is essential that nuisances be well controlled. The creation of urban villages should in itself help achieve this goal, as it puts neighbors in contact with one another and helps to build common ground, a sense of shared purpose, and a place where disagreements can be managed informally. Furthermore, the establishment of urban villages on the basis of value clusters should also help in the regulation of nuisances—in such an environment, the limits of reasonable behavior are apparent to almost anyone.

Coimbra

This will not, however, solve every problem that may arise. The law is a blunt instrument, but occasional recourse to it will probably be required. Since the law is divisive, cumbersome, slow, and expensive, it is useful to establish mechanisms that are more formal than social cohesion and pressure but less burdensome than the law. Condominium associations now routinely manage these issues. The condominium association is a quasi-governmental construction (which has the power of enforcement through recourse to the courts) and is an intermediate stage in the control of nuisances. Most people will not want to fight with the condominium association and will modify their behavior if the association issues an order. These associations are more personal in their workings than the law but less personal than direct contact. They are faster and cheaper than the courts.

Effective community policing may also be useful in some cultures, such as in Britain up until the constabulary lost the community support it had long enjoyed. A word from the local cop can solve a lot of problems informally wherever this kind of policing is possible.

Strides are being made in the art of extra-legal conflict resolution. Third-party facilitators attempt to get the parties to understand each other and to reach a resolution that everyone can accept. This approach is also quicker and less cumbersome than legal action. The agreements that establish an urban village, whatever form they may take, should include provisions for the resolution of disputes without immediate recourse to the law.

In my experience, the most common causes of friction

Basel

Vila Real da Santo António

between neighbors fall into a few broad categories. First are maintenance and construction activities, including jackhammering, hammer drilling, and orbital sanding. Modern tools have increased productivity but most of them are far noisier than older methods. In a concrete building, if a resident decides to take up the floor tiles and replace them, the cheapest way to do this is with a power hammer. The process can go on for days and makes a hideous amount of noise and dust. This practice should be restricted, and compensation of neighbors could be required. A similar situation arises with orbital sanders. Hand sanding is much quieter but appreciably more expensive. It is reasonable to prohibit or restrict the use of some kinds of power tools. Noise is easier to quantify since the advent of inexpensive measuring instruments, and the types, intensity, and duration of noise can now be specified with considerable precision.

Other contentious issues are: the behavior of dogs and their owners (with respect to leashing, barking, and cleaning up droppings); cooking odors (particularly from restaurants and barbecue); sound from telephone, radio, television, computer, and stereo; the handling of trash; and the hanging of laundry to dry. Everyone should accept that an urban village that is home to children will be subject to their yelling at play time. It is not possible to anticipate every nuisance that will arise now or in the future, but if a given neighborhood has clearly-expressed standards regarding most of them, the others will be apparent by extension. In parts of India, it is considered a public service to put a stereo outdoors and play traditional music at very high volumes. If this is accepted during the formation of an urban village as normal behavior, at least everyone will know that.

Before we form urban villages, we must first arrange the basic armature of the district, including its main streets and major squares. This will be a money-driven process during which the best sites will be acquired by those who can pay for them. Village formation will occur along social, not monetary, lines.

SITE PROGRAM

The last major task of urban planning is the adoption of a final site program. The site program is a set of documents that establish final decisions regarding the purpose of the development and the specifications for it. It anticipates the number of people who will live and work on the site and their needs and desires. It sets out the uses to be included, the floor area needed, and the cost of the completed buildings, including land and site work. It reflects the decisions that have been made regarding the ownership structure of the completed project. It establishes the basic character of the completed site, and it normally includes phasing and an approximate schedule for construction.

These decisions will reflect a great many disparate needs that will have come to light during the planning process. These will include the imperatives of the site itself, market studies revealing the need for the project and the desires of its users, regional development considerations, the goals of the project initiators, the availability of financing, the political climate, and the objectives of local politicians.

The site program is thus a detailed specification for a project. The site program does not directly determine the final design but does tightly constrain it. A proper site program is a detailed outline that will be fleshed out during design and construction. Furnished with a site program, designers can get to work on the actual details, street-by-street and building-by-building.

The decisions that inhere in a site program are so important and have such wide-ranging effects that site programs require administrative or legislative review and approval in many jurisdictions. Normally this review will occur at a local level, although regional and even national bodies may reserve the right of review. Once a site program is adopted, the future of the affected area can be anticipated within greater or lesser limits, depending upon the specificity of the site program.

Venice. The fine-grained character of the city is visible from the Campanile.

Venice

Light manufacturing, Venice

An effective site program must respect the needs and desires of users and must be grounded in accurate studies as discussed in URBAN PLANNING. In order to achieve a good site program, the opinions of those people who are expected to live or work on the site once it is completed must be determined. The methods proposed in Part IV in any case require the collection of detailed information from families regarding their preferences (see LAND ALLOTMENT), and there is every reason to encourage their early sign-up. The preferences of each family can be collected during the sign-up process and used in the development of a site program. This gives considerable assurance that important needs of the future users will not have been overlooked.

The same information can be used to determine the overall character of individual districts, if there will be more than one, and of the various neighborhoods within a district. Imagination and an understanding of the residents is necessary to conceive a workable district or neighborhood character, and considerable effort should be devoted to this task. It is worth consulting with a large sample of the people who expressed interest in the project in order to ensure that they will be comfortable in the location that is foreseen for them. Perfection in these groupings cannot be expected, but if a significant number of people are unhappy with the arrangements, they should be reconsidered.

ECONOMIC BASIS & MIXED USES

An important task of urban planning is the identification of the economic basis for an urban area. This is not part of urban design but does greatly affect it. Specifically, the anticipated economy affects the demand for commercial spaces of all kinds and is likely to affect the design of buildings in the project as well. Even rather small manufacturing operations will need comparatively large spaces, often without too many supporting columns and usually with higher ceilings than required for

residential or office occupancies. Of course, most large manufacturing operations will be relegated to utility areas to protect
people from air and noise pollution. This approach is proposed
in the Reference Design, which shows the utility areas tightly
connected to the rest of the city. When the character of manufacturing is such that it can coexist with residential occupancies,
the neighborhood is probably best arranged with larger-than-
usual buildings that have high ground-floor ceilings. Apartments and offices can be located on the upper floors. Freight
delivery must receive special attention in these areas if the
completed project is not to be overwhelmed with truck traffic.
Industrial cities really should adopt metro-freight as proposed in
Carfree Cities. This permits heavy freight traffic while imposing
only minor burdens on adjacent users.

Mixed uses, Venice

As discussed in URBAN VILLAGES, local businesses are important to the development of a sense of community. The needs of
small business owners should be foremost in designing commercial spaces. This is important not only for the health of the
local economy but also for the convenience of people living and
working in the area. This approach also respects the maxim
"access, not mobility"—bring the goods and services to the
people, not vice-versa. Mixed uses allow quick access to goods
and services without recourse to mobility beyond walking and
cycling. This is a solid foundation for a sustainable economy.

Los Angeles

For half a century, North American urban planning was based
on single-use development. Mixed uses were explicitly prohibited in new development even though they had always existed
in most cities. This was perhaps the greatest error of postwar
planning. Fortunately, mixed-use development is finally enjoying a resurgence in US cities.

Centuries of experience with mixed uses have shown that, as
long as reasonable controls are in place to protect against
noxious uses, mixed-use areas are the best and liveliest parts of
any city. This is particularly evident in European cities. In the

simplest form, mixed uses arise by putting commercial uses on the ground floors and residences on the upper floors. The so-called "shop house" is perhaps the best example: a family lives on the upper floors and conducts a business on the ground floor. Life today is more complicated than when this arrangement was usual, but it is still feasible to have residences above commercial uses. This provides a built-in customer base for the businesses in the neighborhood and situates businesses on a street-facing ground floor with high exposure to passersby. The upper floors are less desirable for commerce and provide a stock of comparatively inexpensive residential space. Mixed-use areas are occupied at all hours of the day, so security problems that may arise in single-use areas are normally absent. Although it is in theory possible to develop carfree areas that are segregated by use, this approach makes no sense at all, and I will not consider it further. Jane Jacobs wrote extensively about mixed uses, and those who doubt the wisdom of this approach should read her work. The New Urbanists have employed this pattern extensively.

POPULATION DENSITY & DISTRIBUTION

Once the total population to be accommodated has been determined, it can then be allocated to specific transport halts and districts. It is sensible to build most densely in the districts closest to the city center. Errors in population allocation may lead to an oversubscription in some districts and insufficient interest in others. This question can be assessed by survey, but those being interviewed must be shown drawings and photographs of the various density levels under consideration.

Density can actually be measured in several different ways (see THE DENSITY QUESTION). Many factors affect it. The highest densities are most appropriate for the districts that are shared by all city residents, that is to say, the city center. More distant areas can make somewhat more liberal use of land. Even within a

Venice

district, DENSITY CAN BE GRADUATED. The center of a district will be the busiest part of that district and should be the densest; towards the district edge, densities can be reduced. This simply respects centuries of practice in urban planning.

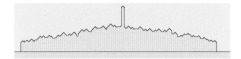

We must keep in mind several trends affecting the demographics of Western civilizations and cities. Increasing urbanization, smaller families, more working women, and an aging population affect nearly all of the richer nations. Even in many developing nations these trends are already visible. Family sizes are plunging in China, Indonesia, and Turkey. Everywhere, more women are entering the work force. The proportion of old people is rising fast in most societies. Urbanization is increasing rapidly in the developing nations and explosively in China. Many people seek larger living quarters than previously and may have enough money to realize their desires, which increases the land area required to house a given population. Flexible buildings can help accommodate the changes ahead. Four-story houses with narrow frontages have proven to be highly adaptable over the centuries.

Nancy

The trend towards urbanization is starting to flatten in most developed nations for the simple reason that most of the population already lives in cities. However, in nations such as China, dramatic urbanization can be expected in the coming decades as people leave subsistence farms for the more lucrative work, richer social life, and wider cultural opportunities in cities. In other countries, such as Portugal, population is stable but the demand for larger living space, migration from the hinterlands, and resort development drive a rapid expansion of existing cities and even the construction of entirely new urban areas.

See, for example, the proposals for the One Planet Living project on the Sesimbra peninsula: www.bioregional.com/programme_projects/ opl_prog/portugal/portugal_hmpge.htm

The Reference Design calls for an average FAR of 1.5 in the built areas of the city. Higher FARs would be applied in the more central districts and near the center of every district, with corresponding reductions in less central areas. I do not believe that a FAR greater than 3.0 can be achieved without its becoming oppressive; this is approximately the value in the most densely-built parts of Venice. Higher values are possible with high-rise buildings, but limited access to light and air do not favor this approach (although it was adopted in Hong Kong). In any case, greater demand will arise for some parts of the site than for others, which will lead to sparser occupation of the less desirable sites as people cluster in the better locations. (If no one wants a location, it can become a park, so long as the allocated population is accommodated somewhere in the project.)

In theory, human density can be increased without limit, if living and working quarters are reduced in size until everyone is accommodated. In practice, of course, the minimum size of accommodation cannot be reduced beyond a certain point. The planning process should include the establishment of minimum sizes. I would plead for permitting quite small quarters for those who are willing to accept them. (Remember that poor people are well served by a small but good house, which will probably be larger than where they had been living and of better quality.)

If the competition for ideal commercial spaces (those fronting on the main squares) is very intense, there may still be too many people competing for frontage on the square even after space allocations have fallen to the lowest permissible levels at the highest allowed FAR. In that case, the only solution may be to enlarge the squares or increase their number. It is, however, possible to make an exception and resort to extremely narrow widths and tiny floor plans. The pattern "Individually Owned Shops" (APL, Pattern 87) states that shops can be as small as 50 square feet (barely 4.5 square meters). I have seen shops LITTLE WIDER THAN A DOOR in the densest sections of Fes-al-Bali. These were barely 2m (7') deep, or about half the size of Alexander's minimum. Such shops might be uneconomic in other societies, but it seemed that these shops, in ideal locations, were profitable enough to support their owners. Organizers should prepare for this eventuality if there is a chance that it may arise.

Many Westerners would, however, be surprised to know just how cramped living conditions are in many parts of the world. Just 20 years ago, citizens of some quite rich nations, such as the Netherlands, were accustomed to living in comparatively small houses and apartments.

PARAMETERS OF THE REFERENCE DESIGN

The design parameters I adopted for the Reference Design for carfree cities were somewhat arbitrary, but I believe they are suitable for a medium-sized city with a non-industrial economy. Design parameters should be formally established for all but the smallest urban projects. Design parameters for the Reference Design were established for each of the four levels of scale at which the design was developed, as follows:

The Reference Topology has the following characteristics:
- 1,000,000 residents
- 256 km² (99 mi²) total land area (only 16% developed)
- 6 city lobes
- 81 districts
- 18 utility areas

The Reference District was located about midway between the city center and the utility areas. Its basic arrangement should be applicable to districts that are not at the center of the city. The following design parameters were chosen for the Reference District:
- 12,000 residents
- 8,000 workplaces (including school desks)
- 5-minute maximum walk to transport & green space
- 760m (1250') district diameter
- Large central square
- Central boulevard
- Freight line parallel to the central boulevard
- Mixed uses
- High-density occupation

The Reference Block was intended to occupy an intermediate location in the district, between the outer edge and the center.

The Reference Design drawings may be found here:

Reference Topology	30
Reference District	128
Reference Block	248
Reference Building	376

Black bars are printed at the edge of these pages.

The amount of green space provided by this design is large, but the overall density of the site is still quite high. The provision of large open areas in a city that still has excellent public transport is a great advantage of the Reference Topology.

Jane Jacobs (1961/1992), 178-186; blocks much smaller than the Reference Block are entirely feasible, although the size of the interior courtyard is disproportionately reduced.

It was an explicit goal to observe Jane Jacobs's dictum regarding short blocks. The block is 85m by 62m (280' by 205') when measured from the centerlines of the adjoining streets. The streets adjacent to the Reference Block are 5m (16.5') wide at their narrowest point. The following figures describe the density of occupation of the Reference Block:

Surface area	5259 m^2	56,591 ft^2
Footprint of buildings	1914 m^2	20,593 ft^2
Gross floor area	7656 m^2	82,373 ft^2
FAR	1.456	
Average number of floors	4	
Building footprint ratio	0.364	
Open space ratio	0.434	
Paved area ratio	0.202	
Inhabitants	139	
Workplaces	93	

Ratios are expressed as the proportion of buildings, open space, or paved area to the whole site.

No Reference Building was presented in *Carfree Cities,* but the per-capita gross area allocation was defined. By the standards of most developing nations, the amount of space was quite large. It would be fairly low by US standards, although residents of Manhattan would regard the allocations as rather generous:

If people demand lower FARs or higher space allocations than envisioned in the Reference Design, larger districts with lower density can be arranged, but this results in longer walks to the central transit halt.

Residence	36 m^2	387 ft^2
Work	18 m^2	194 ft^2
Shopping, health, recreation, etc.	9 m^2	97 ft^2
Infrastructure (sited in utility areas)	20 m^2	215 ft^2
Total	83 m^2	893 ft^2

In this work, I have assigned half of the space that was allocated for "shopping, health, recreation, etc." for the provision of concierge service (discussed on page 180). It is worth keeping in mind that these spaces also supply workplaces for the people who provide the services, so that the per-capita allocation of work space is actually half again as large as it first appears. Some of these uses are, however, quite space intensive, such as the storage space incorporated in the concierge services.

All of these numbers should be established during the planning of a carfree project. They derive fairly directly from data that will already be available. The numbers must be accurate, which requires care in the planning studies and good market-research assessments of demand and the sums that people will pay for building sites.

I believe that the principles of arrangement underlying the Reference District are nearly ideal, regardless of what transport solution may be adopted. A radial district provides the required center with a concentration of goods and services. It is the obvious location for a transport halt. (This assumes, of course, that cars play no role within the inhabited areas of the city; if bicycles are used instead of public transport, then other arrangements may be more favorable.) The only difficult decision is whether to pack the various districts tightly together à la Manhattan or to leave green spaces paralleling the transport routes at a distance of several hundred meters (yards), thereby establishing Alexander's "City Country Fingers" and the quick access to green space that this pattern ensures. As the routes draw near to the city center, the green belts dwindle and vanish.

Baseline Land and Floor Allowances

An important parameter that must be established during the planning of a new carfree district is the baseline per-capita land allowance. This can be derived simply by dividing the district land area by its anticipated population. This hypothetical number gives the area of land to which each person is entitled. That land will be absorbed by the street, courtyard, and house of one person. Few people will actually use an amount of land equal to

Strasbourg

See the appendix "The Bicycle City" in *Carfree Cities*.

APL, Pattern 3

For many purposes, the per-family land allowance is actually a more useful figure, but it changes, of course, as the average family size changes.

Venice

Braga

this average, but these numbers are important indicators of site density. Land used for commerce is not differentiated from land used for residences. However, the development of a baseline allocation implies the need to know what kind of commercial spaces will be required in the district, their total floor area, and whether or not most of this space will be provided in the ground floors of residential buildings.

The urban planners will have determined within fairly narrow limits the amount of floor area that must be built in a given district. The baseline floor area allowance is calculated the same way as the baseline land allowance, except that population is compared to gross floor area rather than total land area. This number also greatly affects the character of the finished district.

Those who value proximity to downtown may have to accept a denser district, achieved by some combination of higher FAR and smaller living quarters. Those willing to pay a travel-time penalty can have a bit more room in a less central district. Some experience will be required in each society before these numbers can be estimated and population targets adjusted accordingly. Polling or market research can help to determine what people want and what they would be willing to accept. The on-line sign-up process proposed on page 427 would be a means to gather this data at low cost in time and money.

If density is very high, there will be scant margin for poor people to trade land to rich people, and everyone will have to make do with something close to the average. A progressive premium can be levied on the lot area if poor people are being squeezed out. This will have the effect of reducing the number and size of large lots while also reducing the cost of small lots.

If the per-capita baseline land allowance is converted to a per-family allowance, it can, in some cultures, be as little as 45 m^2 (488 ft^2) per household, and each household may comprise an average of six people. By building four-story houses with a footprint of 22 m^2 (237 ft^2) on a site of this size, each household acquires 88 m^2 (947 ft^2) of gross floor area. This is just 14.7 m^2 (158 ft^2) per person. I really cannot recommend space allocations any lower than this, but it is actually well above the reported per-capita floor area for Shanghai in 1996. At such high density, a district with the same area as the Reference District reaches a population of 60,000. I would not myself choose to live in such crowded circumstances. In richer nations, an equitable distribution might be 113 m^2 (1220 ft^2) per household. Assuming a family size of just two people, this is 56.5 m^2 (610 ft^2) per person. This is a large range of variation on such a fundamental measure.

Consider how these allocations might work out in practice, as illustrated by these TWO PLOT PLANS. A rich family might buy land 12m wide and 39m deep (39' × 128') for a total of 468 m^2 (5036 ft^2). A poor family might have a plot 3m wide and 24m deep (10' × 79') for an area of just 72 m^2 (775 ft^2). The rich family will pay more than six times as much for its land as the poor family, before any adjustment for premiums, which could themselves become very large.

The range of solutions is broad and can be illustrated by considering four-house PATIO BLOCKS. Houses of acceptable dimensions may range from 5m (16') deep and 8m (26') long to 6m (20') deep and 16m (53') long (even greater or lesser dimensions are possible). The two extremes give the following result per house, assuming that all streets are just 2m (6.6') wide:

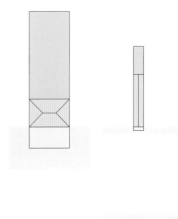

Shanghai International Communication on Residential Design '96

	Metric		Customary Units	
	Small	Large	Small	Large
Street frontage	13m	22m	40'	72'
"Backage"	3m	10m	10'	33'
Street area	14 m^2	23 m^2	150 ft^2	250 ft^2
Courtyard area	2 m^2	25 m^2	24 ft^2	270 ft^2
Buildable footprint	40 m^2	96 m^2	430 ft^2	1030 ft^2
Land/family	56 m^2	144 m^2	600 ft^2	1550 ft^2

Rounding errors are fairly large but not significant.

The small end of the range makes very efficient use of land and gives a plot ratio of 0.71 and a FAR of 2.1 at three stories. If the height of the houses is reduced to just two stories, a FAR of 1.42 is still achieved, and this is an entirely workable arrangement, similar to Burano in the Venetian lagoon. The large end of the range is more generous in its use of land. (Note especially the eleven-fold increase in the size of the interior courtyard.) The plot ratio only falls to 0.67 and the FAR to 2.0 at the same three stories. Of course, fewer households are housed per unit land, although they may have more members. In practice, a district with larger houses is also likely to have wider streets. As already noted (page 113), a relatively small increase in the width of streets results in a large fall in plot ratio, all else being equal.

The extension of living space beyond the walls of a house increases the effective living area at little cost. Even a small INTERIOR COURTYARD or a tiny local square provides important space in this regard. Quite narrow streets can also play an important role, as long as they are safe, beautiful, and inviting. A city like Venice, built to very high densities and with quite small living quarters, still offers a very high quality of life. The lack of cars and the fine outdoor spaces that have arisen over the centuries draw people onto the street.

The side note gives example calculations for the Reference District, in which about 10,000 people would live and work in that part of the district away from the central boulevard. A gross floor area of about 48 m^2 (515 ft^2) would be allocated for each person. They might occupy all of this area themselves or rent some of it to others. Assuming buildings 7.5m (24.6') deep and four stories tall, each person is entitled to 1.6m (5.24') of street frontage. Since the minimum practical width of a building is about 3m (10'), single people wishing to occupy their own buildings would need a building site with almost twice as much frontage as their allocation provides. Alternatively, two single people could share a building, each occupying a floor or two.

Buildings in the Central Boulevard area:

Built footprint	45,270 m^2
Gross floor area	181,000 m^2
Residents	1900
Gross residential floor area	68,000 m^2
Floor area of other uses	113,000 m^2

Buildings outside the Central Boulevard:

Built footprint	119,900 m^2
Gross floor area	502,700 m^2
Residents	10,100
Gross residential floor area	363,800 m^2
Floor area of other uses	139,000 m^2

Keep in mind that even rather shallow buildings, such as the Reference Building, can still yield quite small footprints. This in turn allows VERY SMALL-SCALE BLOCKS, with 2½-story houses like the Reference Building, while still achieving quite high density. These low blocks can tolerate small courtyards without feeling cramped or losing access to air and light. The Reference Building would fit best in a neighborhood for which there is slightly below-average demand, where land cost will be lower than in areas with good commercial exposure.

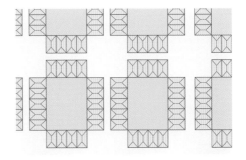

Free-standing ARAB-STYLE HOUSES with very small central courtyards closely resemble the four-house patio block discussed on page 243. These are large houses and usually provide accommodation for an extended family. This pattern has many advantages in hot, dry climates, where it has long been used.

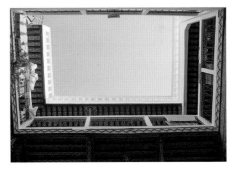

Besides land and floor area, a number of other measures are subject to allowances, including frontage, number of stories, courtyard area, and street width. It may be useful to calculate values for these measures. The supply of any one of them can be adjusted over fairly wide ranges, but only by reducing the supply of some other attribute. For instance, an increase in frontage can be achieved by adopting very small blocks, but this yields small interior courtyards and increases the space required for streets. Taller buildings can be used, but this suggests an increase in street width in order to provide adequate light. As with all things in city design, compromise is required.

FINAL SITE PROGRAM

The unbuildable areas of the site must be defined. There will be reasons to exclude areas from development and other reasons (mainly economic) to avoid certain areas. The limiting conditions will be superimposed on a MAP OF THE AREA. Development must occur in the areas that are not excluded and, to the extent possible, should avoid areas that are difficult to develop.

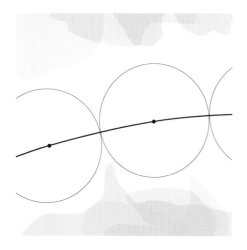

Once the buildable land has been identified, the extent of the districts can be defined within close limits, along with the open space that will surround them. The route of the heavy transport line (and central boulevard) must be determined at this time. This yields the FOOTPRINT OF THE CITY QUARTER, including the location of the transport halts. Each halt will become the center of a district inhabited by 8000–20,000 people. These fundamental decisions also determine the locations of buildings along the central boulevard and the parallel metro-freight line, which form the core of the district. Their locations must be determined before the allotment of the remaining land and the design of major streets, squares, and buildings can begin.

What decisions regarding the site program must be taken before design can begin? This depends on the circumstances, but normally the following decisions must have been reached, documented, and mapped:

- Buildable areas of the site
- Location of transport halts
- Choice of freight delivery mode
- Ultimate population to be accommodated
- Per-capita land and floor area allotment
- Allotment of land for businesses and public services
- Selection of services to be located near the district center
- Allocation of land to various uses along the central boulevard
- Advocated uses outside the boulevard area (see page 423)
- Decisions regarding the provision of concierge services
- Designation of an emergency access street network
- Minimum and maximum street widths
- Maximum building heights
- Options for courtyard ownership and maintenance

Preliminary decisions must sometimes be taken to allow site analysis to continue. As the site comes into focus, these decisions may need minor adjustments. Changes may continue even after the start of construction, as circumstances change.

Madrid

DESIGN OF CENTRAL BOULEVARD AREA

Once the fundamental planning decisions have been made, the urban planners will design the central square, the central boulevard, and the parallel metro-freight line. The building sites adjacent to the transport arteries will have been awarded to successful bidders for these valuable sites. Only the largest and richest entities will be able to afford them. They will usually construct large, unified spaces, each with a single tenant, although some upper floors may include apartments.

Venice

The arrangement of these areas and the sale of the associated land should not occur strictly on the basis of who can pay the most; the needs of the community must be foremost in the minds of the planners. Those who believe that they require buildings on these sites must convince the planners of this need and of the benefits to the community as a whole. Each prospective owner must make a detailed bid for a specific site, including the proposed use, size of the building, general design, and price.

The acceptance of bids is a political process. The planners should analyze the bids and make recommendations. Once the winning bids have been selected, the planners should, in concert with the successful bidders, arrange these buildings and their immediate surroundings. This yields the near-final arrangement of the boulevard area and the paralleling metro-freight line. Some flexibility in the arrangement of the streets cutting across these areas should be retained if at all possible.

Burano

Final design of the buildings would ideally await the design of the adjacent neighborhoods. The patrons of each of these buildings should appoint advocates (see page 423) to represent their interests during the arrangement of the major streets and squares that will adjoin the central boulevard. Once this work is completed, the remainder of the district is ready for the start of the auction process described in LAND ALLOTMENT.

Venice

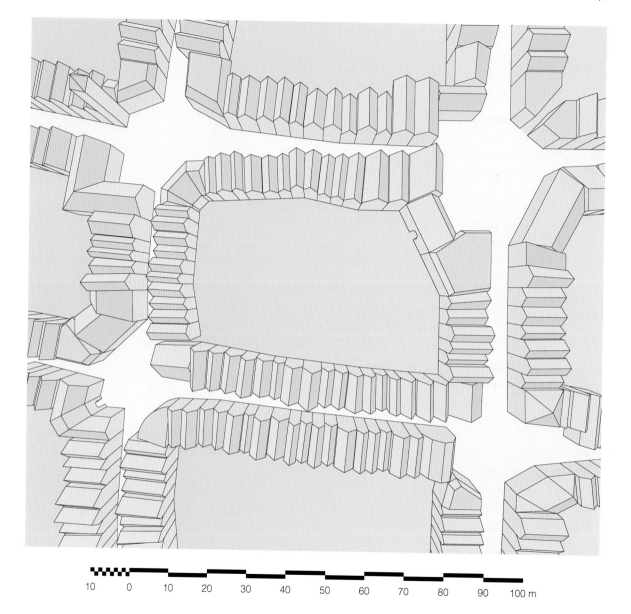

10　　0　　10　　20　　30　　40　　50　　60　　70　　80　　90　　100 m

PART III

ELEMENTS

The fifteen, mostly short, chapters in this Part examine the basic elements of which urban areas are composed, from the large to the small. The strong and weak points of various design alternatives are considered and suggested solutions are given.

Salamanca

CITIES FROM ABOVE
Considers why high places with panoramic views are important to a city and what constraints affect them.

FOUR-STORY BUILDINGS
Proposes the four-story building as the most important element in high-quality, high-density urban areas.

CITY STREETS
Considers city streets as the basic tissue, streets as the stage for community life, proportion & scale of streets & buildings, light and air, circulation, the arrangement of blocks, and pavement.

BOULEVARDS
Considers the boulevard as a grand but flawed element in city design and the reasons for its sparing application.

WIDE STREETS
Examines the importance of wide streets in cities and considers possible arrangements that are effective in carfree cities.

NARROW STREETS
Discusses why the numerous narrow commercial and residential streets are, as a whole, the most important to a city.

Galleries & Arcaded Streets
Looks at arcades & galleries and considers their advantages in high-density urban areas with adverse weather.

Enclosing Streets
Considers the merits of enclosed spaces and the use of curved and tapered streets to achieve enclosure.

Squares
Considers the uses of squares, large & small squares, types of squares, and the arrangement of squares.

Gates
Discusses gates as divisions & entrances, and gates that enclose.

Interior Courtyards
Examines the importance of green interior courtyards for city residents and the various ways to arrange them.

Parks
Looks at city parks as a safety valve for residents of dense urban areas and the factors that constrain their arrangement.

Water
Discusses open water within the city, including rivers & canals, bridges, waterfronts, and fountains & wells.

Major Buildings
Examines the impact of major religious & civic buildings on the arrangement and appearance of city districts.

Minor Buildings
Considers minor buildings, including ground floors, balconies, terraces & roof gardens, privacy, low buildings, and renovation.

Fes

CITIES FROM ABOVE

In the pattern "High Places," Christopher Alexander calls for the construction of high places from which people can obtain a view out over the city (APL, Pattern 62). These should not be inhabited buildings; their purpose is only to provide an overlook and a landmark. High places can take a variety of forms, some examples of which are shown in this chapter. Each community of 7000 inhabitants should have its own high place, to mark that community.

As in so many things, Venice provides a fine example of a high place, the CAMPANILE in Piazza San Marco. It is uninhabited, serves a small community (nearly every parish in Venice has its own steeple), can be climbed, and gives a panoramic view. It is an unmistakable landmark that helps people orient themselves in the city. High places permit people to obtain a view of the city and determine its character. The only shortcoming of the Campanile is that the top is today normally reached by elevator; Alexander would have us climb the stairs, only to be rewarded by the view after having earned it.

In Alexander's view, high places can be either natural or man-made. Naturally-occurring features serve just as well, so long as their access requires a good climb. The ideal high place should have periodic views on the way up the stairs and places to sit and enjoy the emerging view before continuing the climb. They should also have "Open Stairs" (APL, Pattern 158), although this proviso is difficult to attain in many cases.

Alexander thinks that high places should come no less frequently than one in each community, because, if they are less frequent, "they tend to be too special, and they have less power as landmarks." It seems to me, however, that the rarer they are, the more powerful their status as landmarks. On the other hand, more frequent landmarks help people to orient themselves and find their way through the city.

The Campanile, Piazza San Marco, Venice

The EIFFEL TOWER is possibly the world's best-known structure. It is unique and instantly associated with Paris. Here we see the Eiffel Tower in its glory days, soon after it was built. The tower was then even more commanding than today: there was no building in the city even remotely as tall. Only a few cathedral towers and the Ferris wheel also break the skyline.

The view from the top encompasses the entire metropolis. The structure serves only as a landmark and a viewing platform; it has no significant utilitarian function. It is the quintessential High Place.

It is not evident from this photograph of Utrecht just how enormous the tower is. It is farther away than it appears, because the ZADELSTRAAT crests about 50m (150') from the camera and then falls away slightly, which affects the perceived distance. There is also a canal not far in front of the tower, but because it is not apparent in the photograph, the extra distance is not evident from this vantage point. It is always important to bear in mind that perception is not the same as reality, and in the case of design, it is often perception, not reality, that matters. The grotesque spiral staircase at the top right of the tower appears to be only temporary scaffolding (it is not possible to be certain, but it has in any case long since been removed).

PANORAMIC VIEWS

High Places, when accessible to the public, provide a rare vista out over the city. Prior to the advent of aerial photography, only high places permitted an analysis of the city as a whole and allowed people to understand its size and arrangement. We will examine here several panoramic photographs taken from various high places, mainly church spires and clock towers. We will consider how the skylines of our cities appeared a century ago, how they have changed since then, and what these changes have to tell us about the cities they affected.

This view of VENICE, taken from the Campanile on a hazy day, helps us to grasp the very small scale at which Venice is built and its extremely fine grain. Venice has unusually short blocks and the narrowest streets of any city I know except perhaps Fes-al-Bali. It is remarkable how few streets can actually be seen from the Campanile; most are so narrow that even those close to the observer are shielded from view by buildings. The small expanse of the city is, oddly, not apparent from above. The very small elements extend continuously to the shores of the land in a way that makes the city seems bigger than it actually is. Notwithstanding this minor paradox, only a view from above can give such an immediate understanding of the character of this remarkable city.

In this view of NÜRNBERG the only objects that extend above the horizon are churches and defensive works. Compared to modern cities, the influence of the church and the military were great, but the influence of the corporation slight. This gives rise to the question: do we wish to allow commercial interests to dominate our skylines? Do we want to give them the symbolic high ground? Are these the most important institutions? I believe that the answers to all of these questions is "no!" This implies that corporations should not be permitted to build taller buildings than civic and ecclesiastic institutions.

Nearly all the roofs in this city have a very steep pitch (above 45 degrees). The gable end almost always faces the street. Because the buildings are moderately wide, there is a considerable amount of room inside these roofs. In some cases, three stories have been built within the roof.

BORDEAUX is similar to Nürnberg in that only church spires extend above the horizon, but the pattern of the roofs is completely different, giving this city a very different appearance from above. The low slope of the roofs here probably relates to local climate, giving a distinct contrast with the steep roofs of Nürnberg.

This VIEW OF SIENA was taken from the spire of the cathedral. The tall structure in the photograph is the campanile, a civil, not ecclesiastical work, the tallest in Siena.

Siena is the premier Tuscan hill town. It remains fairly small, with only 60,000 residents. Some of the other towns are very small, just a thousand or so. All of them have two dramatic characteristics: the city fabric is quite dense, and it ends abruptly at the edge of the city. In Siena, there are no suburbs, although the city has spilled outside its walls in some places. Their hilltop location gives these towns stunning views of the gorgeous, rolling countryside. Defensive towers were built in many of these towns. All these towns are medieval, with narrow, curving streets and small blocks. This is a truly beautiful way to organize a city. Some regard it as the highest form of urbanism ever achieved. I prefer Venice, but the hill towns are contenders.

LUXEMBOURG is set dramatically on a high bluff above a river. Several extraordinary stone viaducts carry roads and railroads into the city. When the bluff filled up, further development was situated on another bluff on the opposite side of the ravine. The two halves of the city gaze at one another across the ravine, which is now a park. It is important to be aware of flood hazards in siting cities, and it makes sense to put the inhabited areas up high, leaving the parks in the lower reaches, where there is often water to be enjoyed. This protects the buildings from flooding while making good use of the flood plain.

This view from the LARGO DA OLIVEIRINHA gives a dramatic panorama of Lisbon. From a practical standpoint, hills are a curse in a city, but from an aesthetic standpoint they are magnificent. If the streets are arranged with respect for topography, their gradients can usually be held to tolerable values. Where this is not possible, the use of funiculars helps residents to get up the hills, as is done here. Lisbon's old narrow-gauge trams can climb surprisingly steep grades and help people ascend some of the other hills.

FOUR-STORY BUILDINGS

The call for buildings no taller than four stories is based on the work of Christopher Alexander ("Four-Story Limit," APL, Pattern 21). Alexander's arguments are based largely on the mental-health effects of high buildings; people living above the fourth floor are literally "beyond reach and out of touch." They tend to have fewer social contacts, a problem that is especially serious for young children, who have much less social contact than their peers living closer to the ground.

I do not entirely agree with Alexander on this matter: I think buildings of five and even six stories can be fine in the densest urban areas. In smaller cities and towns, two- and three-story buildings can provide sufficient density. Such a town must, however, be small enough to be walkable.

There are two critical issues regarding building height. First, buildings must not be so high that people in them become disconnected from the ground. Although elevators may make it relatively easy for people on upper stories to come and go, the irritation of waiting for an elevator, coupled with the socially uncomfortable spaces within elevators, pose a subtle discouragement to going out. In the case of stairs, the climb to the top floor should not be so great that it discourages people from going out. (This problem can be minimized by building maisonettes at the tops of buildings; these two-story apartments have their entries on their lower floor, shortening the climb to the highest front door; internal stairs probably have less psychological impact that stairs outside the home.)

Second, buildings must be built to a reasonable scale, one that is in keeping with their neighbors and does not overwhelm people in the street below. A five-story building with low ceilings is usually not a problem when mixed with four-story buildings and similar ceiling heights, whereas a four-story building with very high ceilings can overwhelm the street, as is the case

Calle Gradisca, Venice. This minor street in a residential district typifies four-story districts in older cities.

Firenze - Palazzo Davanzati; XIV secolo

with the PALAZZO DAVANZATI in Florence (which counts as four stories only if the loggia is ignored). The building is far too tall and overwhelms its neighbors, which is probably exactly what the original owner intended.

Building height affects the connection with the outside world in another way. From the third or fourth floor, it is still possible to hold a brief conversation with someone in the street, as long as there is no noise from cars, and I have actually heard this quite often in carfree areas. This also relates to the reason that young children from lower floors are allowed to play outside at a much earlier age than those living on high floors. The parents can keep an ear on the child, and in the event of a problem, a mad dash down a few flights of steps will quickly bring the parent to the child's side. In the case of upper stories, it may take a minute or more to reach the child, and it may not be possible to hear his screams so far below. Parents are rightly concerned about allowing small children to play outdoors under circumstances that prevent the parent from quickly responding to a crisis.

Counting stories is not always so simple as it might seem. In older districts, we often see buildings whose height in stories might reasonably be given differently by different observers. In the PRINZIPALMARKT in Münster, all the buildings can be counted, by one method or another, as four stories tall. The use of fractions in counting floors is useful, as when a partial story in the attic might most accurately be counted as half a floor. Counting this way also reflects the visual impact of the building: the story in the roof is considerably less imposing than a full story. The matter is further complicated by inhabited basements. It is common practice for the "ground" floor of a building to be elevated more or less half a story above ground. (This is a poor arrangement, a matter taken up just below and on page 318.) The question then arises at to whether or not to count the half-basement. Finally, there is the question of whether the ground floor is counted as a story or not; in some regions, only stories above the ground floor are counted. (Both Alexander and I count the ground floor). Precision is not, in any case, needed in this matter. It is safe to say that buildings more than six stories or 20m (65') tall are too high in almost all cases.

This photograph of Antwerp's GRAND'PLACE shows a building that, counting the garret, is seven stories tall. I could not find it in me to say that any of these buildings are too tall, although several of them clearly exceed the "four-story limit." Notice the harmony in this grouping: the scale diminishes on either side of the center building. This is also true of the skinny building on the right, which is otherwise dissonant.

It is also desirable to limit the variation from one building to the next. The NIEUWEZIJDS VOORBURGWAL in Amsterdam, one of the broadest streets in the old town, hovers at the limit of comfortable variation. The buildings range from three to six stories and are built in a hodge-podge of styles, yet they form a satisfactory if not entirely coherent whole. Many of the buildings have half-basements, with the ground floor elevated above the street, a common practice in the older parts of Amsterdam. These half-basements (now often inhabited) are cold, dank, and treacherous of access. Having lived for a few months in a half-basement, I would never force this wretched arrangement on anyone. A further reason to limit height variations is that chimneys on the low buildings must become unreasonably tall, to prevent flue gasses from entering other buildings.

Since the horrific attacks of 11 September 2001, anyone inhabiting a skyscraper must feel more keenly the risk of being trapped on an upper floor by some calamity. With low buildings, a ladder can be raised to the front window, making rescue simple if the fire is detected in time. So, while people in low buildings have some chance of escape in the event of a fire consuming a lower floor, those in high buildings are often doomed.

Many people also have a sense of vertigo when they approach the windows on an upper floor of a skyscraper. They aren't

comfortable places to be, and we should stop building them. Their need arises principally because of the space demanded by car parking and circulation; absent that, there is enough space using buildings no higher than six stories in almost all cities, Manhattan and Hong Kong being possible exceptions.

The OPÉRA-LAFAYETTE HOTEL is typical of buildings in the Montholon district in Paris, one of the densest parts of the 19th-century city. By any measure, this building exceeds the four-story limit, as do most of the buildings in the neighborhood. I think this building just succeeds, only because the ceilings are low, so the cornice is only about 18m (60') above the street. The large windows help bring the mass of this building just within the range of what I find acceptable in the densest parts of our cities. When the building was built, it was a long walk up to the top floor, but the building (today still a hotel) is now equipped with an elevator. The streets here are wide enough to permit good light to penetrate into all floors of the building. I find this an acceptable design for those instances when the highest densities are required, in this case equal to a FAR of about 3, double that of the Reference Design.

This RESIDENTIAL STREET in Burano lies near the other end of the continuum of urban story counts. Buildings on this island in the Venetian lagoon rarely exceed three stories, and most are just two stories, with a few single-story buildings. Still, a FAR of 1.5 or a bit less is achieved because the streets are very narrow and little green space is provided except along the margins of the island. In fact, it is principally the *scale* of this area that differs from the Paris example: everything in Burano is much smaller than in Paris. The buildings are narrower and lower, and the street is correspondingly narrower. This is, however, a truly urban space that might be oppressive but for open vistas across the lagoon within a few minutes' walk of any part of the island.

I came to know Manhattan's Greenwich Village during the many years my parents lived there. This is one of the finest urban areas in the USA, with a very active life day and night. Practically any necessity is just a few steps away. Most of the buildings in this area are much taller than four stories, but these beautiful townhouses on the north side of WASHINGTON SQUARE perfectly illustrate the four-story limit. What makes these buildings so fine? Although each is unique, they have a strong family resemblance. The windows are nicely proportioned and of diminishing height on higher stories, which holds our interest. The raised entrances do isolate the buildings from the street, but the stairs are an attractive element, and people sometimes sit on them of a summer's eve. Because the houses are set back slightly from the street, there is room for a small front yard, which permits the stairs to run perpendicular to the street, a generally more attractive arrangement than stairs running parallel to the face of a building.

Judging only on the numbers, the BARBUSSELAAN in Amsterdam Southeast is similar to Washington Square, above. The buildings are the same height, the street is of a similar width, and trees have been planted. However, this development suffers from many serious defects. In the first place, all the buildings on the same side of the street are identical. The view is overwhelmed by the four rows of parked cars. The street seems to have no purpose aside from vehicular circulation and parking. (To be fair, I happened to catch the houses in the Village at a rare moment when there were no parked cars). Although these buildings do stand around attractive interior courtyards with some community social life, the ugly street is dead. This area is served by a nearby metro, yet almost every family seems to own a car, unlike Manhattan, where many families do not. What really kills these buildings, however, is the blank wall at street level. The justification is safety, and this in a neighborhood with a well-deserved reputation for crime. Of course, one of the reasons there is so much crime is that few people choose to spend time on such an ugly street. If the street were a quarter the width

See "Architecture, Money, Graffiti, and Birds" by Richard Risemberg for further consideration of this: www.living-room.org/sustain/graffiti.htm

and the cars disappeared, there would be many more eyes on the street and much less crime. The ground floors can be given over to small businesses, as discussed on page 438. In these buildings, much of the ground floor is given over to storage.

The STORCHENGASSE in Zürich's old town is quite narrow, yet is actually one of the wider streets in the area. Switzerland is a rich nation, and the very high quality of the buildings here is not surprising. The prominent building in the center is actually one story "too high," but I cannot object to it. Would someone be able to hold a brief conversation from the open window on the top floor with someone passing by on the street? I think so. In most respects, this is very fine urbanism, although some car traffic is allowed into the area. Notice the large intrusion caused by a single car, which alters how people use the street.

The RIO TERRÀ SAN LEONARDO is one of the widest streets in Venice. I was actually standing in a square (Campiello dell' Anconetta) looking into the street when I took the photograph. The area is very different in character from the street in Zürich, but it is equally fine. The building on the left is of exceptional quality. It appears to be just three stories tall, but the second story is nearly as tall as two normal stories, and the third floor also has quite high ceilings. This building is situated in a prominent location and is more visible than the plain buildings on the right. I doubt that any society is rich enough to construct all its buildings in a monumental style, and the buildings on the right answer the need for an economical but attractive style, a matter taken up in MINOR BUILDINGS. To my way of thinking, this street is an almost ideal example of a four-story urban area built to quite high density (almost certainly higher than what is proposed in the Reference Design). Only green space is lacking.

We close this chapter with the SPALENBERG, a street in the old part of Basel, a fine city that is often overlooked. I find that the conjunction of curving streets and moderate slopes lends this four-story area an interesting and comfortable feel.

CITY STREETS

Streets are the most important element in the design of a city. In this chapter, we will consider streets generally; in the next five chapters we examine specific types of street. This introduction considers the role of streets in forming a city, streets as part of the public living room, the proportions of streets and buildings, the arrangement of blocks, lively ground floors, and the question of paving materials. A suggested method for laying out a network of streets is presented in Part IV, District Layout.

The way in which an urban area is depicted on a plan affects the way we perceive it. If only black ink is available, the choices are limited. I find outline plans difficult to read and prefer to make either the buildings or the streets solid black. The element that is shown in black is strongly emphasized, so the choice depends on the purpose of the illustration. The color plans in this book are easier to read and show buildings in light orange, streets in light gray, open space in pale green, and water in aqua.

The Basic Tissue

Streets are the basic tissue of any true city. While some contemporary metropolitan areas are built mostly from other tissue (such as shopping malls, parking lots, and freeways), their design was constrained by the need to accommodate the car and to make the resulting spaces as tolerable as possible. These tissues obviously have no place in carfree design and I will ignore them.

Streets occupy much of the land in any city. Land use is most efficient when the space devoted to streets is held to a minimum. The challenge when arranging streets is to make them as narrow as possible consistent with their functions. The VIA OBERDAN in Perugia typifies the narrow, irregular streets found in the oldest districts of European cities. Although only about 3.5m (12') wide in the foreground, the street meets the demands

Via Oberdan, Perugia

Morris, 107

placed upon it. Here and there, it becomes wider (but no narrower) in an apparently haphazard manner. As long as vehicular traffic is kept out, streets this narrow still function well today, although we now scarcely dare to make them so narrow.

Fes-al-Bali is the world's largest intact medina (and a major UN heritage site). The TALAA SGHIRA is one of its two main streets and is in places even narrower than seen here. The only significant changes in design requirements since medieval times are the increase in the volume of freight and the need for good access by emergency vehicles. Major streets today will have to be wider than this example but can be much narrower than the streets laid down since Renaissance times, when the space requirements of carriages began to dominate urban planning. High-capacity, underground rail systems can provide the necessary transport without resorting to broad streets. More land can then be devoted to buildings and open space.

Major changes in the layout of a city's streets are infrequent, so the character of a city is enduringly inscribed on the land once the streets and squares have been defined. The reader will note a persistent bias in this work towards the less regular, more intricate arrangement of streets that characterizes medieval cities. It is not really correct to speak of medieval "design" in the sense we use the word today, as these areas evolved over time and were never formally designed. See the discussion in ORDER & ORGANIZATION IN CITIES.

THE STAGE FOR COMMUNITY LIFE

If one thinks of people on the street as actors and those sitting about the margins of the street as the audience, then the street is the stage for the play of life as here on the RIO TERRA DELLA MADDALENA in Venice. Streets are, of course, similar to squares in this regard. It was long assumed that only residents of warmer climates were attracted to this theater of the street, and few

attempts were made to build stages and set them to the play in northern lands. During the last 30 years, however, city designers have learned that this penchant for watching and participating in the play of life is nearly universal. What happens on this stage tells us much about ourselves as a social species and gives us some insight into our own predilections and behavior. Unwritten standards of behavior develop in these spaces and underpin the culture of the city. Each city comes eventually to have a sense of itself and of how it differs from others. Who, having visited Salzburg and seen this JAZZ PIANIST playing to a street crowd, would be likely to forget it? Would this be tolerated in your city?

One of the tragedies of auto-centric society is that these defining elements are lost in the noise, stink, and danger of traffic, which usurps the very stage of public life. I believe that this is one of the reasons that American culture has become so bland and interchangeable: it is no longer easy to tell one US city from another by observing the way people walk, talk, and interact. This is in part because so many people are in cars that the level of this interaction has declined, as here in front of the BEVERLY CENTER in Los Angeles; while quite a few people are present in the scene, nobody is actually visible. The mall put its shops on the top floors, since there is virtually no walk-in trade, and the location of the parking garage on the lower floors is expedient. This building denies even the possibility of street life.

On warmer days in cities throughout Europe, many people will temporarily move their lives out onto the street. In the spring, the lure of the warm sun after a cold and dark winter draws people out, but many prefer their front stoops to the back garden. It has, of course, to do with where the sun may be falling at that moment, but it seems that most Europeans find it pleasant to sit in the street and watch the world pass by.

In "Children in the City" (APL, Pattern 57), Alexander proposes the creation of a special network of safe bike paths suitable for unrestricted use by even quite small children. It would touch

See page 9 for a definition of "squareness."

Great Streets, 277, citing *Paris Nineteenth Century: Architecture and Urbanism* (New York: Abbeville Press, 1988), 121.

every neighborhood and would allow children to see how their world works, where the newspapers are printed, the bread is baked, and so forth. Alexander believes that this path would offer a unique educational experience for children, and I agree. However, this fine idea is only practical in carfree cities as the pattern calls for the path never to cross street traffic, and this is essentially impossible to arrange in a city with cars. Absent car traffic, children can stand in the street and soak up life around them, as here on the TALAA SGHIRA in Fes-al-Bali. Virtually all of a carfree city can be accessible to children. (Street-running trams are a significant threat and reason enough to put public transport underground.) Children as young as five can explore their own neighborhood. Older children have the run of the entire city and can learn all that cities have to teach about life.

PROPORTION & SCALE OF STREETS & BUILDINGS

Urban areas exhibit an astounding range of variation in the proportions of streets and buildings. The CALLE BALBI in Venice is not much more than a meter (a yard) wide and is fronted by buildings well over 12m (40') tall. On the other hand, some US suburban streets are 60m (200') wide and bordered by houses just 3m (10') tall. This gives squareness ratios ranging from 1:12 to 20:1, an exceptional range of variation for an important design parameter. It must be realized, of course, that few streets in Venice are so narrow, nor are many suburban streets so wide.

Before Haussmann, most of Paris was built to 2:3 (measured to the cornice line), but this became square (1:1) under his direction. To my eye, oversquare streets are generally more attractive than undersquare ones. Some people may find the proportions of Venice claustrophobic, although I have never heard a complaint on this point.

The proportions of city streets began to become less over-square in the 16th century, and this trend has continued until the present day, with important exceptions and some evidence of a reversal in North America, at the urging of the New Urbanists. Otto Wagner proposed in 1912 a new plan for an expansion of Vienna in which no building would be taller than 23m (75') (not counting a roof story or attic) and no street narrower than 23m. He thus required streets to be square or undersquare. Amsterdam's Grachtengordel extension was planned in the early 17th century and approximately tripled the area of the city. Its streets were much wider than those in the old city, where alleys barely a meter (yard) wide were common. The buildings, however, were no taller, so the proportions became less oversquare.

This trend parallels the growth of cities, which increased traffic and demanded wider streets to move increasing volumes of freight. In the same epoch, siege warfare was largely replaced by pitched battles outside the city, and cannon fire greatly reduced the protection provided by city walls. Their importance declined and sometimes they were omitted entirely. As city walls disappeared, more liberal use of space became possible.

At first, as city streets became less oversquare, their scale remained nearly unchanged: the heights of buildings was limited to five or six stories until the advent of elevators. Then, Manhattan's skyscrapers began to rise, but the width of the streets had been fixed years before, so the oversquareness of streets started to increase. We have, very roughly, the same proportions in San Marco as in MIDTOWN MANHATTAN. In both cases, the ratio of street width to building height is as high as 1:12, but in Venice streets are a few meters (yards) wide, and in Manhattan 65' or 100' (20m or 30m) wide.

Our emotional response to a street is affected by its scale, and most people prefer human scale to industrial scale (see page 50). If the buildings are so tall that one could not briefly converse from the street with someone on the top floor, then they have exceeded the limit of human scale, which alienates people from their physical surroundings and also from other people.

Otto Wagner, "The Development of a Great City," in *The Architectural Record*, 31 (May 1912):485-500. www.library.cornell.edu/Reps/DOCS/wagner.htm

Light and Air

Modern skyscrapers do not really need windows, and at least one, a very large telephone exchange building in Manhattan, lacks them. Fresh air is delivered by mechanical systems and artificial illumination is always available and usually turned on during working hours. I think we will need to return to the more efficient past, in which windows provided light and fresh air. This is ultimately a more pleasing arrangement, except, it must be admitted, in very hot weather, when air conditioning is appreciated. There is, of course, no intrinsic reason that air conditioning cannot be provided in buildings with windows that open. Engineers dislike this arrangement because open windows interfere with the operation of the air conditioning system and increase its load. An interlock that turns off the air conditioning in a room with open windows solves this problem.

Traditional buildings get their light and air from the street and from interior courtyards. While it is possible to make an interior courtyard so small that it performs this function poorly, that is rare. However, it does happen that streets are too narrow to bring decent light into the adjacent rooms, although I know of no instance in which a street was so narrow that it seriously impeded the circulation of air into buildings fronting on it.

The problem with dark, dingy streets was brought home to me during a recent stay on the very dark Via Bonazzi in Perugia, which is even narrower and darker than the via cartolari in that same city. My room was on the second floor of a four-story building, with a taller building opposite, and the dark façades reflected little daylight into my room. The deep, narrow room and small windows exacerbated the problem.

Taller buildings should be on wider streets, and in all cases light-colored finishes (including the paving) increase the light, both inside and out. Short blocks help somewhat, as additional light enters from the intersections.

In regions with extreme heat, additional measures have been adopted. See, for example, the "bad-gir" wind scoops of Hyderabad Sindh, shown in Rudofsky, illustrations 113-115. This practical arrangement also gives the city a beautiful motif.

THE CIRCULATION REALM

Among the various functions of streets, none is more important than circulation. We must ensure that the capacity of the street network is not exceeded by the traffic that will use it. In carfree cities, we cannot be certain how many people will be on foot, on bicycles, or on public transport. Traffic levels will vary from season to season, because people are more likely to use public transport during inclement weather.

Origin-and-destination data is routinely analyzed by transport planners, a method that can be applied to carfree cities to project the trips that people will make, the times of day they will travel, and the places they will go. When this analysis is laid over the city's street layout, peak flows by various modes can be forecast accurately enough to determine required street widths. A city of short blocks can have narrower streets, as traffic will spread itself over the many streets. If there is a main axis of travel, it must have alternate routes in case of blockage.

The most difficult traffic to forecast is also the most troublesome: local freight. Even if metro-freight is adopted to deliver most freight, quite a few freight vehicles will still be required for deliveries to locations not directly served by metro-freight. These will generally be the largest vehicles on the streets and there may come to be quite a few of them, as in the Swiss town of ZERMATT. Even though their speeds are limited, they still require considerable space, and they are best separated from pedestrian and bike traffic where possible. Main streets should be designed so that 20-foot shipping containers can be moved through them. Where this is not possible, large shipments will have to be broken down into smaller consignments for local delivery, at considerable cost in time and money.

If trams are used to deliver freight, sidings will be required to allow freight trams to clear the main line while loading. The space requirements demand a case-by-case analysis.

Ayamonte, Spain

See page 172

See page 174

The least desirable method of freight delivery is the use of conventional trucks, which should be restricted to limited hours. If trucks are used, street space must be allocated for them. Amsterdam's busiest shopping street, the comparatively narrow KALVERSTRAAT, has been able to accommodate delivery vans during forenoon hours, when few shoppers are about.

Simply because no cars will be permitted does not mean that parking can be omitted. Freight vehicles, including freight bikes, require loading space and parking when not in use. In most cases, this parking should be provided in utility areas.

Finally, emergency access must be kept in mind. While it is possible to use special, narrow ambulances and fire trucks (see page 140), it will still be necessary to assure the free movement of these vehicles. This includes making certain that corner radii are great enough to permit turns without reversing.

The Arrangement of Blocks

The arrangement of blocks, which are usually quadrilaterals, affects the streets. Blocks cannot be allowed to become too large. Jane Jacobs observed that short blocks provide alternative routes to routine destinations, thereby leading to increased familiarity with the neighborhood. Short blocks also minimize walking distances by providing more direct routes. Block lengths should therefore be held to not more than 120m (400'). (Very short blocks are not a problem except that they leave no room for interior courtyards.) Block widths can be altered to suit the varying distances between major streets, and minor parallel streets can be added as the distance between the major streets becomes too great for a single block. Minor concentric streets can be any convenient distance apart, which gives the flexibility to arrange blocks of the desired size. The size of blocks can increase at greater distances from the center, but always (or nearly always) staying within the 120m (400') limit.

Jane Jacobs (1961/1992), 178-186

Coimbra, Portugal

The length of streets must also be considered in relation to their width. Stübben said that the length of a straight street should not exceed 20-30 times its width as this "awakens a feeling of discomfort." Of course, introducing a degree of curvature that takes the street out of sight within a distance not greater than 10 times its length solves this problem entirely, which is the solution advocated by Stübben:

> For the regulation of streets, straight lines ought not to be exclusively employed. Gentle curves which conform to superficial outlines or to natural boundaries may produce fine effects in the form of the streets.

I agree entirely with this assessment. The matter is considered at some length in ENCLOSING STREETS.

F. [Josef] Stübben, "Practical and Aesthetic Principles for the Laying Out of Cities," first presented at a meeting of the Deutscher Verein für öffentliche Gesundheitspflege in Freiburg, September, 1885, trans. W.H. Searles, in an advance copy of the *Transactions of the American Society of Civil Engineers,* 1893. Available on line at:
www.library.cornell.edu/Reps/DOCS/stubb_85.htm
The citation on this web site has several irregularities of spelling and style that are corrected here.

PAVEMENT

We are often unaware of the paved surface unless it is irregular or in bad repair, but it has an important effect on our feelings about an area. Fine paving is very expensive, and the only way to use it for long lengths of street is to minimize the width. San Marco is paved mostly with large, rectangular stone blocks, as here on the CALLE DEI FABBRI, an important narrow street. The stones are quite smooth but still provide enough grip to minimize the risk of slipping on wet pavement. Although asphalt pavement is the cheapest to lay, it can need repairs in a surprisingly short time, and patched asphalt is never attractive. Stone and brick paving can be taken up and relaid as necessary. Paving issues are considered in STREET ENGINEERING.

Rua Fernandes Tomaz, Coimbra

BOULEVARDS

Few urban elements are more strongly associated with cities than the boulevard. Yet their widespread construction is comparatively recent. The boulevard was first applied in 1667 by Le Nôtre, who laid out the grand boulevard that is today known as the Champs Elysées, arguably still the world's premier example. Widespread application of the boulevard really only began with Haussmann, who used it extensively in his redevelopment of Paris during the mid-19th century. The look of Paris today owes more to its boulevards than any other single feature. Haussmann's plans were the subject of great controversy at the time; he and the "boulevardiers" favored razing neighborhoods to open the way for boulevards, but many residents were opposed. Some feel that Paris was damaged, not improved, by Haussmann's boulevards, but the boulevard was in any case quickly adopted by many other cities.

The medieval city does not know the boulevard. As in the case of Venice, streets wider than about 12m (40') were quite unusual. Boulevards are also straight for long distances, which was rare in medieval streets. The boulevard was foreshadowed by the Renaissance resurrection of the gridded street pattern employed by Roman engineers when laying out colonial towns. The boulevard can be viewed as the ultimate expression of this preference for the grid and its straight streets.

The BAHNHOFSTRASSE in Zürich is my favorite boulevard. It is wide enough to define itself as an important street yet still narrow enough that it integrates well. The two rows of trees are sufficient to give shade and green without overwhelming the space. The street, with pedestrians dotted here and there, is of a highly agreeable width, and the lovely trams and their rails further improve the scene. The sidewalks are of a generous width. The buildings are harmonious but certainly not monotonous. The scale of the street announces that it is a central feature in the

Bahnhofstrasse, Zürich, a century ago

Avenida da Liberdade—Lisboa.

city. The buildings are taller than in nearby areas and in keeping with the width of the boulevard. The BAHNHOFSTRASSE TODAY is little changed and is still one of the vital arteries of the city. The street has achieved a perfect balance of variety and similarity. As boulevards go, it is comparatively narrow.

The planting of trees, more than any other single feature, distinguishes boulevards from other wide streets. Other streets may have trees, but they are usually incidental and sparse, whereas the boulevard always sports at least a twin row of trees. The appearance of a boulevard, even in winter, is affected more by the presence of trees than any other element. It is easy to understand why residents of 19th-century cities were excited by boulevards. There were then few trees in urban settings, except for vast, usually distant, parks constructed in the same epoch.

Although boulevards provide large amounts of useful outdoor social space, they do so at considerable cost, particularly in land and maintenance. The Avenida 9 de Julio in Buenos Aires, reputedly the world's widest street, is a whopping 130m (425') wide. Some boulevards feature eight rows of trees, and, of course, an awful lot of paving to mend and leaves to rake.

The BOULEVARD DES ITALIENS is a typical minor Parisian boulevard, as evidenced by the absence of service roadways and the comparatively narrow width. It is narrow enough that it integrates for the viewer; there is no sense of "the far side of the street"—one takes in the full view. As is usual, it forms a retail magnet, with shops lining both sides of the street. In medieval times, commercial activities were concentrated on squares, which even today still often host markets. This function is less well served by the linear form of the boulevard, because a square with market stalls brings more vendors within easy walking distance than does a long boulevard lined with shops.

The AVENIDA DA LIBERDADE in Lisbon is a classic boulevard, running straight as a rule into the distance. It has two marginal roadways for local traffic and one central artery for through traffic, an arrangement typical of wider boulevards. Rows of trees march its full length. The placement of a large monument at a circular intersection is also typical. There is one deviation from the standard design, and that is the rather narrow sidewalks fronting the buildings, which elsewhere host sidewalk cafés.

The desolate Campo San Polo, Venice

It is important to keep in mind that a city can have only so much outdoor public space; if too much is supplied, then not enough pedestrian traffic arises to make it come alive. Narrow medieval streets rarely suffer from this problem, but it may afflict a city of boulevards, unless the density of construction is quite high. Paris escapes this problem by virtue of its large population. Remember that the need for lively streets is quite different from the requirements of parks, which are usually intended to be calm spaces, islands of refuge and repose. Parks, as distinct from streets and squares, really cannot be too big.

In designing carfree cities, we may prefer to make limited use of the boulevard, or even to omit it entirely. In its place we can have more and much narrower streets with carefully situated public squares, where social activity tends naturally to concentrate. Boulevards have the defect that they provide no clear focus, except for the enormous circles at their intersections, and these are at a gigantic scale, since they must be wider than the already-wide boulevard. The great scale of these spaces often robs them of their rightful function as gathering places. Today's heavy car traffic completes the destruction.

The FRANZSTRASSE in Dessau is about as narrow as a boulevard can be, and it boasts only two rows of trees. In most respects, this is actually a blessing. The street is narrow enough that it integrates for the viewer, and the trees are few and thin enough that the façades of the buildings are visible.

The boulevard does provide a natural artery for public transport, whether on the surface or underground, and for an express bike route. The Reference Design calls for boulevards 33m (110') wide in the outer districts, 40m (130') in the inner

I have since realized that this can be reduced to a more manageable 82m (250'), simply by moving the two outer freight routes outside of the boulevard.

districts, and a whopping 100m (330') for short stretches in the three downtown districts. It would be possible to dispense with boulevards for this purpose, but it is simpler and cheaper to employ them, and their unique character immediately identifies their importance and suggests that public transport may operate on or beneath them.

The question of street trees will be argued forever. I am myself ambivalent about them. They make the street much more comfortable on a hot summer day, but at the same time they hide the face of the city from our view. Shade can also be provided by arcades (see page 292), which have the further advantage that they also offer excellent protection from the rain. That is why I tend to prefer arcaded Italian cities such as Bologna to French boulevards. However, in narrow streets, many of the advantages of boulevards can be had by planting a SINGLE ROW OF TREES down the center of the street, as here in Beja, Portugal.

Boulevards are usually planted with deciduous trees, so that for half the year, the buildings are visible through the bare branches, which affords some opportunity to appreciate the city's buildings. Consideration must always be given to the species of tree planted and the precise location of the trees. They cannot be allowed to interfere with underground works, especially sewers, which their roots will enter and block. See Lynch & Hack's *Site Planning* for a discussion of the various species of trees, their climatic ranges, and their attributes, good and bad.

Promenade des Barques, Narbonne

In any case, the trees must not totally dominate the street. When they are allowed to do so, a confusion arises between the role of the street as an important facility in the city and the role of a park as a quiet, restful retreat, comfortably removed from the center of things. Trees can be added to squares, but preferably as isolated giant specimens like the Asian banyan tree. The resulting "Tree Places" become gathering points and therefore serve a social function. The banyan tree is even commonly used as a symbol by Asian political parties.

APL, Pattern 171

We come next to the AVENUE CARNOT, a rare demi-boulevard in Bagnères-de-Bigorre that calls itself an avenue. The asymmetric row of trees is characteristic of neither a boulevard nor an ordinary street and gives us an opportunity to compare a street planted with trees to one without. On the left, we see a city and can tell a great deal about its nature. On the right, we see a lovely row of immature trees (planted, oddly, in the roadway). In 30 years, the trees will obscure most of the façades of the buildings. The trees are attractive, but do they not belong in the interior courtyards? I enjoyed gazing out the rear window of my old garret in Amsterdam when the trees were in leaf. It was a beautiful and restful scene in the heart of the city. But when the streets are free of trees, they reveal the life and vigor of a city. In practice, we will never reach agreement on this question. We can settle on having some neighborhoods with street trees and some without. This does depend on the climate—in hot climates, trees are a great blessing and should be planted.

The KÄRNTNER RING is part of the ring boulevard thrown around the old core of Vienna in the mid-19th century. Camillo Sitte wrote his *City Planning According to Artistic Principles* because he believed that the design of this new area of Vienna was inferior to that of the older parts. He sought to understand why the older sections of European cities are such wonderful urban spaces and why the newer areas, with their more generous use of space, are less good. Morris remarks:

> The Ringstrasse is about 2 miles long and over 200 ft wide. It was laid out in the form of five straight sections each of which determined the alignment of five gridiron planned districts. Thus, says Rasmussen, the new districts were made up entirely of uniform building blocks except at the corner which would not come out right; the streets had no face, they were simply voids, empty spaces between the cubic blocks, not pleasant outdoor rooms as in old Vienna.

Vienna presents as clear a contrast as possible between the organic growth pattern of the mediaeval Altstadt and the formally planned Renaissance sections of the Ringstrasse. Much criticism of the visual aspects of the scheme—specially that of Camillo Sitte who makes constant reference to his native city in his *The Art of Building Cities*—is derived from this fact.

I would not go as far as Sitte in criticizing it, but I think he is in principle correct. Today, almost any city would covet this beautiful boulevard, which is nearly perfect in its execution. It has the trees, the multiple roadways, and the proportions of a true boulevard. It differs, however, in one important aspect. Because the boulevard encircles the center city, it is formed of a series of straight segments, which yields fairly good enclosure; each segment is closed as the next segment angles off. This defuses one of the usual problems with boulevards: their weak sense of enclosure. (This question is taken up in ENCLOSING STREETS.) The blocks are quite short, and each block comprises just a few buildings, which harmonize well with one another.

The RUE MICHELET in Algiers is not a true European boulevard, but it is clearly a French export. Although it runs straight for a long distance, there are curves in both the foreground and the distance. These were probably made necessary by the topography of the site. Notice that the boulevard has provided an excellent route for the trams and that the width of the street suggests to pedestrians seeing it even from a distance that public transport may operate along it.

Never overlook the influence of military affairs on urban design. Part of the reason for the rapid adoption of the boulevard was military, as it provides a quick and efficient means to move military forces, especially mounted troops, from one part of a city to another. I fear that this consideration will be with us for a long time yet.

Morris, 175-176

WIDE STREETS

Wide streets are distinguished from boulevards largely by the absence of trees. Unlike boulevards, wide streets are a standard fixture of cities, dating back at least to Roman times. Wide streets, as we treat them here, are also generally much narrower than boulevards, although there is some overlap. While boulevards may be more than 100m (330') wide, streets are usually no wider than about 40m (130').

The distinction between "wide" and "narrow" is somewhat arbitrary, and the RUA AUGUSTA in Lisbon (leading to the Praça do Commércio, just beyond the arch) is at the narrow end of the range of wide streets. When it was laid out, this street was probably the widest in the city. While other "wide" streets are four times wider, they all function in a similar manner. In carfree districts, few streets need be wider than 15m (50'), as they carry almost no vehicular traffic. A street just 10m (33') wide can carry heavy pedestrian traffic.

Unlike the boulevard, the wide street is very much an urban form. It makes no attempt to disguise itself as nature. Wide streets are almost invariably the most important and busiest streets in a city, with commercial and governmental functions often clustered along them. It is interesting that in many European cities, major streets are quite narrow in the medieval centers and often become wider as they leave the old center. Paradoxically, this widening is accompanied by a change to less important functions. I have seen this reflected on a map of road traffic densities in Milan. The heaviest traffic is farthest from the center, and traffic volumes decline as the center is approached. Yet the center is the most important part of that city. By "wide street" we do not here mean the 6, 8, 10, 12, or even 14 lane arterials that connect single-use areas in North American sprawl. These streets function more as highways than streets and should be regarded as such. They have no place in real cities.

Rua Augusta, Lisbon

The RUE DE LA PAIX in Paris looks much the same today as it did a century ago, but for the addition of cars. The buildings are little changed, although the signage is less restrained today. Without the Vendôme obelisk in the distance, this street would be boring, even though lined by fine buildings. Consider how much more interesting this view would be if the street weren't perfectly straight: curve it a bit, make it here narrower and there wider, and it would become more interesting.

The AVENUE DE L'OPÉRA is in the same neighborhood as the Rue de la Paix, and the streets are similar, but the presence of the imposing opera house at the end gives it a different feel. (The elevated camera also helps.) This street shows the harmony that can arise when varied designs all stem from a similar style.

Notice the solid chimneys in a consistent style. Today's cheap sheet metal flues and stamped metal caps have removed the chimney from the realm of ornament and turned it into a purely utilitarian element, a blight on the scene.

The street leading to the TUNNEL DEL QUIRINALE in Rome is a typical wide street that is clearly of considerable commercial importance. The tunnel at the far end is an unusual feature that closes the view and makes the street more comfortable. It was built a century ago to provide better tram access to the area.

Note how the building on the right (with the awnings) tapers down to a fairly narrow end. While this is far from the most extreme example of a building in the shape of a fine wedge, it is certainly among the most attractive. Indeed, the rounding of both buildings on this corner, while not cheap, adds interest. Rounded corners (or their cheaper cousins, beveled corners) also help to smooth the flow of foot traffic around the corner.

Lille's fine RUE FAIDHERBE is a wide street with broad sidewalks that accommodate heavy foot traffic. Very few wheeled vehicles can be seen: a few horse-drawn wagons and hackneys, a tram in the distance, a bicycle in the foreground, but there are many people on foot. Ideally, we would return to this level of wheeled traffic in our streets, a change that can only be achieved if passenger and freight transport are moved below grade.

The proportions of the FRIEDRICHSTRASSE in Berlin are just enough different from the street in Lille that it has a different feel; the street is somewhat narrower, but the buildings are about the same height. In particular, the distance between the opposing curbs is less, so the street is better integrated for the pedestrian. This is a street that one would be more inclined to cross on a whim, even though it is not so much narrower than the Rue Faidherbe.

The photograph also shows the German ornamentation that prevailed until the Bauhaus made it taboo. The yearning for ornament probably still lurks in the hearts of most German people. Given half a chance, I think Germany will reclaim its ornamental heritage, as will the rest of humanity. Erik Rauch advised me that "the southern German tradition of decorative painting of building façades is still alive in towns in parts of southern Germany. Even some modern buildings are painted."

The HIGH STREET in Exeter is even more oversquare than the Friedrichstrasse, because the street is considerably narrower and the buildings nearly as tall. In fact, it borders on falling outside the classification "wide," although the name implies that it was the widest street in town at the time it was laid out.

The street has a very old feeling to it, which arises from the wide variety of styles and heights, including the lone arcaded building on the left. I suspect that this street assumed its current form over a span of many centuries. I find that I have a consistent bias in favor of streets that developed through the ages.

The carters must have had an awful time with the tram rails catching a wheel. We need to pay attention to this risk in the design of new tram installations, as tram rails remain a serious threat to bicyclists. Dave Morris advises me that attempts to protect cyclists by filling the flange groove with fairly hard rubber have failed. We will need to consider cycle crossings of tram

tracks and make certain that sufficient maneuvering room is provided, so that a rail never has to be crossed at a shallow angle. Cyclists not familiar with the danger need to be advised of it; once it is known, it can be avoided. The Dutch are accustomed to the problem and it rarely causes them any difficulty.

The CALLE DEL PISTOR is one of the widest streets in Venice (excluding the quaysides). These two blocks feel quite expansive because the buildings are rather low; the apparent width of a street is much affected by the height of the abutting buildings.

Notice the very young children playing in the street. They were less than five years old and seemed to be playing without direct adult supervision. I know of few other cities in the world where small children can safely play in the streets. Here there is no risk from motorized traffic, and the absence of cars and trucks gives clear sight lines, so that the entire street can be overseen by everyone on the street or from a window overlooking the street. Given the very strong neighborhoods characteristic of Venice, the cries of any child in distress for whatever reason would quickly draw adult assistance. James Howard Kunstler tells of having had free run of Manhattan in the 1950s, when he was about ten years old. Few people would allow a ten-year-old child so much independence in Manhattan today. This sad change damages children's sense of self-reliance and restricts their ability to learn about the world.

This street leading to the PALAZZO VECCHIO in Florence is at the extreme lower limit of a "wide street." Many would call it a narrow street, in fact. However, compared to the narrow streets to which we next turn, this is indeed a wide street. Notice that this street is of a similar width to the Calle del Pistor, which does not feel at all cramped. In the highly oversquare street in Florence, however, the taller buildings make the street feel rather narrow. In this as in so many issues in city design, it is appearance that determines our response to an area. The actual width of the street does not affect our feelings so much.

NARROW STREETS

Narrow streets, either commercial or residential, are the most important single element in a carfree city. Few streets need be wider than about 12m (40'), and they may be less than 2m (6') wide. Space is at a premium in every city, especially in carfree cities, where the provision of good public transport depends upon achieving fairly high density. For this reason, most streets will be narrow. Only some major streets and perhaps a few boulevards need be wider. The distinction between "wide" and "narrow" is somewhat arbitrary; the Boulevard de la Tour on the next page is almost as wide as the narrowest streets in the previous chapter.

The streets discussed in the first part of this chapter are in active neighborhoods near the commercial center, although many buildings still provide living quarters in the upper stories. Quieter streets with a distinctly residential character are taken up in the second part. One noteworthy difference between the commercial and residential streets is that the commercial buildings generally carry more ornamentation.

NARROW COMMERCIAL STREETS

The VIA CAIROLI in Ravenna typifies narrow streets in medieval city centers except in two respects: it is straight for quite some distance, and it has overhanging glass awnings, in one case rather elaborate. I have not often seen such awnings and never before in a concentration. They soften the light and give the street a pleasant, luminous feeling, as well as offering partial shelter from rain showers. The street is about 4m (13') wide and is a busy shopping street. It originates in the main square at the center of the city. The buildings on this street are comparatively low for a street so near the center, but this is not such a bad thing on a street as narrow as this.

Via Cairoli, Ravenna

Of the streets in this chapter that escaped wartime destruction, most look much the same today as they did a century ago. Many of them are carfree today, thanks to their central location and narrowness. Some of them may have known car traffic in the 1950s and 60s, but by 1970 Europe was already starting to remove cars from its inner cities, as it became clear that these areas simply could not support heavy car traffic.

Beausoleil is a city on a hillside. The BOULEVARD DE LA TOUR slopes gently in the foreground but gives way to stairs in the middle distance. It is quite a climb to the upper streets.

Notice the pair of cupolas about two blocks down the street. They aren't the same, but they match nicely. We must strive to create this kind of harmony in cities. In the past, it came largely of itself. People building in the same era usually built in the same style and had similar thoughts and values, so their buildings tended to share a family resemblance. Architects today seem intent on leaving their stamp on a city, and most of them design buildings with little thought to how they get along with their neighbors. This kind of egotism is not only destructive to cities, it is antithetical to them: the city is by definition a place where people work together for their common good. One of the greatest challenges that modern society faces is to restore this feeling of shared goals and experience, and to express these common urges in architecture and urban design. A great virtue of Alexander's *Pattern Language* is that it is a tool to identify urban design issues and a context in which to discuss them. Some general agreement on style and a respect for existing buildings is required to produce a coherent district; although this was usual in the past, it has become difficult to achieve today.

Notice the jog at the intersection in Saint Malo's RUE PORCON DE LA BARBINAIS and how the street beyond is narrower than the street in the foreground. Although narrow, this street is able to support a large volume of foot traffic. This area was, alas, heavily damaged in the war, and the reconstruction is less interesting.

It is doubtful if much of this view of RUE THIERS remains, as most of Boulogne was destroyed during the war. Here again we have a major commercial street that is only about 9m (30') wide. It is filled with pedestrians but still manages to pass the odd horse-cart and occasional tram. The buildings are of a very fine character, and apparently built in a hodgepodge of styles over a couple of centuries. Nonetheless, these disparate buildings get along fine with one another, and this was a very attractive street. The consistent use of awnings helps to unify the street.

Notice the early application of plate glass in the foreground. I generally oppose its use, but it does work well for shop windows, and quite a lot of it is found even in Venice. People sometimes do not notice glass and walk right into it, sometimes suffering serious injury. This is especially true if the glass is carried right to the ground, which is favored by some Modern architects. The risk of injury is less with smaller panes, and the mullions announce that there's a window there, making it all but impossible to overlook.

The VIA SERBELLONI is a street of stairs in Bellagio and might be the most photographed street in Italy. I have four different postcards of this photogenic location. This is a minor commercial center that appears to supply local needs. The street wiggles back and forth, but not enough to take it out of our view for quite a distance. The balcony, the lamp, and the stairs marching up the hill are all quiet attractions that help make this street so luscious. The small scale makes it cozy.

Narrow Residential Streets

We now consider narrow streets that have a more residential character. In keeping with the tradition of mixed uses, family businesses are commonly housed at ground level, with the family often living on the upper floors (some call these buildings "shop houses"). The establishment of shops, service outfits, and

Tavira, Portugal

light manufacturing on the ground floor solves the difficult problem of providing adequate privacy (a matter that will be judged differently in different cultures). Many people will not live in ground-floor urban housing because they do not want their windows to face directly onto the street. Even the trick of putting the more public rooms (kitchen, dining area, living room) on the street side is no solution for many people.

At the same time, it is essential to avoid the now-common approach of using the ground floor for storage and parking, with blank walls at street level. This strategy does help to prevent burglary of ground-floor spaces, but it is deadly for the affected street. This form of development should never be tolerated as it actually *encourages* criminal activity by removing the "eyes on the street" that deter crime. We must find good uses for this space, uses that create attractive ground floors, with windows and doors facing the street. The ground floors will be inhabited more by day, the upper floors more by night, but there will always be people about. Unbreakable glazing can protect shop-keepers' stocks while keeping the street attractive and permit-ting the display of the shop's wares even at night, as here on the CALLE LARGA DELL' ASCENSIONE in Venice.

Ground floors are also the location for concierge service as proposed on page 180. This would include facilities for nearby tenants, including bicycle parking, storage, trash collection, and deliveries. This service would be staffed either continuously or from early in the morning until late in the evening, probably by a couple who rely on this business for their livelihood, thus helping to assure eyes on the street near this facility.

Finally, there will probably be quite a few people who have no objection to living on the ground floor, as here on the tight-knit Venetian ISLAND OF BURANO. This approach may be more readily accepted by residents of small communities, but even in cities such as Amsterdam, ground-floor apartments in the center are fully occupied.

The construction of streets as narrow as the one in Burano is possible in new carfree cities, and the reference design does include a few streets as narrow as 3m (10'). Given today's concerns regarding emergency access, these streets must be comparatively short and close to streets wide enough to permit emergency access. Some streets, such as this one in the Italian HILL TOWN OF TREVI, are little wider than the hallway in an apartment building. It is useful to make this comparison, as the functions served are quite similar. Although ambulances and fire trucks cannot pull up directly to the front door of an apartment, they can get close enough to perform their functions. These streets, like apartment hallways, provide access to family quarters from wider streets nearby. There is one critical difference, however. Hallways in apartment buildings are rarely used as social spaces, but very narrow streets are often places where people will sit during the evening or stop to chat on the way home for lunch, especially in nice weather.

Very narrow streets are not for everyone, but many people find them attractive, and they should be available for those who prefer to live on them. A bonus is that houses on narrow streets can have larger interior courtyards, by virtue of the space saved in the street. Alternatively, the buildings can be a story lower.

This street in the CASBAH of Algiers is only about 2m (6') wide. Even narrower streets are common in souks and medinas throughout Africa. Donkeys are the only practical choice for freight delivery in the stepped streets. Emergency access is simply impossible, and I cannot imagine what is done in the event of a fire. Medical evacuations would be possible only by litter. I doubt that we will see further construction of narrow, stepped streets like this except where wider streets are very nearby.

Notice that the upper floors are corbelled out over the street. In hot climates where the noonday sun is to be avoided at all costs, corbelled buildings shade the street below and provide some extra space within the buildings.

The CALLE DE PAMPINOT in Fuenterrabia has a comfortable feel to it despite some deterioration. This does not appear to be a rich area, but it looks like a good neighborhood where many people would be comfortable raising a family. What gives this street this reassuring appearance? Several things, I think. The condition of the paving greatly affects the perceived quality of any street. When it is broken, much patched, or dirty, these defects severely impair our appreciation of the street. Here the paving is in excellent condition and the line of the curbs is well maintained. A few stoops do protrude into the sidewalk, but there are not too many of them and they are in good order. The graceful upward curve near the end of the street is another attractive feature and adds considerable interest to the street. The building that closes off the end of the street is of good quality. Thus, although none of the buildings on this street is of especially high quality, the street as a whole has a decent feel. This is what we need to strive for, and it is not something that can be achieved solely by following a book of rules; it is the ensemble that matters. It seems to me that time-worn streets, when still in a reasonable state of repair, are often reassuring environments.

The CALLE MAYOR, also in Fuenterrabia, is a prosperous street of fairly small proportions. Like the Calle de Pampinot, it is clearly oversquare but not extremely so. Its scale is, however, larger, so the street is wider. I do not believe that many people would find this street claustrophobic, although some people may find the narrower Calle de Pampinot objectionable.

The buildings here announce themselves as belonging to the well-to-do by several features. The ground floor ceilings are lower than those of the second floor, which is where the important, semi-public rooms are almost certainly located. The ground floor will be dedicated to utilitarian functions including the kitchen. The roof overhangs are generous, well detailed, and even, in one case, carved. Finally, the iron railings in front of the windows are nicely made and ornamented. In this practice, windows run nearly to the floor, admitting lots of daylight, and the railings prevent people from falling out. It is doubtful that any of these ledges is deep enough to accept a chair, but people can and probably do lounge in the window openings and watch the world pass by.

The KLINTGASSE in Wernigerode is a lovely example of a narrow street in a mixed-use area that almost certainly includes residences. The street appears to be peaceful despite the evident presence of small businesses. Several minor points help to make this an unusually attractive street. In the first place, its width is not constant: it tapers down in the middle distance. Second, it also curves gently. Third, the view is closed by the façade of a very attractive building. Finally, the signs hung by businesses do not intrude unreasonably into the scene. Small signs are entirely sufficient to the needs of pedestrians; we only need illuminated monster signs to lure speeding motorists.

There is one negative point: the flight of steps that obtrudes into the sidewalk. Notice that the building beyond has its lowest floor just one step above the street, and that building is tightly coupled to the street, with its windows at the eye level of passersby. By contrast, the building in the foreground has its first floor about a meter (yard) above the street, which necessitates the encumbering stairs and disconnects the ground floor from the street.

Notice how each story is corbelled out over the story below. In rainy places like Germany, this helps keep water off the faces of the buildings and their windows, which considerably reduces water damage and maintenance costs.

This quiet area in Amersfoort is known as DE MUURHUIZEN (wall houses) because they are located on the site of the former city walls and were built from stone taken from the wall. This street is nearly perfect for a provincial city of this kind. The width of the street is highly agreeable, given the less urban character of this area. Precisely what is it that makes this street so

attractive? It has one vital characteristic: it curves gently and continuously in one direction, affording the pedestrian a constantly changing view and a good look at each of the façades on the left side of the street. Notice that the buildings on the right are smaller and of a simpler character than those on the left. The curve of the street makes the better buildings more visible. I will relent on the matter of street trees here; the three trees are well behaved, nicely situated, and entirely in keeping with the character of the street. The paving runs nearly unbroken across the street, which helps to unify it. Notice that, despite the presence of a number of single-story buildings, this is still clearly an urban area. That all buildings abut their neighbors has much to do with this. Parked cars today line the right side of the street, blocking the view.

The CALLE ARCOS in Barcelona is the ultimate narrow street. It is not even two meters (6') wide and creates a very intimate space. The curve of the street makes it endlessly interesting. The buildings, although simple, are of extremely high quality, and this is clearly a rich neighborhood. The elements are nicely proportioned, the treatment of the windows is very fine, and the overhead arches serve to enclose the space even more while still admitting plenty of light.

The KAISERSTRASSENECKE in Wernigerode has a freshly-built appearance, so it was probably constructed just before 1900. By that time it had become unusual to build streets any narrower than this. Notice the architectural harmony and variation. Notice also the telephone wires and their supports. Not so long after this photograph was taken, Europe began to bury its utility lines. Today most European cities have their utilities underground, which improves reliability and reduces maintenance costs while greatly improving the appearance of an area.

The paving appears to be entirely of stone. The rich texture of cobblestone paving is very attractive, but it is unpleasant to walk or bicycle over small stones. The use of handcarts is also impeded. Good asphalt paving is an ideal surface for any wheeled contraption, but it is hardly attractive, especially once the inevitable patches have been applied. The best, and most expensive, approach is that taken in the older districts of Venice, where most of the paving is in the form of LARGE, SMOOTH STONE BLOCKS laid tightly against one another. The surface is nearly as even as asphalt and far more attractive. Narrow streets are cheaper to pave, and that is why Venice was able to afford durable, large-block stone paving.

The RITTERGASSE in Basel is not entirely residential; there are some institutions mixed in with housing. It remains a quiet neighborhood despite these non-residential uses. The streets here are narrow but still wide enough to permit automobiles to transit the area, although not to park on the street. The absence of parked cars makes the street highly attractive, but there is just enough car traffic to confine people to the sidewalks.

It would appear that the two buildings were built at the same time by the same hand, as the styles are identical. These are very fine buildings and yet not hugely expensive to construct. Only the stonework of the main entrance is especially intricate; the windows are trimmed in stone, but the carving is comparatively simple. Notice the major and minor divisions of the windows—first the major horizontal and vertical breaks, then the divisions into small panes.

The narrow street is a flexible and essential element in any dense urban area. Narrow streets allow us to achieve high density without resorting to high-rise buildings.

Travesa 1 Maio, Lagos

GALLERIES & ARCADED STREETS

Arcaded streets and their close cousins, galleries, are wonderful urban devices. Arcades make life much more comfortable anywhere the climate is hot or wet, for they provide shade and excellent protection from rain and snow. People within arcades remain in close contact with the street. Galleries *are* the street. Arcades and galleries are graceful elements, based as they usually are on some form of arch.

Entire cities, such as Bologna, have incorporated arcades into virtually every building, which makes for nearly continuous protection against the elements and provides a consistent visual theme. The VIA SAN ROMANO in Ferrara is an excellent arcade. It is nicely paved, with pleasant buildings of good proportions. One point of criticism is the straight lintels on the right, which are less attractive than the arches on the left.

The only significant difficulty posed by arcades is the matter of keeping them bright and airy spaces; they must never become dark or forbidding. This can be ensured by making them comparatively high in relation to their depth, by making the supporting columns round and as small as structurally possible, and by using bright colors within the arcade. When these measures are applied, an agreeable arcade should result.

The gallery is another approach to providing protection from the elements, and one that virtually assures ample natural illumination. Unlike the arcade, which has long been with us, the gallery did not become possible until industrialization made cheap iron and glass readily available. The second half of the 19th century saw a flurry of gallery building, one of the tastier fruits of industrialization.

Either approach, properly applied, should yield a comfortable and attractive street, although the cost of galleries is quite high compared to the much simpler arcade. Modern galleries do not generally seem to be so attractive in their design, alas.

Arcades, Via San Romano, Ferrara

Alexander has much to say about arcades ("Arcades," APL, Pattern 119). His principal argument is that they help to connect buildings with the public realm, which is certainly true. He calls for "simple and beautiful" arcades and gives an example of a lovely, small scale arcade. He warns specifically of arcades that are too high and illustrates this with an ugly modern arcade. I would argue that it is not so much the height that is the problem as the ugly form. Anyone contemplating the use of arcades should review his pattern.

ARCADES

The grandest arcade I have seen is the VIA DELL'INDIPENDENZA in Bologna. Nearly all of central Bologna is arcaded, but this major street boasts unusually fine arcades. The buildings generally are of very high quality, with finely detailed windows. However, the wide, straight street and the overly regular design of the buildings does not hold our interest. Part of the problem is that this street is not carfree at all (I waited for a break in the traffic to take the photograph), and therein lies a clue to the problem. Because the street carries heavy traffic, pedestrians have not taken it over. There is no street furniture beyond the confines of the arcades, and the street seems barren and desolate, a deadly condition in any urban area. Were this street to be made carfree, five years would see a dramatic change in its aspect, and a large improvement as people reoccupied the street and brought with them benches, food carts, potted plants, places for children to play, and so forth.

The protection that arcades provide can actually be extended across intersections. Such continuous protection provides an alternative to the underground warrens found in the center of many Canadian cities, where the winters are long and hard, with heavy snows. In cold regions like this, the inclusion of arcades and galleries would make carfree life more attractive to many people — arcades partially replace the protection against the elements that cars afford.

When designing an arcade, it is important to avoid excessive contrast in the brightness of the street and the arcaded area. The arcade must be bright enough that people on the street can see into the arcade. People in the arcade should not be blinded when looking out. As already mentioned, arcades need to be kept fairly shallow and the arches comparatively high, so that the arcade is bright and cheerful. The walls, columns, ceilings, and paving should be of light colors, the paving especially, as it is normally the first (and therefore most important) surface to reflect light striking into the arcade. The use of round columns is surprisingly important. As can be seen in this photograph of the VIA MERCANTI in Milan, square columns cut off some of the view and the light. A round column that just fits within the footprint of a square column is very nearly as strong as the square one, and only a slight increase in diameter is needed to bring it up to the strength of the square column.

The question of the shape of the arch is an interesting one. We can have elliptical, round, gothic, reverse, and Moorish arches, all in a wide range of proportions. The variation can be fascinating, and there is no real reason not to mix the styles, even in adjacent buildings, although it is better if the stylistic details at least have a family resemblance.

The vault is the highest expression of the arcade. Its complex form incorporates beautiful curved edges and intriguing concave surfaces, which provide a great opportunity for ornamentation, as shown here in the phenomenal arcade of the CHIESA DI SANTA MARIA NOVELLA in Florence. However, even completely plain vaults can beautiful if nicely proportioned, as in the case of LES ARCADES in Bellagio.

Whatever is done, rectilinear shapes should be avoided. When the columns are square, the arches replaced by straight lintels, and the ceilings flat, the arcade loses a great deal of its charm and interest. I believe that ugly modern arcades stem from a change in materials: the replacement of brick and stone by steel and reinforced concrete is probably to blame. (Wood has sometimes been used in the construction of arcades, but is not really durable enough for this use in most climates, as some of it is directly exposed to the elements and will stain, weather, and rot within a few decades.) Steel and reinforced concrete have high bending strength, which stone lacks, so the arches that are necessary in stone or brick construction are merely an added complication when building with modern materials.

The VIA CORRADO RICCI in Ravenna shows all too clearly the graceless modern form; one never sees this in arcades built from traditional materials. The bulky square columns, straight lintels, unrelieved flat ceilings, and graceless window treatment make this space much less attractive than nearby historic arcades. The large plate glass windows with their advertising banners are a further blot. Observe, though, that the white ceiling helps make the space bright.

The best arcades show grace and refinement, with delicate, soaring round columns supporting an arch. This example from Bergamo's PORTICI NUOVI is very fine in many respects, although I prefer an arch that is not round. This arcade is shallow in comparison to its height, so the arcade, with its light-colored stone paving, is well illuminated.

Arcades are most effective when applied along an entire block. When incomplete arcades are built, the building line must be broken to leave room for sidewalks in front of the buildings without arcades. When we remove cars, the streets can be narrowed, making it possible to widen the sidewalks and add arcades to existing buildings. This need not be accomplished all at once; arcades can be added building-by-building, during long-term renovation of a district.

Arcades are economical as well as practical and beautiful. They make efficient use of land and provide high-quality space above the arcade. The ceiling of the arcade must be well insulated from the floor above; otherwise, the floors will be cold in winter. In-floor radiant heating is ideal for this application.

Arcades require good cooperation and sensitive regulation. It is in the interests of store owners to set out piles of merchandise in the arcade during business hours, and the resulting hindrance to pedestrians is actually good for business. In the Italian arcades I have seen, this problem has almost always been managed well, and it is rare that passage is impeded. Bicycles parked in the arcade must also not block the way.

With the largest arcades, like the PIAZZA GRANDE in Arezzo, it is possible to allow restaurants and cafés to set tables inside the arcade, but in this case, the tables completely block the arcade. Here, at least, pedestrians forced out of the arcade by the tables have a large, carfree square through which they can detour.

Earthquake loads must be considered when designing an arcade. Unattractive iron crossbars must sometimes be added to stabilize the structure against hard shaking, as here on the Piazza Grande, which lies in a region susceptible to fairly strong earthquakes. It is possible that reinforced concrete shear walls within the building might sufficiently stabilize the arches without resorting to crossbars. This question may be worthy of further engineering analysis.

When designing an arcade, several important decisions must be made. How many floors is the arcade to span—will it reach only the height of the first floor, or will it rise to the second? Is the height of the first floor to be made great, in order to keep the proportions of the arcade more pleasing? How many floors will be built above the arcade? How deep is the arcade to be made? These decisions greatly affect the final appearance of the arcade. There is no single, perfect solution, a point nicely illustrated by the square of SANTISSIMA ANNUNZIATA in Florence. The arcade on the left is very high and carries no upper floors. The lower arcade on the right carries stories above it. Despite these differences, the two arcades do not clash, because they are built in complementary styles.

The height of these arcaded buildings in Genoa, including the HÔTEL DE LA VILLE in the foreground, is at the top end of the range that is feasible for buildings without elevators. Notice the variation in the dimensions of the arches. The large four-arch building has two different arch widths, although all four are the same height. Other buildings have only two arches, usually the same, but one building has one large arch and one small. A wide range of variations can be rung on the same theme.

Galleries

Galleries ("arcades" in British usage) were built in many European cities during the latter part of the 19th century. Aside from being lovely things, galleries provide good protection from the weather and extend the season for outdoor activities. (Some new galleries are closed off from outdoors and climate controlled, being thus unaffected by weather.) Galleries are closely related to the crystal palaces that were built during the same era and from the same materials. Galleries are coverings for streets, whereas the crystal palace is a free-standing structure.

The GALLERIA MAZZINI in Genoa is enormous; there are four cross streets in this scene, all under the gallery. Notice the lovely quality of illumination: the gallery softens the light and yet still brings a great deal of it into the space.

Wind issues require careful consideration in any construction of this sort. It may blow hard enough inside the gallery to negate some or most of the shelter. Wind tunnel tests may be required. Additional consideration must be given to the question of venting summer heat and possible damage from hailstorms. Gallery projects require comprehensive engineering work by an experienced firm.

The GALLERIA VITTORIO EMANUELE in Milan may be the best-known of all the European galleries. It is built on the same scale as streets in the neighborhood and differs from them only by the glass roof above. Situated in the heart of Milan, this gallery has mammoth portals at the entrances, which are highly ornamented and visible from a considerable distance.

As mentioned earlier, Canada built "underground galleries," starting in the 1960s. They provide full protection from bad weather and are functionally similar to galleries, although often much larger in extent. However, underground malls are dead places: the environment is always the same, night and day, irrespective of weather or season. These underground city centers are often reached by car, and the large garages are connected to the tunnel system. Montréal has over 30 km (20 miles) of underground passages linking more than 60 major buildings. This section at PROMENADES DE LA CATHÉDRALE is typical.

An unfortunate side-effect of underground centers is that, during the brief summer, people do not get to enjoy the pleasant weather. These dark areas may also exacerbate the seasonal depression that afflicts quite a few residents of northern regions; many of these cities have frequent sunny days even in the depths of winter, and residents would be healthier and more cheerful if they were exposed to this sunshine.

Moshe Safdie has proposed the construction of galleries with a modern twist: they would open like clamshells during nice weather. However, fixed galleries are already a prodigious undertaking, and I fear that the costs of making a retractable roof that can withstand a summer squall would limit the application of this technique to very small areas. We might do better to think instead of building arcades and closing them off from the street with glass panels that can be removed during the warmer seasons. Full climate control is unnecessary; simply by providing protection from the wind and a bit of warmth (supplied by heat escaping from adjacent buildings), we can offer an environment that is much less taxing than the icy blasts of Montréal or Edmonton.

Safdie, 158-163

Another approach to the problem of inclement weather was adopted by this SHOPPING MALL in Osaka. Customers have been invited to bring their bikes indoors, where they are protected from the rain, so the saddle is never wet when you return from shopping. Also notice the deadening effect of the metal roll-up door on the right; compare it to the brightly-lit shops on the left. Even though these shop windows are not terribly attractive, they are far better than the steel shutters.

One of the delights of glass roofs is watching the rain splatter and run off them. The patterns of the rain sheeting off the glass

repeat, but never exactly, and it is fascinating and restful to watch. Added to this is the pleasure of keeping warm and dry while watching the rain pour down. These spaces are more lively than underground malls because of the constantly changing light and weather, and this difference has much to commend it.

The COLOMBO SHOPPING CENTER in Lisbon is an example of a modern-day gallery, but there is an important difference. Generally, older galleries did not have loggias, so all foot traffic was concentrated at ground level. In the case of this shopping mall, there is enough foot traffic to provide plenty of activity on all three levels, although there is more on the bottom level than those farther up.

My main disagreement with this kind of modern gallery is that it is not actually a city street; this is a purely commercial enterprise, governed by private interests. This detail is important because city streets should be free from direct commercial interference and must be places where non-commercial and even anti-commercial activity can occur. If a group were to try to protest the activities of any of the commercial interests in this shopping center, guards would stop it immediately, and the courts would probably support the private property rights of the mall owners.

The gallery form can also be adapted to simple construction, as here on the TALAA LEKBIRA, a major street in Fes-al-Bali. This region of Morocco experiences chilly winters and blazing hot summers, when some form of protection from the noon sun is required. The economical solution has been to cover over most of the street with a ragged layer of sticks and reeds, which still allows some air to enter while providing quite good protection from the sun. In this dry region, protection from the rain is not so often needed.

ENCLOSING STREETS

We will be concerned in this chapter with streets that develop a sense of enclosure. Alexander's "Positive Outdoor Space" (APL, Pattern 106) is a crucial pattern. It simply calls for us to create outdoor areas (not just streets, but also squares and gardens) that do not drain off into the distance but have an intimate, enclosed feel. It seems that a few people are uncomfortable in enclosed spaces (and may find them threatening), but the large majority of people seem to have a strong preference for outdoor spaces with well-developed enclosure. Both curvature and taper can help to close the view in streets, and both are dealt with later in this chapter. This arrangement also relates to the need to develop "beady ring" structures (see page 435). Beads are nothing more than swellings in the street, including squares, that are comfortable places to linger and chat. They have very strong enclosure and highly positive space.

In "Building Fronts" (APL, Pattern 122) Alexander calls for the elimination of building setbacks, in order to better define the street. He also says, "let the building fronts take on slightly uneven angles as they accommodate to the shape of the street," which presumes streets that are not straight. This is borne out by his illustration. This is one of the most controversial aspects of Alexander's work, at least to judge by the frequency with which these patterns have been ignored since paper planning began to dominate design 500 years ago. I believe he is correct and that the development of enclosure is one of the most important tasks of the designer.

This minor street near the VIA MAZZINI in medieval Ferrara obeys these tenets. It creates a tight sense of enclosure, which a few people may find oppressive. The street is about 3m (10') wide, and the three- and four-story buildings yield a street that is highly oversquare. The enclosure is completed by the gentle curve of the street, which closes the view in a short distance.

Near Via Mazzini, Ferrara

The IGLESIA DE SANTA MARIA and environs in San Sebastián is a formal space that develops a tight, complete sense of enclosure. While the buildings that face each other across the street are not identical, they are closely related, another hallmark of formality.

The church that closes the view is an extraordinary building, lavishly detailed and beautifully proportioned. It is not precisely centered on the street from which the photograph was taken and stands at a slight angle to it. In medieval times, people were less concerned with rectilinear geometry; they were more concerned with proportion and scale. Balance, not mirror symmetry, was sought. I find this a better approach to building urban areas that hold our interest and win our affection.

The proportions of the street are lovely. The street is highly oversquare but not extremely so. The entire width of the street is unobstructed by curbs, bollards, planters, etc. The stairs mean that cars cannot negotiate this street, so that children can still play safely in it today. In a somewhat wider street, the addition of street furniture (benches, fountains, etc.) will be needed to keep the area from feeling barren. In streets of this width, however, nothing is needed unless the street is straight for a long distance.

Judging by "objective" criteria, the RUE DE L'ORANGERIE in Versailles ought to be excellent, yet it is not. Its rectilinear geometry does not compare favorably with the street above, but this is not its worst failing. Although the buildings here are of nearly ideal height, the street is quite wide, and judging by the use that is being made of it, wider than it needs to be. (The trams will of course use much of its width as they pass.) The street is somewhat undersquare and the sense of enclosure is diffused. In general, I think urban streets should be square or oversquare; anything less consumes too much space and leads to streets that develop weak enclosure. A break in the wall of buildings on the left causes a disturbing gap-tooth effect, further eroding the sense of enclosure.

The enclosure of the RUE SAINT MICHEL in Menton almost fails but does not. The buildings in the distance do close off the street, but if the straight section of the street were much longer, the enclosure would begin to dissolve.

I think this is an excellent width of street, although few would now dare to build new urban areas with major streets this narrow. This street is wide enough to permit a tram to pass, but it has been necessary to run the tram through a parallel street for its return journey, which is no disadvantage.

Notice the pocket park on the left. It is safe to bet that it sees intense use. While it is usual to site squares at intersections, which makes them lively, the placement of a park at mid-block helps to keep it calm and quiet.

The KAMPERBINNENPOORT SEEN FROM DE KAMP is one of Amersfoort's most attractive streets. It has narrow buildings with doorways every 3-5m (10-15'). The steeples, spires, and towers lend great interest to the scene. The sense of enclosure here is excellent despite the undersquare proportions.

Notice that this street does not actually have sidewalks. The small paved areas in front of the buildings are isolated by low railings. The usable width of the street is thus less than it appears. The street is not of a continuous width—it necks down in the middle distance.

Lugano is a gorgeous town of complex topography. The VIA NASSA is an important street that roughly parallels the shore of Lake Lugano, with a steep hill on the left. In some places it is considerably narrower than seen here. This is a fully enclosed space when viewed in this direction. Notice how the buildings have been placed at irregular angles to one another. A detailed study of this area from a range of vantage points would most likely reveal subtle advantages of the arrangement, having main- ly to do with sunlight, skylight, wind, and rain (notice the arcades). The setting of the buildings yields several irregular, quiet areas that are out of the general flow of the street.

The photographer of the BATZENHÄUSL in Bolzano was probably standing in an intersection, as suggested by the break in the sidewalk on the extreme right. This shows that the blocks here are very short, and it seems that the building in the center of the photograph has streets on at least three sides.

In the absence of cars, there is nothing wrong with short blocks and a great deal that's right. The difficulty in arranging them is that interior courtyards are only possible in blocks above a certain minimum size (about 15m or 50'). The buildings in this area probably lack courtyards, which deprives their residents of any greenery except for window boxes and ivy. For me that can be enough (I'm no gardener!), but many people will want more planting. The sense of enclosure in this space is strong.

STRAIGHT STREETS

Straight streets have been used in cities around the world for thousands of years (see ORDER & ORGANIZATION IN CITIES). Rectilinear grids have dominated European city design since the start of the Renaissance. Grids and straight streets were applied almost universally throughout the US West during the westward expansion of the railroads in the late 19th century. Hundreds of new towns were arranged on rectilinear grids.

The disadvantages of straight streets are that they reduce the sense of enclosure, are boring, and make destinations seem farther away than they are. They are disheartening for people on foot (see "Paths and Goals," APL, Pattern 120). Paths should have intermediate goals, separated from one another by a walk of a minute or so. Goals as simple as a statue or a small fountain will serve; they need be no more than minor landmarks. Such goals are more difficult to provide in straight streets.

This street in the ARAB QUARTER of Port Said seems to run out to infinity, even though the distance may be no more than 8 or 10 blocks. It would be a discouraging prospect to start out on a

walk to the far end of this street, even though it is probably only ten minutes away. Even the width of the street is perfectly constant. The only relief is in the variations of the buildings.

Some cost savings and simplifications are associated with straight streets and right angles, but it is possible to maintain rectangular buildings by simply JOGGING BUILDINGS backwards or forwards with respect to their neighbors. This is common in US residential development and allows streets of any shape.

It is possible to preserve a grid pattern while still providing fully-enclosed streets by the simple trick of closing off one block in every few. This eliminates long sight lines down the street, allowing a sense of enclosure to arise. This technique is seldom applied today (because it hinders motorized traffic) but has some merit as long as continuous walking routes are provided.

The RUE ROCHECHOUART in Paris is in many ways a fine street. The high-quality buildings harmonize well with one another. The street is fairly wide, but the buildings are tall enough that it is oversquare and has a good sense of enclosure—except that it bleeds away down the endless straight street. The situation is slightly relieved by the slope of the street and the distant crest. There is nothing terribly wrong with this street, but I find it faintly depressing and uninspiring.

Enkhuizen, in North Holland, is a large provincial town. As is characteristic of Dutch towns, most of the houses on the NIEUWE WESTERSTRAAT are just two stories high, although they are built solid, with no space between the buildings. The houses are typical of Dutch towns and are usually quite shallow. This admits plenty of daylight from both sides, a matter of real importance in places with dark, cloudy winters. This is an excellent arrangement, excepting the long, straight street. Notice how the two lines of trees march off into the distance and finally merge into a solid mass, which creates a degree of enclosure. During the summer, with the trees in leaf, the enclosure will seem more nearly complete.

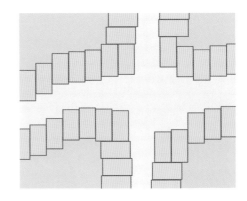

Warsaw is one of the saddest stories in Europe. This was a beautiful city until World War II, during the course of which it was largely reduced to rubble. Some parts of it have been restored to their former glory, but there are no longer many views of the city that look anything like the ULICA MARCHALKOWSKA.

I think wide streets can tolerate being straight better than narrower ones. The vantage point here, from the edge of the street, changes its appearance considerably. Pedestrians will keep to the sidewalks, if only to avoid the streetcars, so they will not often see the view from the centerline, with the street marching off to the horizon in near-perfect symmetry. This is as good a way to arrange a long, straight street as there is.

Is the VIA CAVOUR in Florence straight or not? It isn't straight, but it is straight enough that it works like a straight street: the far horizon can still be seen. Notice, though, that even this small angulation is enough to make the street more interesting.

CURVED STREETS

Curved streets, by their very nature, create closed views, provided that the street is not too wide in relation to the degree of curvature. Curved streets also give more exposure to the façades on the concave side of the street than those opposite, and it is natural to site better buildings in the more exposed locations.

A grid topology is somewhat easier for strangers to navigate than a less regular topology. It is possible to establish a topological grid using SLIGHTLY CURVED STREETS. Such an arrangement is considerably more interesting than a rectilinear grid, and the ease of navigation is retained. The arrangement even permits the use of numbered streets and avenues, as in Manhattan.

The Reference District is based on a radial street arrangement that tends automatically to create curved streets: the concentric streets are by nature curved, and the branching radial streets also create interesting, closed views.

The scale of a space and the degree of curvature can vary widely. At one end of the spectrum are narrow, curving streets such as the JUDENGASSE in Salzburg. This street, which narrows to less than 3m (10'), creates tight enclosure with a moderate degree of curvature. The enclosure is further enhanced by the highly oversquare proportions of the street. However, if the curvature is removed from such a street, a condition arises in which the enclosure is tight in the transverse direction and absent in the longitudinal direction. In fact, this condition is only rarely seen, because most narrow streets were laid out at a time when perfectly straight streets were unusual. It takes only slight curvature to create enclosure in a narrow street, and even streets that look straight on maps often turn out to have just enough curvature to develop a sense of enclosure.

The FALTERSTRASSE in Kitzingen, Germany, is a modest but fine street, better than nearly everything built today. It would be improved by the addition of a gate at the end. The street has a pleasing curvature, the width is comfortable, and the buildings are of a good height. The overhanging sign is a fine touch.

When additions are made to Dutch cities today, they usually end abruptly, just as here in Kitzingen a century ago. The buildings stop and the cow pastures begin. The critical difference between current Dutch practice and this scene is that nearly all new Dutch streets are straight. Here, the opening into the countryside emerges gradually as we round the curve in the street. The end of the street is punctuated by the prominent tower.

TAPERED STREETS

Strictly speaking, a taper implies a wedge shape, and many of the examples in this section are actually jogged, not tapered. The difference is in fact of some importance, and it is taper that one sees most often in medieval streets. (Streets laid out since the 17th century are usually of constant width.) The most

Also recall that when most pre-Renaissance towns were laid out, they would have been enclosed by walls, which themselves create enclosure.

important point is that streets are much more interesting when their width varies, and this is true even when a jog is used to create the taper.

Jogs create breaks, as here in a STREET IN SAN MARCO in Venice, that may be dead space or can be adopted for a variety of purposes, many of which improve the street and add points of interest. Jogs create small public spaces, sometimes in places where a square would be excessive. (We can't have functioning squares at every intersection unless each is very small.) When these spaces are large enough, they can host a sidewalk café or restaurant, a bench or two for people to stop and take the sun, or a children's play area just out of the main flow of foot and bicycle traffic. It is best if the jog has a window in it, so there is no blank wall; this also helps to bring extra light into the building. Better still is to add windows on both sides of the corner, so that it is possible to see through the corner and into the space created by the jog. This lovely touch is easily arranged.

A jog can be employed to provide a more dramatic entrance for a building, as here at the CHIESA DI SANTO STEFANO in Assisi. These small pockets, however they may be created, must be handled well if they are to improve the area. It seems to be particularly important to arrange them so that direct sun falls into them at some time of day.

The RUE POTERIE in Vitré is an important street in a prosperous provincial city, probably near or in the commercial center. (Where are the people? It is probably lunch time or Sunday.) In this case, the jogged street opens up to provide extra space for fairly heavy foot traffic. This also allows a better appreciation of the fine buildings that have gradually accreted in this area.

In the middle distance, the street necks down to a typical narrow width that was doubtless adequate to the demands placed upon it until the advent of cars. This jog is quite large and has a great effect on the appearance of the street. Jogs can also be as narrow as a hand span.

This photograph of the ROYAL COURTS OF JUSTICE in London shows a nicely tapered street. Other photographs of the street make clear that two back-to-back tapers meet in the foreground here, where the street reaches its greatest width. The resulting open space functions as a square. The space is also a clear, and rather large, bead (see the start of this chapter). This arrangement obeys Alexander's "Path Shape" (APL, Pattern 121), which calls for occasional bulges in the shape of a path, creating small enclosures that become places in their own right.

A taper cannot, by itself, create full enclosure—a bend in the street, a gate, or a T-intersection are required for that. A taper does enhance the sense of enclosure even if it is incomplete. Best, of course, is the situation seen in London, where the taper further develops an already complete enclosure.

Fes-al-Bali in Morocco, the largest intact medieval quarter in the world, is also home to the world's largest contiguous carfree population, some 156,000. Metropolitan Fes is actually a much larger city that includes a new quarter from the French colonial period, with the characteristic broad, straight streets. The city has many important lessons for city designers. The TALAA SGHIRA is one of two main streets in Fes-al-Bali; the other runs roughly parallel to it, at varying distances. Both streets begin near Bab Boujeloud, one of the main gates, and run downhill to the center of the quarter. They carry very heavy traffic of both people and beasts of burden. Both streets pass through constrictions less than 3m (10') wide and are clearly too narrow for the heavy traffic they carry.

The streets of the quarter are never straight for more than a short distance, and they exhibit countless changes in width, as shown here. This makes walking through the city a fascinating experience, with constantly changing views. The streets, which are almost entirely free of mechanical noise, bustle most of the day. The comparatively low material standard of living is counterbalanced by the high quality of life.

Rua do Sobre-Ripas, Coimbra

SQUARES

Squares are, after streets, the most vital element in a city. If they function well, the rest of the city can stand significant imperfections. If its squares function poorly, or are absent entirely, a city can never attain greatness, however good the rest of it may be. In huge cities with few squares, such as New York, such squares as do exist are vital to the city. Imagine Manhattan without Rockefeller Center Plaza and its skating rink. Even the highly flawed Times Square, with its torrents of vehicular traffic, is one of that city's vibrant spaces. Consider, too, how much Manhattan would be improved by more and better squares.

Ferrara is an old city of modest size. Its PIAZZA MUNICIPIO is an excellent example of a city square. It lies a scant hundred paces from the Piazza Castello, and the even closer Piazza Cattedrale can just be glimpsed through the center arch. The Piazza Municipio is the civic square and has little commercial draw beyond the two small cafés. The photograph was taken from the middle of a bicycle and pedestrian thoroughfare just where it passes through the arcade at the west end of the square. This path connects the Via Garibaldi, a major commercial street, with the city center. Many people pass through this square, bringing it to life even on a cool and showery early autumn day. This square suffers slightly because there is no entrance into it from the north (left) side, which would link it directly to the Piazza Castello, increasing traffic in both squares.

After having been relegated to the status of "quaint" in many minds and to the function of "parking lot" in many cities, the square has made a comeback in Europe. Even in Italy, where car mania struck early and hard, cars have recently been removed from many once-grand squares, instantly restoring their vitality.

We begin our consideration of squares with a discussion of their uses, followed by an analysis of the various types of squares, and conclude with the details of their arrangement.

Piazza Municipio, Ferrara

Uses of Squares

The city square has a great many uses. It is nearly impossible to predict what use will be made of a given square in the distant future, but squares have retained their utility throughout history. We will consider the most important uses that are made of squares today, along with the design implications for each use.

I believe that the most important use of a square is its function as public living space for inhabitants and visitors alike. I do not believe that any foreseeable development of virtual reality will replace squares as important places where friends meet and new acquaintances are made, as occurs in the PIAZZA IV NOVEMBRE in Perugia. A square is the best location for people-watching, as long as enough people use it to bring it to life. Few squares are lively at all times of day. Market squares are often busiest in the morning, squares in commercial areas tend to be liveliest at lunch time, and squares in entertainment districts are usually most active in the evenings.

Interesting activities and convenient services help squares to come alive. Street performers should be welcomed in most larger squares, and there should be enough spots available that a performer can usually find one. Likewise, the sale of ice cream and "finger foods" should be encouraged, as long as there is no burden from, for instance, barbecue smoke (and even this is accepted in many cities in Africa and Asia).

A successful square must be a pleasant space of comfortable proportions and free from significant annoyances. Drawing a crowd in a square is really quite simple: do something, almost anything, to entice people to stay a while. The MAX EUWEPLEIN, a new square in Amsterdam, had been dead until the chess board was installed; now this is a lively square.

One question that arises is the degree to which the public should be encouraged to concentrate in a few squares, instead of spreading out in smaller squares scattered throughout the city. In

Europe since the end of the war, the population of city centers has fallen appreciably as smaller families seek larger quarters farther from the center. The result is that many squares have become less lively because they are being used by fewer people. There is thus reason to attract as many people as possible to the main downtown squares that are the lifeblood of a city. However, each city district needs a lively square that draws local residents. The challenge is to entice people to spend more time generally in squares, which helps the city to develop and maintain its identity and social cohesion.

The city square became a common site for cafés and restaurants after 1850, as more people had the leisure and money to enjoy this pastime. Even northern Europeans, once thought immune to the lure of Mediterranean street culture, enjoy these uses of squares and will sit out in cold but sunny weather.

Many large squares, such as PIAZZA SAN MARCO, include sidewalk cafés and sometimes also restaurants. There may, however, be reason to encourage restaurants to establish themselves instead in quiet neighborhood squares, in order to help bring them to life. The larger, more impersonal downtown squares can manage with only cafés at their margins. Neighborhood restaurants can be encouraged to locate on squares rather than streets. Squares are, of course, better commercial locations.

The principal requirement for outdoor eating and drinking is that it be comfortable to sit out during as much of the year as possible. In temperate climates, cafés should locate on the side of the square that receives as much sunlight as possible. In hot climates, trees or umbrellas can provide shade, and the space should be arranged to bring the prevailing breeze across the tables. In hot climates with strong afternoon storms, a wide arcade along one side of the square can have tables arranged within it, as in Arezzo's Piazza Grande (see page 295).

Tight regulation of noise and smell from restaurants is essential, to assure that other users and residents are not unreasonably

Not every city is affected by this problem. Venice, despite its population decline, from 200,000 at the end of the war to about 70,000 today, is still a vibrant city. Here, the 12 million tourists visiting each year more than make up for the smaller permanent population.

See especially the work of Jan Gehl and Lars Gemzøe in this regard.

E.g., Gramercy Park in Manhattan

burdened. Many conflicts over hours of operation arise because of noise; what is acceptable at 8 PM may become a burden by 11. Very local regulation is probably most responsive. In Amsterdam, the Greens have proposed the creation of the office of "night mayor" with authority to manage this issue on a largely ad hoc basis. Having lived in a restaurant district, I can attest that this is a significant issue.

Festivals, whether civic, cultural, or religious, define a city in important ways, as here in CAMPO SAN STEFANO during Venice's famous Carnival. Good festivals will draw a large crowd of tourists as well as locals. A few festivals, such as Amsterdam's Koninginnedag, are so large that the squares cannot begin to contain them, and they spill out into the city's streets. The population of Amsterdam more than doubles on this holiday, and the city essentially ceases its normal activities for a day.

Some cities have spaces that are called squares but more nearly resemble parks in both their arrangement and use. Some of these places are actually private property, fenced in and accessible only to a few people living nearby. They typically have large areas of grass and many trees. We will not consider them further.

The square reaches its zenith as a vital urban fixture in Venice. This city has very little open space except its squares. Most of the few small parks are removed from the centers of population, so outdoor life in Venice occurs mostly in its many squares. Venice was organized by church parish, with each parish having its own church on that parish's main square, an arrangement typified by the CAMPO SANTA MARIA FORMOSA, just east of Piazza San Marco. These squares were developed as water catchments over a layer of sand to hold the water and a well to draw it up. Religion no longer plays so central a role in the organization of human affairs in Venice, but the pattern persists and still works.

People identify themselves as residents of a particular parish, and those living in that parish know most other residents. They know who is likely to be troublesome and how to handle them.

This was memorably demonstrated for me one summer evening when I wandered into the CAMPO DEI SS. APOSTOLI and stopped to watch the play of life in this busy, small square. I was soon approached by an obviously tipsy gentleman of some years who began to describe for me the beauties of the square in mellifluous Italian, a language I do not speak. He was obviously harmless and I let him go on, having once made it clear that I did not understand him. We were soon joined by an elderly woman who gave me a wink as if to say, "Don't mind him." She stood by as he carried on for quite some time, although he made it clear that he resented her intrusion. These two people obviously knew what to expect of each other. While I had no need of any protection from him, I was touched by the concern that this woman showed for the welfare of a visitor to her neighborhood. *This* is how a tight-knit neighborhood takes care of people. No police were called, no unpleasant or violent action was threatened by anyone, and a minor problem was dealt with in a very humane way. I had that very day arrived from a conference in which this mode of social functioning in Venetian neighborhoods had been described. I was thoroughly convinced!

In designing cities, we must strive for neighborhoods that serve people's needs as well as do those of Venice. The square is a nearly essential part of any urban neighborhood that functions in this way, and it works in part because virtually everyone in the neighborhood passes through it during the day. People stand around in small groups chatting, thereby nourishing the social bonds that make their neighborhood a place to belong.

LARGE SQUARES

We first take up large squares, although some of them are not large when compared to giants like Moscow's Red Square or Beijing's Tiananmen Square, squares which may seem nearly empty except when huge crowds gather on national holidays.

Coimbra, Portugal

Plaza Mayor, Madrid

However, the squares we consider in this section are large in comparison to other squares in their cities. (In some of the cities illustrated here, the more modern quarters have squares that are considerably larger than those shown. These huge squares are usually less lively than the smaller, more central squares.)

No government should be so fearful of its own people that it will not permit large numbers of them to gather in protest. Any government whose actions are so vile or incompetent as to occasion large and unruly demonstrations might be due for replacement. (There is, presumably, no reason to fear an orderly demonstration.) I had expected that Beijing's enormous Tiananmen Square, site of a prolonged 1989 pro-democracy demonstration that ended in bloodshed, would be broken up to prevent a recurrence, but this did not occur. Although such demonstrations are a large inconvenience and embarrassment for the government, they are also a safety valve for a frustrated people and much safer than the underground plotting that can lead to civil war. China's leaders have been wise to accept this.

A square can host a protest if it is large enough to hold a large fraction of a city's population, even if in packed conditions. I noticed during the PEACEFUL PROTESTS prior to the 2003 US invasion of Iraq that Lisbon lacked a single square large enough to accommodate the huge demonstrations, so the organizers spread the events over two large squares. It is probably sufficient to arrange for one square large enough to accommodate half the city's population in crush conditions, although capital cities may need an even larger square.

The large PIAZZA DEL CAMPO in Siena is that city's principal square. I was standing just in front of the Palazzo Pubblico at the foot of the square when I took this photograph. This square is a large bowl that slopes down to an enormous storm drain just visible at the edge of the gray paving stones. The extraordinary Gaia fountain stands in the distance. Notice that the buildings are unusually tall for the medieval period.

The Piazza del Campo is the venue for the fabulous Palio horse race, the premier cultural event in Siena, an extravaganza that binds the city together while at the same time expressing the rivalry among its 17 *contrade* (districts). The evening before the race, each neighborhood dines in its own streets.

The design of Valladolid's nearly symmetrical PLAZA MAYOR was governed by Renaissance thinking, but the square was fitted into an existing mosaic of irregular streets. The square and the entering streets would likely have been rigidly symmetrical had the square been laid out on an empty site. I visited during warm weather and found the square much too large for the number of people using it; perhaps it is busier at other times.

The PIAZZA CASTELLO in Turin is another very formal square. Everything has been drawn at right angles, and a rigid symmetry has been maintained. The perfect balance verges on static. The people using the square are the one element not in perfect symmetry, and they, of course, bring the place to life.

Notice the long vista down the street, and observe that the space is eventually enclosed by a distant building that terminates this street. We have complete enclosure, although the scale is so large that the square has a very airy feel.

The PIAZZA SAN PIETRO in Rome stands in front of what is known to English speakers as St. Peter's Basilica. The Piazza is one of the most important sectarian public spaces in the world. It is much larger than this view shows, and exhibits a rigid, formal symmetry, although it is not rectilinear. When the Pope speaks, this space is often entirely filled with people.

The gorgeous PIAZZA SAN CARLO in Turin is today used as a parking lot. Rigid formality is expressed by strong symmetry, in particular the two nearly matching churches in the center of the view. Notice the paths that the trams follow. This would only have been so arranged for aesthetic reasons; the curves are an operational inconvenience that slow the trams, which would ideally have been kept entirely out of the square.

LISBOA – Praça D. Pedro IV (Rocio)

The PRAÇA DOM PEDRO IV in Lisbon is one of the largest squares in Lisbon. The arrangement of the square is symmetrical and formal. It is a rather thin rectangle, but the proportions are satisfactory. People will argue endlessly about the trees. In principle, I am opposed to them, and this view shows why: you can't see the city for the trees. (As shown in the view below, the trees have recently been replanted. They are now quite small and no longer dominant.) However, I must concede that in hot, sunny climates like Lisbon, there are sound practical reasons to plant shade trees in public areas where there is room for them.

This CONTEMPORARY VIEW of the square shows the fountain in greater detail. It is an addition that practically no one will quarrel with. Besides offering kids somewhere to play, it cools the air on hot afternoons, if only locally. The paving is laid in the black and white stone so widely used in Portugal. Although this square is now blanketed by traffic noise from all four sides, it remains an imposing space.

I think that Venice's PIAZZA SAN MARCO (seen here and below) is the greatest public space in the world. It is less formal than the other examples of large squares. The buildings on the left and right have a strong family resemblance, but closer inspection reveals differences. The cathedral stands at an angle to the main axis of the square. The square is tapered; here, the photographer is standing at the narrow end. I find this complex, non-Cartesian geometry more satisfactory than that of more highly ordered spaces. This is not a space that we understand at once. There is a subtlety to it that only becomes apparent on longer acquaintance. If we are to live with such squares for a lifetime, is it not better that they engage our senses, instead of offering a dull and predictable order that can be absorbed in one sitting?

The PIAZZA SAN MARCO is technically two spaces. The Piazza joins, on the far side of the Campanile, with the Piazzetta (here just visible in the distance) to form an L-shaped square, with the campanile at the corner (see the plan on page 328).

SMALL SQUARES

The large squares shown in the previous section are beautiful and impressive, as they were meant to be. We now consider smaller squares that are less grand but which should be more intimate and important to the neighborhood. These squares are also excellent locations for small businesses serving local needs.

Overly large squares are almost never lively, as in the case of HET ROND in the Dutch new town of Houten. I first visited it in 1987, when it was a very quiet place even though much of the town had already been built. Ten years later it was still very quiet; the square is too big nearly all the time. On market days, however, it is briefly filled by stands, so there is a sound reason for its great size. Most of the time, though, it is a dead space.

Squares can be too small, as in the case of Amsterdam's Leidseplein (see page 323). This is a lively square most evenings, and during festivals you can't even get into it. The larger Dam Square is not so often crowded to overflowing. Great effort should be made to gauge the level of traffic that a square will see.

The PLACE DE VAUDEMONT in Nancy is a nearly perfect small square. The buildings are of an excellent scale, and the treatment of the storefronts is very fine. The arch in the center and the wall that together enclose the space are of an exceptionally high standard. The arch serves only to complete the enclosure. Notice the statue on the high plinth. There is almost nothing we might wish to add, except possibly some benches.

This square in Urbino, the PIAZZA DELLA REPUBBLICA, has quite a different feel from the previous two. It is smaller and the buildings are taller, so the sense of enclosure is even more strongly developed. Notice that the street on the left tapers down as it leaves the square. Since a taper is generally an interesting addition to a street, the question arises: should a street become narrower or wider as it approaches a square? I think the answer is that it should become wider. The square is thereby

gradually revealed, and the activity of the square bleeds into the street, which then has room to accommodate the higher level of activity. Such an arrangement also contributes to the development of enclosure, as it reduces the deep concavity that is created by a street. This problem can also be resolved by placing arches over the entrances to the square, as in Nancy, above.

Tiny squares can delight if the scale is correspondingly small, as here in front of the beautiful SANTA MARIA DEI MIRACOLI in Venice. The narrow footbridge, the minor canal at the back of the square, the church, and the four-story residential buildings are at an appropriately small scale. This is an intimate area with strong enclosure. In most cities, this square would *constrict* the street, not widen it.

The plan of the GRANDE PLACE in Echternach may at first appear somewhat haphazard, but notice that the arrangement draws attention to the church, which, while not a spectacular building, is pleasing. The buildings on the left conflict with each other. Two of them have their ground floors elevated considerably above the square. The twin staircase on the darker building really belongs on a larger building. The basement entrance poses a danger to pedestrians, who may blunder into the pit in the dark. This arrangement should be avoided.

There is no good reason that the building blighted by the ugly sign on the roof should have had its first floor so much elevated. The building to its right is clearly of some importance (it may even be the city hall). Its arcade is elevated just a few steps above the square and so is lower than the porch of the minor building to its left. This is truly artless.

LE POUHON in Spa is a much happier square. The scale is quite small, and the buildings are excellent and of highly agreeable proportions. The octagonal building with the cupola houses one of the sources of spring water for which the town is famous. The view down the street in the center is enticing, in part because the distant arcade draws the eye.

Notice the odd addition to the left side of the building on the right side of the street. This completes the line of the buildings on that street, so there is nothing really wrong with it, but I suspect that originally the street widened out at that point, which would have helped to enunciate the form of the square.

The SEBASTIANPLATZ in Brig is one of the bigger "small" squares; there is a good deal more of it behind the photographer. It is a lovely bit of city design, and good buildings have been built around it, with the pretty church as a focal point. The fountain is important and strategically placed.

LES HALLES in Lisieux is reasonable in most respects, but it still fails despite good proportions and pleasant scale. The long entering street on the left is tolerable because of the slight jog in the distance. However, the building in the center is dreadful. The triple circular arch is static and the huge parapet serves no apparent purpose. The U-shaped dormer on the left is hideous and does not balance with the reasonable dormer on the right. The hodgepodge of posters doesn't help at all. The sign advertising something for 75 centimes takes us forward a century, to the time when such ugly signs would become so commonplace as no longer to excite notice. All of these errors could be fixed inexpensively.

The classic small square in front of the CHIESA DI SAN PIETRO graces the city of Genoa. It is full of life and no larger than it needs to be. It is obviously a highly successful social space. The surrounding buildings are taller than the square is wide, and they may even be taller than it is long. (The elevated position of the photographer suggests that the square is only as deep as we see.)

The street leading into the square is very narrow. This is probably one of the densest parts of a city that is sandwiched between steep hills and the Ligurian Sea. Space was at a premium here, but the city does not suffer from the necessarily economical use of buildable land. Quite the contrary, in fact—scarcity of land compels the designer to make the best possible use of it.

The PIAZZA VITTORIO EMANUELE in Assisi has an irregular shape that is roughly triangular. However, the side that appears in the center of the photograph is not straight but slightly convex, which usually tends to diminish the sense of enclosure. In this case, however, the degree of curvature is so slight that I don't think it harms the square. This was a difficult site for a square, and a good job has been done under the circumstances.

The classical building in the Greek style is a break with the other buildings, but I do not believe that this harms the space. It is instructive to observe which "mistakes" are acceptable, and which are not.

The ROODE STEEN is the central square of Hoorn, a pleasant Dutch town north of Amsterdam. Six streets come together here. Although this is in many respects a fine square, it suffers from one defect: there is a crown in the surface, which peaks near the large statue. This prevents us from seeing the bases of the houses on the far side of the square, and disembodies pedestrians walking there, as we cannot see their feet. The curvature is slight but sufficient to damage the square. The cause was prosaic: this area began as an intersection of two dikes. When the square was created later, it stood above the surroundings.

MARKET SQUARES

The market square is historically the most important of a city's squares, as the market was once the center of a city's commerce and may have had regional importance. Few European cities lack a central market square, although they are rare in the USA.

The importance of markets to a city's social relations is widely recognized and can be seen in the RIALTO MARKET in Venice. In quite a few cities, market vendors are given some advantage over stores in order to sustain and encourage markets. Although the rise of "big-box" stores on the periphery of many cities has harmed central markets, most have survived.

The market square provides economical commercial space, as these places are neither enclosed nor heated. (Some cities with inhospitable climates have built indoor markets, but, in my experience, they are never heated. In southern regions, markets may be roofed but not otherwise enclosed.) This market square near the CAMPO SAN LEONARDO in Venice typifies neighborhood markets: it is fairly small and serves a limited area. Stall holders and shoppers usually know each other, and the social function is important, especially in close-knit Venice.

Cities often levy a charge on stalls, which do entail some expense to the city, especially street cleaning. However, charges may be waived if the city supports its markets for social and economic reasons. Some conflict exists between the interests of shopkeepers, who pay for their stores, and stall holders, who pay little or nothing, but there is a mutually beneficial synergy at work unless the stall holders compete directly with the stores.

The VIEUX MARCHÉ in Louvain is a typical central market, larger than most. It is unusual only in that the shape is quite elongated and that the buildings average about one story lower than is usual for central market squares.

The MARKET SQUARE in Kiel is of a more typical shape than the Vieux Marché—most are roughly square. Amsterdam's Albert Cuypmarkt is an important exception; it is not a square at all but a long street. This has the advantage that, by virtue of its length, some part of the market lies within easy reach of more city residents, which draws a larger public. Still, a square is more attractive and concentrates everything within a few steps.

The fine HAUPTMARKT in Trier is surrounded by excellent buildings. Although the church is slightly removed from the square, it towers above and is thus present in it. It is not unusual for important civic, commercial, and ecclesiastical buildings to be located on a market square. This lends an urbane quality to the square. Larger cities often prefer to separate these functions, giving each a square of its own. The variation in the scale of

these buildings is right at the limit of what works well. If it were any greater, the scene would start to fall apart.

The MARKET SQUARE of Meissen is a minor failure. The church presents its back to the square. (The front has a square of its own.) Its tower is blocky and unattractive, needs more openings or ornamentation, and looks too large for the church.

Notice the sinister eyebrow windows in the roof of the building on the right, which is a generally poor building. The doubled windows look bad and are not defined by exterior frames. Although this building is a century or more old, it already has elements of the feckless Modern.

The PLACE DE LA MAIRIE in Auray pulls the eye towards a single prominent building. Notice that arms of the square extend into the distance on either side of that building. A tower juts up over the space on the right. I detect the presence of a square opening out from the right of the right-hand arm. Such a conjunction of squares is common, as noted by Camillo Sitte, and constellations of three and even four squares exist.

The gargantuan GROTE MARKT in Bruges serves a medium-sized city and was probably always too large. Overly large squares are a permanent cash drain for a city, even one as rich as Bruges once was. The size of this square probably owes to a misguided attempt to impress.

The tower in the center does not suffer from such severe giantism as it at first appears to; wide-angle lenses with rectilinear perspective exaggerate the size of the elements near the edge of the frame. Still, this is a truly mammoth tower, and the top section really lacks any artistry. The tower is all out of proportion to the building beneath.

Specialized markets also exist, such as the BOOK MARKET on the Spui in Amsterdam. Some of these markets attain regional importance, and all of them help make the city more lively. The Spui is one of the oldest parts of Amsterdam, and this is an interesting and friendly market, fitted into a rather small square.

SQUARES AS INTERSECTIONS

Almost any intersection takes on some of the qualities of a square. There is more space and light. The foot traffic is greater than on either street alone. If some extra space is added to an intersection, it can become a true square, but it only achieves this status if its circulatory functions are subsidiary to other uses. The important point, of course, is to assure that there are calm areas, and that these are large enough to draw some people and comfortable enough to linger in.

A square's function as circulation realm must not come at the cost of the comfort of those using the square. Not only cars but also buses, trams, and trucks are best kept out. If this point is not observed, a situation arises like that in the CALLE DE CORCEGA in Barcelona. Although only a few cars and buses are to be seen, vehicles monopolize this square. Pedestrians have been awarded a few islands on which to cower while waiting for a chance to dart across the traffic, but this square is nearly dead. The space requirements of vehicles are so great that the square must also be made far too large.

Sometimes it is necessary to allow trams to cross squares, but this always brings noise and danger. Often, in Amsterdam's busy LEIDSEPLEIN, the acts of street performers are drowned out by trams screeching around the tight curves in the square. Ideally, trams should stop near, not in, a square, and the tracks should pass close by, not through them. This, however, is not always possible. The intrusion of trams is counterbalanced by the number of people passing through the square on their way to and from the tram. I have observed that the ebb and flow of people in the Leidseplein is regulated by the arrival and departure of trams, and I would be surprised if this condition were not nearly universal in busy squares served by trams.

The PUERTA DEL SOL in Vigo is the intersection of two major streets that meet at a shallow angle, which has resulted in a large

This is traditional German architecture at its best. The buildings are highly varied but do not clash, and they have large windows, appreciated in the gray northern climate. The wooden construction is a fire hazard.

open area that might be a square if there were some provision for people to linger. As it is, it's mostly given over to tram tracks and vehicles. I think that when wide streets intersect, the angle should be steeper than this; otherwise the intersection becomes very large yet still does not become a square; with narrow streets, the effect is more satisfactory. The incoherent building at the point of the wedge is in an excellent location for a store.

The relative width of the streets entering a square is significant to its definition and function. When a square is no larger than its broad incoming streets, we are seeing an intersection. It may look like a square but does not function as such. In other cases, there may be a fair amount of vehicular traffic arriving on narrow streets; in these cases, the intersection may still serve as a real square, despite its function as an intersection.

When narrow streets enter a complex intersection, extra space is usually provided, as at the LUTHERHAUS in Frankfurt. The resultant square is quite small, but the somewhat more open space contrasts nicely with the narrow streets just beyond. People congregate here, if only because there is more sun.

Intersections are always the choke point for street traffic, of whatever kind, including pedestrians. Friction arises at intersections: people and vehicles rubbing against or otherwise impeding one another. When it is people, not vehicles, this friction results in social contacts of a fleeting nature. Millions of such contacts occur at intersections in big cities every day, helping to glue that city's society together.

The GOLDHUTGASSE in Frankfurt is a small-scale intersection at an angle as shallow as the one in Vigo, but here it works out nicely, because the streets are very narrow, which permits the square to be held to a comfortable, intimate size. The photographer appears to have placed himself in the outlet of another street leading into the intersection. There seems to be another street, behind the fountain, that leads off at a shallow angle. Notice the toddler. In the absence of cars, there is no reason that little children should not stand in the middle of the street and absorb the world around.

The PLACE DU MARCHÉ AU BLÉ in Loches is a small, irregular square. Notice that the jog on the left opens this area up by a small but critical amount. Other views show two streets coming in from behind, at the other end of the square, which is perhaps four times larger than what we see here. Behind the camera, the square continues to swell for a few tens of meters (yards) and then one side curves in. This is doubtless an important intersection in the town, but it serves as a functioning square.

The CASA DEGLI ALIGHIERI in Florence is a wonderful urban scene. The photographer used a wide-angle lens to show us two streets leading away from this small square. His back was probably against another building, so we see most of this intersection and its diminutive square. The street on the left follows a beautiful, sinuous course. Notice the luscious flood of light from a small square or street on the left.

Virtually all squares have at least four streets leading away from them, some many more. The more streets that are brought into a square, the higher the level of foot traffic that can be expected. Those few squares with just two or three entering streets nearly all suffer from insufficient foot traffic to make them come alive. This consideration was neglected in the CAMPO SAN ZACCARIA in Venice, which has only two entering streets and little foot traffic. (The two streets do not form part of a good through route.) Whenever I have visited this square it has been as dead as it appears here.

The HAUZEUR MONUMENT in Verviers (Belgium) is sited at a pleasant intersection that forms a minor square. It is evident from the number of people standing in the street that it is still used as a social space and that traffic takes second place.

Notice how the streets first diverge leaving the square, only to converge again in the distance, creating a fine sense of enclosure. This arrangement tends to develop by itself if allowed, as it is

natural for streets to converge on a square. At a certain distance from the square, the blocks between the streets become too wide unless the streets branch or bend back towards each other.

One favored arrangement for streets entering squares is called by some a "turbine," one "jet" of which is shown here, where the VIA CALZAIOLI enters a square in Florence. Streets are supposed to enter at the corners and "inject" foot traffic into a flow around the square. This is thought to make the square more lively. I cannot attest to its effectiveness.

It is evident from the amount of wheeled traffic on the street that the square serves as an important circulation space. Notice, however, that no curbs have been installed. This can play out in either of two ways: pedestrians feel that the whole space is theirs, and vehicles must avoid them, or the drivers feel that the whole space is *theirs* and the pedestrians had better watch out.

OTHER TYPES OF SQUARES

The classification of squares might be expanded to include the religious square, with its imposing church; the civic square, with its city hall; and finally the commercial square, with its many stores. In Venice, two or three of these functions are present on most squares. St. Mark's Cathedral and the Doge's Palace sit cheek by jowl in Piazza San Marco. The Venetian *campo* almost always includes a church, and most are also minor commercial centers. The tiny *campiello* found in Venice is more an over-grown intersection than a real square, but even these are favored locations because of the heavy foot traffic and chance meetings.

The large and wonderful PIAZZA DEL CAMPO in Siena is primarily a civic square, home to the ancient Palazzo Pubblico and Torre del Mangia, the tallest campanile in the city. Many restaurants are located around the perimeter. Siena also has its Piazza del Duomo and Piazza del Mercato, the religious and market squares respectively.

ARRANGEMENT OF SQUARES

A number of points must be addressed early in the design of any square. Although some errors can be corrected after the fact, others become a nearly permanent constraint. It is thus worth taking the time to get these matters right at the start. It is not so difficult to reduce the size of a square, but it is nearly impossible to enlarge one. The irony is that the easiest way to kill a square is to make it too big. We must first determine the size of the population the square will serve. A successful square will on occasion draw almost all of this population at once, possibly supplemented by people from other areas. Taking the example of the Reference District (population 12,000, see page 128), there are two principal squares, one on either side of the central boulevard. I intended that the right side of the district would contain its principal center, so its main square should accommodate 12,000 people. Minimum standing room in crowds is 0.65 m² (7 ft²) per person. We thus obtain a space requirement of just under 8000 m² (84,000 ft²) to accommodate the district's population. This is approximately the size of the square as drawn. The square would, of course, rarely see this many people and could tolerate some packing at that time. At other times there will be far fewer people, but hundreds would use it in the evening of any pleasant day.

Alexander addressed this issue in "Pedestrian Density," where he establishes 500 ft² (46 m²) per person as the upper limit for a square that does not feel dead. It would thus require about 170 people for this square to come alive. This is a high number, and clearly the space will be dead quite a lot of the time. During the day, however, there should be enough people to bring the square to life, particularly if sidewalk cafés are established.

In "Small Public Squares" (APL, Pattern 61), Alexander calls for a limit of 70' (21m) in the short dimension of the square, with a caveat that major squares, such as Piazza San Marco, can

Piazza B. Galuppi, Burano

The main square on the left side chiefly serves that half of the district. It is not intended to host large gatherings and so is much smaller than the main square on the right side, to which the calculations apply.

Lynch & Hack, 461. They say that a "packed crowd" occupies half this much space.

APL, Pattern 123

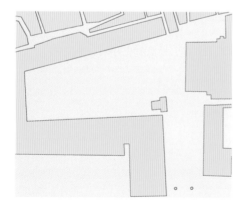

The Piazza San Marco is the large open space in the upper half of the drawing. The cathedral is to the right. The Piazzetta joins the Piazza at the Campanile and runs down to the two columns at the bottom.

greatly exceed this limit. By this criterion, the square we have been discussing is three times too large, being about 70 *meters* (yards) in the short dimension. If experience should show that it is too big, its area can be reduced (see page 331).

Besides the large squares, the Reference District contains about 60 local squares, each serving 100 to 300 people. This is perhaps too many squares, although they range in size from only 9×15m (30'×50') to 15×25m (50'×80'), a size similar to the PIAZZA DEL CONTE in Siena.

This square off the RUE DU BAIN AUX PLANTES in Strasbourg is slightly larger than the smallest of the squares I proposed in the Reference District and, like them, is very little larger than the entering streets. The extra space beyond what is required for circulation ranges from approximately 100 m^2 (1075 ft^2) to 300 m^2 (3200 ft^2). Most of these squares would see enough usage to come alive during large parts of the day, especially if benches or tables were set out to encourage people to linger.

By their nature, squares tend to be concave spaces, but a convex angle can be built into a square. This is the case with some fine squares, including PIAZZA SAN MARCO, which is convex where the Piazza runs into the Piazzetta. The campanile, sited at this junction, helps to maintain the concave shape of both, so that the sense of enclosure is further strengthened in the Piazza and not weakened in the Piazzetta. At the same time, interest is added because there are two separate spaces that work together. Camillo Sitte discusses constellations of squares, most of which were created by the siting of a cathedral to show it off to good advantage, flanked by small squares. The shapes of these spaces are complex, although the individual squares are not themselves unduly intricate. Sitte gives examples in "Plaza Groupings" and "Public Squares in the North of Europe." In some of his examples, the cathedral stands isolated and forms squares on all its sides. Sometimes, the cathedral is so close to other buildings that the space is a street, not a square at all. In other cases, the church is built right into the fabric of the area, but enough space was left around parts of it to produce one or more squares.

Both the perimeter and the ground surface of a square should be concave. Although one or two violations of this rule in the horizontal plane may be tolerable, the vertical plane must be flat (and preferably level) or slightly concave. Squares do not serve well for sidewalk cafés unless the surface is quite close to horizontal, and other functions are impaired by sloping surfaces, including the establishment of market stalls.

See also Unwin, 208, where he gives two informative illustrations, and his pp. 215-220, which illustrates and discusses the central square of Buttstedt, Germany.

In *Urban Space,* Rob Krier exhaustively rubricized the possible shapes of squares and the ways in which streets can be brought into them. Anyone laying out a square should have a copy of his book. His analysis is a useful source of ideas.

R. Krier (1979), 23-60

Overly formal squares don't work very well. Their precise geometry tends to foreclose the uses (such as cafés) that draw people, a problem that afflicts the PRAÇA DO COMÉRCIO in Lisbon. This very formal square, surrounded on two other sides by buildings similar to the one seen here, sees thousands of people passing through, but few people lingering. The Amalienborg Palace square in Copenhagen is another example. It is beautiful in a very formal way, but people rarely stay.

The proportions of a square are also important, even assuming that the square is not perfectly regular. Unwin suggests that the length should not be greater than three times the width, which seems approximately correct to me. Except in the most formal cases, they should not too closely approach a perfect square.

Unwin, 208

The actual arrangement of the edges of a square is also important. Rough edges, such as provided by an arcade, provide the small spaces that seem to enhance the social functions of a square. Salingaros says:

> In urbanism, an undulating urban boundary facilitates human interactions, as for example the edge of a piazza lined with shops and coffee tables. Urban spaces that are

Nikos A. Salingaros, "Connecting the Fractal City," (Barcelona, April 2003), Technical appendix 1, p23: applied.math.utsa.edu/~salingar/connecting.html He cites his own earlier "Urban Space and its Information Field," *Journal of Urban Design* 4:29-49 (1999).

Salamanca

actually used are almost invariably enclosed by a fractal boundary. Removing the fractal structure by making the edge smooth removes the catalytic geometry for pedestrian interaction, and kills the urban space.

I would add to this that the rough edges must never be separated from the main body of the square by a roadway, even one that carries little or no motorized traffic. That is one of the defects of the square in Lisbon shown just above.

Consideration should be given to which buildings are built on the perimeter of squares, and particularly to the nature of their occupancies. Buildings that generate a lot of foot traffic are greatly to be preferred. In practice, this means that office buildings are the least desirable, since they generate comparatively few arrivals and departures for a given floor area. Restaurants, cafés, hotels, churches, theaters, and cinemas are excellent. There is nothing wrong with residences fronting on a square, so long as the building is of reasonable quality, although if a square tends to generate much noise, most people will not see it as a desirable location. However, some people like very active areas and may seek the location. Permission should never be given to build a bad building on a square; this can ruin the best of squares. Even Venice has fallen victim to this in the CAMPO MANIN.

The reasons for considering climate when arranging a square were mentioned on page 311. We will consider here the actual arrangement of a square to make best use of the sun. In any given place, the sun sets in approximately the same position between May 21st and July 21st and in another position between November 21st and January 21st. During the rest of the year, the azimuth of the sun at setting changes so rapidly that it is impractical to design for it. However, we can arrange a square so that, for the month either side of the solstice, the sun strikes into it along a street aligned to the setting sun. In latitudes more than 45 degrees from the equator, it is difficult to arrange for the wintertime noon sun to fall into a small square, but it is possible to arrange for a street to enter the square along the azimuth of the noon sun. Lower buildings on the equatorial side of a square help to warm it, if only by the additional light reflected off buildings on the opposite side.

In some places, the winter wind normally blows from a particular quarter, and it is worth attempting to shield a square from its icy blasts by ensuring that no street enters the square from this direction. If a street must enter from this direction (often the case), then a sharp bend introduced into the street close to the square will considerably reduce the wind.

In the tropics, the need is to protect people from the sun. The sun passes directly overhead at some time of the year, so it will be impossible to keep the sun out of a square even by the expedient of placing tall buildings around it. In these regions, we will need to provide shade trees and arrange the entering streets to convey the prevailing breeze through the square. Remember that social life in these climates occurs mainly in the cool of the evening, so pay special attention to street lighting (see page 196).

A square can only exist if its dimensions exceed the widths of the entering streets; otherwise it is simply an intersection. If we are striving to keep the squares small, then the streets must be narrow. This can be introduced artificially, by narrowing the streets as they approach a square, but this is awkward, and the natural change is actually to widen them slightly. In carfree cities, only the central arteries carrying public transport systems need be wider than 15m (50'). Most streets can be much narrower. Streets in the range of 3-8m (10-26') permit the clear definition of small squares.

A square will sometimes prove to be too large. The simplest remedy is to put a new civic building into the square. However, only top-quality buildings should be constructed in these circumstances, and their design should be governed by the requirement of improving the square.

Salamanca

Ayamonte, Spain

This may not apply to the largest cities.

It is also possible to add semi-permanent uses to a square that is, at least for the time being, too large. A MERRY-GO-ROUND, kiosk, or a restaurant pavilion can reduce the apparent size of a square. Take care that the space can be reclaimed at little or no cost to the city should it later be required.

The furnishing of public spaces greatly affects their use. A square that is otherwise satisfactory may be little used because of poor furnishings. Even Venice can be criticized on this point. The public spaces of Zermatt, Switzerland, have especially fine STREET FURNITURE, with good benches, signage, trash cans, and extravagant fountains. William H. Whyte cautions that street furniture should not be permanently fixed but easily rearranged by users. This caveat applies especially to seating, which people like to adjust to suit themselves (Whyte 1988, 119).

Not every seat must be a bench. People will sit on anything flat and the right height. Stone and metal are awfully cold in winter, but someone desperate for a brief rest will tolerate even this. No furniture installed in the public realm should be designed to make sitting unpleasant or impossible. Railings with sharp points should be prohibited as dangerous, if for no other reason.

See that the squares you design are as comfortable and inviting as your own living room, for they are to become everyone's living room.

GATES

Gates serve a number of functions, which have changed over time. Gates and walls once kept invaders at bay, with taxation as an important secondary purpose. When the Turks used cannons to blast their way into Constantinople in 1453, the nature of warfare changed, and the defensive value of city walls and their gates declined. Most walls were eventually torn down, but gates were often preserved even after their usefulness had ceased. However, FES-AL-BALI in Morocco preserved both the walls and the gates. When city-states were amalgamated into nation-states, taxation of goods entering a city largely ceased, and a further reason for maintaining city walls and gates disappeared.

We seldom build city gates today for any reason, but I believe that we should consider a return to their use. The functions served by gates include: the definition of an entrance, the separation of two districts, the enclosure of a space, and the framing of a view. Many gates serve several purposes at once.

One abuse of gates is commonly seen today. Some form of gate is built at the entrances to "gated communities." These gates are usually just security check-points; the structures themselves are often utilitarian and even ugly. Their purpose is not to define a neighborhood but to exclude people from it.

GATES AS A DIVISION & ENTRANCE

Gates can mark the entrance to neighborhoods and their larger cousins, districts. The need to differentiate between different subcultures and neighborhoods is taken up at some length in URBAN VILLAGES (see page 222), but, to summarize, communities need clearly defined boundaries in order to thrive. Few civic installations provide such clarity of definition as the gate; we know instinctively that we have changed realms when we pass through a gate. Even a minor arch can serve as an entrance.

Fes-al-Bali, Morocco

The ARCO DE SANTA MARIA in Burgos is a truly commanding prospect. Unlike the gate in Nancy (see page 335), it appears to have served a defensive role in the past. It does resemble the Nancy gate in one important respect: it is lavishly ornamented. The city walls in Burgos were demolished at some point, but the buildings that replaced the wall continue to provide a clear demarcation between the areas inside and outside the city's original borders. This pattern can also be seen in the Muurhuizen in Amersfoort, the Netherlands (page 287).

MARBLE ARCH in London is one of the entrances to Hyde Park. It was built from a design based on the triumphal arch of Constantine in Rome and constructed of fine Carrara marble. It, too, is decorated with sculptures of the highest quality. The arch is nicely complemented by the park entrance itself. The detailed columns are topped by large lanterns, and wrought iron was tastefully used for the gates and fences. Imagine this fence if made from poured concrete, galvanized steel posts, and chain link fencing. That's how we would probably build it today.

Many universities have gates, at least at the main entrance. Universities are special settings where different rules and standards of behavior apply, and there is merit in announcing the change through the formality of a gate. The SATHER GATE at the University of California in Berkeley is one such gate, and the division it marks became much more than symbolic during the free-speech movement. In 1964, student activists involved in the civil rights movement came into conflict with university officials regarding their right to use University land and facilities for their campaigns.

In FES-AL-BALI, the boundary between two neighborhoods is always marked by some form of gate, such as the two seen here. Some of these gates are no more than a large wooden beam across the street at a height of several meters (10-15'), but most of them take some form of arch. This obeys Alexander's "Neighborhood Boundary" (APL, Pattern 15).

The GEVANGENPOORT in The Hague was once a city entrance, but as the city grew, its boundaries no longer coincided with the location of the gate. The gate is formidable: it is no light, airy structure. It is only high enough to pass a loaded wagon, and little wider. It has appreciable depth, and so creates a dark and slightly forbidding area that does not invite one to pass through. It also creates a pronounced transition and separation, more than is really required by its modern functions. Notice how the street funnels into the gate, a common arrangement.

GATES AS DESIGN ELEMENTS

We consider briefly the use of gates to close off a view, or, alternatively, to frame a distant view. In the first case, a gate helps build a sense of enclosure, as here with the PORTE STANISLAS in Nancy. Notice that it is entirely ceremonial: it has no doors and so its three portals cannot be closed. This became common in the era after city walls. This gate serves only to define a space and complete its enclosure. This same gate fills a different role when seen from the opposite side.

Gates can also be used to frame a view or a building. This is often done in an artful fashion, with both the location and the form of the gate contributing to the view that it frames. In this view of the PORTE STANISLAS from the opposite side, the gate serves more to frame a view than to create a sense of enclosure (although it also does this). Its function as a frame has been assisted in this case by the photographer's choice of location, which places the distant spire right under the apex of the arch. We often see this in photographs without being aware of it: good spaces have "perfect" vantage points, which photographers seek out intuitively. Good urban design includes making sure that such places are there to be found, for it is by these views that a city becomes known to the rest of the world. Towers and church steeples are especially important in this regard.

It is instructive to compare BAB BOUJELOUD in Fes-al-Bali with Nancy's Porte Stanislas. The two gates are similar in their arrangement, both having a large central arch to pass vehicles and low, narrow arches on either side for pedestrians. I admit to a preference for the Moorish arch, which is more alive than the round arches in Nancy. This gate is decorated with intricate and colorful mosaics, instead of the carving added at Nancy. We see a prominent minaret framed in the gate. In contrast to most modern gates, this one is still furnished with doors that appear to be operational.

As with most things, gates can be over-done, as here in Budens, Portugal, where FOUR SEPARATE GATES can be seen in the space of 50m (yards). The first has twin elliptical arches, the second and third have round arches, and the most distant has a straight lintel with an arched parapet. None of these gates is nicely detailed. True, the first pair of arches has physical relief that is traced by the (rather ugly) pink paint, which gives them some definition. The second and third are really very plain, right down to the square-edged columns that support them. Some effort was made with the fourth, which has raised edging like the first. One or two good gates would have been better than the four impoverished gates that were actually built.

These two gates in Madrid's PLAZA DE LA VILLA form an interesting contrast. This is the seat of government for Madrid, so it is an important locale. The gate on the left provides entry to the inner sanctum. It not only can still be closed, it is actually guarded around the clock and apparently closed at night. It sports twin columns and an intricately carved pediment above a plain straight lintel. The gate on the right is actually formed by an overhead passageway that is carried across the street by a beautiful elliptical arch that has good detailing, including the supporting brackets. The space is perhaps not as coherent as it might be, the buildings having been built at different times, but it is a rich, fine place nonetheless. The gates certainly help.

INTERIOR COURTYARDS

The interior courtyard is a great gift to city dwellers. Courtyards provide high-quality outdoor space of a different character from streets and squares. Courtyards are usually less public (often entirely private) and nearly always include some greenery. Courtyards take either of two basic forms: the formal urban space, with quite a lot of pavement, or the garden. This small courtyard off the GETREIDEGASSE in Salzburg typifies the more formal arrangement, but still with plenty of green.

In Pattern 106, "Positive Outdoor Space," Alexander stresses the importance of creating enclosure. This pattern urges designers to create spaces largely enclosed by buildings, walls, or vegetation, with narrow openings leading to the outer world. The courtyard shown here fulfills these requirements entirely and differs in this respect from many courtyards that are accessible only from the adjoining buildings. This courtyard is accessible from two parallel streets and serves to connect them. The interior courtyard proposed in the Reference Block is much larger than this one and is intended more as a garden than as an urban space. Like this one, it is also connected to the street network.

The smaller the courtyard, the higher the likelihood that it has been developed as a formal space. Conversely, large courtyards are most likely to be pastoral spaces with little paving. In either case, trees may be planted to shade the adjacent buildings, and potted plants are often found.

Interior courtyards are more common than many people realize, because many of them cannot be seen from the street. I noticed in the French Quarter of New Orleans that most blocks had large interior courtyards developed as gardens. Few of these could be seen at all from the street, but they are a great blessing for the residents of that hot, humid city. The casual visitor to Amsterdam's canal belt probably does not suspect that the interiors of the blocks are taken up by courtyards, some of them

Courtyard off Getreidegasse, Salzburg

See other photographs of this space on pages 57, 371, 230, and 524.

large, such as the LARGE INTERIOR COURTYARD behind my old apartment. Even in winter, with the leaves off the trees, the far end of this courtyard was barely visible. The courtyard is about 150m (500') deep and averages about 30m (100') wide. Such very large courtyards carry a subtle disadvantage: they require very large blocks that diminish the richness of the web of streets and the multiple pathways (see page 268) always provided by small blocks with their attendant small courtyards.

On the other hand, even very small courtyards, such as this MINIATURE COURTYARD in Bologna, bring plenty of air and light into the surrounding buildings, including considerable direct sunlight. When a ground-level opening into the courtyard is created, as was the case here, they also form a highly effective ventilation system for the adjoining rooms. Courtyards much smaller than this one are no longer effective in this regard. The deep "air shafts" found in many buildings in Manhattan are no substitute for decent light and air; these openings are often only a meter (yard) or so square and admit hardly any light and little more air.

Amsterdam's BEGIJNHOF is the model that I had in mind while designing the Reference Block, illustrated on page 248. The northern part of the Begijnhof, shown here, is a bit more than half the size of the courtyard in the Reference Block, but it is large enough to provide a considerable degree of privacy. At the same time, a courtyard this small still allows fairly short blocks. I think that a large range of variation is entirely acceptable, even desirable, in the size and style of courtyards and blocks.

The Begijnhof is unusual in one respect: we see here not the backs of houses facing into a courtyard but the entrances, each with its individual front garden. The houses have no other entrances, an arrangement that provided security for the widows who were its intended occupants. There are only two entrances to the courtyard from the street, and even today these are closed at night. This arrangement is thus an inverted form, but that affects the appearance of the courtyard only slightly. Its function, however, is considerably altered: it serves as a common area for those living in the surrounding houses, and sees all the traffic of residents coming and going (plus hordes of gaping tourists, who far outnumber the residents).

One of the most difficult questions in the design of courtyards is: to whom do they belong, and who has access to them? The answer to this question will vary from block to block and district to district. There are three distinct conditions: 1) the courtyard is public and open to all, 2) the courtyard is private and open to those who live around it, or 3) the courtyard is subdivided into private plots. We will consider each of these conditions in turn.

In the first case, the courtyard is public property and is maintained by the city. It is linked to the street network by at least one *sottoportego,* such as shown here on the CALLE DI MEZZO in Venice. If there is but one *sottoportego,* there will be no through foot traffic, but if two or more such entrances are arranged so as to create a shortcut, there may be appreciable foot traffic passing through the courtyard. Whether this is seen as desirable or not will depend in part on the nature of the occupancies in the surrounding buildings and whether or not the reduced street traffic resulting from the shortcut will be seen as a significant loss to the streets. If there is but one entrance, the space will take on a semi-private feel even if it is open to the public. (If the space is inaccessible, such this courtyard, seen through glass, at the HOTEL VICTORIA in Basel, it dies, despite meticulous maintenance.)

If the courtyard is common space shared by all those adjoining it, then it can serve as a central gathering place and a hearth for the local community. Presumably all the buildings that face onto the courtyard will have back doors into it. If the houses are of more than three stories, then it is likely that the upper floors will be separate dwelling units that are accessible only from entrances on the street. The residents of the upper floors will then have no

Siena

access to the courtyard unless a loggia with stairs down to the courtyard is constructed. Alternatively, access for these residents can be provided by a gate opening from the street into the courtyard. This could be arranged in conjunction with the concierge service proposed on page 180. In the case of a commons, all dwelling units and businesses surrounding the courtyard can be expected to share in the cost of maintaining it, probably with higher apportionments for those with direct access.

Finally, the courtyard can be subdivided into private plots allocated to the abutting buildings, with each owner bearing directly the responsibility for the upkeep of his plot. Fences will usually be built or hedges planted to separate one owner's land from the next. (This can be a contentious matter and ought to be specified in the deeds or covenants, to avoid future conflict regarding the type and height of fence or hedge.) The space will then serve only as a shared social space to the extent that neighbors gossip over the fence. Such subdivision precludes the development of the space as a coherent whole. It will instead take on a checkered appearance when viewed from the upper stories. Corner houses may have no frontage on the courtyard and thus no access to it. Those apartments above the ground floor may also lack courtyard access, which was a sore point with me when I lived on the fourth floor in Amsterdam.

My own feeling is that one or the other variety of shared ownership is most desirable, but I know that many will not take this view. I would simply propose to arrange different blocks in the different ways, so that everyone has a chance of finding the right sort of courtyard.

A final possibility is that the courtyard is closed to outsiders but still visible through a LOCKED GATE, as in Venice. Although not ideal, this arrangement is better than a shielded courtyard, whose very existence remains unknown to the passerby.

Coupled with the issue of ownership is the matter of maintaining reasonable quiet in a courtyard. In Amsterdam, at least, this was never a problem. People were aware that their noise affected hundreds of other people and were generally very considerate of their neighbors. Barking dogs were almost unknown.

There is also the special case of the courtyard enclosed by a single building, such as this SCHOOL COURTYARD in Basel. In these cases, the courtyard will belong to the building. This provides an opportunity to create an integrated design for the courtyard. I do not foresee, however, that there will be large numbers of these big buildings. The construction of schools around their own courtyards can certainly work, and housing for staff can be provided in the upper floors if the school is a small one. Similar arrangements for the elderly will be useful.

This large courtyard at the CLAUSTRO DE SAN FRANCISCO in Palma has been laid out as a formal garden, with the inclusion of a full surrounding arcade. The loggia above the arcade provides additional usable space of extremely high quality. Notice that the columns are very slender and quite closely spaced. They admit a great deal of light by virtue of their slenderness, and the close spacing gives the necessary support for the loggia above. When an exterior stairway is included, such a loggia can provide access to the courtyard for apartments on upper floors.

Not every block will have an interior courtyard; a few small, dense blocks near the center of a district may not have them at all. Also, if a large enclosed space is required (e.g., a theater), they will usually be omitted. Otherwise, all blocks should have at least small interior courtyards. (See also the discussion on page 116 for an explanation of the efficient land use that results from the arrangement of hollow blocks with interior courtyards.)

This unusual double courtyard at the PATIO DEL HOSPITAL DE TAVERA in Toledo is interesting because the two halves are separated by a vaulted arcade. (Other views show a remarkable vaulted loggia atop the foreground arcade.) The courtyard is surrounded by an arcade, a highly satisfactory arrangement that allows sitting outdoors, under shelter, on rainy days. This arcade

probably serves as the principal (or even sole) circulation space for the ground floor, dispensing with the need for interior hallways while providing plenty of light and air.

The courtyard of the PALAIS JACQUES COEUR in Bourges has an arcade on only two sides. There is absolutely nothing wrong with this arrangement, which probably arises from the construction of the surrounding buildings at different times. Notice that the inside of the arcade is not vaulted; the floor or roof above is supported by beams instead. This is perfectly acceptable, but the vault is usually a more pleasing form. This arcade exhibits the beautiful elliptical arch. (Many people confuse OVALS AND ELLIPSES. An oval has straight sections on the long sides; an ellipse does not. The oval is a mistake both structurally and aesthetically and should only be used for a running track. Geometry texts describe the simple method of constructing a true ellipse.)

The PALACIO DE LA DIPUTACIÓN in Barcelona is an altogether remarkable space. A gorgeous arch supports the stairway, and perfect gothic arches have been used, supported by very slender columns that must be of unusually strong stone. Notice also that, although there would have been room for the stairs to reach the ground without becoming at all steep, they were brought to a landing, from which a puddle of steps leads to the ground. This arrangement provides a balustrade where it is necessary for safety and places to sit at the lower levels.

The small courtyard and formal garden at the MUSÉE PLANTIN in Antwerp is a fine addition to the building and brings light into all the rooms that front on it. This courtyard might be criticized in the matter of proportion: it is very much longer than it is wide and would have been better arranged in a less elongated manner. Ideally, courtyards are either square or rectangles ranging in proportions from about 1:1.3 to 1:2.5. In less formal cases the courtyard will not be rectilinear. All that is necessary is to give it a pleasing shape that is not excessively elongated—the longest dimension should generally not exceed 3 times the shortest. If, however, tricks are played by lowering the height of the enclosure on the long sides, this ratio can be exceed, as the space will seem wider than it is.

The ALHAMBRA is the great Moorish masterpiece in Granada, an exceptionally fine expression of Islamic architecture. Notice the central fountain and the small watercourse leading away from it. Water, in the dry Arab nations, assumed an importance that most Westerners do not attach to it, even considering their preference to have it nearby. The addition of water improves almost any courtyard. Flowing water is even better, although care should be taken to assure that the sound is not irritatingly loud if people are going to be spending long periods nearby, as in apartments and offices. The sound of splashing water is commonly used to mask the noise of automobiles, but in carfree cities, the ambient noise levels will be much lower than we now consider usual. The masking function is no longer required and the need and desirability of water noise should be reconsidered. A gentle burble is often pleasant, but louder sounds may irritate. Fountains should be shut off late in the evening.

The simple presence of grass and a few shrubs is not enough to perfect a courtyard. Take this COURTYARD in Ravenna as an example. There nothing wrong with the structure itself. The arcade is fine, even if the round arches are a bit static. The loggia on the right is a nice addition. The second floor surrounding the rest of the courtyard has rather sparse windows, but even the nearly blank wall of the third floor is not terribly offensive. What causes this courtyard to fail is that it is a dead space—nothing happens here. A sea of grass isolates the fountain in the middle, which cannot be approached without walking on the grass. People have been trained not to walk on the grass, even if there are no signs expressly forbidding it. Courtyards of this type normally incorporate paths, most often originating in the corners, that cross the courtyard and connect the fountain to the rest of

the space. A few benches beside the paths would invite people to linger on sunny afternoons. The courtyard could certainly stand a tree or two on the north side. This courtyard is clearly under the control of a single entity, so it is curious that these failings have not been addressed; the cost of correcting them would be slight.

The CHIOSTRO DEL SANTUARIO in Vicenza is an arcaded courtyard with a central well. But notice the arches. They are nearly circular, but actually have the gothic form, with a discontinuity at the apex. Lovely as this space is, I think it suffers from the failure to choose distinctly one form of the arch or the other.

Notice also the knee-high column bases, which create benches between the columns. The columns themselves can serve as back rests. (Such use may at times not have been permitted in this particular space.)

The PATIO DE LOS NARANJOS in Barcelona appears, from this view, to lack coherence and a unifying theme. It's a bit of everything: a lovely but incomplete arcade, an attempt at a formal garden, a fountain that is curiously crammed into a small space at the edge, a rosette window that has been cropped at the bottom. Notice the unusual form of the second floor, which has a nearly Japanese character. The panes of the windows are very small, and the windows exceptionally attractive, although the elliptical window arches clash somewhat with the gothic motif. Despite these many incongruities and imperfections, this is still a delightful space.

In fact, we do not need to achieve perfection, nor should we expect to. As long as a space is fundamentally sound, it will work. Future generations, confronting the imperfections, will probably fix them, rather than raze the place and begin anew. I believe that it is from these incremental repairs that some of the finest spaces have arisen. Some spaces, built by geniuses, have been perfect the first time around, but this is too much to expect as a matter of routine.

PARKS

We consider here only parks located in urban settings, such as the LARGO DA OLIVEIRINHA in Lisbon. These are in no sense wilderness areas, and they see intensive use by nature-starved city residents. The carfree city can provide more green space within the city than is usual, but parks will still be needed. We will not take up the design of parks in any depth as there is an ample literature on the subject.

We must provide city dwellers with tranquil, beautiful, green surroundings within easy reach of home. In "Accessible Green" (APL, Pattern 60), Christopher Alexander argues that green space must be situated within three blocks if people are to make much use of it; I think that slightly longer distances are acceptable if the streets are carfree and the walk is pleasant, but large green areas should be located within a five-minute walk. Interior courtyards can meet some of this need if they have reasonable amounts of greenery.

The provision of large open areas near a city is highly desirable from many standpoints, and this was one of the most important criteria established for the Reference Design for carfree cities. Little needs to be done to these expansive open areas: their existing uses can be retained, perhaps with the conversion into parks of some land adjacent to built-up areas. However, large parks that create a sense of rural isolation are not our focus here. In this chapter we will concentrate instead on small parks that are either integrated into the urban fabric or adjoin it. These parks thus have tight connections with their urban areas and, if properly arranged, will serve large numbers of people. We begin with the history of large parks. (The question of parks that are actually called squares is taken up briefly on page 312.)

Space was allocated for large parks when it became clear that rapid urban expansion and the ills of industrialization made a pastoral refuge essential. These heroic parks, in the manner of

Largo da Oliveirinha, Lisbon

Frederick Law Olmsted, were manipulated landscapes designed to improve on nature. Manhattan's Central Park is one of the city's great treasures, but I will argue later in this chapter that its area might better have been divided among 110 smaller parks.

The PARQUE EDUARDO VII is a large park in Lisbon that is completely surrounded by dense neighborhoods. In the manner of the Olmsted parks, this one is probably highly artificial in its arrangement. I have no objection to rearranging urban land-scapes in ways that are pleasing to people, as long as other, larger tracts of nature are left undisturbed. It is sensible for very large parks to be located away from the city proper, in the manner of the National Parks in the USA.

Amsterdam's VONDELPARK (48 ha, 120 acres) is typical of the monumental parks created during the 19th century. It was designed by Jan David Zocher starting in 1864 as a private venture, although the general public was admitted for a small fee. Bicycle traffic soon became a nuisance and was regulated by 1884. Cycling in Vondelpark remains contentious to this day. Such conflicts over the use of parks will be with us always.

The JARDINES DE LA ISLA in Aranjuez is a very formal urban park. The photographer was probably standing on the street, near the head of the stairway that leads into the park. Notice the rigid mirror symmetry of the fountain. This is doubtless a popular gathering place on warm days, as it will be cooler downwind of the fountain. Notice also the finely detailed iron railings and stone uprights with their potted plants.

The KOCHBRUNNEN (hot springs) in Wiesbaden show a fine integration of a good building and an attractive garden/park. It has been laid out with mirror symmetry, which is in keeping with the stiff formality of the space and the building. Small urban green areas can be tended intensively at moderate cost, and flower beds such as these can be replanted several times a year, so they remain in almost continuous bloom. This is an excellent tactic for maximizing the impact of green space.

THE MIRABELLGARTEN in Salzburg is a very formal inner-city park of moderate size. It includes a considerable area of flower beds and some statuary. The provision of parks of this sort is very fine, if the budget will stand it, and if the land can be spared from other uses. This park also serves as a pedestrian thoroughfare, so large numbers of people pass through it during the course of a day, but it remains a restful oasis in this dense, busy city. A park of this type is envisioned in the Reference Topology, right at the very heart of the city, between the three downtown districts. At that location, such a park would see large numbers of people just passing through on their way between the downtown districts. These people would enjoy a tranquil interlude in a beautiful green setting, a refreshing time-out in the middle of a busy day.

The addition of a classical building to a park setting, as here at the VILLA UMBERTO in Rome, is a common device in Europe and one that is entirely fitting to an urban park. Notice the striking sculptures on the roof. The shoreline in front of the villa is cluttered and unattractive, however. There are two ways to fix this problem. A grass apron is perhaps the nicest, especially if it has a southern exposure, as people will sun there. A stone bulkhead is also fine. If the water is much below grade level, there is some risk to small children, with or without a railing. There are many place in Venice where a child could fall into the water (and few railings), but the risk has been accepted for centuries. If a railing is wanted, it can be of either rustic wooden design or of solid stone balusters with a stone cap railing. A grassy apron is safer and requires no railing if a gentle slope is maintained below the shoreline. Then, as long as there is no current, even very small children will not get themselves into serious trouble. (Consult "Still Water," APL, Pattern 71, on this point.)

The fanciful PARC MONCEAU in Paris was certainly an entirely man-made space. It appears to have been first constructed in the 18th century and extensively rebuilt during the 19th. It was doubtless intended to fascinate, and it does.

Thirteen badly-needed pocket parks were recently created in Lower Manhattan.
"No Man's Land for Parks, No More"
New York Times, 5 Nov. 2003, page B1.

One of the wonderful things about urban parks is that we can include such fanciful constructions as this footbridge in Berlin's TIERGARTEN. What a delight to the eye!

Pocket parks can be integrated into side streets, where they are restful and provide an oasis for nearby residents, but larger parks ought to be on the fringes of the city, not in the middle. Consider the case of Manhattan's huge Central Park, which occupies about 150 city blocks. It is a fine park and offers beautiful vistas for those lucky enough to enjoy an overlook, but it meets the needs of most residents of Manhattan rather poorly.

The 150 blocks of Central Park could have been broken up into, say, 10 parks of 10 blocks each and another 100 parks of half a block each (which would be about half the size of New York's Bryant Park, behind the main public library, or roughly the size of PIAZZA ARIOSTEA in Ferrara, which is big enough to cater to the needs of a considerable number of people).

Using this scheme, the banks of the Hudson and East Rivers could have had five large parks each, where the peaceful riverside location would offer a real haven from the city's noise and bustle, as well as beautiful views out over the river. The 100 small parks would have been scattered throughout Manhattan. They would have been located in the middle of a block, with buildings at both ends of the block to shield the park from the busy avenues. Such an arrangement would have provided local parks within easy reach of all residents while providing larger parks within a half-hour walk. I believe that this would have been a better and fairer allocation of this precious space. At the time, though, the focus was on monumental parks, and Central Park is certainly a wonderful example. In all fairness, by the time Central Park was developed, most of the island south of it had already been fully developed, so that it was no longer possible to provide dozens of small parks in the lower half of Manhattan.

Even very small urban parks are a great boon to those who live nearby. This POCKET PARK in central Zürich is little larger than what we see here, yet it finds considerable use and relieves the dense urban construction encircling it. Small parks will fit into even the densest neighborhoods, precisely the places where they are most needed. In cooler climates, tall buildings must not shade the park at lunch time. When carefully arranged, these small parks can see intense use. In southern Europe, a court on which *jeu de boules* is played will almost invariably be found; the game requires nothing more than bare, dry, level ground.

The JARDIM DE SANTA BÁRBARA in Braga, Portugal, is a fine example of an urban park. It will require a lot of work per unit area to keep such an elaborate park looking so good, but the total area is not so very great (it is little bigger than we see here), and the cost of the work has apparently fallen within the budget of a city that is not especially rich. Never fail to consider trading quantity for quality.

Larger parks, such as PARC DE LA PÉPINIÈRE in Nancy, are also needed, but their use is less opportunistic, and their catchment area far exceeds that of a pocket park. These are the parks that families visit on the weekend, where they go for a picnic and a game of catch or frisbee. They are, of course, very important, but they will see less intense use than neighborhood parks.

The JARDIM DO CORETO in Tavira, Portugal, nicely illustrates another of Alexander's patterns, "Sleeping in Public" (APL, Pattern 94). This pattern will be controversial in many Western nations (although not in Iberia, where it is widely seen). He says, "In an environment where there are very few places to lie down and sleep, people who sleep in public seem unnatural because it is so rare." The pattern calls for environments with comfortable places to lie and sleep, sheltered from wind and passersby, where people feel comfortable taking a nap.

Graveyards share many of the attributes of parks and are used in some of the same ways. I suppose that cremation and scattering will soon replace burial and the setting of tombstones—we really do not have land enough for graveyards in cities.

Rio di San Trovaso, Venice

WATER

Water makes almost any urban area more attractive. People seem to have a strong need to be near water, and we should strive to bring open water into our cities wherever possible. Even small streams, ponds, and fountains greatly improve the quality of a neighborhood. We first consider rivers and canals, then bridges, next urban waterfronts, boat landings, and piers, and finally fountains and wells.

RIVERS & CANALS

Venice and Amsterdam are famous around the world for their canals. Bangkok once had an equally extensive canal system, but most of it was filled and paved. These canals were once the main transport arteries in all three cities, as they still are in Venice. In Amsterdam, dozens of tour boats still ply the canals.

Venice's Grand Canal is by far the widest of the city's canals. Much more typical is the RIO DELLE MUNEGHETTE. It differs in one respect from most Venetian canals: it has a walkway running alongside the canal itself. In general, the two circulation realms of Venice, the streets and the canals, cross each other rather than running alongside one another. The arrangement shown here does occur with some frequency, though.

Space is at a premium in Venice, and both the streets and canals were made as narrow as possible consistent with their functions. Only narrow boats can navigate the minor canals. Bridges, like the one seen in the distance, are low and limit the height of vessels that can pass beneath. The result is that freight delivery in Venice, except to locations along the Grand Canal, is conducted using boats only about the size of the one moored in the bottom-right corner of the photograph. This means that the usual crew of two is delivering a comparatively small amount of freight, which makes the service expensive.

Rio delle Muneghette, Venice

Ideally, the Venetian canal system would permit the direct delivery of standardized shipping containers, but this would require wider canals, higher bridges, and quays to offload the containers, so that merchants could unload while the boat crew moved on. This arrangement would spoil Venice.

The GRAND CANAL sweeps through the heart of the city in a great S-curve and is the best address in Venice. The canal creates a full sense of enclosure for most of its length; it is only near the ends that distant vistas come into view. The Grand Canal is also the route of the most heavily used ferries and thus the axis of Venice's pleasant but slow public transport system.

When this photograph of the RIO PRIULI in Venice was taken, most of the water traffic was still powered by oars, although there would have been steam-powered ferries by this time. Small, single-oarsman gondolas are now used almost exclusively by tourists. Obnoxious water taxis have replaced gondolas for private transport, and this is a most unfortunate change, as the taxis are noisy, stinky, and create heavy wakes. In their own way, they are worse than cars, but fortunately there are not many of them (due mainly to the prohibitive cost of using them). They are responsible for severe damage to the foundations of buildings along the canal, a cost not paid by their users. Although other boats also leave wakes, they, at least, carry many passengers or a considerable mass of freight, and their speeds are intrinsically low, so their wakes are comparatively small (the taxis are speedboats and are supposed to slow down in the canals).

In the middle distance is one of the hundreds of arch bridges that knit the dozens of Venetian islands into a city. These bridges constitute a formidable obstacle for anything on wheels, which explains why Venice was never overrun by cars. Today, these bridges make the city almost totally inaccessible for anyone in a wheelchair and considerably hinder the passage of freight on handcarts. When designing new carfree cities, we must make certain to avoid this problem.

Islands often develop in the middle of rivers, as here with the ISOLA TIBERINA in Rome. These sites have commonly been used when bridging the river and were sometimes the earliest inhabited locales, owing to their inherently good defensive situation. Here, not all of the island has been walled against periodic flooding; a small triangular beach has been left, where fishing skiffs are landed. Examine this scene carefully. For me, it evokes a sense of almost perfect peace, of permanence, and of security. Yet it is not a highly ordered place, even though it may be highly organized. The attractive, natural shape of the site was the underlying primary organizing force, I believe.

The HERENGRACHT in Amsterdam is one of the four famous concentric canals. Its construction was an expensive proposition, one that was undertaken during the Golden Age, the height of Amsterdam's fortunes, in the 17th century. These four canals are crossed by narrower radial canals, one of which branches off under the bridge to the right. Unfortunately, several of these radial canals were filled in and today serve only as parking lots. Beautiful stone-trimmed brick arch bridges are nearly universal but vary from one another in subtle ways. They give the inner city a harmonious appearance.

This excellent plan was, alas, abandoned when Amsterdam expanded during the 19th century, and no expansion conducted since the Golden Age achieves the quality of the glorious Canal District. Much of the rest of the city is actually quite plain, but tourists see little of it.

Amsterdam's OUDEZIJDS ACHTERBURGWAL is one of the city's earliest canals. It is considerably narrower than the grander canals built later, but it is still entirely serviceable. Today, this view is dominated by parked cars. Fortunately, not much else has changed, so Amsterdam could still recover its beautiful past. So far it stubbornly refuses to do so, despite the passage of a referendum more than a decade ago that mandated large reductions in parking and car use.

The entire Dutch coastal plain, about half of the country's land area, is criss-crossed by canals, most of which are still in use today, some only for drainage but many also for shipping. Delft is part of this coastal district and so boasts a canal system, like other cities in the lowland region. The arrangement of this canal in the HYPOLITUSBUURT is typical. A comparatively narrow canal with vertical walls is flanked on both sides by rows of trees. Next comes a roadway, then a narrow sidewalk, and finally the buildings, which form a continuous wall. Bridges are found every 100-200m (300-600'). Delft differs from Amsterdam in that the buildings run about one story lower, but the pattern is otherwise very similar, as indeed it is throughout the region.

The DONKERE GAARD passes through the center of Utrecht, another old city on the Dutch coastal plain. However, the ground level here is slightly above sea level, and the canals may in fact follow the route of natural watercourses, which would account for the pretty S-curve we see here.

Notice that the street is a full story above the canal, and that a quay has been included at the base of the wall. This arrangement once kept the freight system separate from the surface streets while allowing the delivery of freight directly from barges into building basements along the quayside. This removed the clutter from the streets and allowed the merchants to handle freight conveniently and on their own schedule. Unfortunately, this practice disappeared with the advent of trucks.

Waterborne delivery is making a minor comeback, at least in Amsterdam. Oddly, it is the express service DHL which first reverted to WATERBORNE FREIGHT. The streets had become so congested that their package delivery service had been significantly slowed and costs increased. The solution was to use a boat to haul the packages to a quay in each district, from which bicycle couriers make the final deliveries. The service appears to be working well for both the company and the city. It remains to be seen if other shippers will also adopt the practice.

BRIDGES

Bridges, when nicely designed, add much to an urban setting, especially when the bridge crosses a watercourse. Both Venice and Amsterdam abound with bridges crossing narrow waterways. Highway bridges rarely improve an urban scene, especially given the usual poverty of their design, which is necessitated by the cost of the vast breadth demanded by cars.

The Grand Canal in Venice is crossed by only three bridges, two of which are on sharp bends, probably so as not to block the long vistas down the canal. One of them is a makeshift wooden affair. The bridge near the train station is a classic, unadorned arch. The third of these is the great RIALTO BRIDGE, one of the principal landmarks of Venice. The bridge is situated at a sharp bend in the canal and is a vital link between the two major halves of Venice. But it is more than a bridge. What I had never realized until I saw it myself was that the arches atop the bridge are actually the backs of small shops facing the center walkway, an exceptionally fine location due to the heavy traffic. The balustrades on the outer walkways are of Istrian stone (similar to marble), which has been polished smooth where people have leaned against it over the centuries.

When Florence's PONTE VECCHIO was reconstructed in 1345, bridges were commonly inhabited, as this one still is today. The houses on the bridge are actually cantilevered over the edge, to maximize the usable space. Here, too, the heavy foot traffic makes this a prime location for shops. The zigzag gallery that starts in the foreground and runs over the bridge was built as a private walkway for one of the Medicis.

Another view of Florence shows the PONTE SANTA TRINITÀ, with the Ponte Vecchio just visible in the distance. We are looking in the opposite direction from the photograph above. This must be one of the world's most beautiful bridges. Its simple, elegant form could only have been improved by carrying the

arch of the full bridge across the center span, which is flat. This was probably done to minimize the grade that had to be climbed by wagons crossing the bridge. Each of these bridges is commendable in its own way, and we enjoy the variety.

Much of lowland Europe is served by a network of barge canals still used today. The requirement that waterways permit the passage of barges has considerably affected the design of both cities and their bridges. In this view of the PONTS DE L'ILL in Strasbourg, five bridges span a canal. The land has been raised (or the canal dug lower) so that the bridges can connect at street level while still permitting barges to pass beneath.

When a waterway passes through a city, a critical decision must be made: should a street run alongside, or not? Here at the LEIE EN PREDIKHEERENLEI in Ghent, both choices have been made. What is apparently a factory on the left fronts the canal directly, for easy loading of barges. The opposite bank has a quayside street. There are advantages to both treatments. When crossing a canal, one has a brief view down the waterway. When walking alongside a canal, one has a constantly changing view of the water. The decision is usually made on practical grounds, as was likely the case here.

Most bridges in Venice are built on the model shown here, along the RIVA DEGLI SCHIAVONI. They start low, about half a meter above the level of high tide, and arch up fairly steeply to provide about two meters (7') clearance for boats passing underneath. This bridge differs only in being wider than usual. It needs to be, as this is the busiest walkway in Venice.

Venice is built on a tidal lagoon, and the low-lying quays sometimes flood at high tide when weather conditions raise the water level in the northern Adriatic Sea. Flooding not only inundates the streets; boats can no longer pass beneath the bridges. Unless the proposed flood barrier is actually completed, Venice will continue to suffer from frequent flooding that impairs passage through both its streets and waterways.

WATERFRONTS

Waterfronts are always special places in cities. The busy waterfront at the PUERTA DE LA PAZ in Barcelona is typical. Notice
how people are drawn to the waterfront activity. I can recall as
a child being fascinated by ships locking through the old
Lachine canal in Montréal. The locks were open to the public
and drew crowds who delighted in watching as ships from
around the world transited the canal.

The MOLO AND PIAZZETTA SAN MARCO is the principal water
gate in Venice. Notice the raft of gondolas in the foreground,
still there a century after the photograph was taken. The quay
that begins just west of here and runs far to the east (as the Riva
degli Schiavoni) is the principal point of embarkation for ferry
service throughout the lagoon. The coming and going of ferries
makes this area a hive of activity from early in the morning until
late in the evening. The ferries are reasonably quiet, so, despite
the heavy water traffic, the local environment remains attractive.
The southern exposure helps to make this one of the most pleasant spots in all Venice except during hot weather.

The JUNGFERNSTIEG in Hamburg and its surroundings
achieve a formality appropriate to their importance without
becoming stiff. The buildings are of similar character, modest in
size, and nicely varied within the constraints of the style. Notice
the three spires breaking the horizon. The liveliness of the area
derives in part from heavy foot traffic to the ferry landing.

The PIAZZA CAVOUR DAL LAGO in Como is a simply magnificent square of its type. The size and proportions are about ideal,
the buildings appropriate in scale and design, and the steps on
the embankment the best treatment for landings on waterways
with only moderate changes in water level, usual for lakes and
even quite a few tidal estuaries.

The handling of the waterfront in cities with a tidal range in
excess of about two meters (7') is a great challenge. At low tide,

ugly, smelly mud flats are often exposed. It is difficult to moor small vessels to a wall where there is a large range of tide, so it becomes necessary to install floats that rise and fall with the tide. These require gangways to the shore to provide low-slope access to the floats at all stages of the tide. These requirements are difficult to handle attractively.

Here, on the THAMES EMBANKMENT in London, the challenge has been handled well, and this is one of the most attractive waterfronts in the world. Just about everything is perfect: the buildings, the bridge, the promenade, the ferry, and even the landing are all beautiful. London has rediscovered its waterfront, and sights like this are returning. The boat in the foreground, or one very like it, is today moored nearby.

At the QUAI DU LAC in Lugano we have an example of a concave shoreline that has been nicely treated. Trees have been planted in a double row fairly close to the shore but do not obscure the urban character of the scene. I imagine that on a hot summer day, it is highly satisfactory to sit on a bench in the shade, perhaps with a cool breeze coming off the lake, and certainly with a luscious view out over the water. The fountain also has a cooling effect. The distant hill provides a pleasing contrast with the mass of the town.

The PORTO DI BALBIANELLO on the shores of Lake Como is a scene of enormous power, which, I believe, owes largely to the welcoming statue on the left. This place is actually part of the mainland but is normally accessible only by water. This is not a formal setting, but the elements have been wonderfully integrated in a fluid manner that works better than a more rigid style would permit.

The contrast of the boats on the AUSSENALSTER in Hamburg with the church spires in the background is striking. There is a much-used urban park in the foreground. Certainly, whenever possible, parks should include a watercourse, although few will attain the beauty of this one.

FOUNTAINS & WELLS

Even today, in many parts of the world, people still draw their water from communal wells. This makes for a great deal of work (and economical water usage), but it does build an active social life centered around the wellhead, as people wait their turns. The modern equivalent is the office water cooler. The presence of pools of open water in the city center is comforting and restful. This is easy to arrange, and we do it frequently.

This EXTRAORDINARY FOUNTAIN in Basel stands just inside the entrance of a school. I find it a simply astounding sight, and this in a city renowned for its beautiful fountains, many of which are far more elaborate than this one. However, this fountain is not only approachable (some of the others are, for some reason, well above the ground), but it is exquisite in every detail. It is inconceivable to me that mere chance has caused the ivy to grow in a pattern that complements the fountain. I expect that generations of gardeners have nipped the ivy back to maintain this shape, which resembles a Japanese character. Such beautiful places beg to be photographed.

When I urge people to bring beauty back into their surroundings, it is this sort of beauty I have in mind. This fountain is not extravagant. Only the column is in any way elaborate, but it is small and would not be hugely expensive to carve even today. All the other materials are quite ordinary, but they have been assembled and maintained in a manner that creates a quiet, enduring beauty. Hundreds of people pass this way every day, and I would wager that few of them fail to glance at the fountain as they pass. Great wealth is not required to create beauty, only sensitivity and love of place. Ugliness is a modern poverty.

Also to be found in Basel is this whimsical fountain on the THEATERPLATZ. It includes a number of playful sculptures in a wading pool near the city center. It is a great gift to the residents of this fine city, who seem to appreciate it.

This well at the PALAZZO PRETORIO in Florence stands in a very formal interior courtyard. The well is classical, rather spare, and elegant. This was probably never a very busy well, as it appears only to serve the surrounding building, not an entire neighborhood.

Although few wellheads can be seen in the USA today, they remain quite common in much of Europe, and many of them are still places where anyone can get water, which is handy if you have a kid with freshly smeared ice cream. As far as I know, all the wells in Venice are now sealed off (although there are still many working fountains), but the wellheads remain, and they are still social spaces, even if at reduced level. People tend to sit on their steps, set their knapsacks and lunch on the well covering, or just lean against them.

Technically, the ZAHRINGERBRUNNEN in Bern is a fountain or spring, not a well. This distinction is not very important from a social standpoint, except that people spend more time at a well, as they must draw up their water. This fountain forms a good counterpoint to the extraordinary clock tower beyond.

MAJOR BUILDINGS

Major buildings are those by which a city comes to be known in the wider world. These are the cathedrals, museums, city halls, and other buildings of great cultural significance. These are usually large and expensive buildings. Few cities will build more than one or two of them in a decade.

Sometimes these buildings are the very *raison d'être* of a town, as in the case of the BASILICA OF ST. FRANCIS in Assisi. This church, completed in 1230, was damaged during an earthquake in 1997 but had been restored by 2002, when this photograph was taken. The luminous church is sited on the flanks of a steep hill and is visible from the far side of the valley, an hour's bus ride away. The main façade, obliquely visible on the right, is simplicity itself, although the building as a whole is complex. Double doorways beneath a large gothic arch form the entrance. Above that is an intricate rosette window, with a plain round window above. The façade is completed by two drip courses of moderate complexity. The same white stone is widely used in the town.

When we build large, impressive, and expensive buildings, they offer an opportunity to create an icon for the city. Truly distinct buildings may eventually become an icon that is known around the world, as in the case of Sydney's fanciful Opera House. Even a building that clashes completely with the rest of the city, such as Bilbao's Guggenheim Museum, can become an instant icon for that city. How much better, though, if a landmark building harmonizes in some way with its host city, as in the manner of Assisi's Basilica, which mirrors the character of the town. We can be certain that Bilbao will not be redeveloped in the image of its crumpled-tinfoil museum, and that for as long as it stands, this museum will draw attention to itself not as an amplification of the city's culture and history but as a foreign body stuck onto the city like a leech. Let's try to avoid such errors in the future.

Basilica of St. Francis, Assisi, Italy

Monumental buildings are best sited in or beside a square, where the square and the building complement one another. If a major building must, for some reason, be sited on a street, it is common to set the building back from the street, giving it a forecourt that serves, in essence, as its own square. Major buildings usually need some room in order to be appreciated; there is not much sense in putting up a fine façade on a narrow street where there is not enough room to back up and obtain a good view of the building. This problem afflicts the CITY HALL in Budapest. Even with a very wide-angle lens, I could not back up anywhere near far enough to get the façade of this building in the frame, and to see the upper stories of this fine building requires craning your neck. In fact, this is a curiously modest façade. The COUNCIL HALL is an astounding space, the splendor of which is not suggested by the staid façade.

RELIGIOUS BUILDINGS

Churches, cathedrals, mosques, and temples are often a city's most cherished architectural treasures. Many are ancient, and those that have survived are usually impressive structures. (The ruins of others are often nearly as impressive.) Great churches and mosques affect an entire city, because their towers are visible from all over town, and locally they are dazzling. Only occasionally does a secular work (a city hall or museum) actually overshadow the best sectarian building.

Construction of the CATHEDRAL of Cologne began in 1248. It has the standard transecting wings, the twin spires, and the third, lower spire at the intersection of the two wings. To be in the presence of one of these cathedrals is to be overwhelmed. Even today the construction of such a church would be a stupendous undertaking that would tax the resources of any city. When these beauties were built, cities were much smaller and their resources far less. What a phenomenal dedication to an ideal!

The MONASTERY at El Escorial is another staggering undertaking. By dint of phenomenal effort, it was finished in just 21 years. The scale is deceiving. The paving and its intersecting marble courses make the building look smaller, but the doors and windows give the scale away. Seen from the train, this is a huge building. The echoing shapes of the spires are delightful.

What place do buildings like this have in modern society? Their cost is not so much in their materials as in the effort of their construction, stonework especially. A great challenge to society today is to provide full employment, and the construction of fine buildings like this one is a solution. These long-lived buildings have low environmental costs, and this helps to meet the challenges of sustainability.

We often see photographs of the LEANING TOWER of Pisa, but how common is this view, which takes in most of the site? The tower is a fanciful work, a curiosity, made unique by its lean. Integrated sites like this, where all the buildings serve one end, are comparatively rare in old cities; normally, churches are mixed in with other buildings and even share common walls with them. Here we have truly monumental architecture, of the highest quality, in a dedicated setting. Oddly, this is not really an urban scene despite its location within the city center. So much land has been devoted to a few buildings, each surrounded by open space, that no sense of enclosure arises. This treatment may be reserved for exceptional buildings like these.

I have seen the CATHEDRAL in Strasbourg from this same vantage point. It is overwhelmingly large; the building makes the people around it look like ants, as you can see here. It is built out of a bright red sandstone that must be very strong and of highly reliable structural properties, as many of the elements are amazingly thin (you can't quite see them in this photograph). The scale of the cathedral utterly dominates the buildings around it, which are not small themselves. A skyscraper built near this site would greatly diminish the cathedral.

JANAKI TEMPLE in Janakpur (Nepal) is actually less than a century old. The city is a major Hindu pilgrimage destination and plays a role in the epic Ramayana. It is said to be the birthplace of Sita. The *Lonely Planet* guide dismisses it as having "no great architectural merit" and says it "was built in 1912 and might be described as baroque Mughal." None of this seems to deter the pilgrims, and the guide says that the temple is a very lively place during the evening. However poor its pedigree, I find it an enchanting and fascinating building.

MAJOR CIVIC BUILDINGS

By their very nature, monumental buildings can only be commissioned by wealthy entities. Usually this means governments and religious orders, but in more recent times, corporations have also amassed the means to build monumental buildings, usually, alas, alienating skyscrapers.

The Piazza San Marco is one of the great monumental squares of Italy. On the right is the DOGE'S PALACE, which was both the residence of the sitting doge and the center of civil authority in Venice. In the background stands Saint Mark's cathedral; on the left the towering Campanile. Vast sums were expended on these buildings, which certainly pass the test as monuments.

Size alone does not make a monumental building. A big-box store is large enough to qualify but lacks all the other attributes, including good design, quality materials, and fine workmanship. Monumental buildings exhibit generosity in their arrangements: broad staircases, ranks of columns, towers, grand entrances. The rooflines are variegated and the roofs topped with ornaments, turrets, and usually some symbol to identify the building's patron. There is nothing about these buildings that was done meanly or cheaply; that was never the objective.

PARLIAMENT in London is one of the most intricately detailed buildings in the world and without doubt the most important building in all Britain. Badly damaged during the last war, it was fully restored to its original condition. Big Ben, the clock tower, is Britain's leading icon.

The CÂMARA MUNICIPAL (city hall) in Lisbon is a formal building standing on a formal square. It is not an especially large building, but it is unmistakably a major building. If classical architecture is to be applied in modern cities, this is certainly the place to do it. The design of this building is timeless, and the structure can be expected to withstand the ravages of time. This building for the future is already 130 years old.

Grenada's ALHAMBRA is the greatest Moorish work in all of Spain. Christopher Alexander noted in *The Nature of Order* (TNO, I:187) that while the smaller elements of this large complex of buildings are often symmetrical within themselves, the complex as a whole lacks any symmetry. This probably arises from its gradual assembly over a span of centuries. However, this does reinforce my growing notion that symmetry is more important and more desirable at smaller scales than at larger scales. (Alexander coined the term "local symmetries.") I am fairly certain that symmetry at scales larger than can be seen from the ground does little to help the design of an urban area and may actually damage it. Even in this view, the Alhambra is not perfectly symmetrical—the doorways on the left are not mirrored on the right.

Paris has never lacked for monumental buildings, and L'OPÉRA (now called Opéra Garnier) is one of the best. This building was given a most prominent location. Not only does it command a space of its own, it stands at the end of a great boulevard, as can be seen in the photograph on page 278. It would have been difficult to find a more imposing site for this building. As with so many of the majestic areas of Paris, this is Haussmann's work.

The PRAÇA DE TOUROS, the principal bull ring in Lisbon, is a remarkable building, and the entrance is unmistakably defined. The roofline is unique as far as I know and makes the building

instantly recognizable. Notice the Moorish character of the main entrance arch, which clearly reflects Portugal's long Maghrebi heritage.

The RIJKSMUSEUM in Amsterdam is not a particularly old building, having been constructed in a new district of the city at the end of the 19th century. When new, it stood almost alone, but the remainder of the area was developed soon after this photograph was taken. The appearance of the building today is much changed by the presence of a few large trees, which have softened its sharp outlines. Nearby buildings have filled in the skyline on either side, eradicating the cake-on-a-serving-platter appearance in this photograph. The twin towers are an unmistakable landmark throughout the city.

A weakness in this building is that the main entrance was not located where it would be expected. The four archways in the center of the building lead not to the entrance but to a passageway for pedestrians and cyclists beneath the building. The actual entrance has for years been just off to one side. Even as I write, controversy rages over the location of the entrance. The city refuses to close the major thoroughfare under the building, and the museum wishes to locate the main entrance where it belongs, inside these arches. The question is whether or not room can be found for both functions. Pierre Cuypers, the original architect, designed many fine buildings, but his mismanagement of this entrance is an enduring problem.

The POST OFFICE in Ghent looks like a very old building but was actually constructed in 1910. The stepped gables with their ornaments are a rich form that is echoed in the turrets. The windows are exceptionally graceful for such a large building. Their number has been kept rather small by making them unusually large, and they are headed by elliptical arches. The main entrance can be immediately identified, even from a considerable distance. The stories are very high, which yields rooms with the high ceilings befitting an important building.

MINOR BUILDINGS

The bulk of any city is composed of minor buildings. These are the apartment buildings, town houses, small offices, minor factories, and family shops. An efficient economy requires that these buildings be reasonably inexpensive to build, maintain, and operate. At the same time, they must be safe, comfortable, and attractive.

We will never be able to build more than a small portion of our buildings in the monumental fashion, and to do so would diminish the truly important buildings. In any given city, we must find a way of building that is well suited to local conditions, uses local materials as much as possible, and reflects local culture and history. In many places, a designer need only review the vernacular architecture used prior to 1900 and update it to meet modern requirements. Certainly, we will make some changes, but most local vernacular styles are uniquely well suited to the needs and resources of their region.

These houses on the PIAZZA GRANDE in Arezzo typify the kinds of buildings we consider in this chapter. As befits their prominent location, the detailing of these buildings is more elaborate than most other small buildings in Arezzo, but their size and layout are typical. There are hundreds of similar buildings in that small city. They are, like these four buildings, mostly about four stories tall and quite narrow. The only expensive element is the stonework, which is actually fairly simple. The walls are probably built of rubble and may not fare well in an earthquake; we would today almost certainly substitute reinforced concrete. These are buildings that we could still build today, with some structural advances.

One of the most damning curses an architect can bestow upon the work of a fellow architect today is to call it "derivative." But all architecture is derivative. No building is entirely without precedent, and so what if it were? Does the abnegation of our

Houses on the Piazza Grande, Arezzo, Italy

architectural heritage somehow improve a building? Is it a good thing if there is "not another building like it in all the world"? On the other hand, should we not avoid the 20th-century error of building hundreds, even thousands of houses that are exactly the same? Can we not have individuality without uniqueness? Is there no middle course?

There obviously *is* a middle course. It is simply the course we followed for thousands of years as we constructed buildings in the local vernacular style. These buildings tend to have a strong family resemblance, as seen in these TWO STREETS IN ASSISI, even though no two are alike. This arises because they are built to serve similar needs using similar materials assembled by similar methods. People look to neighboring buildings, find the things they like, make minor changes to meet their own needs, and hire the same builders to construct their building. Paper plans are not required. A long discussion with the builder, a few stakes in the ground, some sketches in the dirt, and a review of standard details are all that is needed before construction begins. Adjustments might be made as the work progresses.

The result of this approach was coherent towns, with common themes, common adaptations to local circumstances, and common underlying values expressed in the finished buildings. Only an architectural snob would find anything wrong with this approach, and the fine results were usually superior to anything we build today. This practice is still followed in many places.

Sadly, vernacular styles are no longer widely respected in many Western nations, and, where they remain in use, the fundamental logic of their design has been forgotten. Modern examples of vernacular styles are often hardly more than a burlesque. In the USA, stud-framed houses are a maladaptive vernacular form. Centuries ago, this construction technique was well suited to MASSACHUSETTS, with its once-vast stands of old-growth softwood. The framing, siding, and roofing were all made of locally-available, rot-resistant softwood. This timber was logged-out years ago, so the high-quality lumber on which this design relied is only available at an exorbitant price. The basic framing method is still used in most of the USA, despite serious termite problems outside the cold areas where the style originated. Wood-frame houses built today have a relatively short life expectancy. (Wood is in any case unsuitable in urban areas due to the fire risk.) Roofing and siding are made of plastic, aluminum, or asphalt and mimic the forms of their old wooden counterparts, but the eye immediately discerns the fakery. Real, operable shutters have been replaced by bolt-on plastic or metal imitations that are often not even the right size to cover the windows they adorn. Thus was a practical and attractive vernacular style misappropriated over the span of decades.

Besides the unsuitability of contemporary lumber for this construction method and its use in regions where it rapidly decays, the quality of design has steadily deteriorated for two centuries. The reasons for this are not entirely clear. The matter may have to do with the Cartesian errors of several centuries past, which were exacerbated by industrialization and mass production, and further compounded by today's corporate greed and consumption frenzy. More investigation into the decay of design abilities is badly needed. Alexander has attempted in his many books to restore good design skills to everyone.

Several important considerations affect the design of minor buildings. They are the subject of the rest of this chapter.

Ground Floors

We will want to keep the ground floors of most buildings busy during much of the day. I propose to use ground floors mainly for commercial occupancies, which will keep them busy during business hours. It is not out of the question to have some, or even many, residences on ground floors if people are prepared to live with the inherent privacy limitations (see page 372), and

Woodstock, NY

Jonathan Hale took up this question in *The Old Way of Seeing* and offered some interesting thoughts on the matter, although it is too early to draw conclusions.

Some US houses are torn down after just a few years, only to be replaced by other houses of similar (large) size and character. This is probably the most extreme form of conspicuous consumption in history.

Coimbra, Portugal

this has the advantage of keeping eyes on the street at all hours of the day and night.

Most commercial users benefit from having ground-floor show windows, even if these are not always expansive plate glass affairs. If commercial use is contemplated but not immediately required at the time the building is designed, it is possible to frame the windows floor-to-ceiling, but to fill the bottom meter (yard) with a window sill until such time as larger window openings may be required. A later conversion to French doors becomes a simple matter. If plate glass is used, it should not be brought too low, as the risk of someone walking into it will arise. Even Venice has some instances where this is an issue, but in most cases VENETIAN PLATE GLASS is safe. I usually object to plate glass windows, but less often in Venice. This is probably because repeating, identical windows are rare and because of the high quality of Venetian shop window displays. The use of stone framing in Venice, instead of the aluminum so common today, also helps a great deal.

A perennial problem is the desire to store bicycles and other gear at ground level. Entryways tend to get cluttered with junk and become difficult to pass through with a load of groceries. Only the proposed concierge service really seems to offer a solution to this thorny problem (see page 180).

BALCONIES, TERRACES & ROOF GARDENS

Balconies are a gift to residents of dense urban areas. For many, it is the only way they can pass time outdoors without leaving home. I have never had one and have always felt the lack acutely. When my parents lived in a Greenwich Village apartment, they used their balcony every evening during warm weather, as did many other tenants of that large building. The only point to watch with balconies is that they must be at least six feet (1.8m) deep if they are to be useful.

Faro

"Six-Foot Balcony," APL, Pattern 167

Occupants of ground floors may have to give up some privacy, but they should in return have direct access to a terrace on the interior courtyard. For many, this will be enticement enough. Although most of the courtyard may be in public or semi-public hands (see page 339), the first 2-4m (6-13') can be reserved for the abutting occupants, as here at the BEGIJNHOF in Amsterdam. These spaces will see intense use in warm weather, and we should ensure that they are made available.

One trick that can be played is to make the ground floor of a building a bit deeper than the rest, so that occupants of the floor above have a terrace on the roof of the extension, perhaps with a spiral stair giving access to the courtyard. Commercial tenants on ground floors should also have access to the courtyard, where they will often prefer to take their lunch during good weather. The placing of storage sheds in courtyards should be prohibited under most circumstances. Again, the concierge service offers an alternative.

The use of roof-top space varies enormously from culture to culture. In Western nations, it is relatively uncommon. In arid regions, rooftops are a vital part of living space. In Fes-al-Bali, virtually all buildings have ACCESSIBLE ROOFTOPS. In very hot weather, people will sleep there, as these regions cool off rapidly after sunset under the prevailing clear skies. In addition to their use as gardens, rooftops are valuable for prosaic activities such as laundry drying, water catchment, or the installation of solar collectors. It is important to have coherence in the design of the roofs of any given block (or larger area, if possible), and so roof usage should be addressed from the outset of design. Heavy snow loads can be expensive to accommodate on flat roofs, so roofs in snowy regions are normally pitched and hence unsuitable for use except as a location for solar collectors.

In the arrangement of any rooftop space, safety is a serious consideration. It must be impossible for small children to fall, and anything left out on the roof must be of such a nature that

Faro

All this assumes a location in the northern hemisphere.

it cannot possibly blow away, even in a violent storm. Large umbrellas are a particular risk. Their frames should be so strong that the cloth will rip out before their fixing blows away.

One appreciable disadvantage of dense construction is that sunlight cannot reach all floors during all seasons. Although buildings on the south side of a street should have sun on the back side all winter, ground floor spaces on the north side of a narrow street will have no sun during many months of the year. This is the most suitable location for the concierge service. The floors above will also be in shadow some of the year, but there should be decent light all year. Of course, the backs of these buildings will have fine north light from the courtyard.

PRIVACY

Privacy is a sensitive issue in dense urban areas. When ground floors are given over primarily to commercial uses, the privacy of ground floors becomes less of an issue. (To some extent, this is a cultural matter; in Holland, it is common for people to leave their ground-floor living and dining rooms open to public view, with their more private spaces at the back and on upper floors.) The reflections from window glass significantly obscure the view of the interior by day. The use of curtains, even thin, gauzy ones, provides good visual privacy (but little acoustic privacy when the windows stand open). Operable shutters (see page 530) provide almost the same degree of privacy as walls, and I commend their application, which continues unabated in much of the world. Heavy curtains are an alternative means to provide visual privacy after dark, but they interfere with ventilation in hot weather.

Adjustments can be made in the floor heights of buildings on opposite sides of narrow streets, so that floor levels are about HALF A STORY DIFFERENT. When this trick is combined with the lateral staggering of windows, so that they do not look directly

into one another, reasonable privacy is created in the deeper recesses of the facing buildings. If the front wall of a building is quite thick, then part of the window is hidden when viewed from off axis. If the sides of the window openings are kept a light color, then plenty of light is still brought into the room. Reducing the size of windows is also possible, but I do not recommend this approach.

Privacy on the back sides of houses is an easier problem to tackle. Interior courtyards will generally be at least 20m (65') in the narrower dimension, and this distance is sufficient to provide a considerable degree of visual privacy. Trees, when in leaf, provide far more. At the cost of some visual coherence, the backs of the buildings can be STAGGERED (by varying the depth of the buildings), and this provides a surprisingly large improvement in privacy, even if the variation is only 2m (6') or so. If balconies are provided on the back sides, they provide additional privacy, especially once potted plants have been set out on them.

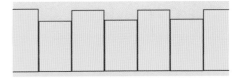

Privacy issues have found various solutions over the centuries, but it must be admitted that residents of dense urban areas have less privacy than those in rural areas. Many people accept this circumstance and some don't seem to mind it at all.

LOW BUILDINGS

You may ask what place low buildings have in a city. The short answer is "not much," but the matter is more complex. Two-story buildings have a place in small cities and towns, and they are occasionally useful in larger cities. The advantage of low buildings is that we relate immediately to them and that their scale is hardly ever daunting. Families especially will prefer them if a single family can occupy an entire house. The following examples are of unusually fine low buildings.

The lovely FERME DU LIEU MAROT in Houlgate is probably quite old, certainly in style if not in fact. The small scale and

elegant setting would make it a delightful place for a weekend getaway. I have imagined that the green areas surrounding a carfree city might include places like this, accessible only by bicycle, to provide a tranquil retreat in the countryside. Switzerland has a number of isolated small inns in hiking areas, where several trails converge.

The AÎTRE DE SAINT MACLOU in Rouen dates to 1527. It once belonged to a cemetery and today houses a school of fine arts. Notice that the building is built to a very small scale despite its fairly large size. The ceilings are low on the upper story and only moderately high on the ground floor. The small panes in the windows contribute further to the pleasing small scale. This is a warm, friendly building.

Lisieux is an old provincial French town. From other views it is apparent that this low house on the RUE ORBEC is unusual; much of the rest of the town was built a story or two higher. Despite its modest height, this was an expensive building, with elegant stone carving. Notice that the windows are of very small panes set in lead. This is an old and very beautiful technique.

Notice also that the upper story is nearly as large as the ground floor; the faces of the dormers actually come right out to the main façade of the building, and little room is lost to the sloping roof, which is steep and intersects the front wall above the level of the attic floor. There may even be a small third floor, with dormers out the back.

Adaptive Renovation

Let us not lose sight of the importance of adaptability; good buildings are not recycled, they are reused, often many times. We simply cannot afford the resource drain involved in demolishing and replacing buildings every few generations. Although renovations are often extensive and sometimes cost nearly as much as new construction, a far smaller mass of materials is needed, and the amount of waste created is correspondingly small. We should attempt to design buildings that are suitable for uses other than those intended by the original owner. In particular, it is useful to arrange them so that several adjacent buildings can be merged if a larger space is required, as in the case of the COMMERZBANK in Amsterdam, where five different buildings were fused to make an office. The only thing that makes such a conversion difficult is variation in floor levels. If the floors are kept at the same height (which may be a bit boring), then such fusions are comparatively simple to effect. It is merely necessary to add lintels to the side walls and punch doorways through to join the spaces. Undoing this change is even easier.

Many buildings in the centers of European cities are centuries old, and most have known major changes in their usage over the years. This is even true of monumental buildings, including churches that have been adapted for secular uses in the face of declining church membership; without this change, these wonderful buildings would have had to be demolished, as there are no longer enough parishioners to pay for upkeep.

When renovation is done with sensitivity and respect for the building's past, the essential character of the building is preserved even though the changes (particularly to the interior) may be extensive. High grade RENOVATION WORK is conducted in many cities, such as the Alfama district of Lisbon, where most of the building stock requires rehabilitation and especially increased earthquake resistance.

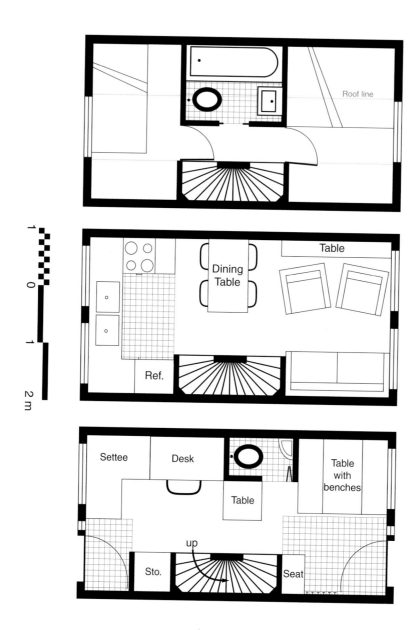

PART IV

DESIGN

This Part begins with a more detailed introduction than the others, as the methods proposed are new and unfamiliar, based as they are on design by users rather than design by experts. The chapters will be difficult to comprehend in isolation and should be read in order. The objective of this Part is to synthesize practical methods for conducting user design of beautiful, functional carfree urban areas, working on the site. The sequence given will require tailoring to fit local cultures and circumstances.

As shown in the FLOW CHART, the process occurs in three phases, which I call the "auction phase," the "commercial phase," and the "village phase." During the auction phase, families bid for prime sites on major squares and main streets. The winners will arrange these areas during the commercial phase. Residential areas are designed during the village phase, which starts with families gathering into urban villages.

The design process actually begins during urban planning, with the establishment of the site program for the district. Late in the planning process, planners will solicit bids for the building sites along the central boulevard and metro-freight lines, where design flexibility is constrained by the rail corridor and transport halt. The location of these buildings will be nearly final by the time the auction phase begins (see page 247).

Preparation for on-site design should begin during urban planning. An understanding of the needs and desires of the future inhabitants can most easily be obtained by opening the sign-up process early and collecting each family's preferences, which can then be allowed to influence planning decisions.

The methods I propose have never, so far as I know, been attempted, although the cohousing movement and the work of

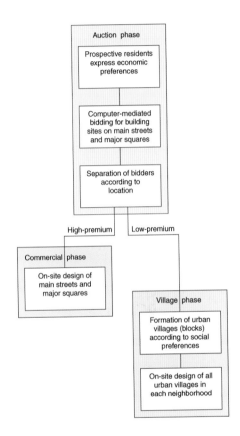

Livingston NJ

Christopher Alexander suggest the way. The first attempts will be pioneering and subject to difficulty, but as experience is gained, the process should flow more smoothly. Initial difficulties may be offset by a demand for carfree living that will outstrip the supply of lots, giving rise to a large pool of applicants. I base this optimistic view on the success of NEW URBANISM PROJECTS (see page 97), which have sold for high prices to eager buyers. I anticipate an even greater improvement in the quality of life from carfree projects, and I hope great demand will arise. This is especially true if the process is economically more efficient than developer-built housing and therefore less costly. The highly efficient use of land will itself significantly lower costs. Enthusiasm should sustain families through some delay and difficulty in their quest for a way of life that is still rare.

During the auction phase, the cost of the land and the premiums that will be charged for prime commercial sites will adjust until demand comes into balance with supply. At the end of the auction phase, families are divided into two groups. Those in the commercial phase will have elected to buy prominent commercial locations for which they will pay hefty premiums, and they will be the pioneers on the site. They will design the major squares and the main streets, which divide the district into 12 to 20 neighborhoods. Families in the village phase will gather into groups along social preference lines, with each group becoming an urban village occupying a single block. All the urban villages in a particular neighborhood will gather on the site at one time to design their minor streets, small squares, and blocks. The process is complete when each family has its own building site. The process involves the following principal steps:

- Families make economic choices regarding their budget, needs, and willingness to pay for high-value locations with good exposure and any other attributes in short supply.
- These choices affect and are affected by other people's choices in a process that resembles a slow-moving auction.

- The demand for high-value sites comes into balance with supply over a span of days or weeks, during which people may change their preferences as a solution emerges.
- Those who will pay high prices for premium sites bordering on the major streets and squares will become pioneers on the site and will design the most important features of the district.
- The main streets demarcate the district's neighborhoods, which will be more residential in nature.
- Those who did not wish to pay high premiums for their sites (which will be the majority of families) will gather into urban villages once the pioneers have designed the main features.
- Each neighborhood will comprise about a dozen urban villages, each of which will take the form of a single block.
- All urban villages in a given neighborhood will gather on the site at one time to design their neighborhood.
- A cooperative process allows villagers to design their blocks and houses to yield an excellent outcome for everyone.

Fes-al-Bali, Morocco

DESIGN TECHNIQUES

Discusses the work of Christopher Alexander, wholeness, design sequences, the universal gift of design, observation, site assessment, climate & weather, evolution vs revolution, paper plans, charettes, models, and the virtues of on-site design

LAND ALLOTMENT

Proposes a method whereby families decide whether or not to pay the premium for a prominent location with good commercial prospects. I call this the "auction phase."

DISTRICT LAYOUT

Discusses design objectives, strategy, street topology, street path, design approach, street layout, on-site design, advocates, assistants, initial design, initial position, major streets, and squares. I call this the "commercial phase."

Coimbra

Village Formation

Considers space allocation, explaining density to participants, district arrangement, design by villages, land, design phases, village formation on the basis of social preference, physical features, advocated buildings & squares, economic decisions, values clusters, and software. This chapter describes the first part of the third and final phase, called the "village phase."

Neighborhood Design

Discusses neighborhood scope, design principles, method, initial position, final definition of villages, arranging minor streets, siting & arranging squares, and the handling of the perimeter. This chapter describes the second part of the village phase.

Building Layout

Discusses the arrangement of floor space, building frontage, varying story heights, roofs, entrances, windows, stairs, utilities & storage, greening the street, and basic building types.

Building Design

Considers materials, style & design, the vernacular, properties of good design, detail, culture & tradition, local themes, roofs, floors, doors, windows, signs, craftsmanship, design regulation, urban form & architectural style, and code enforcement.

Case Examples

Two case examples are presented, a clay maquette in Budapest and a field test of user design in Prague.

Poetry

This Part concludes with a discussion of urban poetry and gives some comparative examples.

DESIGN TECHNIQUES

The methods and techniques used to design an urban area have a large influence on the final result. Many approaches have been employed through the ages. But why do we design streets and buildings at all? What are we trying to accomplish when we do? Is anything more than sound engineering actually needed, or does design, whatever it may be, actually add something to the completed whole? For me the answer to this question is self-evident—we have only to look around at the dismal failures of postwar design to see that there is more to construction than making sure the roof doesn't fall in. But what are we trying to do when we design a building or an urban area? What methods can we use to help us visualize the completed spaces before they are built? First, we must briefly consider what design is and how it attempts to achieve its objectives.

I believe that city design is an effort to satisfy basic human needs in a way that also pleases the senses. I also believe that practical functions are better served when the design is also aesthetically pleasing. For one thing, people are more likely to take care of places they love than places they hate, which reduces vandalism and improves the chances that a place will endure. In fact, this may explain why time seems to be an effective filter for good design: the best buildings and places are preserved, often at huge expense, because we cherish them. Places nobody likes often get the bulldozer treatment, in hopes that the next effort will be better. Imperfect but promising attempts may warrant improvement by later hands.

The field is in a state of rapid change as I write. It is not only the availability of cheap computing power that is causing some of these changes but also whole new ways of thinking. Much new thinking actually expresses age-old ideas that fell out of favor during the automobile age. Christopher Alexander and his colleagues led the way in reviving traditional methods.

Corner of Keizersgracht & Reguliersgracht, Amsterdam

The Work of Christopher Alexander

Alexander has provided us with powerful new design techniques that seldom even employ computers. Alexander has sought, above all, to give the people who will use a project a voice in its design. I have adopted this revolutionary notion and will expand upon it in DISTRICT LAYOUT and NEIGHBORHOOD DESIGN, where I propose a step-by-step method for design of a site by users. The advantages of small urban communities were discussed in URBAN VILLAGES. The assembly of urban villages is taken up in VILLAGE FORMATION, three chapters on.

Alexander has spent a lifetime reflecting on the nature of design and has proposed new methods to achieve better results. His task has been especially challenging because he has worked during an era that is probably the worst in history in terms of design quality. I will discuss briefly some of the tools he has given us. I must note at the outset that Alexander rejects my position on carfree cities. He says:

> The temptation to say—keep the cars out, make it all pedestrian—is far too harsh. In many places, it is just the cars which create life in a place: the freedom of access that they permit which brings vivacity, energy, imagination. But undoubtedly, the pure pedestrian space in which there are no cars is also vital, allowing us to walk, dream, play, unhurried and uninterrupted.

Now, maybe Alexander is correct when speaking of rural areas and perhaps suburbs, but I think it is pedestrians who bring life to city streets. Cars bring only death, literally and figuratively. I think it can be simply stated that any truly urban space can always be improved by removing whatever cars may be passing through or parked there. If there is too much space left after the cars are gone (and this will be a common condition in North

Braga

TNO, III:77

American cities), then the area can be redesigned to find new uses for the extra space, including the addition of new, high-quality buildings. These new buildings bring new uses, new life, and new income to areas that were once dead car spaces.

So, while Alexander and I do not agree on the matter of cars, I believe that nearly all the patterns he identified in *A Pattern Language* are almost essential to achieving the poetic carfree spaces I want to see built.

Another caution is that Alexander has generally worked on projects with considerably lower density than I am proposing, and Alexander talks more about making good gardens than I will. In fact, I think that he, like most designers, believes that good design is easier at low densities than at high densities. I do not think that this is the case. If we adopt the hollow block with a solid wall of buildings around it as being the most practical way to arrange acceptable urban areas at FARs above 1.0, then the remaining design issues are considerably simplified. It remains only to make good dispositions of the streets and to arrive at a successful design for an enclosed interior courtyard.

Alexander was disappointed by the results of *A Pattern Language* notwithstanding the enduring popularity of the book. The patterns he identified were not by themselves sufficient to generate good design and the quality he calls "wholeness." The patterns were the ingredients in a good recipe, but they didn't explain how to cook it up, how to assemble the elements in a satisfying way. I think this failure is even to be found to a degree in Alexander's own buildings. Many of them are somehow unsatisfactory, even though they possess many patterns that are in themselves right. His buildings are often distinguished by brilliant ornamentation, but the larger elements may seem plain, even drab. It is, ironically, sometimes the whole that fails. To be fair, Alexander's results have been better than those of almost any other contemporary architect.

Alexander stresses the importance of local symmetry, which is

His two high-density apartment proposals in Japan were important exceptions; the denser of the two had a FAR of 1.44, a plot ratio of 0.48, was built only 2½ stories high, and still managed to accommodate cars. The green spaces were tiny.   TNO, III:316-330

Known by some as a "perimeter block"

Venice

TNO, I:187

TNO, II:447-478

Venice

found in his buildings. At larger scales, he believes that balance, more than symmetry, is to be sought. He gives the example of Granada's Alhambra, rich with local symmetries but lacking any overall symmetry. I think that the relationship reflects human symmetry. At the scale of an individual, we are quite symmetrical, but as soon as we gather in groups we almost always assume asymmetrical arrangements. At roughly the same scales, our buildings should do the same. He gives a wonderful illustration of a building in Copenhagen where "uneven, syncopated, local symmetries form a perfectly harmonious whole" in a building that lacks any overall symmetry.

Alexander has not adopted the order & organization plane of analysis that I have used here, although the concept is certainly not foreign to his work, which exhibits very high levels of organization. (This, in fact, is really what *A Pattern Language* is all about.) High levels of order are usually confined to the smaller elements of his buildings.

Some will criticize the lack of perfect finish in Alexander's buildings, but I have no objections whatever to the handmade imprecision of his buildings. The result is human and interesting, not mechanistic.

I summarize below what I think are the four most important works Alexander has written during the course of a remarkably productive life.

A Pattern Language

I regard *A Pattern Language* (APL) as one of the most important books of the 20th century. If you read only a single work on the design of the built environment, make it that one. It is packed with practical, easily-accessible advice. A few parts of *A Pattern Language* are either dated or unsuitable for application to carfree cities, but otherwise this book gives citizen designers the most important concepts of good design. Even though it is over 1100 pages long, the gist of it can be gleaned in just a few hours, as the book is a true handbook, with the important points emphasized. The 253 patterns identified in this book will help in the design of projects that exhibit deep, organized complexity.

A New Theory of Urban Design

In this book, Alexander proposed a method for achieving good neighborhoods that exhibit wholeness and an evolved character, without having to wait centuries for this result to appear. The method uses a maquette plus paper plans to achieve rapid, evolved design that approaches the quality of spaces that emerged over the centuries. The method depends on first establishing features that anchor the space; successive work fits in adaptively. Design does not start with one grand idea; it evolves, each piece strengthening what has already been done. Alexander himself admits that the trial effort presented in the book (and never built) does not achieve the high level of wholeness he sought, but the result is clearly far better than the usual grand plans devised in the conventional manner.

Venice

The Production of Houses

Alexander helped a small group of families in Mexicali to design their own houses. He devised construction techniques that allowed considerable flexibility in design, which was performed on the site by the future residents. He helped them to arrange their five houses on a single small block while anticipating the use of these construction methods. The result was inexpensive, high-quality, user-designed houses. He describes the methods he used to reach rapid compromise and agreement among the future residents. Although the precise construction techniques proposed are not suitable for multi-story buildings, the concepts are fascinating and can doubtless be altered for taller buildings.

Alexander developed a new codified structural engineering solution based on locally-available materials and suitable for single-story buildings. See page 519 for a general discussion of this approach.

The Nature of Order

Unlike the earlier works, this one is exasperatingly full of minor production errors.

Alexander's rambling four-volume *The Nature of Order* (TNO) is a problematic work, as it verges at times on mystical. However, the many case examples are interesting and illuminating. I have seized upon those ideas that I find useful. Reading the three earlier works mentioned above will give you the foundation you need. Most of *The Nature of Order* can simply be skimmed.

WHOLENESS

Wholeness is really the central theme of Alexander's *A New Theory of Urban Design*. All seven of his fundamental rules are directed specifically towards the generation of wholeness. Although the methods he uses are different from those that I will propose, I accept this concern with wholeness, or coherence, or whatever you may wish to call it, as being of central importance to good urban spaces. He begins *A New Theory of Urban Design*:

Porto

Alexander (1987), 2. Ellipses in original.

> This feeling of "organicness," is not a vague feeling of relationship with biological forms. It is not an analogy. It is instead, an accurate vision of a specific structural quality which these old towns had ... and have. Namely: Each of these towns grew as a whole, under its own laws of wholeness ... and we can feel this wholeness, not only at the largest scale, but in every detail: in the restaurants, in the sidewalks, in the houses, shops, markets, roads, parks, gardens and walls. Even in the balconies and ornaments.

Until now, wholeness has mainly arisen through centuries of evolution, as in Piazza San Marco, cited by Alexander as an example. However, some instances of wholeness did not evolve, they were designed at one stroke. I am thinking here of the many grand Renaissance plazas in Spain, which certainly exhibit wholeness, although I do not find them to be the best examples of design in the cities they grace. These spaces did not evolve. One man had the power to implement his vision. There are many clear examples of this, where a medieval district stands cheek by jowl with a district planned according to Renaissance sensibilities. I think here of Lisbon, Léon (Spain), Sfax (Tunisia), Fes-al-Bali (Morocco), and so forth.

The very nature of "planning" may cause failures in urban design. In a discussion of large-scale projects, Alexander says:

Piazzetta San Marco

> And there is a further sense in which such planned communities, and indeed nearly all developer-built artificial communities, are based on structure-destroying transformations. This comes not from their failure to be consistent with the land, where they are built, but merely from the fact that they are planned *at all,* rather than "grown."

TNO, II:122

Alexander identifies the four fundamental and essential features of growing wholes as:
• Piecemeal growth
• Unpredictability of the final whole
• Coherence
• Strong feeling

Alexander (1987), 14

The most noteworthy of these is, I think, piecemeal growth. The idea that everything should be influenced by what has gone before and should affect everything that comes after is a central notion in urban design, and one that is not widely accepted at this time. (This says nothing about the tempo: decisions should follow one another, whether closely or over the centuries.)

Stuart Brand has also tackled the question of design that achieves a satisfying and enduring wholeness:

> The most admired of old buildings, such as the Gothic palazzos of Venice, are time-drenched. The republic that

Venice

lasted 800 years celebrated duration in its buildings by swirling together over time a kaleidoscope of periods and cultural styles all patched together in layers of mismatched fragments—an aesthetic practice that may be appropriate to our own multicultural age.

Brand, 63

Despite this potpourri of styles, Venice achieves a wholeness that is rarely found on such a large scale. The superior result stems from a steady and sensitive adaptation to what has gone before.

I don't think we are yet ready to synthesize a grand theory of wholeness. Nevertheless, this concept is one to keep in mind when designing urban spaces.

The processes I propose in this Part are based more on social and economic commonalities that will drive the formation of urban villages than on aesthetics per se. I certainly hope that beautiful spaces will emerge; they are indeed necessary, but design will be driven by the needs of the users, not by abstract theories of design. Design that is informed by some inner need is almost always better in both its appearance and its functioning than design that is driven by abstract philosophy.

Burano

DESIGN SEQUENCES

The method I propose is based on the four works of Alexander just described. One of his more surprising findings is that design decisions can be guided by "morphogenic sequences," a concept borrowed from developmental biology. It has long been known that all mammalian embryos look very much the same until a certain point in gestation, when they begin to differentiate themselves according to the species they will become. Each change springs from the differentiation that preceded it. Alexander proposes that spaces can also unfold following a set sequence of steps in which a single question is taken up at a time.

If Alexander's hypothesis is approximately correct, and I believe that it is, then he has made a real breakthrough in design technique. This method is described, with examples, in a chapter in *The Nature of Order.* The process is perhaps best characterized in his description of the design of Guasare New Town in Venezuela. There, the process was complicated because few buildings touched each other, and the decisions regarding the handling of the open space between the houses were complex.

The task of arranging a district would be simplified if morphogenic sequences could be applied; correct sequences should lead to a good unfolding of the space, as long as the sequences are properly executed. The use of sequences is a great simplification, without which the number of possible design combinations can become essentially infinite. However, if a workable morphogenic sequence can be defined, then the number of decisions that must be taken becomes fairly small, and the possible choices for each decision are limited. The task is thus made manageable. Alexander's process is, rather surprisingly, *not* iterative: you take each decision in order and don't go back.

> The essence of the successful unfolding is that form develops step by step, and that the building as a whole then emerges, coherent, organized. The success of this process depends, always, on sequence. (TNO, II:129)

However, the designer knows the sequence and will anticipate decisions soon to come. His awareness of the later steps will likely influence the current decision. This causes no problem except for the minor violence it does to the neat theory.

Alas, lacking the actual experience of building a carfree district, I am unable to propose morphogenic sequences for their design. The best that I can offer for now are more generalized suggestions for design methods and processes, coupled with the advice to study and apply the examples given in Part III.

"The Sequence of Unfolding," TNO, II:300-322
Guasare project, TNO, III:340-348
See also the project in Santa Rosa de Cabal, Colombia, in which families designed their own streets and houses. These were single-family houses one or two stories high, many but not all of them abutting the neighboring buildings. TNO, III:398-408.

Beja, Portugal

The Universal Gift of Design

In *The Old Way of Seeing,* Jonathan Hale tackled the question of why the quality of building and street design has declined so precipitously in the industrialized nations. Although he does not arrive at a very satisfactory explanation of the cause, he correctly identified a crisis in Western design.

He attributes the decline to weaker community values and to the rise of acquisitive values. I do not think he is too wide of the mark, but there is more to it.

I have observed that the ability of people in pre-industrial societies to design the objects in their lives has not seriously deteriorated, although their abilities may have declined since they have been exposed to Western ways. As I mentioned on page 41, the fractal processing capabilities of the human mind may really lie at the root of what we find beautiful and what repels us. It is also quite possible that good built environments closely resemble good natural structures in the character of their arrangement; biological processes long ago discovered and expressed efficient structural design. Again, we may have evolved to effortlessly process such structures in our minds, since they abound in the world around us. More research into these vital questions is clearly needed.

Fractals in nature

Alexander has sought to restore the universal gift of design:

> In this vision, the craft of the architect—the forming of the environment in its beauty, in its majesty, in its humanity—is to be assisted by semiautonomous generative sequences that help millions of people to become creative.

TNO, II:560

Although Alexander's work may contain some internal contradictions and some flawed reasoning, I believe that his prescriptions are fundamentally correct. This body of theory has far to go before it matures and can be held as proven, but, in the absence of anything better, we can follow his methods when trying to put design into the hands of ordinary people, and we can have reason to anticipate success.

Observation

Whoever may actually conduct the design, sensitive design that is responsive to the site depends upon good observation at the start. The data that is collected during urban planning studies forms the foundation of this data, but it is not sufficient. Other observations of a more contemplative and subjective nature will be required. As Lynch & Hack put it:

> The basis of any design project must always rest upon observation of the users and their needs. Such observation is a matter of life-long preoccupation by good designers. City designers need to know people and how they use city spaces. They must understand that other people differ from themselves and each other in a great many ways. While it is not possible to know everything about everybody and their tastes, an effort should be made to extend this understanding to the greatest possible extent, as it influences everything that a designer will do.

Lynch & Hack also devote a chapter to this issue in *Site Planning*.

There is really no substitute for direct inspection of the site, and this process should last at least through all the seasons of a year. All parts of the site should be inspected at least once, and the areas thought suitable for building should be visited frequently, during all hours of the day.

Take detailed notes, make sketches and photographs, record audio and video footage. After-the-fact review of this material will give rise to insights that do not occur while standing on the site. It is best if several people make independent observations and later compare their findings. Where disagreements arise, the site should be revisited to resolve the question before design begins. Volunteers can make and summarize most of these observations, although some training may be helpful.

Venice

Lynch & Hack, 86. See also Lynch's *The Image of the City* and *Managing the Sense of a Region.* William H. Whyte's *The Social Life of Small Urban Spaces* and Donald Appleyard's *Livable Streets* are both valuable.

Lynch & Hack, "The Site" 29-66

Salema, Portugal

I only became aware of the din made by thin plastic shopping bags while recording in Piazza San Marco. I had only been subliminally aware of noise from this source until I was listening through headphones as I recorded. By this means you will hear things of which you have never really been aware.

"Site Repair," APL, Pattern 104

Do not neglect the ambient sounds, which are surprisingly difficult to apprehend. I have found the use of a digital recorder and a good stereophonic microphone invaluable. While recording, monitor the sound through headphones. For some reason, the simple act of listening to live sound through headphones makes the acoustic environment far more evident than listening to it directly. I cannot explain why this should be so.

Site Assessment

Be certain to understand the limitations of the site. Alexander calls for the early identification of the damaged and inferior parts and suggests that these are usually the best places to build, thereby leaving the good parts intact. When we are working in a dense urban context, we will not always have the luxury of following Alexander's dictum, but we should be aware of what is good and worth preserving and what is damaged and would be better altered. If the site has natural watercourses, consider trying to retain them, rather than burying them in culverts.

Mundane issues are often important, for they will affect the quality of day-to-day life. Will the night-time noise from a distant highway disturb your rest? Will the north slope remain cold until late in the spring? Does the earth turn muddy after a light shower? Do the winter winds blow unobstructed into the site? Will the glare of late-afternoon summer sun off the water be intolerable? Study the site until you understand every aspect.

The character of the site should be allowed to exert a large influence on the design. When street plans are established without regard for the site, poor results are likely. See page 78 for a discussion of the consequences of the mindless application of grids to San Francisco. However, when design responds to the site, the results can be not only functional but beautiful. Take, for example, Lisbon's ALFAMA DISTRICT, where the steep slopes affected nearly every aspect of design.

Designers need to know the slopes of a site and understand which areas are steep enough that streets should not ascend them head-on but by crossing their face. This will have major implications for the arrangements of streets, as it is the wider streets that must be arranged to cross the faces of steep slopes; minor streets can be steep and may even be arranged with stairs, as in the MEDIEVAL QUARTER of Coimbra.

Lynch & Hack call for the design of both the site and the buildings on it to be developed by the same individual or team. They see problems arising when different groups take responsibility for these two tasks. If, however, design involves the future inhabitants, this problem should not arise. Do remember that a conflict between urban planning and final design may arise when experts are employed for the former. Outsiders must work closely with the ultimate users and gain a thorough familiarity with the site. And always remember that a difficult site invites a brilliant response, as in Tibet's memorable POTALA.

CLIMATE & WEATHER

Design must accommodate local climate and weather. Remember that climate averages are a poor substitute for full data. An average wind speed of 15 knots takes on new meaning if this represents calm half of the time and a near-gale the other half of the time. Climatic data should be presented as ranges and frequencies. GRAPHICAL REPRESENTATIONS are easy to comprehend, and rare conditions stand out clearly. Preliminary design should always at least consider the traditional regional solutions to climate challenges, as they may still remain the best approach to the problems.

Ideally, those doing this work will have lived on the site for many years and be intimately familiar with the climate and the extremes of weather. Do understand that 30°C (86°F), 75% relative humidity, and no wind in New York feels very different

Lynch & Hack, 133

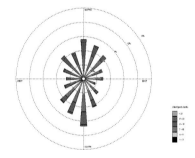

Valladolid

Lynch & Hack, 54

from the same 30°C in Lisbon but with 30% humidity and a good breeze. New York summers are difficult without air conditioning; almost no one in Lisbon has it and most see no need for it. This owes in part to the heavy masonry construction used in Lisbon, which is well suited to hot days and cool nights.

Designers must have an almost intuitive understanding of the effects of climate, and this comes most directly from long experience living in a place. This is yet another reason for design to be conducted by local people. Those who have lived for a time in San Francisco will refer, without irony, to the different climates in different parts of the city. The western part of the city can be cold and foggy on a day when it is hot and sunny downtown, a rather short distance away. Even the east and west sides of the same hill can have markedly different climates. Few places experience such extreme variation in microclimate, but the effect is common, and the circumstances are usually known to people who live in the area. Do also be aware of cold air floods, in which a layer of cold, night-time air slides down a slope to pool at the bottom. These pools of cold air can be much colder than nearby areas.

The latitude of the project must be considered. Even in the relatively mild climate of northern Europe, the very low winter sun angles will affect many aspects of design. In particular, it is essential to bring good daylight into homes and offices during December. In a more southerly location, such as Morocco, the sun will be fairly close to overhead in June, and pedestrians need to be shaded from it to avoid becoming overheated in what is already a hot climate. In intermediate latitudes, such as Venice, these problems are moderated, but the NEED FOR DAYLIGHT must be kept always in mind.

Regions with significant accumulations of ice and snow pose a very different problem from those places where frozen water is rarely or never present on the ground. The maximum depth of frost affects the design of foundations and may, by itself, determine whether or not buildings should have basements. Always keep the extreme events in mind.

Rainfall also imposes design constraints. Many arid climates are subject to occasional torrents. Some wet climates, such as Florida, have so much sunshine that extensive irrigation is required to keep lawns green in summer. The falling water tables in this region testify to the need for a different approach to landscaping, open space management, and water retention.

EVOLUTION OR REVOLUTION?

Good spaces most often arise when a long series of good design decisions has been taken over a span of centuries. Some spaces have been great as they were first designed and have since been left alone, but I think that most of the best spaces have evolved over time and show traces of the many hands that shaped them.

Piazza San Marco is a great space despite the rather ordinary, even monotonous, buildings of the PROCURATIE that enclose it on three sides. The design of the campanile is quite plain, and the cathedral is an odd hash of somewhat conflicting styles. The Doge's palace is one of the weirdest monumental buildings in the world. Yet this RATHER STRANGE ENSEMBLE works exceptionally well. It evolved into its current form over the course of a millennium. The hypothesis is that each change was based on repairing the shortcomings of the then-existing state and adding new, desirable elements to the mix. This is supported directly in a fairly long discussion by Alexander, and implicitly by Edmund Bacon, as well as by simple reflection on the history of this extraordinary space.

In his discussion of the Piazza Annunziata in Florence, Bacon enunciated the "principle of the second man":

It was the great decision of Sangallo to overcome his urge toward self-expression and follow, almost to the letter, the

Alexander TNO, II:251-255; Bacon, 101-105

design of the then eighty-nine-year-old building of Brunelleschi. This design set the form of Piazza della Santissima Annunziata and established, in the Renaissance train of thought, the concept of a space created by several buildings designed in relation to one another. From this the "principle of the second man" can be formulated: it is the second man who determines whether the creation of the first man will be carried forward or destroyed.

Clearly, the "second man" ought to think long and hard before demolishing what has been done before. Even the most hopeless situation may offer scope for salvation. Take the work of Michelangelo on the Capitoline Hill as an example. Bacon shows the rather mangy and incoherent form of the site when Michelangelo took it on. The buildings were not well related to one another and the enclosure was weak. Without more than incidental demolition, he completely reshaped the plaza by adding new, deeper façades to the existing buildings. Thus was created one of the great urban spaces of the world.

When some element of the existing constellation violates the underlying organization of the site, do not fear to remove or dramatically reshape it if that is necessary to make a coherent whole. Often, however, a way can be found to redeem some or all of the existing construction. It may not require the genius of Michelangelo. Lynch & Hack say:

> Adaptation is the preferred method of designers who believe in the virtues of familiarity, and that truly great environments are the product of accumulated understanding. It can be an especially powerful method when carried out in the field, that is, when modifications can be made to an environment in use, the results observed, and another round of adjustments then be carried out. A close fit between form and purpose is achieved. But except where

Bacon, 108-109

Bacon, 114-119

This space actually exhibits the hand of a "third man," as the work was finished after Michelangelo's death by those who understood his ideas and brought them to final realization by building the palace in the location and style needed to complete the composition.

Venice

there is a decentralized management of small settings, the cost and scale of normal site operations makes this difficult to do. Working directly with the real product rather than with its simulation is the privilege of painters and potters and small builders. Site planners usually wrestle with more unwieldy institutions.

Lynch & Hack, 131

This has been Alexander's greatest frustration. In *The Nature of Order,* he discusses the problems he has encountered during a lifetime of trying to build great places. He has devised quite a number of new construction business practices with the objective of restoring precisely that "privilege of painters and potters" to construction projects, in which not everything is detailed to the last nail in construction plans, before the first shovel is ever turned. Rather, the design is adjusted during the course of the work, in response to the problems and opportunities that become apparent as the site takes form.

Guimarães, Portugal

Building in this manner was, in fact, the norm in history. Today, however, the slightest deviation from the construction drawings leads to expensive "change orders," or to damage claims if the contractor makes the slightest mistake (or even improvement). I will not delve into the methods Alexander has developed but do recommend that his work be consulted on these matters. Of course, when citizens not only do their own design but also much of the construction, many of these problems simply disappear.

See especially TNO, II:499-529.

The virtues of evolution are gradually being recognized. Jay Walljasper studied the renewal of the Nørrebro and Vesterbro neighborhoods in Copenhagen. In Nørrebro, riots flared in the 1980s when the city demolished 19th-century streets and apartments to replace them with contemporary street arrangements and buildings. By contrast, in Vesterbro, the existing fabric was maintained and improved. The new apartment buildings of Nørrebro are less popular than the old, improved Vesterbro.

Jay Walljasper, "New Lessons from the Old World: The European Model for Falling in Love with Your Hometown"
www.emagazine.com/view/?2307&printview

Gubbio, Italy

In the end, it comes down to a choice between a conservation ethic, which retains good things, and a new-is-better ethic, which demolishes everything at the start. For a great many reasons, economy among them, I believe that the conservation ethic is to be preferred, although not slavishly. (After all, many of those dreadful Modern buildings cannot be fixed, and we will be wanting to demolish them.)

As discussed in ORDER & ORGANIZATION IN CITIES, evolution was the usual method of development during the millennium between the fall of Rome and the start of the Renaissance. I believe that we should attempt to retrieve the refinement of medieval urban design and that we need to find ways to speed up the tempo without harming the results. In DISTRICT LAYOUT and NEIGHBORHOOD DESIGN, I propose a method that combines several techniques. The remainder of this chapter considers the urban design techniques in general use today.

PAPER PLANS

The history and problems of paper plans were considered in ORDER & ORGANIZATION IN CITIES. A century ago, Camillo Sitte condemned "modern" paper-based design:

> [City builders] could attain naturalness easily by judging and arranging everything right on the spot for its actual effect. We, on the other hand, work on the drafting board, and often we have never in our lives seen the plaza for which a competition project may be intended.

Sitte, 75

The real problem with paper planning is that it is a 2D (two-dimensional) method applied to a 3D problem; the inherent flatness of paper is self-defeating. The further danger of paper plans is that it is very tempting to make a plan that is itself beautiful and seductive but which may in fact be poorly adapted to the demands of the site. In particular, the straight line is very easy to draw and looks good on a sheet of paper. On the ground, however, straight lines are boring. Perhaps a few true geniuses have been able to build up 3D structures in their minds and translate them into 2D drawings, but the poor results of modern design suggest that these geniuses are rare indeed.

See APL, "Paths and Goals," Pattern 120

Alexander argues, and I agree, that paper plans may be necessary, but that they should be derived from marks on the site made with stakes and string (see the discussion on page 402). The resulting design can then be recorded on paper, which will be necessary for permitting, land sale, and construction.

Charette

The charette is an intense process that lasts a few days to a week. It brings together everyone interested in a particular design problem. The hope is to generate a design solution that will be adopted by consensus and thereby short-circuit some of the contentious political wrangling that so often bedevils development. Various methods are used and may include site visits, progressively more detailed sketches, and crude maquettes. The core of the method is intense, protracted consultation with everyone who will be affected by the final design. Developing a sense of community is an explicit goal of the method, and a well-managed charette should usually accomplish this goal. Some leaders have turned to the charette in the face of intractable conflict over an important design question, an approach that often resolves the conflict. At the end, the professionals return to the studio to complete a design that ought to reflect the final intent of the charette. The New Urbanists have made extensive use of the charette as a primary design tool.

Coimbra

Alexander considered the charette and rejected it. He has used methods that may resemble the charette, but they are distinguished by being on-going processes that run throughout design and construction. His consultations are probably not as intense and energetic as a charette, but they may yield a deeper and better-considered solution for the project. He said:

> Because the drawing comes too fast, it is playful, creates a sense of participation. However, the actual design is then inevitably drawn by the architect in charge, and is at best an interpretation—often differing widely from what people meant—that gives enormous license to the architect to draw his/her own fantasy in place of the real intention of the community members.

TNO, III:264

I don't see this problem as intrinsic to the method, but it clearly is an issue to be watched.

Alexander's more serious objection to the charette is that the method does not work, because it is mainly based on paper drawings. He also does not believe that the method is suitable to cases where a difficult issue, such as higher density, must be debated and resolved, because of the inherently playful nature of the method and because many issues need to be talked about, rather than sketched. I have myself no direct experience with the method and can only point out these issues as problem areas to be watched when it is employed.

TNO, III:264-265

Physical & Virtual Models

The construction of a scale model (maquette) is a time-honored design technique. It has the great advantage that the impact of the finished site can be assessed from almost any vantage point, not just the one vantage of an isometric drawing. Traditionally, maquettes are built in great detail, sometimes even with fully-developed façades applied to each building. They can be built in wood, papier-mâché, clay, plaster, foam, aluminum, stiff plastic sheet, cardboard, and paper. They can be painted, sheathed in

Venice

paper printed with the building's exterior details, or left raw. Some of Alexander's preliminary maquettes were little more than wads of tissue paper, made in a few moments and as quickly changed. Presentation maquettes are the products of skilled craftsmen working for weeks, with costs to match.

For our purposes, the rough-and-ready maquette made of cardboard or clay may serve just as well, at a fraction of the cost in time and materials. What we are trying to assess with a maquette is mainly how the masses of the buildings will interact with one another and whether the shapes of the resulting streets, squares, and courtyards are satisfactory. We can assess the sense of enclosure. The addition of a few stick figures and trees at true scale certainly helps people to grasp the scale. Lines marking the levels of the floors may help.

Stewart Brand described Alexander's use of maquettes:

Clay maquette

> Chris Alexander believes in making models. Not just one fancy presentation model but whole lineages of rough models, with everyone who will use the building getting a chance to study and critique the best of them as they evolve. Gradually the models grow in scale until they are life-size and at the site—chalk lines on the ground or the floors, tentative portions of the building jury-rigged of cardboard or cheap plywood.

Brand, 200-201

Alexander prefers to assess such details such as truss layouts, column capitals, and window mullions in place and at full size. With a little skill, models can be improvised with cardboard, tape, battens, and staples in fairly short order. The results seem much surer than trying to get it right on a drawing.

At the Towards Carfree Cities V conference, I led an intensive maquette building exercise that lasted a full day of the conference. We adopted some of Alexander's methods, in particular the use of easily-worked clay rather than wood or cardboard to

Budapest, July 2005

make the many individual buildings required. The results of this process are presented in CASE EXAMPLES.

I am of the opinion that the maquette method works, at least to a degree; I doubt that it is suitable as the sole design method for any but the smallest projects (and only then when created at a larger scale than I propose). It is, however, useful as a means to help groups explore design questions and get a feeling for how the site must be built upon in order to reach density targets.

Computer modeling techniques are unfolding rapidly, and 3D renderings are no longer such an immense amount of work as formerly. Even though this method lacks the inherent flexibility of working directly on the site and is slower and more expensive, the ability to "fly through" a design while sitting at a desk should give a good sense of how the space would feel.

ON-SITE DESIGN

I believe that in medieval times, cities were seldom designed in the sense we use the word today (see discussion on pages 84-86). Rather, small decisions were made over the years by the people who were directly involved. This led to complex, satisfying, and highly-organized arrangements. Some of these arrangements may seem quixotic at first glance, but my experience has been that the greater my familiarity with a medieval space, the more facets of its design are revealed to be driven by opportunities and needs. Some nuances remain mysterious even after an exposure of several weeks, and the ingenuity of their design might require years to discover. Other elements may be accidents of history that arose for reasons now lost to us.

Three major changes since medieval times affect the layout of streets in modern cities. First, the transport system must be adequate to the needs of a large city, not a comparatively small town. If metros are used, passenger transport occupies very little land, which allows us to provide the required capacity while still

Near press time, Google announced that it would be linking Google Earth with Google Sketchup, enabling users to add 3D details to buildings with relative ease. The city of Amsterdam is to be the first that has the volume of all its buildings made available on Google Earth. Right at press time, Procedural, Inc., released its CityEngine software, which promises to bring great power and flexibility to 3D modeling.

On-site design exercise, Prague, 2006

employing streets as narrow as we may care to make them. This approach does require sufficient density of habitation in the vicinity of the halts to permit frequent service to be provided at reasonable cost. Second, access for emergency vehicles is now required. This is not difficult to arrange, but it does demand wider streets than were common in medieval quarters. Third, we must provide for the delivery of a larger volume of freight than in the past. The proposed metro-freight system permits this without burdening the streets with large numbers of trucks. In carfree cities we are thus free to return to the narrow, meandering streets of the medieval era

Alexander has again led the modern adoption of old methods. Many times, he has gone out with an armful of stakes and worked with his clients to lay out buildings right on the site. This allows direct response to the properties of the site—its grades, existing vegetation, light, weather, and surroundings. I myself have almost no experience with this method (but see CASE EXAMPLES). However, I have no hesitation in recommending its use, on the strength of Alexander's experience and enthusiasm for it. This approach is amenable to bringing large numbers of people together for simultaneous, on-site design. By bringing them together, it is possible to achieve a more tangible display than is given by sticks and string, simply by asking families to line up at the face of the building they have staked out. If everyone does this at once, the shape of the street will be made quite clear.

If on-site staking is combined with surveying and the development of a 3D computer model, then people could take a virtual walk through the proposed neighborhood and examine it from any vantage point they may wish.

A method for on-site design is proposed in detail in the next chapters. This method is predicated on the formation of urban villages that will design, build, and occupy individual blocks on the site. The rationale for this was given in URBAN VILLAGES.

Coimbra, Portugal

This is well explained in TNO III:173-177 and 270-273. In some cases, Alexander did some staking *after* the construction of a simple maquette, to check the results on the site.

Prague, 2006

Expert Assistance

Alfama, Lisbon

Citizen planners, acting from their knowledge of their own needs, know instinctively how to decide many issues, but experts have an important advisory role in the design process and may be asked to guide it, under the direction of a citizen committee.

Great care must be exercised in the selection of experts, many of whom may be uncomfortable working with citizen designers and unable to serve their needs effectively. It is also essential that experts be philosophically compatible. It is no good bringing a Modernist architect into a project that will be built in the local vernacular style. Traditional architects have usually been willing to work cooperatively with citizens, and their familiarity with the virtues of vernacular style can be assumed, although most buildings will be designed by the owners themselves, with some help from architects and engineers. The proposed method is taken up in BUILDING DESIGN.

Major buildings are a special category both with respect to their importance to the completed district and the manner of their planning and design. Small buildings can be treated in aggregate right up to the point of their actual design, but large buildings must be identified early in the planning process and space reserved for them.

Major buildings must have both patrons and advocates (roles that may be fulfilled by the same people). Planning for these buildings must include the use of and need for the building, the required size, the desired location (mainly with respect to distance from the district center), and any peculiarities of the use. The advocates for these buildings should not be allowed to make demands, but the buildings should be accommodated if they give a significant public benefit. Design constraints will have been negotiated during the urban planning phase. These buildings will almost certainly be designed by architects.

Doge's Palace, Venice

LAND ALLOTMENT

The process described in this chapter is the "auction phase" as shown on the flow chart on page 377. Land will be allotted to families and businesses using a slow-moving auction process mediated by a computer. Money will thus have a significant role to play in the allocation of specific sites to their final owners.

Within the constraints of urban planning and the allocation of sites, a great deal of design freedom exists. However, the design freedom of the future inhabitants working on the site is subject to some constraints. For reasons discussed in URBAN PLANNING, many important design decisions will have been made prior to the start of user design. I will take these earlier decisions as a given, although they may be subject to minor adjustments.

The allotment of building sites begins during urban planning, when planners, civic leaders, and business owners will identify major features they think are needed in the district. The disposition of land along the central boulevard and the metro-freight line is constrained by the adjacent rail lines. These are the most valuable areas of the site. Businesses that need high exposure and excellent access to freight service will want these sites, which will be allocated during the urban planning phase, probably with the local government selecting the winning proposals.

Important uses that are tightly constrained will also exist outside of the central boulevard area. Planners will be thinking of large squares, schools, fire brigades, municipal offices, police stations, and the like. Civic leaders will identify theaters, churches, and community centers. Businessmen may seek to locate a large office or store in a good location. Patrons of major projects cannot make demands; they may only submit a proposal that states their needs. Winning proposals will be incorporated in the basic design of the district, as described on page 247. The patrons of the accepted projects will designate advocates (see page 423) to represent their interests during the design phase.

Street intersection, Siena, Italy

Venice

Those who seek high-premium locations will probably have many common interests, as most of these families will be running some kind of business, and so they tend to form natural communities.

Beja, Portugal

The allocation of all the remaining land to families and organizations occurs during the auction phase. By the time the auction begins, all people and organizations seeking a building site in the district will have indicated their preferences by completing forms on the Internet. These preferences include not only total land area but many other preferences, most of which are actually social, not monetary. The urban planners will use this information to ensure that the basic arrangements they propose will support the needs and desires of the future residents.

Those who are willing to pay high premiums for prime sites with good commercial exposure will bid for locations along the major squares and major radial streets. The winning bidders will usually be constructing comparatively large and expensive buildings. They will be the ones to design the basic armature of the district during the "commercial phase," as described in DISTRICT LAYOUT. They will arrange the important public spaces—the big squares and major streets—which are also the best commercial locations, while siting their own buildings.

Main streets defined during the commercial phase form the boundaries of neighborhoods with a more residential character in the areas behind the main streets. During the "village phase," families will gather into urban villages organized on the basis of values clusters derived from social preferences using methods proposed in VILLAGE FORMATION. These urban villages will then design their own neighborhoods using the process described in NEIGHBORHOOD DESIGN. This concludes the design of the streets, squares, and blocks of the district.

I assume that, by the start of the auction phase, urban planning will be complete and all the land will be in the hands of a single entity, the "developer" (see page 203). I assume that the local government will exercise significant control over the process and that the developer's freedom of action will be constrained by agreements with the municipality. The design processes could be managed by either the developer or the municipality.

Process Overview

Specific building sites will be allotted using different mechanisms in the commercial and village phases. Before the auction ever begins, each household seeking a building site in the district will state the amount of land they wish to acquire and their willingness to pay for each of the various attributes that will command premiums, such as a location along a major street or square, proximity to the center, a corner location, and probably quite a few other attributes in high demand. This process is described in detail starting on page 426. At the end of that process, the future owners of the high-premium land will have been identified, including those who are willing to pay for expensive sites along the district perimeter. Those who choose not to buy expensive sites in the commercial phase will join with neighbors to design their neighborhoods in the village phase, when social rather than economic considerations will predominate.

Many different approaches to allotting land and charging for it are possible, but whatever system is chosen must be fair, transparent, and acceptable to the participants. I propose to sell land at a single price per unit area and to charge variable premiums for more desirable sites, in order to balance demand for these better sites with supply. (Premiums are discussed at length starting on page 411.) Each household will exercise great control over the cost of its lot, which is affected by the amount of land purchased and the level of the premiums to which it is subject.

Premiums are charged only on the land, not for the house that is built upon it. Some premiums are unitary (e.g., for a lot on a given corner) but most are charged either by unit length (e.g., street frontage) or on the total area of land (e.g., proximity to the center). Each family will construct its own house, along the lines described in Minor Buildings, on the lot that it buys,

Siena

Venice

See 397 for a discussion of the proposed contracting mechanisms, derived from the work of Christopher Alexander, which diverge widely from common practice.

If lower-density districts with longer walking distances to the center are desired, a FAR of 0.5 is sufficient.

Perugia

subject to the agreements that govern construction in that area. Most small buildings will be occupied by one, sometimes two, households who do not want to pay a premium for their land and who will represent themselves during on-site design. Although the density of these areas may be somewhat lower than the density of the main streets and squares, it will still be quite high, achieving a FAR of at least 1.0.

The method by which prime locations and the area of land for each building are allotted to individual families is subject to many arrangements and is ultimately a political question. I will assume that the money economy is in play and that those with more money to spend will be able to obtain larger plots and better locations than those with less money. Other arrangements based on power, social class, merit, order of application, or uniform allocations are possible and might eventually be applied in some societies.

Economic stratification is a circumstance that I and most New Urbanists expressly seek to avoid. Their strategy has been to place principal residences on the street front, with garages opening onto a back lane. "Mother-in-law" apartments are built above the garages, creating a supply of inexpensive rental housing, albeit in a less prominent location that is arguably of lower quality as well. My approach is similar. The wealthier families will take up the best locations along the big squares and main streets, but plenty of inexpensive land will remain just behind these locations. Families without much money will find affordable sites near the more expensive locales. Unlike in the New Urbanist projects, the quality of their environment will not be degraded by the presence of garages and cars.

Not every family intending to operate a business in its new house will wish to pay a premium if the nature of the business is such that it will tolerate an obscure location. Since both density and premium levels will be highest near the center of the district and on the major streets and squares, people willing to accept less convenient and prominent locations can acquire a site in one of the lower-density neighborhoods subject to little or no premium. Such sites will be abundant in most districts. These will be quiet, narrow back streets at a distance from the district center. These sites are, in fact, excellent residential locations. It will be necessary to ensure that the neighbors are seeking similar street widths, courtyard sizes, and permitted uses. These are ideal locations for small community services, such as day-care facilities, that will be known mainly within the neighborhood and found by word-of-mouth.

Most blocks facing a major street will have several quiet sides. (A few blocks near the center may have major streets on two, three, or even four sides.) The back streets will be less desirable for most kinds of retail operations and will attract much less competition, with correspondingly low premiums. People who are comparatively affluent may live on one side of the block and those less well off may live on the other sides. This only causes conflict if the two groups do not agree about the interior courtyard; the richer families may want larger courtyards and might want some of the space privately allocated. It is possible to make more room in back of some of these buildings and permit their buyers to pay for additional land disposed in a narrow band of private gardens abutting the shared part of the courtyard. This is not a difficult problem to solve, but it should be anticipated during planning.

During the village phase, the results of the auction phase must be respected while social preferences are being matched (see page 464). Matching in the village phase is non-monetary by default (i.e., social), but cash premiums could be applied to a particular attribute, such as privately-held courtyards, if supply cannot be adjusted to meet demand and it is otherwise impossible to reach a balance. Once a provisional village composition has been reached, urban villages will gather on the site to refine their composition and the sequence of families along the sides

Amsterdam

Braga

Amsterdam

Basel

of the block that comprises the village. The urban villages so formed will then design their local streets, squares, and the location and size of each building.

The auction process commences with each family indicating its preferences. This will include the amount of land the family wishes to buy and the premiums it is willing to pay for scarce locations that will draw a premium. Once every family has expressed its initial preferences, the most desirable sites will be allotted in a process during which premiums for the better sites will be adjusted over a span of days or weeks until demand comes into balance with supply. Each day, premiums will be adjusted to reflect demand and bring it closer to supply. Quite large premium changes may be required to reach a balance. Families will have an opportunity to react to changes by adjusting their preferences.

Matching on economic preferences is complex and includes more than just land area and premiums. Each family should indicate the nature of any business it intends to establish, along with attraction to or repulsion from specific other kinds of businesses. This allows businesses to situate themselves in ways that improve their commercial viability. A computer will make the best preliminary matches possible.

When the process comes into balance and all families are willing to accept the result (or leave the process, to be replaced by another family), this part of the process is complete and each family should know within close limits the ultimate cost of the land it will acquire, even if, as in the case of low-premium land, its location is not yet known. There may be further adjustments to the cost of an individual site as the on-site design emerges, but these changes should be comparatively small and are subject to acceptance by the affected family.

I have given much thought to the question of how to charge for land and the total amount of money to be collected. The usual tendency will be to raise the total district land price in order to recoup any evident "excess" value. The resolution of this matter will be affected by the type of project ownership. The method I have devised has the advantage of simplicity: set a fixed amount of revenue to be realized from the sale of land in the district. From this amount, deduct the money raised from premiums. Spread the remainder evenly across the area of land in the district. If, as I expect, there is a great deal of competition for superior sites, then the money that must be raised by selling the underlying land is comparatively little, and people who accept less desirable locations will not have to pay too much for them. This provides many low-cost sites that are, in essence, subsidized by buyers of the best sites.

Every patch of ground is unique. The best neighborhoods usually arise when the land distribution process maximizes total land values. The high-value sites, those that will be subject to premiums, will be occupied almost entirely by families and organizations that need and can afford prominent locations. They will enjoy the right to design these areas in ways they prefer, and their choices will necessarily be driven by economic considerations. As already mentioned, their scope of action will be limited by agreements reached during the urban planning phase, and it is in their interest to develop attractive places, as this will draw the largest clientele and maximize the value of the land and buildings constructed upon it.

Venice

LAND PRICE & PREMIUMS

I am personally uncomfortable with the concept of land as a commodity, but the prevailing economic systems in most of the world treat it as such today. The methods I propose therefore reflect this reality, and I will treat land as something that can be bought and sold at prices that reflect the relative desirability of one plot as compared to another. However, do remember that in cities the value of any given plot of land is greatly affected by

Prague

See Likely Scarcities, page 414

An alternative method would be for families to trade away land in return for a better location; other families in worse locations would receive extra land. Money-based societies will probably prefer the simplicity of the market as a regulating method.

Venice

the nearby uses and by proximity to transport systems. Public and private investments result in values rising more on some plots than on others. In an entrepreneurial system, those who are clever enough to figure out where the desirable plots will be and buy them will gain the benefit of increased value without having to pay for it. The levying of premiums is intended to capture this value for the general treasury, whoever may own it.

The fundamental question is thus how to allot land, especially the more desirable sites, to individual businesses and families. Each family will buy a greater or lesser area of land at a greater or lesser price, both possibly subject to some limits. Inherent in the land are a number of scarcities, which must somehow be allocated. Using premium pricing to balance supply with demand seems the most direct method. Minor changes of location during the on-site process will cause equally minor changes in premium levels as families move slightly closer to or farther from the district center. However, as the center is approached, comparatively small location changes might result in large premium changes, reflecting the very high value of sites near the center. If a family should decide to move around the corner to another side of the block, they may be moving into a main street with high premiums that reflect its commercial value.

Once the willingness to pay premiums in exchange for better sites has been expressed by each family, the initial solution can be derived quite simply. Take the example of major streets. Households are placed on the major street of their choice at the lowest available premiums consistent with their preferences. Households are arranged in order along the street according to their willingness to pay for proximity to the center. Corner locations are allocated in accordance with the premiums households will pay for these excellent retail locations. Frontages are adjusted within the range indicated by each household until the best solution is found. If supply and demand cannot be brought into balance, the software shows a "no solution" condition, and planners or the developer will need to adjust supply to bring the situation closer to balance. A consultative urban planning process should help to forestall these impasses.

We must determine precisely what attributes are to be sold for a premium and what uses are permitted for the land. We must decide whether or not each family will pay for the land in front of its house, land that will become a street. If each family is required to buy a minimum of one meter (yard) of street width, then all streets will be at least two meters (yards) wide. In the case that a family buys a greater width of street (presumably in conjunction with other families seeking sites on the same street), that family might obtain limited rights to use the extra width for a sidewalk café or outdoor sales display. Families might be permitted to use only part of the extra width, which amounts to charging a premium. There is also the matter of who will pay for infrastructure and street paving. These questions must be answered at the urban planning level before the process begins.

Large squares serve important civic functions. It is possible that the abutters will not be willing to underwrite the cost of these squares at sizes as large as the urban planning process has determined to be necessary. However, these squares are such excellent commercial locations that I think people will not only pay for their share of the square but will also be willing to pay a premium as well. In the case of arcades, the abutters would pay for the land beneath the arcade because they obtain usable floor space above it. They might gain limited rights to use the arcade.

If not all street frontage subject to premiums is spoken for, premiums for the less desirable areas will fall to zero. The extra length will be absorbed in two ways: households may elect to increase the length of frontage they wish to acquire, and additional households may be attracted to sites that are cheaper than had been anticipated. Reducing the supply of these sites might be required to bring supply and demand into balance.

Some of the people with whom I consulted during the

Ayamonte, Spain

The question of infrastructure funding is important, but I will not address it except to say that local practice will probably govern. This could be in the form of lot assessments, value assessments, or income tax. The costs could be included in the land price, or general-obligation bonds could be sold to raise the capital.

Guimarães, Portugal

Basel

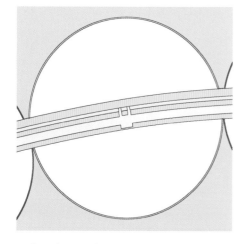

Central areas, allocated during urban planning

development of the methods proposed here were concerned that the extreme speculation that afflicts housing markets from time to time would lead to people scheming to get rich by buying up land in a carfree district. Self-centered behavior of this kind is damaging to both the design process and later neighborhood life, but I am unable to suggest a way of tempering avarice; I can only suggest using premiums to keep it in check. This matter is especially difficult to manage during a real estate bubble, but at least plenty of cash is chasing land, and high premiums may be allowed to arise. This has the effect of making cheap lots available for people willing to accept less desirable sites.

LIKELY SCARCITIES

It is not possible to predict all of the attributes that will become the subject of competition and therefore scarce relative to supply. Some attributes will be amply supplied and will not give rise to competition; these would not be subject to any premium. If something that was believed to be of value is not sufficiently sought-after to generate a premium, it may be useful to reduce the supply of it, especially if this permits an increase in the supply of something that *is* in short supply. For example, if the demand for corner locations in quiet neighborhoods is low relative to supply, larger blocks can be used, which reduces the number of corners and allows larger interior courtyards.

We cannot say for certain what scarcities may draw enough interest that a premium must be charged to regulate their distribution. Some scarcities are nearly certain to draw premiums:

• Locations along the CENTRAL BOULEVARD
• Locations on major squares
• Locations on main streets
• Locations at corners
• Locations with metro-freight access
• Locations on a preferred side of a block or square

- Locations at the perimeter
- Proximity to the district center
- Building frontage
- "Backage" (i.e., courtyard frontage)
- Allowed building height
- Attraction to specific physical features

Sites fronting on major squares will be in great demand, because these are ideal for commerce. They will also be popular with people who enjoy the energy and bustle of a big square. Demand for these locations will probably be great enough that they should be arranged at the maximum permitted number of stories and with the smallest interior courtyards. These locations will require premiums to balance demand with supply.

Premiums will arise wherever they are needed. Any attribute to which significant value is ascribed will become the subject of market-driven negotiations. Demand for locations on small neighborhood squares might be managed simply by requiring the abutters to pay for the land of the square. Space for small squares should be reserved during the auction process. Households can request a square-front location and express a willingness to pay for a part of the square in their land allotment. These households would then have more say in the disposition of the land for which they had agreed to pay. If payment for the land of a square is not by itself sufficient to manage demand, then a premium will have to be added. The mechanism for establishing a premium and managing its level needs to be simple enough that there is no great barrier to creating a new premium when an unanticipated scarcity arises.

It is important to avoid "stickiness" in pricing mechanisms. If, for instance, a premium is charged for proximity to the center, broad price bands will encourage people to cluster at the inner edge of each band. If the price bands are only a meter (yard) wide, then this stickiness is for all practical purposes averted. Until the advent of computers, such fine-grained pricing would

Guimarães, Portugal

Coimbra

The technical term is "boundary effect."

have been too computationally intensive, but today it requires little additional effort to implement.

Each attribute to which a premium is attached becomes an "axis," of which several types are identified (see page 431). We can make an assumption regarding the market value of a given axis and then conduct a trial run. If families tend to cluster at one or the other end of the range of prices, then the formula for computing the premium can be adjusted and a new trial made. Once a good distribution is obtained, we have probably found an equitable mechanism that accurately reflects the market value of this axis.

Increasing the supply of scarce attributes increases the total value of the project without necessarily increasing the cost. For instance, in some parts of China, south-facing frontage is considered auspicious. It is possible to increase the supply of this by reviving the LILONG HOUSING PATTERN that has fallen into disuse but which provides a south-facing entrance to every house. Even lilong housing can be laid out with radial streets, as shown.

The following table compares two different types of locations: wide radial streets and main squares. For each, the likely scarcities and the methods available to manage them are given:

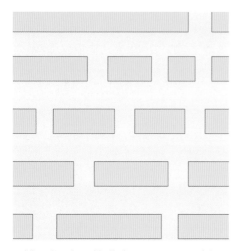

Lilong housing with district center near top right

The land occupied by a square increases as the product of its dimensions, so relatively modest increases in frontage lead to quite large increases in land area if the proportions of the square are retained.

	Wide Radial Street	Main Square
Scarcity		
	Frontage	Frontage
	Corner location	Best orientation
	Proximity to center	Proximity to center
Supply constraint		
	Number of major radials	Fixed area
Increase supply		
	Articulate to add length	Elongate to add frontage
	Add more main radials	Add more squares
Allocation mechanism		
	Premium for frontage	Premium for frontage

Premium for location	Premium for location
Premium for center proximity	Public interest
Typical starting condition	
14 radial streets	Square 20 × 30m
Spaced every 150m	Rough location known
Moderate articulation	Irregular oblong
Location choices	
Select a street	Select a square
Distance to center	Select a side
Frontage	Frontage
Min/max premium	Min/max premium
Extra street width	Add arcade

Venice

All privately-owned advocated buildings should be required to pay a premium for their location and to contribute to the land cost of their streets and squares, as these buildings command choice sites and preempt the design process to some degree. Public buildings that require advocates may or may not be subject to premiums, depending on local political and economic structures. Premiums for advocated buildings can be quite high, as their owners will be anxious to secure a good location.

See page 423

Apportionment of Street & Courtyard Area

Each family would pay for one-half of the street width in front of its house, all of the land occupied by the house, and its share of the interior courtyard. Corner locations may have little or no enjoyment of interior courtyards, and this lack would be reflected in the charge for courtyard land.

There are two possible approaches to apportioning street and courtyard land to adjoining houses. One is to make a fair extension of the wall that divides them and the other is to bisect the angle between the two façades. The result is often identical but differs if the demising wall is NOT AT A RIGHT ANGLE to the

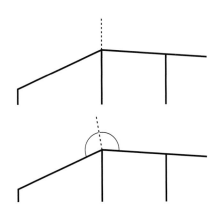

façades. Any increase in the land at the front of the house is usually counterbalanced by a decrease at the rear, but the two may not exactly cancel out. The angle-bisection method seems to work better. Whatever mechanism is used, it must be simple and transparent to avoid conflict.

The division of courtyard costs will also require careful handling. If people will actually own their own backyards, then the method is not so important, as a smaller plot gives a lower price. In the case of courtyards that are shared by all abutters, the matter is not so simple, and people will be seeking to minimize their costs. The two simplest approaches are to divide the area of the courtyard equally among the abutters or to allocate the cost according to the length of backage, which seems fairer to me.

PREPARATIONS

Preparatory work can begin before the urban planning tasks are even complete. As already noted, an understanding of the needs and desires of the future inhabitants can most easily be obtained by opening the sign-up process as early as possible and collecting each family's preferences, which can be allowed to influence urban planning. The distribution and review of information about the site and the design process should occur as early as possible. Informal urban village formation can begin any time.

The site should be open for exploration months or years in advance of land allotment and on-site design. All available information about the site must be easily accessible. The methods to be used to allot land and design the district will require a detailed explanation, as no one will be familiar with the process.

Families will design their own houses, subject to constraints imposed by the urban planning process or adopted during the formation of urban villages. Families must agree that all the houses in a given neighborhood will be constructed at the same time and that construction must begin by a certain date and be

Venice

Near Utrecht

complete within, say, one year. This permits economies of scale during construction, as many different builders and tradesmen will be working in the same area at once, which holds mobilization costs to a minimum. Noise, dust, and disruption are concentrated into a short period during which comparatively few people will live in the neighborhood.

Citizens will need help understanding the physical arrangement of the neighborhoods they will be designing. In many cultures, these arrangements will differ considerably from what is customary; it will therefore be necessary to show future residents how these areas will look and in particular the density at which they will be built. It is not easy for laymen to translate density numbers into a sense of how a place will look and feel at completion. We must provide each family with thorough, comprehensible density comparisons. We will need illustrative materials in various media. Ideally, we would conduct tours of comparable neighborhoods and their buildings to give people direct experience of the choices. In the beginning, we will have to settle for carefully prepared materials.

Certaldo Alto, Italy

Those guiding the process must explain what range of density is required and what choices people will have. Families not willing to live at the densities in question would not join the process. This book is, of course, intended to serve as a starting point. Participants should read THE DENSITY QUESTION, BUILDING LAYOUT, and BUILDING DESIGN before they are asked for their preferences regarding land area and building heights. This will give them an understanding of the range of possibilities and how the various options appear at completion. Additional useful materials are:

- An urban transect (as pioneered by the New Urbanists)
- Photographs and videos of Venice, Fes, and Freiburg
- More comparisons like those in THE DENSITY QUESTION

The feasible types of housing differ from those with which people may be familiar, and a thorough introduction to these

For more on the urban transect, see for instance: Andres Duany, "Introduction to the Special Issue Dedicated to the Transect," in *Journal of Urban Design*, 7 (3):251-260, 2002. Reprint at: www.dpz.com/pdf/03_Journal_of_Urban_Design.pdf Thousands of urban photographs are available in the Design Library at Carfree.com: www.carfree.com/library.html

Coimbra

If streets in the range of 2m (6.5') are used, the scale streets are just 20cm (8") wide, which presents a problem during building, as it is nearly impossible to walk through the maquette. As soon as the streets are 4m (13') wide, the scale streets are 40cm (16") wide, and it is possible to walk through the streets with care

Squares near the perimeter may have merit in isolated carfree districts with external car traffic to garages at the periphery. Even in this case, however, there should be at least one large square near the center.

forms is essential if people are to act with real understanding of how the finished houses will appear and function, both inside and out. Ideally, we would build model houses on the site to show people what is possible within the constraints of the required densities. Another approach is to mock up some floors of typical houses using stage-set techniques, which would be adequate to show people how the spaces would feel. Once the first neighborhoods are constructed, members of later neighborhoods need only examine them.

The building of small-scale clay maquettes, prior to the actual design of neighborhoods, would help people to understand these issues; this process is described in CASE EXAMPLES. Be sure to respect the observation in that chapter regarding the importance of keeping all objects at true scale, so people get an accurate feeling for the space. An alternative is the construction of a 1:10 scale maquette using cardboard boxes. An entire district can be modeled at this scale on a football field, and the boxes can have façades inked on them, to enhance the sense of scale.

BASIC DISTRICT ARRANGEMENT

Urban planning must be complete before the auction can begin. For the purposes of this discussion, I will assume that the district under design broadly resembles the Reference District (see page 128). That is to say, a diameter of about 750m (2500'), a transport halt situated on a square near the district center, open space surrounding most of the district, adequate access for emergency vehicles, narrow streets, many small public squares, interior courtyards within most blocks, and density high enough to support good public transport. This leads to the following typical design conditions:

- Two or three main squares per district, near the center
- Blocks no longer than 120m (400')
- Nearly all blocks hollow in the center, forming courtyards

- Major streets radiating from the center
- Minor radial streets just a few meters (yards) wide
- Minor concentric streets of similar width
- Broad open space outside the perimeter
- A concentric street about 15m (50') inside the perimeter
- A row of houses facing open space at the perimeter

The last two points require explanation. Buildings at the district perimeter will enjoy nice views, and demand for these sites will exceed supply. Additional perimeter sites can be produced by wrinkling the district edge, thereby lengthening the perimeter. By reducing the "house in the woods" feeling, wrinkling may reduce demand while increasing supply. The height of houses at the district edge might be limited to two stories, thereby giving the next rank of buildings an overlook from the top floor. This should also lead to a pleasing graduation of roof heights (see page 236). Reducing the allowed height of buildings reduces their total floor area and hence their value.

Constructing only a SINGLE ROW OF BUILDINGS at the perimeter also helps to manage demand for this location. If a street is arranged right at the perimeter (which is advisable on a number of points, including the provision of emergency access), then the outer row of houses will have streets both front and back, without courtyards, which is compensated for by the view of open space. The rear street ensures adequate light and air. The depth of this row of houses can be increased to raise the total floor area, permitting more but narrower houses. The practical limit is about 15m (50') deep, with frontages down to 3m (10').

Families who choose a site on the perimeter may also have expressed a further preference for a specific part of the perimeter, say, the south-facing side, which would get good winter sun (in the northern hemisphere). Let us assume that along the 800m (2600') of south-facing perimeter, only 200 households can be established. There may be some premium variation even within this rather narrow group (the perimeter with southeast

Certaldo Alto, Italy

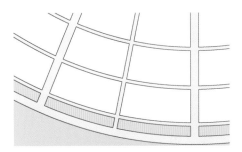

The maximum thickness of a block should be limited to a value that allows some daylight to penetrate into the depths of the buildings. As long as the spaces run the full depth of the building, reasonable ventilation is assured. I would suggest an absolute maximum depth of 20m (65') for residential occupancies.

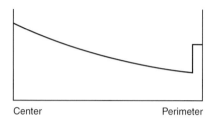

Center   Perimeter

The height limit excludes high places that are for observation only. A city could decide to accept buildings 10 stories tall in the most central districts, but I believe that this is not necessary and better avoided. Recent observations in Spain make clear that buildings even higher may be acceptable in some cultures. It must be noted, however, that this was accompanied by quite wide streets (and many cars). Some interior openings are no larger than air shafts.

exposure might be more desirable than the perimeter that faces southwest), and people might not be willing to shift very far along the perimeter. Premiums can be adjusted to manage demand along the various sections. The perimeter is an unusual case in that its buildings will be arranged in rows, rather than blocks, thereby reducing the number of households that can be grouped into urban villages, simply by virtue of the limited physical extent of the location.

I anticipate that the density of the central part of a district will be the highest and that a DENSITY GRADIENT will emerge as families express their location preferences. From a commercial standpoint, the most desirable locations are those closest to the center, on the major squares, and along the inner segments of the main streets. Lower premiums at greater distances from the center will probably induce families to be a bit more liberal in their use of land, reducing densities at greater distances from the center (excepting the perimeter). This is a desirable result, as it provides a greater range of variation in the housing stock.

Limits on some parameters are required. They would be adopted during urban planning and would almost certainly include (with typical limiting values):

- Maximum story height (2 to 5 stories)
- Maximum building height to cornice (12m, 40')
- Maximum block length (120m, 400')
- Minimum courtyard width (3m, 10' per adjacent story)
- Minimum street width (2m, 6.6')
- Maximum building depth (for residences, 20m, 65')
- Windows on at least two sides of every building
- Minimum area of local squares (per person 2 m^2, 22 ft^2)

Other limits can be adopted as needed. It may be thought that a minimum footprint for houses is required, but I would argue that people should be permitted to build houses as small as they may wish. Some consistency in the height of buildings along an individual block should be enforced, probably as a two-story range (e.g., 3-to-4 stories). This also applies to the buildings on the opposite side of the street, although it is sensible to encourage buildings on the equatorial side of an east-west street to be a STORY LOWER than those on the polar side, so as to increase sunlight on that side. This condition can be imposed during the urban planning process or negotiated during land allotment.

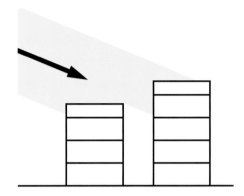

PHYSICAL FEATURES & ADVOCATED USES

Most sites have important physical features—such as hills, watercourses, or a fine grove of trees—that have such a large impact on design that their constraints must be managed even at the urban planning level. These features must be included in the site database as objects that cannot be intruded upon. Their locations and extents must override other considerations. This will have the greatest effect on the routing of major streets, which in the case of hills cannot be steeper than some given value that ideally does not exceed about 6%. In severe cases, an envelope of permissible street routings will have to be developed and included in the database; this will limit adjustments to the route of the affected street to a certain range of locations. Some of these features can be slightly intruded upon and others are subject to minor alterations. This information, too, must be included in the database. Generally, though, these features are best left alone and simply permitted to influence the design.

Major squares and large buildings (see note) will require advocates. (The owners of small buildings will advocate for their own needs.) Advocated buildings must conform to the nature of a district and not unnecessarily restrict the on-site design process. High premiums will be attached to their sites for three reasons: their needs are comparatively inflexible, they often require specific locations, and they will usually be located on prime sites. Urban planners should negotiate premiums in a transparent process (see page 247).

The following is a representative list of building types that require advocates:

- Buildings abutting the metro-freight line
- Transport station
- Hospital & clinic
- Swimming pool/gymnasium/arena
- School & university
- Hotel
- Theater
- Dance hall
- Meeting hall
- House of worship
- Indoor market
- Department store
- Bank
- Library
- Museum
- Fire department
- Government agency
- Small factory
- Concierge service
- Apartment block

Any use that requires a large, unified space, such as a meeting hall, qualifies as "large" for our purposes.

Advocates will participate directly in the on-site design process. They may be architects, urban planners, or others very familiar with the requirements, including location, size, and purpose, of the feature for which they advocate. Large squares can draw their advocates from among the urban planners associated with the project. Advocates for large buildings can be nominated by patrons of those buildings. Planners may advocate for speculative buildings, based on the need for specific kinds of buildings and the present lack of a patron.

Any square larger than about 500 m^2 (5500 ft^2) should be identified during the planning phase and should become an advocated use. Like all advocated uses, the size and location must be recorded as an entry in the site database. Any building that is larger than usual and needs a frontage wider than, say, 10m (33') should probably have an advocate, whether that building is identified during the urban planning process or later.

The largest buildings will usually be the best and most expensive in the district and will enhance a square if situated on it; they in turn benefit from a prominent location. Concierge service (see page 180) is an important advocated use and occupies a considerable amount of land. Space for this service must be allocated even if no family has yet been identified to operate it, as the service is essential (unless some other method has been devised to provide concierge functions). Concierge services will be sited in the least desirable locations and are the one advocated use that will be arranged during the village phase.

The ADVOCATED BUILDINGS will have some precedence on the site, but no more than is essential to their function. In some cases, even the shape of the building will have been determined before land allotment commences, but requirements should be no more restrictive than necessary. A private organization that proposes an advocated building could be required to post a bond to ensure that it will not abandon the project, thereby creating a gap in the district and causing a revenue shortfall.

Ferrara

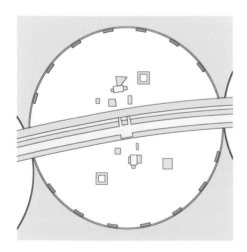

Basic Auction Process

No family can be expected to buy a lot without first knowing the price and location. It is during the auction itself that building sites are allotted to families and organizations. In some cases this will be a specific site, and in other cases the location may be more generalized, as, for instance, at an unspecified location a particular distance from the district center. During the auction, the demand for scarce locations will become apparent, and premiums will adjust to balance supply and demand. At the end of the auction, each family will know the price of its lot (perhaps only within a narrow range).

Each family will already have stated how much land it wishes to buy and what level of premium it would pay for each of the attributes that will likely be subject to some level of premium. This information will already have been collected using forms on the Internet and stored in a database.

Some locations will be more desirable from a commercial standpoint than others, even in areas away from the district center. Locations on minor street corners or small squares have better exposure than buildings situated mid-block on a narrow street, and small premiums for these corners will probably be required to balance supply and demand. The supply of corners can be increased by using what might be called the "double corner." FOUR DOUBLE CORNERS arise when a square is placed at the center of an intersection. Each "corner" then yields two corner buildings. The premium for these corners might be no more than paying for the land occupied by the square. This has the further advantage of spreading the cost of a square's land over more households without posing a significant disadvantage to any of them.

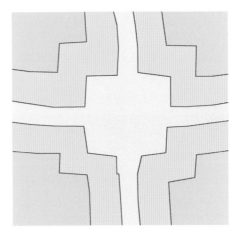

The major radial streets that provide emergency access are necessary for everyone (see page 448 regarding the details of their arrangement), and it is not strictly fair that only those who

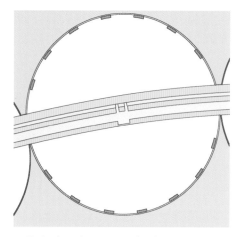

Red stripes show ranges of main street origins

build along them have to pay for their extra width. These streets must start at the perimeter from a LIMITED RANGE OF ORIGINS. These streets will be good commercial locations, and it is likely that only at the outer ends, where foot traffic will be less, will there be any shortage of families willing to pay for the extra width. If insufficient demand for these sites arises, the process will have to stop until the problem has been addressed. It may be necessary to allocate some of the cost of the street to all land in the district, as these streets are needed by everyone. In the case of strong demand, the abutters will pay for the extra width and perhaps a premium as well.

A mechanism is required to ensure that spurious claims are not made; if a site is claimed, it must be built upon, if not by the family staking the claim then by another family. The obvious mechanism is to sell the building site, with payment due soon after the claim is staked in final form. This will be an appreciable sum for most families, who will have arranged financing before the process begins, with the lender reserving the right to inspect the claim and determine its viability before lending the money. This gives some assurance that the site is viable, as lenders will not loan against a property that cannot be resold.

COMPUTER-MEDIATED AUCTION

The proposed method is a complete break with the normal developer-driven process, which treats housing as just another commodity. Success in that system depends upon the accuracy with which the developer anticipates the needs and desires of house buyers. Costs are minimized and profits maximized by mass-producing dozens or hundreds of nearly identical buildings or apartments. None of them perfectly fits the needs of any one family; the design is "good enough" if people will buy the completed dwellings. We need an approach that yields better results and lower prices.

Alameda da Guia, Cascais

The methods I propose have never, so far as I know, been attempted, although the cohousing movement and the work of Christopher Alexander suggest the way. The first attempts will be pioneering and subject to difficulty, but as experience is gained, the process should flow more smoothly. I anticipate that the initial difficulties will be offset by a demand for carfree districts that will outstrip the supply of lots. This would give rise to a large pool of applicants for sites in the district under design. This has been the experience of New Urbanism projects, which have typically been oversubscribed. Given the even greater improvement in the quality of life in carfree projects, I think high demand will arise for building sites in new carfree districts, so long as public transport, cycling, and walking conditions are good. Enthusiasm may sustain families through some delay and difficulty. Certainly the German experience with a handful of early carfree projects has demonstrated the willingness of hundreds of families to stick with a process that has sometimes lasted for years. I hope that less patience than this will be asked.

Before the start of the computer-mediated, auction-like process, families will specify attraction (and repulsion, if necessary) to physical features and locations. They will express the premiums they are willing to pay for each of the attributes that are expected to draw a premium. Premiums for each axis will be expressed as a range the family is willing to pay and their preferred value within that range. Families will express their choices on a FORM ON THE INTERNET. The data will be stored in a database for later manipulation.

Computerized matching is a conceptually ambitious goal, but the computational problem is not too difficult. The mechanistic determinations of the computer will often be wrong, but the magnitude of errors should usually be small, even though they may be quite important to a given family.

Each household will make several monetary decisions at the start of the process. In many cases, these decisions will be driven

Lisbon

See: www.autofrei-wohnen.de/proj-d.html

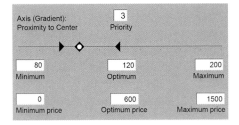

Venice

Negative premiums could be applied if demand is low and people are otherwise unwilling to pay for the extra width of the remote part of a wide street.

A real-time auction is also possible. The software requirements for this option are considerably more demanding, and I would in any case prefer not to place such important decisions as these under heavy time pressure.

by the desire of the family to own a ground floor and use it for commercial purposes (or rent it to others for commercial use). These decisions may hinge on the ability of the family to secure a loan on the property. Expensive locations will usually be worth more in the marketplace because of the higher rents they command. Some commercial activities, such as warehousing, will not tolerate high-value locations, whereas some others, such as newsstands, will not succeed without them. The market is often quite effective at determining prices and allocating better locations to those operations that most need them.

Initial premiums must be estimated by those running the process. The first assessment is whether or not any given attribute actually *is* in short supply—demand may be less than supply. If, for instance, a given radial street has 400m (yards) of frontage and only 300m (yards) are demanded, premiums for the more distant parts of the street could fall to zero, causing demand to increase. Obviously, a solution has not been found until all frontage is allocated, even if some of it is at zero premium.

Unexpected demand may give rise to new attributes that require premiums to balance supply and demand. It is also possible that later changes, during the social matching process, may give rise to premium changes. Here again, families will not simply be required to accept the changes but are free to respond by altering their preferences as they see fit.

Once the auction begins, an iterative process with distinct rounds will ensue, with the rounds separated by a day or two. This gives people time to consider the situation and decide on their next move, which may include alterations in any of their expressed preferences. At the end of each round, the computer will develop a best-fit solution on the basis of current monetary preferences and the land area desired by each family. On major streets, households are placed first on the street of their choice, if any. (This might itself be the subject of a premium.) Those with no preference join a pool that will be divided among residual locations on major streets. Households are placed along each street according to the premiums they are willing to pay for proximity to the center. Corner locations are then allocated on the basis of each family's willingness to pay a premium for one of these prime retail locations. Frontages would then be adjusted within the range indicated by each household until a solution (if one exists) is reached.

The computer reports to each family the current size of its lot (including interior courtyard and street), the current price of the raw land, and a breakdown of all premiums that apply to the lot. For locations that will be designed during the commercial phase, the computer also reports the lot location. This allows families to find and inspect their hypothetical lots on the site. (These locations will change somewhat during the actual design of the streets and squares on the site.) Families seeking inexpensive lots in neighborhoods that will be designed in the village phase will not yet know the location of their lots, as this will only be determined once urban village formation begins.

The process continues until premiums reach stasis. Premium levels would change as the demand for various attributes becomes clear. As supply comes into balance with demand, changes in premium levels would become progressively smaller until they reach insignificant levels. If some households hamper the process by making frequent and large changes in their preferences, they might have to be excluded from the process, in order to allow a solution to emerge.

Once premium stasis is achieved, the computer will display the location that each family in the commercial phase will take on a main street or major square. These locations are best considered as topological: each family is located with respect to the families who are to be its neighbors, but its precise location on the site is not yet determined.

Once the auction process is complete and people are satisfied with the location and price of the lot they are seeking, the

Venice

Possibly, near-stasis is all that can be achieved, but this should be adequate in the real world.

Lisbon

commercial-phase design can begin on the site, with each family starting from its agreed location. There, they will meet their neighbors and conduct face-to-face negotiations that culminate in the design of their immediate vicinity. They will design the streets and squares, altering the paths of streets until the design looks right and functions well. The shapes of squares will be adjusted until they feel right and fit well with the streets that enter them. This process is taken up in the following chapter.

Software

Updates will be posted as software design evolves, at: www.carfree.com/book2/software.html

The software should allow urban planners or the developer (depending on who is managing this part of the process) to intervene in both the establishment of premium-attracting axes and the setting of initial premium levels. Some of the facilities described here are needed in the auction phase, and others may only be needed in the commercial or village phases. The underlying design of the software does not particularly depend upon which axes are balanced in which phase. The addition of a new attribute to the list of premiums should be a simple matter, as the need can emerge at any time in the process, and it is not possible to anticipate every premium that might arise.

As already mentioned, there are at least three basic classes of premiums: unitary, by unit length, or on the total area of land. At least these three basic classes must be included in the software; others may eventually be needed.

There are two major groups of data in the computer-driven part of the process. The first defines the AREA OF LAND that each family wishes to buy. Four basic parameters affect the area of a site, wherever it may be located. They yield the amount of ground that will be purchased by the household. This is directly calculated from a few simple measures:

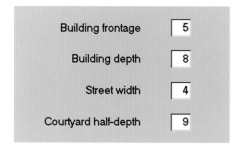

- Building frontage
- Building depth

- Street width
- Courtyard depth

Once these parameters are established, a family has determined, within narrow limits, how much ground it will buy. For rectangular plots not bordering on a square, the formula is simply: land area = house width × (½ street width + house depth + ½ courtyard depth). It will be helpful if families can accept some variation on the measures of street width and courtyard depth. This enables better matching of families on social preferences. An additional monetary preference is the amount each family is willing to contribute towards an adjacent small square.

The second group of data expresses the premiums people are willing to pay for a site at their preferred location. These will be expressed as attraction to or repulsion from physical poles, which exist in several types:

- Point (gradient around a point)
- Spot (a point with a limited range of attraction)
- Gradient (linear)
- Bifurcation (binary)

The axis by which people will express their preferred distance from the center is a point pole, with the point at the district center. A bifurcation pole would be used for the house-on-the-periphery axis (a site is either at the periphery or not) and the light-manufacturing-allowed axis (permitted on one side of a dividing line and not on the other). A gradient would be used for the absence-of-dogs axis, which need not be absolute; a range of dog-aversiveness can be mapped on a plane across the district. The spot pole could exist in multiple, with each pole having a limited reach (locations beyond this limit are neither attracted to nor repelled by the pole). This will be useful for the courtyard-ownership axis (which is trinary: private, shared, or public). Other pole types, such as stripes, can be imagined, but as yet I see no need for them.

The organizers would assign a pole of the appropriate type to

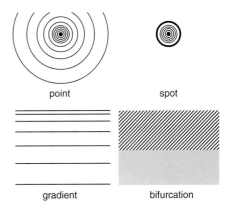

point spot

gradient bifurcation

"Pole" is used here in the sense of a field that has attraction and repulsion, somewhat akin to magnetism.

In fact, the distribution of preferences can be more complex than a simple gradient across a plane. It may prove difficult to match families unless more complex shapes (e.g., curves) are available in the software. Their mathematical description is usually quite simple.

each axis. They would designate the initial pole locations and, in the case of bifurcations and gradients, the axis angle. It should be possible to designate some types of poles (e.g., courtyard ownership) for automatic optimization by the computer, as an aid to reaching a solution without interfering with the expressed preferences of families. Auto-optimization should include both the number and location of the spot poles. The software would need to incorporate all of the necessary types of poles to allow organizers to assign whatever type of pole may be useful to match families on a given attribute.

The list of poles will include some that are non-monetary. For instance, an attraction/repulsion algorithm must be provided to permit grocers to space themselves out evenly (i.e., repulsion from other grocers). This same algorithm must also permit office areas and universities to attract copy shops. Some business will do better if they are situated next to one another—rare book dealers may all benefit from being located in the same block. Woodworkers will want to be near hardware stores and lumber suppliers. Ideally, the software would know most of these attraction/repulsion mechanisms and suggest their use by those who plan to establish businesses that benefit from locations near to, or distant from, the same or related businesses. Each of these relationships can be expressed by its own pole, although most households will assign it a priority of zero, causing it to be ignored in calculations for that household.

The software will generate solutions that maximize the number of households with good fits for their highest priorities; it allows some of their lower priorities to slip out towards the ends of their ranges of preferences (and even beyond, as long as the household is warned).

Finally, the process must yield a fixed-sum outcome, whereby all of the allocated population is accommodated on the site. If the neighborhoods are designed in phases, each phase must accommodate its share of the population.

Salamanca

DISTRICT LAYOUT

This chapter marks the beginning of physical design on the site. This is the "commercial phase," during which the main features will be arranged. Once the economic questions of the auction phase have been resolved, the buyers of premium-priced land will gather on the site to design the main streets and major squares in a cooperative process. The planners and the developer will have only minor roles to play, as their principal decisions will already have been made.

At the start of the commercial phase, families and organizations that acquired rights to premium sites will already know the sequence of their lots along the streets and squares, even though their exact locations have not yet been determined. They will now design their local neighborhood, working with stakes and string on the site itself. My original vision of this process had been to design an entire district at one time, but I realized that the high-premium sites need to be designed first. This allows a natural unfolding of design in which the principal elements anchor the rest of the design. The process is subject to many limitations, including the need to ensure that the arrangement does not impose unacceptable hardships on design in the village phase. Those working in the commercial phase must therefore remain aware of the needs of all the inhabitants.

The basic armature of the district as designed in this phase will become the foundation for the "village phase," as described in VILLAGE FORMATION and NEIGHBORHOOD DESIGN. During the village phase, those families who decided not to buy a premium-priced site will enjoy the benefit of good matching on social preferences. Families will first group into urban villages (i.e., blocks—see URBAN VILLAGES). They will then gather on the site, where each village will act with nearby villages to lay out its own small streets and squares. The basic design techniques in the commercial phase and the village phase will be similar.

Narrow, winding streets, Alfama district, Lisbon

DESIGN PROCESS

See page 140

See page 402 for the rationale for user-based, on-site design.

Lisbon

Urban planning is by its nature a centralized process, but the *design* of districts and neighborhoods is not. Once a regional plan is adopted, those who will live on a site can, with professional help, design their own locale. Planning must be complete down to the approximate routes of emergency access streets.

I propose a return to design methods that I believe were used during medieval times, when neighbor worked with neighbor to arrange pleasing streets (see page 84). The success of this proposal depends upon finding a way to accelerate the process, so that what once took generations to evolve can now be arranged in a brief, intensive effort involving hundreds or thousands of people working on the site to stake out their future in a literal sense. In this phase, the main elements of the district, which will serve everyone, will be arranged over a span of days or weeks.

The final computer output from the auction will show how families negotiated to arrange themselves along the major streets and squares, but this arrangement is primarily topological; the exact shape and location of the streets and their adjoining buildings remains to be determined. Once on the site, families will design the major streets and squares and designate the exact location of each building. Computers will be used only to calculate the land area allotted to each household and its associated premiums, reflecting the design as it emerges on the site.

Those who have chosen high-premium locations will have many common interests, as most of these families will be running some kind of business. There is thus reason to think that they can work cooperatively on the site to design good spaces. Individual families will advocate for their own interests and needs. Major buildings will have the interests of their patrons represented by advocates. As long as the constraints imposed during the urban planning process are respected, the design of a district is limited only by what people want and will accept.

Design Objectives

The processes in this chapter and Neighborhood Design do not directly address the creation of beauty, but it is central to the goal of making joyous places to live and work. The material in Part III, Elements, should be consulted by families before and during design for help in understanding their many choices. The City Design library at Carfree.com offers many resources, some of which are reproduced throughout this work, but far more material is available on the web site.

Streets and squares are the primary hearth for community. Hillier & Hanson identified the "BEADY-RING STRUCTURE" (just above) as vital for good social functioning. A beady-ring structure consists of closed-loop paths (e.g., city blocks) with frequent convex, enclosed spaces (e.g., small squares). Streets lacking the beady-ring property are less effective in facilitating social contact. Consider this MAJOR STREET in Siena. Although it does show a single "bead" on the right in the middle distance, this is not enough, and the street seems not to encourage people to pause during their passage. There are too few places that invite people to linger just there, in preference to somewhere near by. Contrast Siena with this bead on the VIA GARIBALDI in Venice, which encourages neighbors to sit for a chat.

Beads relate to other patterns, including "Activity Nodes" (APL, Pattern 30), "Small Public Squares" (Pattern 61), "Public Outdoor Room" (Pattern 69), "Street Cafe" (Pattern 88), "Activity Pockets" (Pattern 124), "Building Edge" (Pattern 160), and "Column Place" (Pattern 226). These patterns all have in common the creation of niches (beads), where people are comfortable lingering. "Positive Outdoor Space" (Pattern 106) is the grandfather of them all. We will especially be needing these beads on major streets, but the quieter streets will want them too, as this is where neighbors will first get to know one another. Parents out with their toddlers will start to chat while

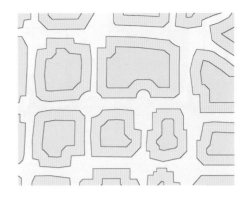

Alexander, TNO, I:416

Záttere, Venice

their kids play together. Old folks will commiserate with one another's aches and pains. Teenagers will look for somewhere to hang out and meet their agemates. This is *not* loitering, in the mean sense of that word. We actually want to *encourage* people to sit around with nothing particular to do except meet people, make their acquaintance, and pass some time together.

There is a growing literature on bringing streets to life, which can be summarized simply as "people, the more the better." Designers should be familiar with Allan B. Jacobs's *Great Streets,* the works of Jan Gehl and Lars Gemzøe, William H. Whyte's œuvre, and Donald Appleyard's seminal *Livable Streets*. To summarize, activities that involve a lot of coming and going are especially helpful. Stores are great creators of street life. Local enterprises are better at building community than large, impersonal operations managed from afar, because the operators of local businesses have good reason to care about the health of the local community: it is *their* community, too.

Frequent entrances (which always arise from small buildings) and windows at street level make for lively, human-scaled streets. The sight of people at work in their shops and offices adds life to a street. People are the best known protection against street crime. Even when few people are on the street, their nearby presence is apparent, which is reassuring, especially for women walking alone at night. The CALLE LARGA SAN MARCO in Venice is a busy shopping area, but there are apartments and hotels on upper floors, and it feels safe even in the wee hours of the morning, when the shops are all closed. It is possible to have large numbers of people nearby without their presence being felt, a condition that arises when ground floors are composed of long expanses of BLANK WALL with few entrances, also sometimes seen in Venice. This makes a street feel unsafe even if it is not.

Frequent entrances also arise naturally when commercial spaces are on the ground floor and individual family residences or apartments are located on the floors above. This arrangement normally yields two exterior doors per building, and buildings may be as narrow as 3m (10'). Doors are as good as windows at relieving the façades of buildings and making them interesting.

See *Great Streets* by Allan B. Jacobs for more on this.

Keep ground floors close to ground level, in order to maximize the connection of buildings with the street (see page 497). For the same reason, windows on the lowest floor should not be above eye level; passers-by should be able to see into the ground floors as they walk along. This is one reason to devote most of the ground floor occupancies to workplaces rather than residences, as people in many societies will not want their living quarters visible to everyone who happens by. (The Dutch are notably different in this regard, and their living rooms are often open to public view.)

Sidewalk cafés keep people on the street, as do all places that invite people to sit for a while. Anything that encourages people to leave their homes and go for a stroll among the neighbors adds life. Vendors selling snacks, drinks, and newspapers are also a draw, as are street entertainers and playgrounds. Never omit benches. Clean, safe toilets should be within easy reach, as should drinking fountains and trash cans. Some of these facilities can be provided in the concierge services.

Venice

DESIGN STRATEGY

The frame of reference for design greatly affects the result. Most urban planning has been done by architects who, by the nature of their training, tend to focus on individual buildings rather than entire blocks. (There are important exceptions, such as Léon Krier.) In *A New Theory of Urban Design,* Christopher Alexander proposed an urban design process that is, in some ways, the inverse of what I propose. In that work, streets arise as buildings are placed, even though the placement of those buildings is expressly intended to create good exterior spaces. I propose a simpler method that establishes the edges of the streets

"We may express this rule simply as follows: 'Buildings surround space,' NOT 'space surrounds buildings.' It has become a habit of thought in our century that buildings are simple-shaped volumes, floating in a sea of ill-formed space. If we compare a plan of a typical modern city, with, for instance, the great Nolli plan of Rome,... we see there that it is the *space* which is made up of simply-formed shapes, while the buildings are more irregular, loose relaxed shapes, whose primary function is to surround and shape their space." Alexander (1987), 67-68

Braga

The rationale for this is discussed in Building Layout. Apartment houses are also possible, as shown in that same chapter, but single-family occupancies reduce the points of friction between neighbors.

The construction of larger office buildings is possible, but they are not easy to integrate into a fine-grained urban area.

and determines the height of the abutting buildings so as to shape a space that feels good. The difference arises in part because Alexander has usually worked at densities lower than the carfree city requires. High density does not permit open space between abutting buildings. If all buildings abut their neighbors, design is considerably simplified. Nearly all blocks will have interior courtyards, and once the widths and locations of the streets are defined, there is little left to do but position the demising walls between buildings and determine the size of the courtyard. Small squares can be added as the need and opportunity arise. The major streets are best laid out all at one time in order to ensure coherence and good functioning.

I would prefer to provide each family with its own house, whereby it would obtain a full floor at ground level. I call this arrangement the "ranch house on end" because it provides about the same usable space as the many ranch houses that were built in the USA during the 1950s. The rooms are stacked on several floors, rather than sprawling out on just one. The garage, which often became the site of a family business, is replaced by inexpensive ground-floor space that is used for a business or as additional living area. I anticipate that most ground floors would be used for business activities of one kind or another, whether directly by the families themselves or by businesses that rent the space from families.

When a large organization seeks to establish a group of offices, it will rent clusters of comparatively inexpensive ground-floor spaces. This arrangement is actually quite efficient. Someone needing to consult with a colleague in another office simply walks for a minute or two along the streets to the other office, instead of waiting for an elevator in a high-rise office building. The total trip time is about the same as in an elevator building, and the trip is certainly more pleasant and invigorating. In areas with inclement weather, this is a further reason to build arcades. Most office-based businesses can be located on quiet streets and have no need for a prominent location on a major street or square, except perhaps for a reception area from which people would be directed to the various offices.

Most retail businesses can function well if they are located in the ground floors of adjacent small buildings. Amsterdam offers many examples, such as the CONCERTO RECORD STORE on the Utrechtsestraat. In this case, openings have been made between the buildings to link up the shop internally. This task was complicated by the varying heights of the ground floors, but even this difficulty was overcome. In a new district, ground floors should be at the same height unless the street climbs a hillside. Very large retail operations will typically take the form of multi-story department stores, still common throughout Europe.

Once the most desirable ground-floor space is taken by shops and then by offices, the remainder will be available for small manufacturing and warehousing operations of a character that mixes well with residential uses. (Manufacturing operations that require large, unified spaces should probably be located in a utility area, where this can readily be provided, although they can also be accommodated in the large buildings adjacent to the metro-freight line.) Ground-floor rents would adjust until supply and demand came into balance, but I would expect that a good supply of reasonably inexpensive space would be available, particularly in the more remote parts of the less central districts.

STRAIGHT VS CURVED STREETS

The alternation between straight and curved streets through history is taken up at length in ORDER & ORGANIZATION IN CITIES. The benefits of curved streets are discussed in several chapters in Part III, in particular ENCLOSING STREETS. Those chapters explain why I strongly advocate curved and articulated streets that create a sense of enclosure, which can be secured if the relationship between street width and curvature is such that

Coimbra

long vistas are not created. An exception is required in the case of the central boulevard, as the degree of curvature is limited by its use as a rail corridor. The great width of the boulevard further reduces enclosure, and most locations along it will afford a view hundreds of meters (yards) in either direction. This will help to orient people, as there will be only one wide street with long vistas in any given district. Since some people seem to prefer these more open streets, this is not a serious defect.

The street in front of the MAISON DES QUATRANS in Caen is a good example of a curved street with a closed view. The rate of curvature is moderate, but the street is fairly narrow, and the view is closed in about a hundred paces. It is usual with curved streets to make the façades of individual buildings straight, with each building standing at a slight angle to its neighbors. The resulting interior spaces are not perfect rectangles, and the façade will not form an exact right angle with both side walls, which are in turn not quite parallel to one another. This is somewhat more expensive, but I think the improvement in the quality of the streets is worth a small increase in the cost of construction and the minor inconveniences from out-of-square interior fittings (shelving, carpeting, etc.). Surveying is more complicated, but modern techniques allow us to neglect this problem. The strategy proposed on page 496 largely eliminates the extra cost.

Arranging the Street Network

The design approach proposed in this chapter is predicated on the assumption that an irregular but loosely radial street pattern will be employed. A geometrically-regular arrangement is possible, but I believe that more relaxed shapes are more adaptable, humane, and pleasing. When local constraints and opportunities are allowed to influence the design, more complex layouts arise by themselves.

See, for example, the spiral design for a city on a hilltop, page 49.

Most European towns were laid out when earth was still moved entirely by muscle power, so great economy was to be had by minimizing the volume moved. In these towns, we see streets that climb hills at a steady grade by crossing the contours of the land at a low and constant rate. These streets are rarely straight for any great distance, as they follow the folds in the land. Today, we rearrange the topography to suit us, but this expensive work does nothing to improve the quality of the finished place; it merely simplifies the design task by permitting whatever arbitrary street arrangement the designer may prefer. Better is simply to lay out the major streets so they approximately follow the contours of the land, always keeping in mind the need for a full network of emergency access streets. Minor streets can be as steep as necessary, as here in GUBBIO, and vehicles can detour along the lower-slope major streets. When streets are moderately steep, it may be advisable to provide auxiliary stairs, as was done in the PFALZGASSE in Zürich.

We must arrange a reasonably direct network of pedestrian and cycle routes to adjacent districts. This can be accomplished using a combination of the central boulevard and smaller streets that run roughly parallel to it. It is desirable to provide at least two parallel routes, so that passage is still possible if one street is blocked for some reason. Within the built-up area, cycle routes fall into two categories: through routes and local routes. Speeds on through routes should be unrestricted and stop lights avoided. This requires relatively wide streets, at least 10m (33'). On local streets, cyclists will mix with pedestrians, carts, and all other street users. Speeds will be low if many people are about. In very narrow streets, cyclists may have to dismount and walk the short distances involved. In somewhat wider streets, cyclists may ride at a speed that does not endanger pedestrians, as on the VIA MASSIMO D'AZEGLIO in Bologna. Remember the need for travel to other lobes of the city, which may require bike paths through natural areas; these may be graded gravel (see page 186).

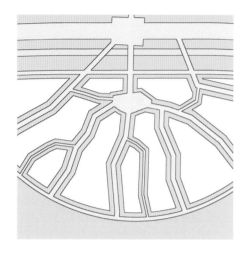

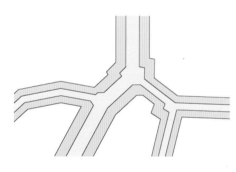

My experience in laying out the 81 inhabited districts of the Reference Topology was that the obvious approach works: start with the major streets and move on to successively narrower streets. I first determined the route of the transit system (and thus the central boulevard). Next, the widest streets were laid down, most of them with curves and jogs to maintain enclosure and make them more interesting. The process was continued down to the smallest streets. As long as the basic layout of the major streets is reasonable, it is rarely necessary to adjust them when laying out the minor streets; it seems fairly easy to adapt the smaller streets to the preexisting wider ones.

If the district is roughly circular and the transport halt is near the center, a REASONABLE LAYOUT requires that the radial streets branch at some distance from the center, as they cannot all be brought to the center for simple lack of space. The best approach is to bring about half of the major radial streets to the subdistrict square. Of the other half, some can branch off from the main radials about 100 meters (yards) from the subdistrict square and some can be brought to the central square/transport halt or to a point on the central boulevard not too far from the center. All major streets running direct to the center require a minor street that connects them to the subdistrict square.

The BRANCHING OF A MAJOR STREET is best arranged so that the major street bends away from the new minor street at the branch, as this gives better angles at the intersection. A small square also eases the junction and will enjoy considerable foot traffic. Ideally, streets should not intersect at angles of less than about 30° because the resultant intersection functions poorly (even in the absence of car traffic) due to the limited sight lines. People rounding the corner may blunder into one another unless something is added to slow them down, such as these steps at a sharp intersection on the CALLE TERESA in Valladolid. Blunting the point of the wedge reduces the problem, as on the RUA TENENTE VALADIM (see next page) in Faro, and the excellent "double-aspect" shopfront, with display windows on two (or even three) sides, is a bonus. Still, it is usually better to make a broader branching, bending the two streets back towards one another after fifty paces if necessary.

Alexander insists that design be done in the field, and I propose to adopt this method. Families should arrive on the site with a bundle of stakes, some lengths of string, and a clear idea of what needs to be done. Once the stakes have been set, engineers can measure their positions and prepare a survey that shows the precise locations of the streets to come and the individual building lots that have been established along them. This yields a paper plan, but the paper is used only to record the design, not to create it. The difference is, I believe, of critical importance to the quality of the completed design. It seems clear that the fine medieval arrangements that have come down to us were devised on the site, without benefit of paper plans.

The adjustments required to create a satisfactory arrangement may change the area of land occupied by any given family and may also slightly affect the associated premiums. These changes will in turn affect the total cost of land for each family, usually within a narrow range. Consensus regarding the final design is required; it is otherwise invalid. No family may be priced out of the district as a result of any changes made.

Each household that has spoken for a site that will be designed during the commercial phase will start with a length of string equal to its agreed frontage (see page 478) on a particular major street or square. These strings will be connected into façades for one side of a square or a block. (The remaining sides of a block will be designed in the village phase, excepting blocks that are bordered on two or more sides by major streets, which will occur in some areas close to the center. In these cases, all of the major sides of a block will be designed in the commercial phase.) These façades define a major street or square, and it is their arrangement with which we are most concerned here.

Alexander, TNO III:70-84, 272-273, 336-337

Rua Tenente Valadim, Faro

Venice

ADVOCATES & ASSISTANTS

See the discussion of advocates on page 423.

Brig, Switzerland

The payment of their fees must be arranged by the project sponsor, but this money will ultimately have to be recouped from the sale of land.

Advocates for major buildings and squares will be on the site at the start of on-site design. Some advocates will need to maintain the positions of the buildings they represent within narrow limits. Other advocates will have the responsibility to arrange a square of a certain area at an approximate location but will be free to adjust the shape and exact location to fit with nearby uses. Some buildings will need to be a specific size, and other buildings, such as a theater, may even require a specific shape, subject to only minor adjustment. Yet other buildings will require a specific location, such as fronting on a particular square.

It is best if agreements with building patrons allow as much room for adjustment as possible; avoid allowing them to place a predesigned building in a specific location with no changes permitted, unless there is some compelling reason for this, which should be one that has important benefits to the public.

Advocates can carry bamboo posts for each corner of their square or building, with straps connecting the tops of the posts at the needed length and far enough off the ground that people can walk underneath. The size and shape of the building or square are thus visible to all, and it can be shifted without disturbing its size if the straps are kept taut.

Also needed will be volunteer assistants with a weekend's training. They will facilitate the process and help people to understand their options and the implications of various choices. I foresee the need for one assistant for every 25 families, but experience will reveal what adjustment to this number is required. They can be drawn from among the families who will live in the district.

Experts will also be needed to assist (see the discussion on page 404). Experience will show how many architects and planners need to be on the site during the design process. The time required is not great, so the cost should be reasonable.

DESIGN OF MAJOR ELEMENTS

The main squares and major streets will be arranged at this time. The on-site design process will bring onto the site all of the households that have negotiated for a site on one of the major streets, advocates for larger buildings and squares, and businesses that have negotiated for locations along the central boulevard. (Advocates for central boulevard sites are needed because minor adjustments will require their approval.) Any other location for which a high premium arose, such as sites along the perimeter, will also be designed at this time, with their owners on site.

Beja, Portugal

The design process given here assumes a North American or European context; it would require adjustment before being applied in other regions, but the general principles should remain valid. I am presuming that large groups of people are capable of making comparatively rapid design decisions that will affect their lives for years to come. What makes this possible is that despite the considerable design freedom, most of the important and time-consuming decisions have already been made. The participants have already decided how much land they want to pay for and what locations they will accept. They will have spoken for a given length of frontage and agreed on the order they will take up along their chosen street or square. What remains to be determined is only the exact course that a street will follow or the precise arrangement of a square. Given also that a known length of frontage must be disposed of, the design is actually quite constrained despite the freedom within those constraints. The use of frontage strings makes it possible for families and businesses to take up their positions and then work with their neighbors to obtain a satisfactory design.

Venice

Most of the households seeking locations on major squares and streets will intend to establish retail businesses; the high premiums for these sites will discourage others from seeking them. Most advocated buildings also need good public exposure

Beja, Portugal

Venice

In fact, it is probably useful to permit anyone to be on the site during this phase of design, even though their capacity would be purely advisory. The merit of this approach is that it helps to avoid the deadlocks that may arise if aspects of the commercial-phase design impose unreasonable burdens on the village phase.

to achieve their purposes. Corner locations are, of course, especially advantageous, and some households and organizations will already have elected to pay hefty premiums for these scarce locations. During the on-site design process, it is possible that some corner locations may be deleted or that new corners may be created. These changes will have to be agreed to by everyone concerned and will also affect premiums, which might necessitate a further round of computer-based adjustment.

As noted in the previous chapter, frontage on major radial streets is one of the scarcities in district design that is actually susceptible to an increase in supply. This requires curving a street so as to increase its length. This process must be restricted in order to prevent these streets, which provide primary access to the district center, from becoming unreasonably long. As the same time, some curvature will help a sense of enclosure to emerge and is therefore desirable. Additional length may be applied to longer frontages or additional households. In practice, it may be found that all available space will readily be absorbed and that the process will be limited only by the additional length of street that is permitted. The increase in length does not affect walking times as much as might be expected, as pedestrians will take the shortest route, cutting the corners (see drawing on page 473).

(see drawing on page 473)

Advocates for major squares will have instructions to keep their squares within a fairly narrow range of locations, but considerable flexibility in shape exists and perhaps some also as to size. I think that the best approach is to locate the approximate paths of the streets first, then to site the squares to accommodate the paths of the streets, and finally to adjust the streets. In actuality, both processes can run in parallel if they are as fluid as I hope. The location of the central square is probably inflexible, but its size and shape may be subject to change within some limits. Representatives for residents of minor streets should also be on hand to ensure that difficult conditions are not imposed on families during neighborhood design.

INITIAL POSITION

Before households take up their initial positions as determined during the auction phase, the location of the large buildings along the central boulevard must be staked out, including the streets that will cut through to the central boulevard at intervals not greater than 100m (330'). These are the largest buildings that fit comfortably in a standard carfree district, and most of them also have valuable access to metro-freight.

The approximate routes of the radial emergency access streets forms part of the initial position (see also page 184). A certain minimum width will have been determined, probably at least 9m (30'). There may be reason to make a few streets as wide as 15m (50'), but more than that would only be required where unusually heavy foot and cycle traffic is expected. Remember that the central boulevard is at least 30m (100') wide and the heaviest flows will travel along it. (If trams are used, the central boulevard may be split into two one-way streets; see *Carfree Cities,* pages 176 and 183.)

The INITIAL DISPOSITION OF ADVOCATED BUILDINGS might be as shown in light orange, with major streets and squares in light gray. Radial streets would have to strike the perimeter at the locations shown, subject to the degree of adjustment shown in red. Considering the buildings in this example, a full block in the northeast quadrant is the site for a school, the exact location and shape of which would be subject to change within some limits as long as the required footprint and courtyard areas were maintained. The shape of the theater on the north side of the northern subdistrict square would be fixed within narrow limits, as would its required location on that square. The other buildings are assumed to be somewhat flexible in their shape and location, but most of them need to be relatively close to the central square. Each family's starting position is given simply a direction and distance from the district center.

In the case of manufacturing facilities, it may be useful to allow the buildings to bridge over the streets, so that continuous space is created on the upper floors, allowing unbroken production lines. These buildings are 30m (100') thick, which creates a tunnel that is longer than desirable. Ideally, the buildings should narrow where the streets pass through, to avoid creating large, dark, inhospitable spaces beneath. Making the ground floors of these buildings higher than normal admits more light to passageways.

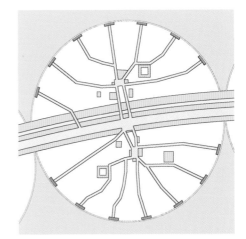

Burano

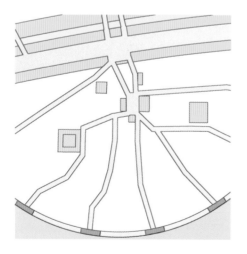

MAJOR STREETS

The first task is to establish the routes of the major radial streets, keeping in mind their use for emergency access. This will pose few limitations in the inner parts of the district, but must be watched carefully in the outer hundred meters (yards) or so, to ensure that no location lies more than the permissible distance from emergency access. Even low buildings require extensible fire ladders that are still fairly long when retracted, and this limits the minimum allowable turning radius along emergency-access streets. Intersections of the main streets should either receive small squares or should have the corners beveled, to allow long fire trucks room to turn. If the fire is not on an accessible street, ladders will have to be carried to the scene, which is only possible if the ladders need be no longer than those required for four-story buildings.

An emergency-access street is needed at the perimeter of the district. If the perimeter street is not a continuous gentle arc (such as envisioned in the Reference District), then its corners must be arranged so as not to impede emergency access.

The spacing of the major radial streets will depend upon the maximum allowed distance between a front door and an accessible street. Probably 90m (300') can be negotiated in most jurisdictions. As long as the row of houses at the perimeter is penetrated at intervals of not more than about 80m (265'), then the SPACING OF MAJOR RADIAL STREETS can be 160m (530') at the perimeter. This further requires that blocks are not more than 40m (130') long in the radial direction and also presumes that the outer row of houses is only about 15m (50') deep. The problem largely disappears as the center is approached, because the wide streets are quite close together there. In some cases, a concentric street wide enough for emergency access is needed about 100m (33') inside the periphery of the district, which is the most difficult area to reach with emergency equipment. The range of points at which the major radial streets must strike the perimeter should be indicated on the site. The locations of adjacent radial streets are somewhat interdependent.

At least one continuous street is required parallel to the central boulevard and distant from it by the width of the rows of buildings on the METRO-FREIGHT LINE, about 65m (215'). This is an important street and should be at least 10m (33') wide to allow emergency access. The other side of the central boulevard can be arranged with a parallel street just behind the buildings, or it can be fashioned into blocks, as was done with the Reference District; this decision should be made during urban planning. The locations of buildings and streets associated with the central boulevard are subject to little change, and their final locations must be staked out before on-site design begins.

The minimum length for each radial street will have been established by the time on-site design commences, and we need to ensure that the street reaches this minimum length. This is accomplished by inducing bends in the street until its length is sufficient; the location of bends can be arranged to suit the households designing the site. It would be natural to situate bends in the streets at the points where other streets will intersect them. This in turn suggests including squares of moderate size at the bends, as squares are best arranged with the greatest possible number of streets entering them. As shown on page 442, larger streets should join the major streets at the outside of the bend. (It will not be possible to avoid having minor streets join at the inside of bends.) This tends to yield an efficient route network and adds life to the squares as people pass through.

Careful attention should be paid to the slope of the land. If the site is hilly, the bends in the streets should be arranged so as to minimize the maximum gradient on the street, snaking around the sides of hills. Otherwise, these streets can be arranged in whatever manner the future occupants find attractive. Do, however, review WIDE STREETS and NARROW STREETS in Part III

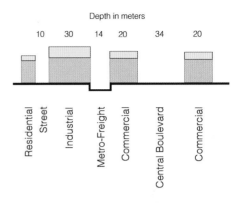

It is to be hoped that the penetrations of this wall of buildings can be adjusted to suit the requirements of streets entering the central boulevard.

Braga

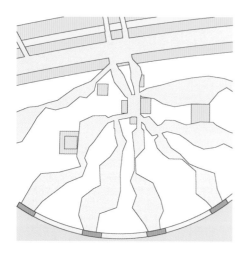

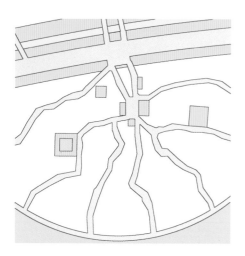

for guidance. The task is only complete when the full length of the street has been staked out, every household that has spoken for a place has been accommodated, and the requirements for emergency access are respected.

When all of the households with frontage on a given street are on the site in the correct order, each will join its frontage string with those of its neighbors. (The openings of side streets need to be represented by strings of suitable length.) The first thing to do is to take up all of the slack in the string by moving backwards or forwards, in small groups, until the street TAKES ON AN INTERESTING SHAPE. It will be instructive to allow the opposite sides of the street to act independently at the start. This could lead to a circumstance where at some places the two sides of the street are facing each other with no gap and at other places the gap between the two sides is a hundred paces. The first thing to do might be to ask those groups that are nose-to-nose each to step back by half the width of the street, thereby giving a tentative working street arrangement. The groups that are separated by great distances should drop their strings and meet in the middle of the gaping street to discuss why they chose their locations and how they might cooperate to reduce the street to its necessary width.

As THESE ADJUSTMENTS OCCUR, the need for other adjustments may arise. The location where the street strikes the perimeter can be changed within certain limits. The precise location where two major streets intersect is subject to some adjustment, particularly if some of the affected families are willing to take up a bit more or a little less frontage than they had negotiated. The lengths of the major streets are subject to some change as well, simply by adopting a more direct route or one that is more sinuous. These changes can help to provide each family with the length of frontage that it desires. The scope of these changes is actually affected by the solution that is arising on the adjacent streets, as the major radials may not be more than some given distance apart where they strike the perimeter.

The grade of the street should be kept always in mind and the path of the street altered to eliminate unreasonably steep sections. This is also the time to pay attention to the points at which the streets enter the main squares and where two streets join. The shape of the space at the junction should be arranged to give a block that is rather short on the side that forms the root of the fork but of a shape that allows a reasonable arrangement of the buildings. (See the drawing on page 442.) Arrange adjacent main streets so that they are not too far out of parallel with one another, because this makes it easier to shape the blocks behind these streets, particularly where the major streets are not far apart. Streets cannot be truly parallel for any great distance as they must radiate out to different points on the perimeter.

As a workable arrangement begins to arise, consider how squares can be arranged at the principal intersections to smooth the flow of traffic and shorten routes to the center. These will be relatively important squares even if they are not so very large. Plenty of foot traffic will pass through them in the course of a day, and their arrangement will have an appreciable influence on the functioning of the district. It is also necessary to coordinate the arrangement of the main streets with the subdistrict square, upon which most of them will converge.

LOCATING & ARRANGING MAIN SQUARES

If a formal square is preferred, it is probably best to arrange it first, including the locations of streets entering the square. For a formal square, the streets must be subservient to requirements of the square. As already discussed, informal squares have much to recommend them, including the flexibility to adapt streets and squares to one another. The arrangement of squares should, at the very least, be highly influenced by the route of the streets. The most common locations for streets to enter large squares are

Braga

Venice

Many Renaissance squares in Spain were imposed on existing medieval districts, resulting in irregular entry of the streets to the squares, thus spoiling the ideal form. These "errors" do little violence to the design.

See Camillo Sitte's discussion of multi-function, multi-part squares in his "Plaza Groupings" chapter.

from the corners and at or near the centers of the sides. This rule is often violated, however, and without apparent harm. A more demanding rule is that the surface of a square should be flat and level, or very nearly so. A bowl shape can be excellent, as it creates a space that resembles an amphitheater, as seen in Siena's wonderful CAMPO. Convex and appreciably sloped sites must be avoided, unless money is available to level the site, which can be very costly in a large square.

I anticipate that most districts will want three main squares, one at the center and one in each of the two subdistricts on either side of the central boulevard. The subdistrict squares should be one or two blocks from the central square and connected to it by direct streets. The central square is probably the most suitable one to receive a formal design, as it is here that most institutions serving both subdistricts will be located, including buildings of the local government, often in a formal style. The subdistrict squares, on the other hand, belong to their own communities and help to define them. These squares should be unique in their arrangement, perhaps with an important community building intruding into the square, as with the church on the CAMPO DI SANTA MARIA FORMOSA in Venice. An intruding building can divide the square into two or more parts with different functions. This arrangement allows a large increase in the perimeter of a square without a corresponding increase in its area. Complex shapes, such as the L-form of Piazza San Marco, also make for interesting squares. They should be adopted without hesitation, but the treatment of any convex corners thereby created require careful attention. (The campanile in San Marco stands at the convex corner and helps to define the two spaces that make up the square.)

If a square is still too big, the best of the large buildings fronting on the square can be moved right *into* the square, giving that building a highly prominent location. This excellent medieval arrangement can be seen in the PLAZA DE SAN BENITO in

Salamanca, where the church is engulfed by the square. It should be reserved for buildings of the highest quality.

Squares are better if their proportions do not exceed about 3:1 (length:width), as noted on page 329. The more nearly circular a square, the less perimeter length is created for a given area, so oblong arrangements do have an advantage.

The streets that connect the central square with each of the subdistrict squares must be defined early in the process. It is possible to have only one such connecting street, but two or three roughly parallel streets give alternate routes and are to be preferred. (Trouble will probably be saved if a decision regarding the number of these streets is taken before the land allotment process is complete.) This is the time to decide whether or not the central square will be visible from a given subdistrict square, which determines whether the connecting street is to be straight or articulated/curved. If the squares are very close together, it will be impractical to close the sight lines between them. These streets can have no sharp corners, as they form a part of the emergency access network. Gates can be added to strengthen the definition of the squares and to avoid any sense that one square runs into the other. (That would not really be a problem except that we are wanting to define the subdistrict squares as distinct and individual spaces that help to set the tone of their subdistricts.)

As the location of a square and the entering streets begins to settle down, advocates can consider the shape the square will take. Especially important is the location and direction of streets entering the square. If the square is informal, allow the streets to PULL ON THE BOUNDARY OF THE SQUARE in the manner of a string stretched around pins. This will tend to give the square a positive shape that has a logic of its own, arising simply from the pull of the streets.

If there remains a shortage of floor space in the buildings surrounding a square, an increase in height to five or even six stories

Coimbra

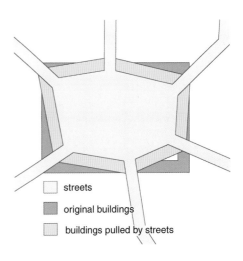

☐ streets

■ original buildings

☐ buildings pulled by streets

Venice

Faro

can be accepted. This is no bad thing, as can be seen on Siena's Campo, but it does require a fairly large square if the result is not to feel somewhat claustrophobic. I suggest that minimum dimension of the square be at least 30m (100') for five stories and 36m (120') for six stories. It is best if the buildings on the equatorial side of the square are lower in order to ensure good winter sunlight. The taller buildings may also have to be larger, in order to support the cost of providing elevator service to the upper floors. These choices probably belong to urban planning.

As with streets, those who have spoken for a location on a major square should join their strings in the agreed order and move about, in concert with groups of neighbors, until interesting shapes begin to arise, all the while making sure that the full length of the string is expressed. See the SQUARES chapter in Part III for examples and inspiration. There may be a tendency for the square to assume a circular shape that is rather vague and lacks clear orientation and definition. I think that, unlike streets, curves should be avoided in the edges of squares. (Convex curves are particularly to be avoided, as they damage the emerging sense of positive space.) Rather, allow as many sides to emerge as may be convenient, but keep those sides straight, or nearly so. Resist the temptation to form a more or less regular polygon, as this reduces the relative amount of frontage for a given area of square. Consider instead, if the square is large enough to support it, an L-shape or even an S- or U-shape. This allows the creation of relatively a lot of perimeter for a given land area and also permits multipart squares to arise, each part with a different function.

Encourage families whose buildings will form the length of a façade between two entering streets to move together to create interesting and functional shapes. It is not essential that a street enter a square evenly; one side of the street can reach the square before the other side, and this arrangement is seen quite often in medieval squares. There is nothing wrong with it, especially if it solves a problem. Likewise, there is no need for streets to enter a square at right angles to the façades, although it is better if the angle is not too acute.

At least one of the three major squares should have a High Place (Pattern 62). I think *either* the central square should have one *or* each of the two subdistrict squares should have one; three may be too many. The high places can best take the form of an observation tower perhaps 30m (100') tall, incorporated into one of the major advocated buildings surrounding the squares. (The towers do not actually have to be on a square, but this is their historical location and a pattern worth preserving.)

The siting of small squares is opportunistic and will be conducted during neighborhood design.

Venice

DESIGN AT THE PERIMETER

Perimeter locations are a special circumstance but pose no particular difficulties. As noted on page 421, the best way to arrange the perimeter is as a single row of houses with their gables facing onto the open space outside the district. Another street is laid out behind this row of houses, with the usual hollow blocks being arranged on the inner side of that street. The computer should have placed adjacent to one another those families seeking a perimeter location and desiring a given depth of house (there will be little room to match social preferences for these families). This area nearly designs itself, and the only real flexibility that arises is the penetration of minor radial streets through the row of buildings, which may be best accomplished with a *sottoportego.* The disadvantage of this arrangement is that it provides only a small "keyhole" view of the natural areas from inside the district. This can be turned into an advantage if the pattern Zen View is employed. The best design may require angling the radial streets one way or the other to focus on an especially attractive view. This imposes only a minor hardship

Venice

APL, Pattern 134

on the households affected by the change, who will enjoy the improved view every day on their walk home.

Perimeter buildings will almost certainly have their concierge service provided in the block to the rear, as the perimeter space will be too valuable to dedicate to utilitarian uses. Do be certain to guard against the urge to place buildings in the open space reservation, although exceptions like tea houses, gazebos, band shells, and the like may be accepted. Any structures ought to be light, low, and airy so as not to completely block the view.

At the conclusion of the commercial phase, all the major radial streets and the three main squares should be in final form, possibly subject to small adjustments made during the village phase with the object of enhancing the connections to minor streets. Small squares along the main streets will also have been arranged, possibly also subject to some alteration as the minor streets take shape. I envision that this process might be conducted in a single day or weekend, but participants should anticipate the need to return to the site several times in order to reach a satisfactory conclusion that will endure.

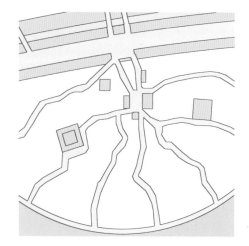

The FINAL POSITION must be accurately recorded and entered into the computer. This data is used to generate a plan showing the street and square frontages as well as the locations of the individual buildings along them. Land prices will be recalculated on the basis of this staking, which must include building depths. Final land prices cannot be computed yet, as courtyard depths will not be known precisely until neighborhood design is complete and the blocks with their courtyards are fully defined, but the range of further price changes should be small by this time. The urban villages that will arise behind the frontages of the main streets will only achieve definition during the NEIGHBORHOOD DESIGN process. First, however, we turn to the task of VILLAGE FORMATION.

VILLAGE FORMATION

The "village phase" comprises two steps: the formation of urban villages (discussed here) and the design of minor streets and squares by those villages (discussed in the next chapter). I propose to use urban villages as the basic design entity for new carfree neighborhoods because of the strong sense of community that arises in villages (see URBAN VILLAGES). Whether or not these villages will take root and thrive as I envision is impossible to say. The best we can do is to form good groupings and supply the necessary hearths for community: public spaces, local services, local enterprise. If this is done at small scale, among groups with natural affinities, common roots, and shared purpose, I think that a village society will develop. Designing their neighborhood together should help forge an initial bond.

For the same reasons that I want to permit families to design their own houses, I want them to design their urban villages and neighborhoods, the better to meet their needs. Each urban village will arrange itself as its members prefer, so long as basic requirements for health, safety, efficient functioning, and the needs of adjoining groups are met. This has to do with empowering people and also with achieving better design. I believe that the best urban design arises when driven by the imperatives of the site and the needs of the users. It is conducted on the site, not on paper, in order that the character of the site be fully reflected in the design. This approach will yield neighborhoods with a handmade feeling that may be less polished and neat than we have come to expect. At the same time, I anticipate that a deep sense of satisfaction, a feeling of rightness will arise in the completed neighborhoods. This feeling is one that many people have experienced in medieval districts, most of which emerged over time and under the influence of the generations of families who lived in them. The site and the people exerted their own forces, which shaped the neighborhood.

Calle de l'Ogio, Venice

Families enjoy a major advantage by waiting out the commercial phase—they will be able to match with a large pool of other families, which greatly increases the chances for good matching on social preferences; families who have chosen high-value locations will have to forego this. The families who participated in the commercial phase should nonetheless be present for urban village formation and neighborhood design, as they will become members of these villages, and their streets will form sides of many emerging blocks. It might also be useful to alter the major streets slightly to improve the blocks behind them.

I think that urban village formation should be conducted for an entire district at the same time, because this maximizes the population pool that is to be organized into villages and gives the best available fits. If, for logistical reasons, this cannot be done, then the largest possible units should be chosen for the village formation process. Attempting to organize diverse populations into urban villages becomes essentially impossible below a certain population, as the population pool is too small to permit good matching. A single neighborhood comprising at least ten urban villages is probably the smallest practical unit for both matching and design, unless the population is unusually homogeneous. Once the villages are formed and located on the site, design and construction can occur neighborhood by neighborhood if that is more convenient.

The proposed method does not employ experts to conduct design beyond the earliest possible moment in urban planning. This allows future residents the greatest latitude in design. Professionals have only a consultatory role to play during the design of neighborhoods and individual houses, except that major buildings will be designed by architects in the usual manner. Even here, however, the location and orientation of these buildings will be affected by user-driven, on-site design. Urban planners will develop performance specifications (e.g., minimum widths of streets) and leave the actual design to users.

Praça Marquês de Pombal

Faro

Urban villages will be developed on the basis of social preferences and fitted into the NEIGHBORHOODS delineated by the major streets and squares laid out during the commercial phase. Great flexibility of arrangement still exists when matching social preferences, despite these prior constraints, and families can expect good matching on social preferences. This chapter focuses on the formation of those urban villages.

Basic Process

Central to the process is the provisional identification of urban villages by a computer on the basis of the expressed social and economic preferences of the people who will live in the entire district. Only those parts of the district that have already been designed are excluded. Families must also be matched on their preferences regarding the frontage and depth of buildings, the width of streets, and the size of interior courtyards. The computer will make the best available matches on these expressed preferences. The constraints of the commercial phase must of course be respected, but these limitations still allow broad scope for creating good neighborhoods. Once provisional urban villages have been formed, their members will meet on the site to form final urban villages.

Matching on social preferences is by default non-monetary, but a given measure could be monetized if supply and demand cannot otherwise be balanced. The goal is to produce a starting position that matches families with like-minded families while respecting their preferences for physical locations. Families will have made certain choices that will draw small premiums, such as proximity to the center, but these choices can be respected during village formation without this exerting too great an influence on the process.

This approach offers some important advantages over today's demographics-based mass-production of commodity housing:

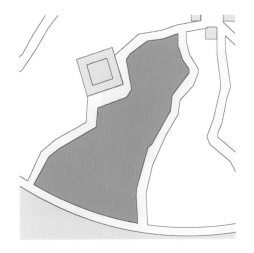

Venice

- Households adjust their preferences to reflect their needs
- Communities (urban villages) are formed before-the-fact
- These urban villages cooperate to arrange the neighborhood

The results will differ dramatically from today's mass-produced housing and will, I anticipate, better meet people's needs. The design should be responsive not only to the needs of each urban village and all of its families but also to the limitations and opportunities of the site. We can expect this to lead to the design of beautiful, functional neighborhoods.

Each urban village will normally comprise a single block. The computer output will show families arranged along a specific side of a block, in the order that best fits their preferences. Social affinities differ from monetary choices and location preferences in that they are not attracted to or repelled by physical locations. The software optimizes social preferences by minimizing the total length of connections, giving extra weight to the high-priority axes. The parameters that must be optimized have force (priority), preference (optimum value), and elasticity (range of acceptable values). Some axes will require the provision of poles of affinity as well as poles of repulsion. The list of axes may include some that are not, strictly speaking, social.

Each household will already have indicated its preferences on a survey conducted during the auction phase, and this information will be available in a database. Families will have ranked various axes as to priority, minimum and maximum value for each axis, and the optimum value for that family. The initial identification of values clusters and prospective urban villages will be based on a computer analysis of these preferences.

The process depends upon the ability of groups of families to reach consensus during the design of their neighborhood. Consensus-based decision-making has been more successful than many people would anticipate. Given a strong enough reason, people will work together for the good of the group. This allows consensus to be reached even in fairly large groups.

Salamanca

See page 431 for an explanation of poles.

See page 220 for a discussion of the concept of values clusters.

I was, in fact, rather pessimistic about the workability of this method for governing World Carfree Network. However, we have succeeded in reaching consensus at our Annual General Meetings despite some contentious issues demanding resolution.

The process cannot be said to have yielded an acceptable result until the range of preferences for all users on all axes has been respected. (It might be permissible to offer solutions where some of the lower-priority values are identified as out-of-range; people can then decide whether or not to accept this result.) A solution may fail to emerge because erroneous assumptions were made during the planning process regarding what people would want. The process will stall until adjustments are made. Since these changes are virtual, not in physical space, this is no great hardship; all that has been lost is some time. In fact, regular returns to the computer can be expected until some experience with the process has been gained. If, for instance, more people wanted to live in dog-free areas than had been anticipated, the axis that separates dog-aversive families from dog-loving families might have to be shifted to increase the dog-free area.

A family who feels mistreated may withdraw from the process. One advantage of forming urban villages is that some level of cohesion should arise very quickly, which would encourage the group to find a workable solution to a problem faced by one member. If this mechanism should fail, and the place of a departing family cannot be filled by a new household willing to take over the site, then the process will have to begin anew. If some people become impatient with the process or decide that they do not like the emerging arrangements, they would drop out, to be replaced by another family from the pool of applicants. It is by this means that I hope to meet the challenges that will arise during the first attempts. If people are a bit flexible in their requirements, the process will be facilitated. Willingness to change the orientation of a house is very helpful, as a problem can sometimes be solved by slipping a house around the corner to the next side of the block. In similar fashion, if some families can accept slightly smaller or larger courtyards or wider or narrower streets than they had wanted, a good deal of maneuvering room is obtained. It is my hope that the formation of

Salamanca

Salamanca

urban villages will encourage cooperation during design, which in turn would make for a good start on village life.

The village formation process will define a number of urban villages that will be accommodated in a given neighborhood, the bounds of which are delineated by the major streets and squares already arranged. The design of individual neighborhoods can be conducted in any convenient order. An advantage of working with a single neighborhood at a time is that succeeding groups can visit completed neighborhoods to observe the choices made and their ultimate effects.

Once computerized matching has reached a promising solution, the members of all urban villages will gather on the site to complete village formation. I propose here a generalized method that would be suitable for most societies, with adaptations for local culture, politics, and economics. The provisional computer-generated matches will almost certainly change once people actually meet each other on the site, starting at the locations identified by the computer. Although the computer's mechanistic determinations will often be wrong, I expect that most errors will be small. The initial placement will have no further influence once people gather on site and start to make their own choices regarding the membership of their urban villages. People will be free to change village as they may wish, subject, of course, to premium changes applicable to the new location.

It will probably be necessary to devote several weekends to on-site matching of families into urban villages. Families would start at location coordinates found by the computer to be the optimum for each family. Each prospective urban village will raise a literal standard at the center of the village, depicting the preferences that members of the village have expressed on the survey. No family would be obliged to remain at its designated starting location, but everyone would be encouraged to begin there. It is likely that many adjustments will be made in the field, but if the software works well and the preference items have

Alfama, Lisbon

Standards will carry iconic representations of the preferences of that village's members. The information on these standards should be permanently recorded on the street signs to be affixed to corner houses. Even though the character of the district is likely to undergo considerable change over the centuries, it will be interesting to have a prominent record of how the urban village began.

been correctly identified, most changes should be relatively small. As urban villages form, their members should confer with neighboring villages to ensure their mutual compatibility.

As urban village membership firms up and families take up their locations with respect to one another, the computer would track changes, which may affect both the applicable premiums as locations change and the cost of building sites as street widths and courtyard sizes change. After each weekend's field work, the computer would calculate the adjusted lot price for each family. These changes must be within the range that each family will accept. If changes are small, premiums probably will not change by enough to have an appreciable effect, especially given that premium levels in this phase are generally low. Final lot prices would only be determined once the on-site design is complet-ed, but final adjustments ought to be small and surprises few. If a family decides that its lot has become too expensive and the situation cannot be renegotiated, they may abandon the site to another family from the pool of applicants. If no such family can be found, then the process will have failed, and the situation will have to be reconsidered.

It is possible that more families can be accommodated on the site than had been foreseen during the urban planning process. Some families designated as alternates might be accommodated if the members of a given urban village were willing to use less land than had been expected, thereby making room for that village's alternates. This would save every family some money.

Urban villages may vary greatly in size, so we need block layouts in many sizes, as discussed on page 218. If a group forms that is too large (i.e., their block would be too large), it might break into two adjacent blocks along some internal division. Oversized blocks can be permitted if a public passageway through the interior courtyard is established, keeping walking distances short while requiring only slight extra distance for cyclists and any service vehicles using the streets.

Salamanca

Venice

COMPUTERIZED MATCHING

Venice

Lagos, Portugal

The results of the commercial phase must already have been entered into the database as predetermined locations. Computerized matching will require that each family's preferences be collected and stored. This can probably be most easily accomplished during the initial sign-up, as this information is needed throughout the process. The use of Internet forms makes it possible for each family to change its preferences as the process continues. Most of this information requires the same data structure as for premiums: minimum, optimum, and maximum values for each axis on which families will make choices. Each axis must be weighted by the family as to the priority they attach to that axis.

On the basis of this information, the computer generates a best-fit solution. This includes lot size requirements and all preferences, including social, side-of-block, and proximity-to-corner. The process is dynamic and consists of several or many rounds. Families can review the situation daily and change their preferences in response to the emerging village formations.

The matching of households on their social preferences is not entirely straightforward. Some preferences need only be matched with near neighbors; others must be matched with others living in the block and even within an entire neighborhood. Some must be matched on both sides of a street. Others must be matched within courtyards. For instance, the management of dogs will affect both streets and courtyards, and hence all households in the neighborhood. Matching families on the basis of preferred street width must obviously occur with neighbors on both sides of the street. Equally obvious is that matching families on the basis of the preferred type of courtyard ownership must happen within the block itself and is independent of the decisions made by adjacent blocks. A family who wants to run a small business that is not especially sensitive as to its precise location and need not have a prominent site can achieve a good match on social preferences during village formation.

One peculiarity exists in the formation of values clusters: two households that have expressed the same preference for a given axis may have given it a different priority. This will lead to one family being more strongly attracted to the other family because of the difference in assigned priorities. This presents no great difficulty, but it is a subtlety to keep in mind.

The initial location and orientation of at least some of the poles will most likely have to be determined by the planners on the basis of their best guesses as to what basic arrangements will satisfy the largest number of people. These decisions probably ought to emerge slowly and from fairly early in the planning process. Citizen consultation should be sought. It cannot simply be assumed that all land at a given distance from the district center has the same value. The land has its own benefits and drawbacks, and these demand attention. If people perceive that some of the best attributes have been assigned to groups other than their own, the process may strand. It might, in some cases, be necessary to introduce new premiums to regulate the demand for certain areas of the site deemed to be particularly attractive for whatever reason.

The addition of new poles of social attraction that urban planners had not anticipated should be as simple as possible. The following social poles are needed in the standard software package and will be used in virtually every formation:

- Urban village size (population)
- Courtyard ownership (public, shared, private)
- Home businesses (including allowable uses)
- Degree of reserve or gregariousness
- Tolerance for pets
- Sound levels for music, TV, dogs and cats, manufacturing, etc.
- Hour of expected evening quiet
- Use of intoxicants (none, slight, ample)

Madrid

Lido, Venice

If, as I foresee, districts are divided in half by the central boulevard, with metro-freight service paralleling it on only one side, the side that has metro-freight service will favor manufacturing and warehousing operations, which are inherently somewhat noisy. The other half is by nature the "quiet" part of the district.

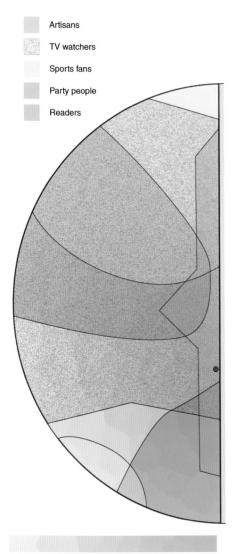

Artisans

TV watchers

Sports fans

Party people

Readers

Pole of dog aversiveness ⊕

- Desire for private garden plots next to houses
- Common interests: sports, affinity clubs, etc.
- Desire for street trees

I have not included an axis for children or old people as I believe that a healthy community requires a full range of ages (see APL, Pattern 35, Household Mix, and Pattern 40, Old People Everywhere). If people demand child-free or elders-only neighborhoods, these can be provided, but I urge against it.

As to the other axes that must be negotiated at this time, there are some that are monetary and some that relate to preferred locations such as corners or the south side of a street. The software must simultaneously optimize all of the axes in play during village formation. Although adjustments will certainly occur on the site, the number of axes is large and the problem is too complex to solve unless the field work starts from an approximately correct solution. Preferences related to social class, wealth, educational attainment, political affiliation, or religion might also be included as axes, although there are risks of social stratification associated with their use.

Those households who chose sites on major streets during the commercial phase will have only a weak voice in the formation of urban villages. Still, the kinds of shops and businesses they will establish act as elements in the urban village matching process—the heavy drinkers will prefer to locate near the bars and liquor stores. By contrast, those households that seek low-premium sites and are flexible regarding their location within the district should benefit from GOOD MATCHING ON SOCIAL PREFERENCES. (Effective graphics that help understand social fits require color overlays that can easily be turned on or off, as the number of axes considerably exceeds the number that can be differentiated in a single view.) The bustling part of this sample district is in the north. The "party people" section (light blue) intersects with a part of the "artisans" section (green) along the central boulevard and a large part of one of the "sports fans" sections (yellow). (The smaller sports fans section in the south is perhaps golfers and sailors of a quieter nature than the larger section.) "Readers" (purple) are in the quieter southern part of the district. The "TV watchers" (speckles) cover most of the district, with a small area of non-viewers (real athletes with little time for television) at the top and a larger one at the bottom (where the readers will live). "Dogs" (crystal-faceted red) are represented by a polar gradient centered on the red dot, with greater levels of dog-aversiveness represented by darker red.

Coimbra

Matching will be performed first for each household's top priority, which will generate powerful attractors to other families with similar preference on that axis. The strongest attractors will be for households that have not only the same optimum rating but have also given the axis top priority. Next will come families whose priority for that axis is not as high but who have given the same preferred rating. If not all preferences can be optimized for all people with respect to their highest priority, then attempts will be made to match people at least within their range of acceptable values. If even this fails for high-priority choices, the problem will have to be analyzed, with realignment of one or more poles as a likely path to a solution. People might also be asked to be more flexible in their acceptable ranges on some axes.

At the finest level of detail, the computer should establish blocks in which various physical and social parameters are arranged in the OPTIMUM SEQUENCE. Although computerized matching is a conceptually ambitious goal, the computational problem is not too difficult. Social affinities differ from monetary choices and location preferences in that they are not attracted to or repelled by physical locations. By grouping families into urban villages situated at their optimum locale, a good on-site solution should be reached without too much searching.

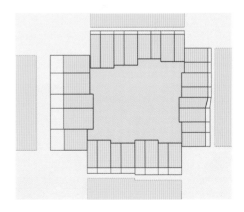

The process must be open and records should be public and searchable even if most users find no need for this capability. If

An odd computational difficulty arises if one family is attracted to another, which is in turn repelled by the first. Repulsion should probably take precedence.

Once high-resolution, hand-held GPS (Global Positioning System) units become available, positions can simply be given as latitude and longitude that can be entered as the end point. Cell phones and cameras may soon incorporate GPS.

a family wishes to express an aversion to some other family, this record could be confidential. The software will recompute the state of play every night based on changes that have been made during the day in the expressed preferences of all the families. Each day's results can be viewed by anyone. Old runs would be archived. The computer reports each family's lot by its location coordinates, which allows any family to quickly find and inspect its notional lot.

Once the process has reached stasis, the computer's role in the initial formation and arrangement of urban villages ends. It will only be used to keep track of lot size and cost. From then on, changes are negotiated directly between households working on the site. During on-site negotiations, unrestricted rearrangement would be permitted. These changes may affect premium levels slightly, and land cost to a somewhat greater degree, as changes are made in lot location and size.

The detailed computer output of the makeup and starting position of each urban village must include for each family:
- Which subdistrict (i.e., side of the central boulevard)
- Proximity to center
- Land occupancy
- Street frontage
- Street width
- House depth
- Courtyard area
- Side of the block
- Whether or not the lot is on a corner
- Whether or not some of the cost of a square is to be paid
- A breakdown of the applicable premiums

The computer output is considered mainly topological. That is to say, the computer proposes only the relationships between the various households within an urban village and the relative position of nearby villages. Precise physical locations will only be determined on the site, during neighborhood design.

Venice

Once a good formation has been achieved, the computer will shorten the frontage of all the houses by some arbitrary amount, probably about 30%, so that the district will be loosely arranged, with the blocks considerably smaller than they will become. The computer will direct each family to its location on the site. The graphical output will take the form of SIMPLIFIED BLOBS that leave a lot of room between the blocks.

ON-SITE VILLAGE FORMATION

On-site village formation will take some time. When it is complete, the compositions of urban villages and their relative locations on the site will be known. Families should be encouraged to at least explore the location they were assigned by the computer and meet their prospective neighbors. If the computer process has been successfully concluded, families ought to be a fairly good fit with one another and reasonably well matched on their preferences. However, many families may find that they would prefer to have as neighbors a family who is not immediately adjacent to their starting position. A few families may find the proposed arrangement not at all to their taste, and they may seek another location that better meets their needs or drop out of the process entirely.

Significant changes from the starting position are not only to be expected but actually encouraged. People will meet their prospective neighbors and get to know them. The final designation of urban villages, their members, and the sequence of families on the various sides of each block must be determined. Location changes must be recorded and entered into the computer. Changes that affect land area or premium levels will affect lot costs, probably only slightly. Families will have to know about these changes before they can agree to them.

Families will negotiate with their neighbors until the final order of households along each side of the block has been

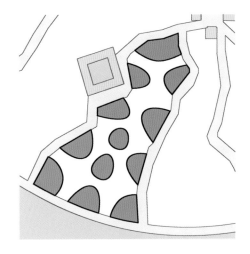

There is, of course, no reason that families should not meet informally before the on-site process begins. This may help the process to move forward. The attraction/repulsion mechanism discussed on page 410 could be applied to pairs of families that wished to remain together.

Valladolid

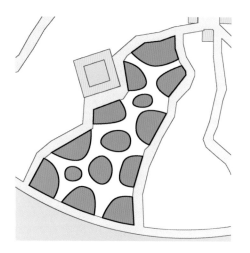

agreed. It is also important that people meet the families who will live across the street, in the adjacent urban village. These relationships must also be congenial. This task is somewhat complicated because the starting positions place families who will be on opposite sides of the same street at a much greater distance from one another than will be the case once the blocks and streets have taken shape. Families who start out facing one another across the street may well end up some distance apart as BLOBS START TO BECOME BLOCKS, so families should endeavor to meet other families who will live anywhere nearby. There is, of course, no disadvantage to this.

During the on-site matching, villages may split or fuse as it becomes apparent that this provides better matching. This will have small effects on land use as new streets are created or old ones eliminated by changes in the number and size of villages. These effects should be small enough that they do not greatly interfere with the overall land allocation.

This process might take on some of the aspects of a festival, with families cooking a meal on the site and perhaps sharing it with others. Some members of a family might remain at their provisional site while other members roam the neighborhood seeking a more congenial urban village than the one the computer picked for them. Picnics on the site before the actual start of this process would help families to meet one another and at the same time become familiar with the character of the site.

As urban village membership firms up over several weekends and families take their final positions, changes in the area of lots and the associated premiums ought generally to be small. Fine adjustments to premium levels may be required to maintain a balance between supply and demand. After each round of in the-field adjustments, the computer would provide an updated lot price to each family. Final lot prices can only be determined once on-site design has been completed, but any last changes should be small.

NEIGHBORHOOD DESIGN

We now consider a process to complete the design of neighborhoods down to the arrangement of blocks, streets, courtyards, minor squares, and individual house lots. This process can be conducted a single neighborhood at a time. Groups of families will already have formed into final urban villages as described in the previous chapter. All members of urban villages in a given neighborhood will meet on the site at the same time, where their task will be to create beautiful, functional spaces that will delight people for generations to come. Part III of this work, Elements, introduces the various design elements available to those conducting on-site design. This material must of course be adapted to suit local climate, economics, and culture.

When the process described in this chapter is complete, the layout of streets, squares, and interior courtyards will have reached final form, and their locations and dimensions will be staked out on the site. Individual building sites will have been marked out precisely and can be surveyed on the basis of this final staking. It then falls to individuals and organizations to design and construct their buildings, about which some final suggestions are made in the two following chapters, BUILDING LAYOUT and BUILDING DESIGN.

The process must respect the location and arrangement choices made during the commercial phase. Families will make decisions that will affect the exact land area they will occupy, which will slightly change premiums and perhaps appreciably alter the area of land for which they must pay. These changes will, of course, affect the final price that each family will pay for its land. Care must be taken to ensure that no family is priced out of the neighborhood by these changes.

Almost certainly, some parts of a district will be denser than others, and the same will probably be true of individual blocks. This assures variety in the character of the housing stock.

Quiet residential street, Alfama district, Lisbon

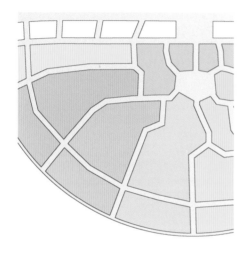

Neighborhood Scope

Neighborhoods will normally be delineated by major radial streets. If a concentric emergency access street was arranged during the commercial phase, it can be ignored for the purposes of establishing neighborhood boundaries—these wide streets will actually be rather quiet. They do not intrinsically separate neighborhoods.

Each district will comprise 12 to 20 neighborhoods, each with populations ranging from 300 to 1200 people. If we consider one quadrant of a district, we see how it might be DIVIDED INTO NEIGHBORHOODS of 4 to 15 blocks, each with populations of 30 to 250 people. (A much larger number of blocks is possible if very fine-grained blocks in the Arab manner are chosen for a given neighborhood.) We must remember that neighborhood boundaries are porous and that neighborhoods affect each other even when they are separated by the width of a main street.

Design Principles

A number of design principles and conditions must be established before the start of the process, and these must be respected as it continues. We consider here the design principles, which must be clearly understood and accepted by the participants if the process is to succeed.

Even though the major radial streets have already been arranged in final form, the layout of minor streets will have a large impact on the district and is critical to the success of the neighborhood. The minor streets must form a complete street network that provides fast walking routes to all destinations in the district. In point of fact, this is not hard to arrange as long as blocks are kept small and all streets run through (i.e., there are no culs-de-sac). As long as no block is too large and no dead-end streets are created, the final network cannot be too terribly bad.

Madrid

An advantage of districts with true centers is that most foot traffic will be moving in a given direction (i.e., to or from the center), so we can optimize walking paths for that trip. If the blocks are small and the minor radials arranged in an efficient pattern, the arrangement of concentric streets has but slight influence on walking times to the center, although they should lead quite directly to a radial. It is helpful if the minor streets connect fairly directly with one another, as offsets where they cross a radial street will somewhat lengthen the walking time to destinations not located near the center.

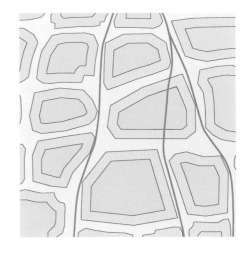

Because much of the traffic is to or from the center, we want a street network that SHORTENS WALKING TIMES to the center as much as reasonably possible. This in turn requires minor radial streets to complement the major radials. Given that these minor radial streets will not actually reach the center (there simply isn't room for them), they will have to join up with the major radials. The shortest practical routing will normally be achieved by applying the street-branching pattern described on page 442. Another approach is to make some of the inner blocks permeable, so that pedestrians can take shortcuts through them on their way to the center. In general, the issue of path-creating will not drive local design; it merely needs to be kept in mind and checked before a final design is accepted. An additional 30 seconds of walking time to the center is a small concern.

If minor squares are arranged on the more central side of an intersection, then small shortcuts are created that fractionally reduce walking times to the center. The problem is more difficult in a homogeneous layout without clear centers. This condition exists in LARGE PARTS OF BARCELONA, where a grid was imposed during a city expansion. (The grid was rotated from the usual north-south orientation in order to minimize summer solar heat gain.) Squares were obtained simply by beveling *every* corner, creating diamond squares at each intersection. The benefit of this arrangement has largely been lost to heavy car traffic, but

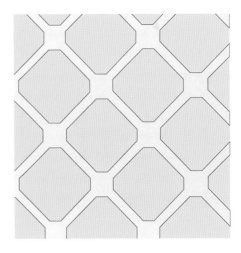

it does create frequent squares of appreciable size. It also reduces the apparent scale of the whole area, because the block frontages are noticeably reduced, even though the amount of land given up to the squares is quite small. This approach is worth keeping in mind, although there is no particular reason to follow a regular layout of the minor squares; they can be omitted when there is reason to do so, and they may be rectangular, triangular, circular, or quite irregular without harm.

A VERY SMALL SQUARE like this one in Guimarães, Portugal, can be added to a layout with little disturbance. It occupies only about as much space as a single building. The total area of small squares should have been allotted before on-site design begins, as the adjacent households will, in most cases, be the ones paying for the land and must therefore agree with the need for and extent of the square. (Squares, like streets, will be public property even though abutters will have paid for the land.)

Recall that many basic design decisions have long since been made. These include frontage, "backage," number of stories, depth of buildings, depth of interior courtyards, and so forth. The computer solution ought to have ensured that the arrangements to which people have agreed will, in fact, fit on the land available. This is no great computational chore, but accurate results are essential. Do notice that it cannot be done with absolute precision until the full street layout is complete, as the exact shapes of the blocks that are designed in the field will affect the "geometric efficiency" of the plots. By this I mean that blocks that depart very far from rectilinear or are noticeably oblong can increase the area that must be devoted to streets by an appreciable percentage.

In fact, if perimeter strings are used as the basic design tool, blocks will generally occupy less rather than more land as their shapes become more irregular. Rectangles of a given perimeter can go quite far away from square before there is a large change in the enclosed area. Increasing the aspect ratio only reduces the

Madrid

area to 98% for a ratio of 1.5:1, to 94% for a ratio of 2:1, and to 87% for 3:1. Even 4:1, which is beyond normally-desirable values, only reduces the area to 80% for a given perimeter length. Only by adding sides to a block does the enclosed area actually increase as compared to a quadrilateral. A circle has 127% of the area of a square with the same perimeter. Note, however, that a right isosceles triangle with the same perimeter as a square has only 69% of the area of that square. Blunting the point of the triangle and swelling the sides, as recommended on page 476, brings the percentage up considerably.

Design in this phase soon resolves to the delineation and shaping of individual blocks. During this phase, it is necessary to take account of the space requirements for the concierge service that will serve each block. This is the one significant advocated use that is not arranged during the commercial phase, because the final location of concierge service cannot be known until each block is designed. Also, concierge service will be arranged on the lowest-value land, which will draw no premium, and this distinguishes it from other advocated uses. Space for this use must not be omitted.

During this phase, it is important to pay attention to wind and solar access. In temperate regions, buildings on the equatorial side of a street are ideally one story lower than those on the opposite side of the street. This reduces shading of those buildings and brings more light into the street (see page 423). This can be part of the process of trade-offs that are made during design.

In the far north, winter sunlight is a critical consideration. Sweden requires access to it in new projects. Given the very low winter sun angle in these regions, this is a difficult challenge to meet. The problem must be specifically addressed during the urban planning phase, but the blocks shown in this SCHEMATIC DIAGRAM yield reasonably high density while still meeting the requirements for solar access for all residences. The interior courtyards must be very large, and so openings have been intro-

Venice

It is entirely reasonable for one concierge service to serve two adjacent blocks. However, I think it slightly better if each block has its own concierge service as this is a hearth for each community. Economics will dictate, and this question must be resolved before neighborhood design can begin.

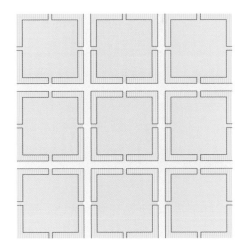

duced into the perimeter buildings in order to create pedestrian shortcuts. The buildings on the north side of the street would have to be reserved for non-residential uses as they will have no direct winter sun, although they would have ample daylight from the large interior courtyards. If the actual need is only for every family to have some winter sunlight, then it might be acceptable if only the top floor of row houses gets sun, which is much easier to arrange than sunlight on every floor.

Irregular sites and the shapes of their buildings will require attention so as to avoid a circumstance in which it only becomes apparent too late that an impossible design condition has been imposed on a particular building site. It will thus be necessary for families to anticipate the issues raised in BUILDING LAYOUT. Given that each family will be advocating for itself, problems from this cause should rarely arise.

Wherever two streets converge at a shallow angle, a problem arises. A WEDGE THAT BULGES is easier to manage, as this makes the angles less acute. The situation is further improved if streets are not brought together at a point but rather enter an intersection or square at a sufficient distance from one another to create a truncated point (see also page 442).

Most of the streets that are laid out during this phase of the work will be quite narrow. I anticipate a range of about 2 to 7m (6.5'-23') between facing buildings. If the resulting streets are to be comfortable and attractive, they must be given interesting shapes that also bring good daylight to street level. Complex shapes are interesting, and this is especially true when those shapes arise from the demands of the site and the requirements of its residents. In particular, I have noticed that narrow streets seem to work best when blocks are quite short and the NARROWEST PART OF THE STREET IS AT MIDBLOCK. Under these conditions, and assuming light-colored buildings, quite good light penetrates to the street along its full length, some of it reflected from the wider spaces of the nearby squares.

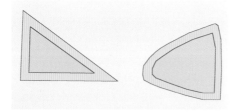

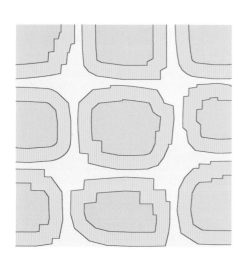

Irregular shapes do not in themselves pose any special difficulty, as discussed in ORDER & ORGANIZATION IN CITIES and SQUARES. Streets should therefore be arranged in whatever pattern helps to solve a particular design problem, even if that problem is faced by just one household. Allow the opportunities and constraints of the site great influence on its design. Indirect routes that skirt natural obstacles or specific features of the site that warrant preservation should be adopted without hesitation.

Coimbra

METHOD

The method proposed is similar to that for district-level design. Instead of yielding a network of major streets standing alone, each neighborhood will now be fully developed, within the bounds of the major streets. Although quite a few people will be working in a comparatively small area, it will by no means be crowded. This concentration of effort means that the experts who assisted at the district level can disperse over a much smaller area; there should be no shortage of available experts.

This process principally involves the design of blocks, but streets of course arise between blocks, and one of the objectives of the village phase is to give these streets good shapes that also function efficiently. The definition of the streets will depend to a substantial degree on the street widths that people chose during the village formation process. The members of each urban village will determine, in cooperation with adjoining groups, the location and shape of their block and the arrangement of the adjacent streets. This also includes the location, size, and arrangement of small squares, nearly all of which will be shared with other blocks. (In theory, a square can be the product of one village, if it is arranged entirely out of land paid for by that village, but there is almost no advantage to this.) Nearly all squares will be established at street intersections and will thus affect the design of several urban villages at once. Each neighborhood

Venice

Note that, unlike many parameters, the total amount of frontage can be adjusted over a fairly wide range. Simply by adopting a fine-grained arrangement (with the resultant small interior courtyards), the amount of frontage can be increased without changing the amount of land occupied.

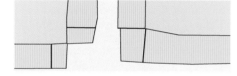

In the case of chamfered corners, the corner building may have a short back exposure if the buildings are not too thick in relation to the chamfer.

ought to have its own minor square not too far from its center. This will be appreciably larger than the other squares in the neighborhood but still a rather modest space. It can be a minor commercial center with local shops and services.

One of the principal agreements negotiated during the computer-driven village formation process is the length of street frontage that each family has reserved for its house. Each family can go out onto the site with a length of string equal to the length of its agreed frontage. If each string is arranged with a loop at one end and a toggle at the other, the strings of adjacent families in a block can quickly be connected to one another, creating a loop of string equal in length to the total frontage of that block.

One point must be watched: HOUSES ON THE CORNERS can be arranged in either of two basic ways, as shown. On the left is the arrangement that arises when a small square is included; on the right is the arrangement when a single house occupies all of a corner location. It will be seen in the first case that the houses have a great deal of extra frontage and the normal amount of "backage." In the second case, the house has about double the usual frontage and no exposure to the interior courtyard. In order for string to serve as a useful design tool, it will be necessary for this extra frontage to be included in the length of string for corner houses with double frontages. The arrangement shown on the left is preferable, as it does not give rise to houses lacking access to the interior courtyard and at the same time creates a small square of good shape. This does, of course, require somewhat more land.

If each family's allotted frontage has been temporarily reduced by 30% from its agreed value (see page 469), about half of the site will be occupied by the open space between the blocks. The distance between blocks will be on the order of 10m (33'). The streets at the starting position will thus be much wider than they will be once all slack in the perimeter strings has been taken up. Ultimately, the area dedicated to streets will usually fall in the range of 15-25% of the district. Values well outside this range are possible, but the final percentage should be known quite closely from the computer output.

People must understand the slack-string arrangement and the appreciable effects that it will have on the appearance of the neighborhood as the slack is taken up and the streets become narrower. Families may perceive this as a rather small amount of space to be absorbed, but once the strings have been lengthened again to their agreed values, people will move outwards to take up the slack. There will be just sufficient land available, although localized shortages requiring adjustment will arise.

The residents of a block will hold their string at waist level and walk slowly outwards until the string is taut. (String is relatively stretchy, but cheap polypropylene string is quite good in this respect. Since final measurements will be taken from the staking, a little stretch in the string is of no great consequence. In any case, the string should be tensioned only enough to take up the slack.) If all urban villages do this at the same time and move towards each other until the strings nearly meet, both the blocks and streets are defined at the same time.

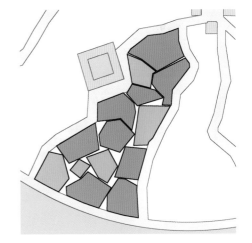

It is not to be expected that all the villagers will come to an exactly correct meeting with other villages in the neighborhood. Indeed, the initial result will almost certainly be unworkable. In some places, strings will meet, giving streets of zero width with BLOCKS THAT ARE NOT YET LARGE ENOUGH (those shaded in red). In other places, the streets will be too wide even though the blocks have already reached full size. Some shifting of shape and position will be required before all of the villages are arranged into blocks that satisfy all of their residents. Other blocks may have to shift as changes are made, and even distant changes may affect a given block. However, a solution should exist if an accurate length of frontage was allocated during the land allotment and village formation processes.

Adjustments will be difficult to make unless people know where extra space exists and where streets are too narrow. If those assisting the process are in contact by walkie-talkie, then villages can be asked if they would shift the shape and position of their block in a direction that leads towards a solution. As the villages shift, the assistants should help to avoid positions that produce unsatisfactory layouts (such as a sharp point at an intersection, or a block that is too long and narrow). Real-time aerial imaging would be exceptionally helpful and could be provided by a wireless camera suspended from a tethered balloon.

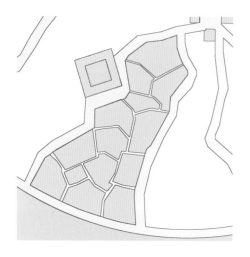

It is possible that no satisfactory solution can be reached on the first attempt, but a SOLUTION MAY EMERGE even in difficult circumstances if people will be a bit flexible. Some households might accept slightly more or less frontage than they had received in the computer-generated solution. (This can be compensated by making their building site shallower or deeper.) Streets might be made a bit wider or narrower than people had expected. It may prove helpful if some families will shift to another side of the block, permitting a needed change in the shape of that block. It might even be helpful if a few families would agree to move from one village to another. In extreme cases it might prove necessary to split an urban village or to fuse two of them. No change should be imposed: people must agree on the need for the change and its acceptability to their family. It is to be hoped that the formation of urban villages based on common interests and values will help families to reach agreement. Families who agree to shift to another side of the block may be moving into an area with different premiums, which would affect the cost of their site, and they must understand and accept the consequences before they agree to move.

The process will require creativity, flexibility, and compromise, and the process of attempting to reach consensus should help to show whether or not the formation of an urban village is viable. Remember that if one household is dissatisfied with its

Madrid

situation, some other household might offer to trade places with it; if no family is willing to occupy the site, then it is evidently untenable and the problem will have to be addressed by the group as a whole.

String and stakes have their limitations. In particular, they give no sense of how the height of the buildings will affect the feeling of space; people cannot visualize the completed street simply by staking out façades. As a child, I inspected dozens of houses during their construction and noticed that the sense of interior space changed several times, starting from the ground-floor platform upon which the house is built. The first change occurs when the studs go up, then when outer walls are sheathed, again when interior walls are sheathed, and once more when doors and windows are added. Even paint and final trim have subtle effects. The rooms seem smallest when the exterior sheathing has been applied but the interior walls are only studded out. This is counterintuitive, as one can still see the full length of the house, but somehow the rooms seem very small.

Madrid

Ideally, we would mock up buildings using painted theatrical flats, but the logistics are formidable if the whole thing is not to blow away in the first gust of wind. I expect that a mock-up would reveal the same sorts of changes as with houses under construction. First, the streets will seem very narrow when laid out with sticks and string. They will feel larger once the ground floors have been erected and later still they will feel smaller as the façades rise. This matter is worthy of a field test during which the various states would be experienced and recorded by observers. Such an example would help people to grasp how the feeling of the streets will evolve as the buildings rise.

The only practical way to visualize a street is to develop a 3D computer model based on the staking. Whether this is thought to be worth the cost is another matter, although the locations of the stakes must in any case be recorded, and once this data is available, it is not so difficult to build a 3D wireframe model

Faro

GIS = Geographic Information System

This technique is used by "first-person shooter" computer games, starting with *Doom* more than ten years ago. The design of that software was elegant, and it is exceptionally fast in execution. It might be possible to adapt such software to this new use. Right at press time, Procedural, Inc., released its CityEngine software, which promises to bring great power and flexibility to 3D modeling.

Venice

from the GIS data. Mapping images of building fronts onto the wireframe is a bit more difficult but would give quite a good sense of how the completed street would feel. Alternatively, it might be useful to make an accurate maquette of the neighborhood. Other approaches are possible, including stacking straw bales to the height of the first floor. Styrene foam blocks and bamboo skewers can be used to build a temporary wall that is light enough not to threaten anyone if it should topple. It might be worth experimenting with this approach to model the ground floors of houses.

People will be better able to visualize the completed streets if members of all the villages stand immediately behind the taut string. The expanse of the streets will be apparent, even though the sense of space will change as the buildings rise. The sense of density for a given street width will vary if building heights decline by one or two stories from the district center to the edge. Streets will feel more open among the lower buildings near the perimeter. Block sizes will tend to increase at greater distances from the center, giving larger interior courtyards and subtly affecting the sense of density by virtue of the longer blocks. Good recording of the first design efforts will help members of later projects to anticipate the changes that will occur.

Once a final arrangement is agreed, each family will set corner stakes, and an accurate survey of the stakes will be made. Areas will be computed from this plot and final lot prices calculated. This removes any benefit from cheating by stretching or splicing onto the string—people must understand that they will be paying for the actual area of land they occupy.

INITIAL POSITION

On the first day of on-site design for a neighborhood, all of the households in that neighborhood gather on the site. The locations of all buildings, streets, and squares that were established during the commercial phase must be accurately staked out. The frontage of these buildings must be delineated by string, so that their location and arrangement are clear to all. Families then move to the position they agreed to during village formation, with the families in the prearranged order. Frontage strings are connected, forming the block's perimeter but using the shortened length of string as described above.

Those who negotiated a site on a major street or square that passes through or touches on the neighborhood will already have arranged their streets, squares, and building, but they, too, are needed, to represent their own interests and assist in the formation and arrangement of the blocks of which they are members by virtue of their location. Advocates for the larger buildings and squares that directly affect the neighborhood are also needed on the site. Some advocated buildings may not have been situated in their final locations, but most of them will stand on a major street or square and will thus have had at least their frontage arranged during the commercial phase. Any remaining advocated buildings should be free to float within certain limits along minor streets and squares in a neighborhood.

Coimbra

ARRANGING MINOR STREETS

The members of each side of every block will have spoken for streets of a particular width, which must closely agree with the preferences of those in the blocks facing them, although these values may be different for different sides of the same block. When everyone is in position, each family will lengthen its string to the agreed value, and the string will now hang slack. Families will start to move outwards, slowly taking up the slack in the perimeter string until this becomes taut. Families who have negotiated for corner locations will need to walk farther than families near the center of one side of the block, in order that the corners take on definition.

Venice

Valladolid

Faro

The process will at first yield some streets that are too narrow and others that are too wide. The blocks must shift around until the agreed street widths have been achieved. Blocks will shift in the direction of available space. The assistants will advise members of each block where extra space exists and where more is needed. The block can move as a whole, or some parts can stay in place while others move, altering the shape of the block. The method chosen will depend in part on how the streets on the other sides of the block are faring—if their width is already good, and if there are no pressures against those sides of the block from other blocks, then they can remain in place, with other sides of the block shifting as needed. All the while, the perimeter strings are kept as near to taut as possible. There are some limits to this process. If the block is taken too far out of square, it will begin to lose appreciable amounts of area (for a constant perimeter), especially in the courtyard. It is to be hoped that the villages will be willing to give up a little in the interests of reaching a solution for the neighborhood as a whole, but a given urban village should not be asked to sacrifice street, square, or courtyard space beyond small amounts.

Even once all the strings are taut and the streets have reached the desired width, the design is incomplete. Minor changes in the shape of the blocks are needed to move space from the streets to the squares at the intersections, or vice-versa. The streets can be given more interesting shapes if families move slightly to increase or decrease the width in front of their house or to improve the shape of the interior courtyard. Jogs can be introduced into the street if one group of families moves a pace forward or backward. Flares are introduced if a group of families agree to back up from the street by progressively larger amounts; the slack thus created is taken up as other families move outwards. The actual amount of movement may be quite small, but the effect of even a one-meter (yard) change will seem large.

Corner locations are excellent for small, neighborhood

businesses. The ownership of corner locations will have been negotiated during the village formation process and must be respected during on-site design. It will sometimes be helpful if one or two families will agree to move to a location around the corner, allowing the shape of the block to change without changing ownership of the corner location. Minor manipulations of premium levels might be needed to encourage this kind of shift, which would necessitate another day of on-site design, once the computer-based negotiations were completed.

As with all steps in this process, changes must be made voluntarily. Some changes in premium levels and lot size may occur, with a resultant change in the cost of a site for a particular family. If that family does not wish to accept the change, then some other solution to the problem must be found.

I think that the necessary, subtle adjustments will cause blocks to take on interesting shapes. The design will be driven by needs and opportunities, which as I have said tends to be a better basis for design than abstract theory. The quirks that will arise are not arbitrary; they have a reason for being. This is better than efforts to introduce some particular design quality, such as curved streets, merely for its own sake. I believe that internal logic gives rise to "right" design: even long after the initial reason for a particular choice has been lost, the rightness of the arrangement will still be apparent.

Siting Squares

The larger squares were arranged during the commercial phase, but SMALL SQUARES are arranged during the village phase, their land having been spoken for during the auction phase, when households may request a square-front location and express a willingness to pay for their part of the square. These households would then have more say in the disposition of the land for which they had agreed to pay and probably the right to make

Coimbra

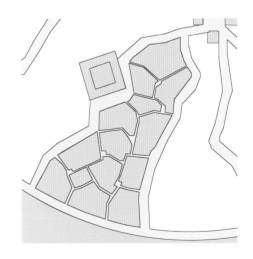

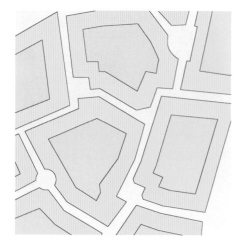

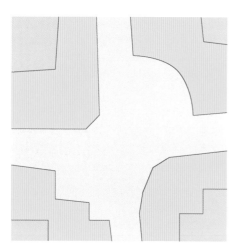

some commercial use of that part of the square that abuts their building. Alternatively, the two sides of a block that will share a corner square can agree to pay for the land it requires. This is a process that could take place on the site and might simply involve trading some street width or courtyard space for a square. If the squares are kept small, their cost is low.

In most cases, squares will actually be SHAPED FROM SPACE taken out of more than one of the adjacent blocks. (See the Reference Block on page 248 for examples.) One way or another, the land of the square must be paid for. Given that even a very small square is a substantial improvement in a neighborhood, it should not be too difficult to convince people to pay for it. The mechanism may allow those who sponsor a square to exert some permanent rights of control over the square, limiting its uses. If the adjacent corner building(s) are not to pay the full cost of the square, then it is to be expected that they would gain no special right to use the space thus created. This might actually be desirable if people want a quiet square with no abutting commercial uses. The non-commercial nature of the square would be recorded as a condition in the deeds of adjacent buildings.

The mechanism by which the land of a square is paid for affects the shape of the square, of course. Blocks that do not wish to pay for a square will not be cut into to provide space for it. The square will be disposed away from that block. In this EXAMPLE, the blocks on the northwest and southeast have given up very little land to the square. This does not greatly reduce their enjoyment of the square, and they should probably contribute a small amount to its cost. The willingness to pay for small squares can be handled as a preference during village formation. In any case, owners of corner locations should probably be required at least to bevel the corner, which substantially improves the intersection at a tiny cost in land. A mechanism to handle these circumstances is required and probably will have to be devised to reflect prevailing land laws and culture.

Arranging Squares

Once land for a square has been allocated and people found to sponsor it, the question arises of how to dispose of the space. It will be useful if the definition of squares begins early in the on-site design process, when streets can still be shaped to give advantage to the emerging square. The chapter Squares in Part III addresses their arrangement. That discussion will not be repeated here, but some further advice can be given.

The first consideration is the size of the square. In most cases, it can be remarkably small and still have a great influence on the immediate vicinity. In some cases, just a swelling of the streets will be enough to create one of the "beads" (see page 435) that we want to arrange.

Venice

If the entering streets are very narrow, say two meters (yards), then the square need only be about two or three times this width to exist as a place in its own right. The amount of land thus required is really very small. Resist the temptation to make the square too large. If squares are established at most or all street intersections, there will come to be a lot of them, and no square may see sufficient use to come alive (see page 327). Most of these squares will serve best if they are intimate spaces where clutches of neighbors will gather from time to time during the day. This function is actually better served by less space, not more. Of course, if streets are wider, say five meters (yards), then the amount of land required to define a square is much greater, which is yet another argument in favor of quite narrow streets. Still, squares even 10 meters (yards) on a side occupy only as much land as might be allotted to a single family.

Venice

Try to arrange at least one quiet corner that will not draw too much pedestrian traffic. Plan on a bench or two, probably in a sunny spot unless the climate is very hot. Consider planting a tree in the quiet area. Bevels function differently from hollows, as traffic will hug the face of a bevel, which is the shortest route

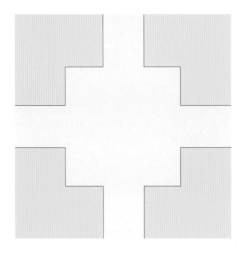

Guimarães

around the corner. Foot traffic will tend to cut across hollows, which will not be disturbed even by foot traffic.

Great care should be taken in arranging these small squares. They will set the tone for the vicinity, more so than the streets, which actually occupy much more space. Even small squares can be given a FORMAL (i.e., highly ordered) design, but unless the neighborhood is very stiff-necked, this is probably not the appropriate treatment. Few back streets will meet at right angles in any case (this geometry is poorly suited to a radial district, although it can be imposed on small sections if people insist). Streets will intersect at odd angles, and many will be articulated or slightly offset at squares. The irregular square shown on page 486 is in nearly all cases better suited to the radial street pattern and more responsive to local needs and opportunities.

When designing these squares, ask some people to stand along the building façades (to reveal the shape) and others to act as if they were actually using the square (to give a feeling for the scale). Fiddle with the details until they are exactly right. This includes adjusting the angle, width, and flare of the entering streets. These arrangements can affect emergency access, an issue with which assistants must be familiar, but few of these streets will be part of the emergency access network. If access is required, remember that the swept area is affected by the degree of turn, with acute corners requiring considerable extra turning room, and obtuse corners requiring much less.

Do not forget the adjacent uses, especially if these are sidewalk cafés or restaurants. Consider where the street furniture will stand. Just as with a living room, sometimes small changes in dimensions will determine whether a bench just fits (or doesn't). This is, in fact, a good analogy. The space that is under design is similar in size to a living room and will serve similar functions.

Consider adding a partial or full arcade if heavy rain characterizes the local weather. Cafés will prefer these locations for the respite they offer from sudden squalls. When arcades are fitted with blinds, they can also offer protection from hot afternoon sun. If an arcade is to be built on only one side of the street or square, it should probably be the sunny side, to provide shade for buildings and pedestrians (the other side of the street will probably be in shade nearly all the time).

Arrange somewhere for children to play while their parents enjoy an afternoon coffee or an evening glass of wine. A full playground is not needed. Include a drinking fountain if children are to form a part of the square's regular population—they are always thirsty, and water is better for them than soda.

Depending upon the urban planning arrangements, it might fall to citizen designers to decide such matters as street lighting and paving. If these decisions can be left to local residents, this gives another opportunity to make a local square feel just right.

Venice

Interior Courtyards & Building Sites

The INTERIOR COURTYARDS must also be arranged at this time. As on-site design progresses, it will be necessary to keep an eye on the area of the interior courtyard. As already mentioned, changes in block size and shape can considerably affect the area of the interior courtyard, even while the perimeter of the block maintains its agreed length. As long as people are willing to accept changes in courtyard area, this poses no special problem, as the families in the adjacent houses will pay for any extra area and save money if there is a reduction. However, most urban villages will not be willing to see their courtyard area change beyond a certain point.

It is of course true that the area of the courtyard is greatly affected by the depths of the adjoining houses, and we may be wishing to make some changes in house depth to accommodate a shortage or surplus in the perimeter length of the block. It is probably best if a quick check on the courtyard size be made as soon as the first provisional arrangement of streets and blocks is

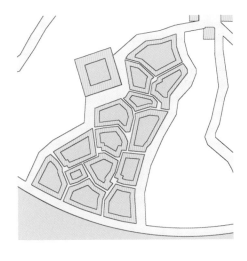

Madrid

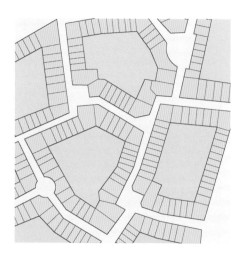

done, as any great error will require rather large changes in the arrangement of the block and surrounding streets, which will in turn affect nearby blocks. All that is necessary is for each household to pace off the depth of their house, moving away from the current location of the perimeter string. If every family does this at once, the size and shape of the interior courtyard will be fairly accurately defined by family members standing at what would be the back of their house. If the children then run out to play in the emerging courtyard, the feel of that courtyard will be quite well revealed.

If there is a serious shortfall, the block might need to increase its perimeter, make its houses shallower, and make the sides of the block more convex (which has a large effect on not only the size but the feeling of the space). If too much space exists, this could be retained, except that it is likely that this surplus indicates a shortfall in some other block. The opposite measures can be applied to shrink a courtyard if need be.

Remember also that adding or removing just a few buildings from the side of a block exerts a very large effect on the size of the courtyard. It might be possible for a village with an undersize courtyard to take in one or two families from another village that had too large a courtyard, assuming, of course, that the families are willing to move.

As the design of the streets and squares comes into focus, the area available for situating individual houses will become clear. In conjunction with managing the size of the interior courtyard, it will be necessary to ensure that each family is obtaining a building lot of a reasonable shape that is within the size limits the family will accept. Families should keep in mind the discussion in BUILDING LAYOUT while making these decisions.

As all of these matters are refined, the FINAL ARRANGEMENT OF THE NEIGHBORHOOD will emerge. People should not be too hasty to accept the arrangement and should tinker with it until it feels exactly right. They will be living with it for a long time.

BUILDING LAYOUT

We take up here the layout of the buildings that will comprise new carfree districts. Families engaged in on-site design need a mental image of the houses they wish to construct while they are helping to lay out their streets, courtyards, and their own building site. The material in this chapter should be provided to families before the on-site design process begins.

The focus in this chapter is on smaller buildings that will be designed by their owners. Larger buildings will almost certainly be designed by architects. We consider first the important aspects of building arrangement and conclude with an overview of some types of minor buildings that are suitable for carfree districts. These types are not adapted to a particular climate or specific construction resources but in most cases are versatile enough that adjustments to meet local requirements are feasible. A range of types is presented that is indicative of the possibilities that exist for house design.

It may be that people are not interested in designing their own houses or even their own blocks. If that proves to be the case, there is no real reason that developers cannot buy a full block to design and build for sale or rent. As long as the right conditions are imposed on the developer, there is nothing really wrong with this practice, although it does not yield all of the benefits that I foresee from user-designed blocks and buildings.

It is essential to consult with local officials regarding not only the type of house to be built but also the construction codes that must be observed. Much of what is proposed here conflicts with zoning and building codes in US jurisdictions, and variances will have to be won on a case-by-case basis. The New Urbanists have succeeded in implementing new design codes (although the construction codes are unchanged). If a jurisdiction really wants a carfree project, political pressure should suffice to allow necessary variances.

Small buildings in the local vernacular style, medieval quarter, Nancy, France. These buildings are considered by many to be "quaint," which is a disservice to their enduring practicality and simple beauty.

Concrete is a comparatively energy-intensive material. However, it is fireproof and durable when properly
constructed. Wood is in many ways preferable, but the
supply of high-grade framing lumber is now very
limited following centuries of unsustainable logging
practices. The fire risk from wood is significant.

The construction techniques are generally in line with the
reinforced concrete methods widely used on all continents
except North America. I propose to allow both the arrangement and structural design of minor buildings to be undertaken
by anyone, subject to the requirements of simple codes. This
controversial proposal is supported by Alexander's experiment
in Mexicali (see *The Production of Houses*). Remember that, in
the past, few buildings were the subject of either architectural
design or structural engineering. Failures certainly did occur,
but they were rare enough that people tolerated the risk (having
little choice). The North American practice of referring the
structural design of residences to simple tabulated engineering
solutions can be broadly applied to most places and methods.

Per-Capita Floor Area

One difficult choice I made when developing the Reference
Design was the per-capita floor area allocation. This decision
affects the area of land that the city occupies, the cost of
construction, and the arrangement of public transport. (The
allocations I adopted are given on page 239.) These allocations
are somewhat low by contemporary American standards but are
comparatively high for the rest of the world.

The space allocations are for *gross* area; net, usable area will be
20% or even 30% less (see note). If there is no basement, some
use may be made of the space beneath the stairs, and the top
floor will not have an ascending staircase (unless routine access
to the roof is required). If there are many interior walls or large
utility spaces, usable space is still further reduced.

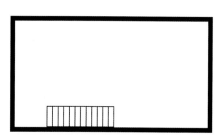

Consider this plan of a building with a footprint
9.14×5.03m (30'×16.5'), an area of 45.98 m² (495 ft²).
If the walls are 20cm (8") thick, then the floor area is
8.74×4.63m (29.58'×15.08'), with an area of 40.5m²
(435 ft²). Even without any allowance for stairs, about
12% of the footprint has been lost to exterior walls.
Stairs occupy an area 0.91×3.05m (3'×10'), further reducing the net area by 2.79m² (30 ft²), bringing the
floor area down to 37.7m² (405 ft²), for a total reduction
of 18% before any allowance for interior walls (which
may sometimes be omitted) and utility spaces. Low-
rise buildings may have thinner walls, however.

Although working with gross area is a necessary simplification
when planning neighborhoods, we must explain that net spaces
will run 20-25% lower. Most laymen think stairs occupy just
half the space they do. They will be surprised by the magnitude
of these losses and must be specifically warned about it.

In Western societies, people are occupying far more space than formerly. Reliable figures are probably unobtainable, but if we compare a US working-class family of a century ago, when it was common for a family of eight to live in a single room, with a family today whose income level falls in the same percentile, we might find a family of four living in a house with six rooms, giving a 12-fold increase in per-capita space. Whatever the exact number may be, families today comprise fewer people and occupy more space. Rising energy prices may soon impose a more modest way of life in the rich nations, but I hope not to return to the extreme overcrowding of the early industrial era.

Westerners have become casually wasteful of space, especially in new suburban housing. A perfectly functional KITCHEN or BATHROOM can occupy a small fraction of the space usually devoted to them in new housing. I lived with the kitchen and bathroom shown here for 14 years and found only storage to be an annoying limitation, and that only because I never troubled to build in more shelving. The tiny kitchen was actually big enough for two people to work in, and the bathroom was entirely functional. The short tub was big enough to soak in and used less water than a full-length tub. You will find no kitchens or bathrooms this small in standard architectural reference works, but many buildings in Venice and central Amsterdam have examples this size or a bit larger. These smaller rooms are cheap to build, cheap to occupy, and easy to keep clean. We simply need to display the same ingenuity as the architects and craftsmen who know how to fit these functions into tiny spaces.

The US "McMansions" are no less than 3000 ft^2 (270 m^2), and often only two people live in them. Without immigrants working at low wages to maintain them, their owners would spend most of their free time in upkeep. As has happened in the past with overly large houses, they may eventually be subdivided into apartments, with many more people living in the same space. (There will certainly be plenty of bathrooms!)

Building Frontage

In true urban areas, the streets are defined by the façades of the buildings along them. It is possible to allow one or two meters (yards) of garden between the house and the street, but normally no green space intervenes between buildings and the street. Frontage is the most valuable part of an urban plot and also the most expensive to supply, as it requires the construction of streets and utilities corresponding to its length. Historically, those places where land was most valuable had the narrowest buildings. Land in cities built on reclaimed land or protected by defensive walls was always expensive to provide. The narrow houses of the REGULIERSGRACHT in Amsterdam are typical.

In the pattern "Row Houses," Alexander proposes two-story row houses oriented with their long sides towards the street. He suggests buildings with a 30' (9m) frontage and 20' (6m) depth. The back yard is just 15' (4.6m) deep, and the width of the lane in front is 14' (4.3m) This provides excellent light and densities of 85 houses/ha (35/acre). At 2.5 persons/family, this gives an occupation of 214 residents/ha (86/acre), compared to the 264 residents/ha (107/acre) in the Reference District, which also includes 176 workplaces/ha (71/acre), giving a net human density of 440/ha (178/acre). The Row House pattern thus yields only about half the density proposed for the Reference District, which is predicated on four-story buildings.

The relatively low densities proposed by Alexander in Row Houses can be accommodated in carfree cities, but only if people will walk seven minutes to the transport halt, instead of five. This similarly increases the walking time from the center to the large green areas beyond the perimeter. If people are willing to accept longer walking times, the task of selling carfree districts to North Americans may be simplified, as the density can be brought down to much lower levels that may be easier for people to accept.

APL, Pattern 38

Net human density is simply the number of residents and employees living and working on one hectare. See especially the work of Vincent Fouchier on this.

Alexander explored this pattern in two projects for Japan which were to have been built at 3-story height and would have allowed each family to park one car. Very little usable open space remained, even after putting about one-third of the cars in underground garages. Final densities reached 200 dwellings/ha (81/acre) in the denser of the two projects, which is a net human density of 500/ha (202/acre) without commercial occupancy. This is about 15% higher than the Reference District.

We have seen the advantages of curving streets from both topological and aesthetic standpoints. As already mentioned, this introduces irregularity into the layout of buildings, which are no longer arranged using right angles exclusively. Building fronts are not usually curved; rather, each building stands at a slight angle to the next. Take for example these OLD STREETS in Santarém, Portugal. The one on the right has been made very attractive and interesting by its articulation. The one on the left, while not perfectly straight, is much less attractive. (This has in part to do with the much plainer façades.)

It is possible to develop irregular streets while maintaining rectilinear plots and buildings. Buildings are kept aligned to a grid but jogs (offsets) are introduced between adjacent buildings, to create the desired street path. However, a more coherent effect is achieved when building fronts are continuous, without jogs (although jogs do create "beads" and also allow windows on two sides, giving more and better light). My view is that jogs should be employed sparingly, and then mainly in the service of creating beads where people will congregate.

Non-rectilinear plots are somewhat more complicated to survey, but modern surveying techniques reduce the added cost to almost negligible amounts. A more serious concern is that the building interiors are no longer rectangular. One or both of the side walls will make an oblique or acute angle with the gable, and the side walls may no longer be parallel. If the angles are not far from 90°, which is normally the case, the layout is little

TNO III:312-327 & 382-384

The space allocation for a workplace in the Reference District is half that for a dwelling place, so the net-human-density comparison is not entirely valid.

Illustrated on page 303

See page 435

This has advantages as far as acoustics are concerned. Rectangular rooms have resonant peaks that are difficult to damp.

Alfama, Lisbon

TNO III:562-570

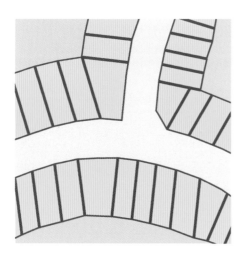

affected, and the rooms are often subtly more interesting. The complications introduced into construction are more serious. Modern materials (such as plywood) are manufactured with precise right angles, to simplify construction. Tooling can be set at 90° and left there. If the floor plan is not rectilinear, the tools will have to be adjusted frequently.

The advantages of non-rectilinear buildings in permitting the arrangement of attractive streets are so compelling that a method must be found to cope with construction of buildings that are not rectilinear. Any journeyman builder is capable of this work, but costs will rise. Computerization has been slow to reduce the cost of non-standard building elements, but this is starting to change. Alexander gives an example of a floor made of thousands of small pieces of stone, each cut to a precise shape by a computer-controlled tool. Cost and time were reduced by an order of magnitude.

The increase in construction costs can be reduced by keeping the demising walls (the wall that separate one building from the next) parallel to one another. In that way, only the façade is at an angle, and the rest of the building is still based on right angles. When the angle of the façade gets more than, say, 15° out of square with the demising walls, one building is arranged with its DEMISING WALLS WELL OUT OF PARALLEL, correcting all of the accumulated error. This minimizes the total increase in the cost of the buildings.

One practice should be avoided. In the UK and the eastern USA, it was once common to build row houses in which two adjacent buildings shared a common wall. This approach reduces construction costs but introduces several problems, including building-to-building noise transmission. Ownership of the wall is shared, complicating later redevelopment. Impairment of the structural integrity of one building may propagate to the next.

We consider next how some of the principal elements of minor buildings affect their layout.

VARYING STORY HEIGHTS

After irregular streets, nothing makes an area more visually interesting than varying story heights. It is not necessary or even desirable to achieve large differences in story heights; all that is required is some variation between buildings. The REGULIERSGRACHT in Amsterdam has a fairly wide but still pleasing range. This can be achieved simply by allowing people to choose their story heights, within some specified range. It is particularly useful to encourage lower ceiling heights on upper stories, which makes them feel more intimate and private. Lower stories benefit from higher ceilings with respect to the admission of daylight. Upper stories are already brighter because less light is cut off by neighboring buildings and trees. Another important benefit of this arrangement is that areas with this characteristic lose all association with mass-produced, one-size-must-fit-all housing.

The elevation of the ground floor with respect to the street also exerts a profound influence on the character of an area. The closer that ground floors are to the level of the street, the better the quality of an area. A centimeter or two (half an inch) is enough to keep out rainwater, as long as the basic drainage is good. At-grade ground floors are also a boon to anyone with mobility limitations. When ground floors are at ground level, we usually find inviting streets, such as this SHOPPING STREET in Amersfoort. Besides being easy of access, these buildings feel connected to the street. So, to the extent possible, build ground floors at street level. When all ground floors are at the same height, the buildings are more adaptable to changes in use and it is a simple matter to join several buildings together into a larger office or store.

This is related to Alexander's "Connection to the Earth," APL, Pattern 168. The joining of adjacent ground floors is discussed on page 439.

Above the ground floor, there is some reason to introduce variation in story heights. In the photograph of Amsterdam just above, notice that no two buildings have the same arrangement of floor heights. The adds further interest to a street and can give increased privacy in narrow streets if opposing windows do not to look directly into one another.

In general, we will want to make story heights as low as possible, in order to minimize the scale of a building and reduce its cost. Lower buildings allow more daylight to reach the street and create rooms with a cozy feel.

ROOFS

We will be concerned here with the general arrangement of roofs as related to the layout of buildings. The design details of roofs are taken up in the next chapter. Roofs are also discussed in passing on page 370.

Roofs fall into SEVERAL BASIC TYPES. We will not delve into every possible type of roof, but those types that are useful in small buildings are worth considering. (The use of domes and other elaborate types is highly desirable in major buildings, as it helps to make these buildings even more distinctive, but they are too expensive for routine use.)

Probably the oldest and certainly simplest type of roof is the SHED ROOF, a pitched roof that reaches its highest point at one edge of the building. These roofs are generally only suitable for the smallest buildings, as the rafters become expensive if the span is very great. Most other types of roof can be built with thinner supporting members owing to their shorter spans and self-supporting properties. Only the flat roof is an exception to this rule. The shed roof suffers from its unbalanced appearance and generally should not be used as a main roof, although there may be times when its application solves a specific problem. They are excellent when a secondary roof is needed.

Simple GABLE ROOFS, like these in Amsterdam, are probably the most common. They are easy to lay out and construct. The ridge normally should run in the long dimension of the

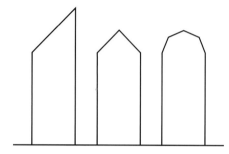

Shed, gable, and gambrel roofs

building. They make quite efficient use of material as long as the width of the roof does not exceed about 8m (26'), at which point only a truss can carry the load without extravagantly large framing members. Trusses, however, break up the attic and render the space useless for habitation, although storage is still possible. By avoiding the need for trusses, the interior space is kept free of obstructions. This type of roof has gables at both ends, which should always have windows, however small.

HIP ROOFS are probably nearly as old as gable roofs and do not differ greatly in their basic engineering. They do, in fact, make slightly more efficient use of materials and are by their nature self-reinforcing in both directions. The disadvantage of the hipped roof is that it admits no daylight to the interior unless dormers or skylights are added. Low-angle hip roofs are widely used in hurricane country because they resist storms better than other types, but these shallow-pitched roofs provide standing headroom only if the building is quite large.

The gambrel roof is a compound form, with a steep pitch on the lower part, breaking to a low pitch farther up. It is often known as a "barn roof" in the USA. The ends are gables. This form of roof provides a large amount of usable floor space, as seen here in an APARTMENT INSIDE A GAMBREL ROOF.

The MANSARD ROOF is a related form, with gambrels on all four sides. It provides a bit less usable floor space than a pure gambrel, and is more attractive in a building that might otherwise appear too massive with gable-ended gambrels. (The apparent height of a building is the height of its eaves, not the peak of the roof.) The large mansard roof in the center of the photograph is an attractive example. Both mansard and gambrel forms permit the use of small and economical framing members. The mansard roof provides good usable space when dormers are added to admit light. (The alternative, skylights on the steep slope of the lower roof, is not at all attractive.) Note that this example is not a pure mansard; a dormer has been added to the

Alfama, Lisbon

upper level of this large roof in order to provide another partial story of habitable space. There is no reason to avoid this approach, and many roofs in older parts of cities are compounds of various forms. Sometimes this is almost unavoidable, and if the roofs are arranged with artistry, the result is highly satisfactory.

Some fire codes forbid the mansard for reasons I have never discovered. The concern may date back to a period when flammable roofing materials were used and a fire could spread between close-facing mansards. Consult local codes before choosing a mansard or gambrel.

Flat roofs are the devil's choice. They are the least attractive type of roof (when viewed from the street) and are expensive to construct and maintain. I have lived and worked under them and have nothing good to say about them. Even when they have the recommended slight pitch to allow water to drain off (a refinement often omitted), they have a great propensity to leak. The slightest break in the roofing membrane can cause serious leakage. However, they do provide usable space and a place to take the cool evening air in hot climates. They are useful for laundry drying and sunning. It may be expedient to provide a small area of flat roof, with the remainder of the roof pitched, as in this VACATION HOUSE in Portugal. When so used, all the roofs in an area should be about the same height above the ground, so as to maximize the view for everyone while affording some privacy by the use of waist-high parapets. This practice is common in desert regions and well suited to them.

Buildings whose floor plans are not quadrilaterals generally require complex roofs based on conjunctions of standard forms. Although these roofs are often more attractive than a simple roof, they are complicated to build and have more flashing, which is a common point of leakage.

The selection of a roof pitch requires careful consideration, and local conditions exert a large influence. In many ways, a low-pitched roof is the least practical. It provides no useful space beneath it, nor does the surface of the roof provide usable area. Low slopes are also generally less attractive, but may be advisable in stormy regions. In areas with heavy snowfall, steep roofs will shed heavy snow loads, preventing an uncleared roof from collapsing under extreme snowfall. However, steep pitches can endanger people walking below, as an avalanche of roof snow may carry ice. If the ridges are arranged perpendicular to the street, this hazard is avoided. In many places, the first meter (yard) of the roof surface above the eave includes loops around which ice will grow, securing it against sliding. Local practice should usually be followed. Steeper roofs increase the amount of usable space within the roof while consuming only slightly more material in their construction. A pitch of 40-45° seems to me optimum for a simple pitched roof, particularly from the standpoint of outside appearance. Very steep roofs are difficult and dangerous to work on, although work on the very steep lower section of a gambrel can often be performed while standing in the gutter between two buildings.

Unless flat roofs form part of the local vernacular style or are otherwise essential, roofs should be designed to permit the habitation of space within them. This space is economical to develop, reduces the volume of a building for a given amount of floor area, and allows the use of economical pitched roofs. This approach also maximizes the amount of daylight reaching the street for a given level of building density. Very steep pitches may even provide room for several occupied floors within the roof, such as at the MUSÉE ALSACIEN in Strasbourg. These spaces have sloping walls, of course, and get very hot even in temperate climates. However, having lived in several garrets myself, I find them generally agreeable and often cozy spaces. The heat problem is solved by adding openable skylights as high up as possible. When this is combined with a window on the stairs leading up to the garret, a remarkably strong draft is created that rapidly exhausts the hot air that builds up when the space is closed on

Strasbourg

Valladolid

a hot summer day. Skylights give lots of light and air, but they are not sufficient by themselves; a conventional window is required, if only to see out.

A further advantage of inhabited roofs is that they provide the cheapest possible living space (saving aside basements, which I regard as unsuitable for human habitation due to the dampness, cold, and lack of light). We must attend to the need for inexpensive housing, and attic spaces offer an excellent solution.

The "green roof" has gained some popularity in recent decades. It is simply a very strong roof structure covered by a layer of earth on which grass and other vegetation are planted. They have excellent insulating properties and help to retain rainfall while providing substantial green space within the city. Their structural requirements are very high, and the heavy load at the top of the building should probably be avoided anywhere that strong earthquakes occur.

In "Dormer Windows" (APL, Pattern 231), Alexander explains why dormers with windows are almost the only possible means to make space inside a roof inhabitable. However, it is possible to develop an inhabited roof in a building with a simple pitched roof and GABLE ENDS, as long as windows are set in both gables. Dormers must always be tall enough to stand underneath. They come in the same three principal varieties as main roofs: shed, gable, and hipped. All are acceptable, although the roof of a shed dormer is more prone to leak owing to the usual shallow pitch. The style of dormers generally ought to reflect that of the main roof. This FINE BUILDING in Basel has six small dormers and one large dormer that can also be used to hoist heavy objects into the building, a common pattern in Basel. All seven dormers have hipped roofs, in a building with a hipped main roof. The overall effect is highly satisfactory. Dormers can be quite elaborate in their detailing. Normally, their windows should be in a similar style to the rest of the building, although this rule is often broken to good effect.

When the need for more living space arises, attics can be converted into bedrooms at low cost. Dormers may have to be added, but if proper stairs were provided at the outset, the conversion of these spaces is fairly simple and inexpensive. In the Netherlands, many buildings constructed during the 1920s had full attics, giving each tenant in the building a large enclosed storage space. Many of these spaces have been converted into small apartments today, increasing the supply of cheap housing.

A good roof arrangement includes a HOISTING BEAM. This permits furniture to be hoisted in through the windows on upper stories. This is much faster and easier than heaving things up the stairs. Care must be taken to ensure that the beams do not rust or rot away, only to fail the next time they are used. The Dutch practice in this matter is a good guide, as hoisting beams are still installed in new buildings. Small roofs are placed above the beams, to keep the water off them, which, along with inspection at long intervals, seems to be all that is required.

Eaves should be kept low, to minimize the mass of the building and allow more daylight to reach other buildings and the street below. To achieve this, story heights should be kept low, which requires that floor structures be made as thin as possible.

"Sheltering Roof," APL, Pattern 117

Alexander would prefer that the roof come low enough that someone passing by can touch the edge of it. Roofs in dense areas are normally much higher, as the buildings must be at least two stories tall in order to achieve sufficient density. It is possible, however, to provide a SMALL ROOF OVER THE ENTRANCE to shelter waiting visitors. This roof can be low and within reach.

Parapets should generally be eliminated from urban construction except in the case of flat roofs, where they are advisable to keep someone from falling off the roof. Parapets are prone to falling during earthquakes, when they endanger anyone in the street. They also block the sun to a greater degree than is otherwise necessary. If parapets are deemed essential, keep them as low as possible and see to their reinforcing.

Entrances

Entrances to narrow buildings are problematic, especially when there are multiple occupancies. The most common solution is to provide two entrance doors, one for the upper stories and one for the ground floor. This is rather awkward, as a large part of the building façade is taken up by doors. The installation of glass in at least one door makes them less forbidding.

Another approach is to build a small foyer inside a single front door, with access to both the stairs and the ground floor from the foyer. It is possible to close off the foot of the stairs with a door, but this arrangement is inconvenient unless some room is left between the foot of the stairs and the door. (I myself lived with this for years and never found it to be much of a bother.)

A clever trick, rarely applied, is to install a shallow showcase at the foot of the stairs, as here on the UTRECHTSESTRAAT in Amsterdam. A side door provides access to the space behind this showcase and thence to the stairs. The store has a deep showcase on the opposite side. Increased display area is thus provided.

Windows

There is no substitute for natural light. Aside from its perfect economy, it is the most practical, balanced, full-spectrum illumination available. (Advances in lighting technology are finally overcoming the awful quality of artificial light that has afflicted us since the gas-discharge lamp came into use a century ago.) Even if a perfect source of artificial light becomes available, we still want natural light in every inhabited room. The changing light keeps us aware of the time of day and kind of weather.

Alexander calls for "LIGHT ON TWO SIDES OF EVERY ROOM" (APL, Pattern 159). This arrangement results in highly satisfactory illumination. Unfortunately, it is not possible to arrange this in a street of town houses unless the buildings are jogged with respect to each other, permitting a window in the side wall thereby exposed. The best that can normally be done is to keep the floor plans as open as possible, so that light from both the front and rear of the house illuminates most spaces.

Until quite recently, windows were the only way to cool and ventilate a building. The advent of refrigeration and mechanical ventilation is not entirely an improvement. Serious health problems can arise from microbial colonies in ducting. Forced-air systems always make some noise. In auto-centric cities, rooms facing the street are usually quieter when sealed up and air conditioned than when the windows are open. Carfree cities will be far quieter and most of the sounds will not be unpleasant. We should, therefore, always provide opening windows in our buildings, even if they are air conditioned. They are simply too important to our health and well-being to omit. I doubt if air conditioning can be sustained in the face of energy constraints.

Tavira, Portugal

STAIRS

Small buildings with stairs giving access to upper floors provide wheelchair access only to ground floors, and only then if that floor is at street level. Elevators are impractical for small buildings due to the cost in both space and money. It is possible to install stair-side lifts where handicapped access must be provided. The cost is considerable but not huge, and most buildings will not need them if publicly-accessible spaces are on ground floors.

Otherwise, stairs are not a serious constraint. In Dutch cities, where land was always at a premium, virtually all buildings are several stories high, and until recently most buildings had STEEP AND WINDING STAIRS. These stairs are today prohibited by most building codes, but I think there is merit in a return to their use. They occupy less space than anything except a ladder and are actually less dangerous than commonly believed. A fall on a long, straight flight of stairs can be serious even if the rise-over-run is

Companionway ladders on boats are very steep, often wet, and used while the boat is moving in a seaway. They are provided with good handrails, and the hatch provides another hand hold. The narrow passageways help prevent falls, and accidents are uncommon despite the highly adverse conditions.

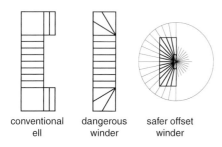

| conventional ell | dangerous winder | safer offset winder |

The layout of the stair illustrated above-right is more complex than a simple offset radius, as can just be seen. The point from which each tread radiates is farther offset in the middle of the stair than near the ends.

8/9 (the steepest now generally permitted) or less, whereas with narrow winding stairs, there are many ways to break a fall, and longer falls are stopped or retarded by the walls where the stairs change direction. Consider the building in Amsterdam where I lived for many years. The first flight of stairs was straight and long (due to the high ground floor). For years this stairway had no hand railing, but even after one was added, the prospect of a fall remained frightening. The other two flights were tight, steep, narrow winding staircases, as shown on the previous page. There were no railings but plenty to grab for in case of a stumble. I found it safer both in prospect and practice. It is, however, essential to use an "offset winder," in which the treads do not come to a point at the wall. Rather, the point from which the treads radiate is offset from the side of the stair, resulting in treads that are wide enough to give a toe-hold at the narrow end. In an offset winder, all the treads are nearly the same width along the path followed by someone climbing the stair, and the small changes are gradual. The change in direction is continuous, and the complex geometry yields a stair that is comfortable to climb.

The more common plain winder is deficient in this regard, as even are ell-stairs with flat landings, as the turn has to be taken all at once. It requires great skill to lay out and build an offset winder, but the arrangement saves a great deal of space while providing good safety. Badly-designed winders invite a fall because the tread depth varies erratically. The errors in laying out this CONTEMPORARY WINDER are small and not even easy to see, but they are all too apparent when using the stair. If hoisting beams are used to move furniture (see page 503), stairs can be quite narrow, which is safer because it is easier to catch a stumble—the instinctive reaction is to spread one's arms in an effort to regain balance. In narrow staircases, this is usually sufficient to stop a fall. Stair treads must have excellent anti-slip properties. Well-secured carpet of medium thickness seems to work best and provides some cushioning in the event of a fall.

UTILITIES & STORAGE

Spaces for utilities are troublesome to provide, and future requirements for area, volume, and ventilation are impossible to anticipate with certainty. Chimneys are becoming smaller and even unnecessary. Mechanical ventilation and air conditioning have imposed new requirements, particularly for disposing of heat. Whatever may be done, the noise and sheer ugliness of STREET-LEVEL HEAT EXCHANGERS should never be allowed. Changes in energy sources may make old installations obsolete, and new installations may be larger or smaller. The adaptation of existing buildings to new systems has often been awkward and expensive. Basements are often useful for these conversions.

In regions where frost penetrates deep into the ground, basements are a cheap source of additional space. The space they provide is of low quality due to dampness and the lack of daylight, but there is merit to building them where they are cheap. If deep foundations are already demanded by the frost depth, the additional cost of digging a bit deeper and providing a concrete floor is quite low. Basements simplify the entry of utilities and also permit the use of composting toilets, which may answer the need to recover human wastes for use as fertilizer.

Not so long ago, a house was a shell in which to live. Fireplaces and stoves were added for heating and cooking. They required only chimneys. No other utilities were installed. As each new system came along, ad hoc arrangements were made to accommodate it, and many installations were exposed and ugly. Over the years, utilities were hidden away in walls, which makes repairs disruptive and expensive. Fortunately, modern plumbing and wiring rarely require attention.

Much of the cost of modern buildings lies in the utilities. Until quite recently, many houses had no more piping than a sink drain and a cold-water tap. We then added (and sometimes later removed) piping for gas light, electrical wiring, sewer pipes

Consider space heating. The shift from fireplaces to wood stoves to coal-fired hot-air furnaces to gas-fired hot-water furnaces was accompanied by big changes in the space required for chimneys, furnaces, piping, and ducting, to say nothing of wood and coal bins, which gas made obsolete. As we shift to solar heating (probably with gas-fired auxiliary capability), large heat storage tanks may be needed.

Only in recent times and only in rich nations have human wastes been discarded. In other times and places they have been recognized as a valuable source of fertilizer. We almost certainly need to return to this frugality, sooner or later. Modern techniques permit the control of disease vectors in wastes.

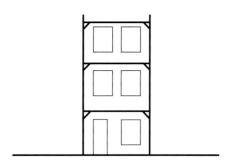

The Dutch Koninginnedag was for years the symbol of a thrifty nation. On this day, which celebrates the birthdays of the past three Queens, a "free market" is held in most Dutch cities. Anyone can set a blanket or table out in the street and sell off their old junk. It usually goes for a trifle, but many goods find a second life. In recent years, the market aspect has declined and the holiday has become more of a festival, but it still serves the admirable purposes of encouraging reuse and clearing the attic and basement. It is even a rite of passage for kids, as they sell off their "baby stuff."

TNO, III:205

and vents, running hot water, central heating ducts, piping for radiators, telephone cables, air conditioning ducts, television cables, and computer data cables. Fiber-optic cables are in the offing. Who knows what may come next.

Utility chases were unknown 150 years ago and are still uncommon today. They simplify the addition and maintenance of utilities. Alexander has called for the provision of "Duct Space" (APL, Pattern 229), to accommodate utility runs in TRIANGULAR CHASES at the junction between ceilings and walls. This may not be the right solution for every building, but the notion that present and future utility requirements should be anticipated is eminently sensible.

The demand for storage seems inexhaustible. Many people cannot bear to throw out, give away, or sell off things for which they have no immediate or prospective use. Although second-hand shops are common in many parts of the world, people in many rich nations have become accustomed to either storing junk forever or throwing it away. Resource constraints probably signal an eventual end to this practice, and reuse of old goods will probably again become the norm. All of this would ease the demand for storage space. One of the functions of the concierge service is to provide additional storage as needed. Since people would have to pay for it, this would encourage them to recycle their junk to people who can find a use for it. Storage space, except in basements, is actually fairly expensive to provide, and basements are unsuitable for things that may be spoiled by damp. Since attic space is likely to be used as living space, the requirements for inexpensive storage space are not easy to meet. Built-in storage is popular and, when designed into the building from the start, is not difficult to provide. Alexander has argued that rooms should be arranged to best shape the principal spaces. The remaining awkward interstitial spaces are then used for storage, bathrooms, and other small spaces. This works well in larger buildings but not in the small row houses I envision.

GREENING THE STREET

Most people need green plants in their lives. They will have them in their homes and gardens. They may set them out on the street, as here in Lisbon's ALFAMA. Buildings are often adorned with plants by one means or another. The municipality may be called upon to plant and maintain street trees. Plants are a natural and normal addition to a city's face. Climbing ivy, potted plants (set on the stoop, at the foot of a building, or in brackets on the façade), plants trailing down from roof gardens, and window boxes can all help to bring green onto the street and give the city a soft, warm face.

During the recent maquette-building process in Budapest (described in CASE EXAMPLES), many people spontaneously added street trees. They are very attractive but bring with them an assortment of problems that is not limited to the expense of their planting and maintenance. In very narrow streets, there will be no room for them. The lifetime of street trees is often quite short (although this may have more to do with automotive air pollution than any intrinsic problem with trees in cities), and they sometimes cause fairly serious damage when they fall during windstorms. Their roots break up the pavement. Ultimately, the decision for or against trees on any given street must be made on the merits of the situation. People will probably want them for most streets that are wide enough. The TREES ALONG THIS CANAL in Amsterdam are a vital part of its appearance and feeling. Even during the winter, the trees are an important aspect of the street. The city spends a great deal of money on upkeep, and every heavy storm topples trees, sometimes with secondary damage and even injury. The trees are thought to be so important to the city's beauty that these problems are simply accepted. During the half of the year that the trees are in leaf, the aspect of the canals CHANGES COMPLETELY. (See also the discussion of street trees in BOULEVARDS.)

Having once come within two steps of being killed by a falling window box, I would urge communities in which these are common to hold annual "window box days" which include an exhortation to make sure the boxes and their fixings are still sound and secure.

BUILDING TYPES

Architects refer to "typologies."

The following four pages show some types of buildings that are suitable for carfree areas. These buildings will not be familiar to people who live in suburban areas, but buildings like them have been built in cities since time out of mind. They are known and understood all across Europe. The courtyard house, discussed last, is a staple of the Mediterranean world.

All floor plans are printed at a scale of 1:250 so the reader will grasp their relative sizes. I have assumed that narrow offset winders, discussed on page 505, will be used; contemporary stairs occupy about twice as much space. Hoisting beams (see page 503) are needed to bring large objects into these buildings, as they will not pass up the stairs. This in fact simplifies moving.

REFERENCE BUILDING

Coimbra

Plans of the Reference Building are shown on page 376. This building has a footprint of just 3.2 by 5.7 meters (10.5 × 18.7') and is quite a lot smaller than people in richer lands will accept as reasonable housing. It actually provides 54.7 m^2 (586 ft^2) of gross floor area, which is adequate to the needs of a small family running an office-based business on the ground floor. (A small store would also fit.) The building really was intended for construction in developing nations, where it would generally be considered to be quite comfortable housing. Even in Tokyo, the floor area would not excite comment, as apartments in that city are normally very small. The size of the Reference Building is suggested by the narrow building shown on page 116. Even smaller buildings are possible, but this is near the limit of what is practical in a building that must include a staircase.

The volume of the building is held to a minimum by putting the bedrooms under the roof, which may be counted as a half story, because standing headroom is only available in the middle.

BUILDINGS 6 TO 9 METERS DEEP

This is Western urbanism at the small end of the scale. Buildings of this size are not uncommon in smaller cities, where the lack of a third story is not unusual. (Larger cities have been built at least four stories tall since the Roman *insula,* about 2000 years ago.) The plan shows a building 7.1m (23') deep, which is nearly as deep as Alexander's suggested maximum of 25 feet.

Very shallow buildings allow single-family row houses with façades as narrow as 4m (13'), giving just 28 m^2 (300 ft^2) per floor, or 84 m^2 (900 ft^2) for a three-story building. These buildings have about the same floor space as the millions of 1950s-era US ranch houses, but turned on end. They can be built at densities of up to 200/ha (80/acre), contrasted to suburban US single-family housing, which rarely exceeds 25/ha (10/acre). This does not, of course, leave very much open space, and the streets are quite narrow, but the small scale of the area can be comfortable, as in this EXAMPLE FROM BURANO. Unlike Burano, however, I propose interior courtyards of decent size.

These shallow houses in Burano are just 6m (20') deep, which is near the practical lower limit for houses.

With buildings just 7m (23') deep, blocks can be as small as 26m (85') across (not including the adjacent streets). A block just a bit larger than this is shown on page 245. This yields an area with an exceptionally fine-grained character. The useful space in 2½-story buildings is actually often nearly as great as in 3-story buildings, because the top floor will be bedrooms. Beds and desks can be placed under the sloping parts of the roof, yielding nearly a full usable floor, as in the Reference Building.

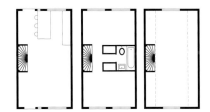

If the buildings are instead 9m (30') deep, considerably larger living spaces can be arranged, and flats become possible. Notice, though, that at this scale, stairs and halls still occupy a considerable proportion of the total area. In the case of flats, common halls and stairs are required. Together they take up nearly half the width of the building. If flats are desired, the hallway and stair arrangement shown on page 513 serves better at lower cost.

Buildings 9 to 12 Meters Deep

There is always the temptation to make buildings deeper, and this is certainly the least expensive way to add floor area. The costs of land and infrastructure are unaffected if the extra depth is taken from the interior courtyards, a practice often seen in old neighborhoods—people have extended their houses over the years, gaining space at comparatively little expense.

The problem that arises is the one suggested by Alexander's Wings of Light (APL, Pattern 107), which calls for buildings to be no thicker than 25 feet (7.5m) in order to ensure good daylight. When buildings are appreciably deeper than 9m (30'), dark interiors become a problem that is compounded if the layout is like that in Amsterdam's GWL CARFREE PROJECT, where a central hallway gives access to apartments on both sides of the hall. A glassed-in external stairway provides access to the upper floors. The apartments are not flats with windows at both ends. They may be shallow enough that light penetrates far into the apartment, but in no case is there light from more than a single direction. When flats are properly arranged, light strikes into rooms from both the front and back. Having lived for many years in a building with this arrangement, I can testify that the improvement is real and important.

I therefore suggest the layout shown here when more floor space is desired. It remains a single-family house with the good privacy that this provides, and if no wall is built entirely across the width of a floor, an appreciable amount of daylight (and plenty of air) diffuses through the full depth of each floor. This is a far superior arrangement to apartments along a central hallway. The only disadvantage is that more space is lost to stairways than with central halls, and the provision of elevator service is made too expensive, as each elevator serves only a single family. When apartments are needed instead of houses, flats, such as shown on the next page, are a better arrangement.

Center-hall apartments, GWL project, Amsterdam
www.gwl-terrein.nl

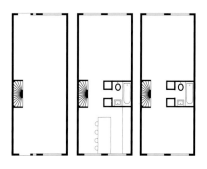

Twin Flats

I recently lived for two years in this APARTMENT BUILDING in Cascais, Portugal. It was 17m (56') deep, which is far deeper than Alexander would recommend and close to the limits of what is acceptable as far as natural lighting is concerned. By locating the stairwell and bathrooms at the center, the effects of the dim light are minimized. Almost no light penetrates from one end of the flat to the other but the rooms were tolerably well lit because large windows were provided and the walls were white. With internal light shafts, even deeper spaces are possible and indeed common in Spain, but I really cannot recommend buildings as deep as this. The living room was very deep and quite narrow, giving it quite uncomfortable and inconvenient proportions. (The kitchen was even worse.)

I give here not the plan of the Cascais flats but a generalized design for this type of building. It is about the same width as the Cascais design, 6m (20') excluding the stairway, but is only 10m (33') deep. The staircase layout is quite efficient but works best if the third and fourth floors are joined into large maisonettes, with two staircases giving access to the top floor, one from within each apartment. These can rise from the center, one rising towards the rear of the house and the other rising towards the front. Notice that the landing is quite long, which is necessary to break a fall from the third floor; it is otherwise possible to fall the full length of two flights. The large landing also provides room for the twin top staircases. I pay so much attention to staircases because their arrangement has a great impact on small buildings that are more than two stories tall.

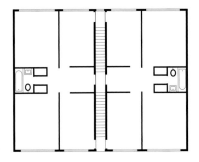

The arrangement shown permits some daylight to penetrate from one side of the house to the other, and the rooms are reasonably proportioned and of useful size. As has been done for centuries in Amsterdam, large windows should be provided to maximize daylight and give good natural ventilation.

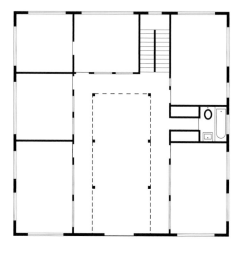

COURTYARD HOUSING

The courtyard house commends itself to wider usage. The HOTEL ESSAOUIRA in Marrakech is a fine example, and similar houses are found in Andalucia, Spain. (See also page 244.) The hotel is only three stories tall but has a well-used roof with a café and comfortable seats from which to watch the sunset.

The courtyard is no larger than we see here; I was sitting at the desk in my room when I took the photograph. The dimensions of the original section of the building (seen here) are approximately 9×12m (30×40'), and the courtyard is about 4×7m (13×23'). The courtyard occupies only about 25% of the area of the site, which is surrounded on two sides by narrow streets and on the other two sides by buildings. The cool and shady respite provided by this courtyard, with its plants and fountain, is a great blessing in the long, hot summers.

There are two choices to be made when designing courtyard housing. The first is how big to make the building. Does it provide housing for a single nuclear family, or is it large enough to house an extended family? In North Africa, these are normally extended-family compounds housing quite a few people. Western adaptations of the form are more likely to house a single nuclear family in what is sometimes called a "patio house," with a tiny courtyard. Per-capita space allocations affect the design.

The second choice is whether the building is entirely free-standing or surrounded on one, two, or three sides by other, similar buildings. Usually, these compounds abut others.

A common defect of courtyard housing is that the outer walls lack windows, due to privacy and security concerns. If windows on the street can be tolerated, both the house and the street benefit, and if the building is freestanding, then exceptionally good light can be provided in every room. Even if just two sides border on streets, excellent light can be provided in most rooms, and the bedrooms can be darker and free from street noise.

BUILDING DESIGN

This is not a work on architecture, but building design must be taken up here if people are to design their own buildings. They will need help with this unfamiliar task. It can come in the form of pattern books, treatises on design, and experts. A short course in methods and styles would be very helpful to most people.

MATERIALS

Materials have such a large influence on design that I will take them up first. Durable materials from local sources are not a matter of plain thrift; they have a significant benefit in achieving sustainable cities. Not too much energy should be invested in their production and distribution, and they should be reusable in later buildings. Stone, brick, and roof tile have always been reused, and the pleasing character of used brick often makes it more valuable than new. Other materials, such as plaster, cannot be reused but are made from widely-available raw materials. Although these materials are not strictly sustainable, we can make fairly liberal use of them, at least for now. The use of local materials reduces transport energy consumption. Lightweight materials and structures further reduce transport energy.

The nature of a material affects both the way we perceive it and the length of time that we will accept it without renewal. Again, stone and brick score well in this regard and usually wear in ways that we find agreeable. Most modern materials wear poorly, although there are exceptions, such as Corian artificial marble. Many modern materials will scar when dented or chipped, which makes them ugly. Any material that is not homogeneous is unlikely to wear well, whereas homogeneous materials can be damaged without changing their essential character. Solid wood wears well; plywood does not. Stone countertops may chip, but only to reveal more stone. But chip

Leiden, The Netherlands. These row houses exhibit many details that will be considered in this chapter.

Some "natural house" builders use straw bales, rammed earth, or earthen bricks cast with gypsum. These materials may be fine for low-rise buildings but generally lack the strength for multi-story construction.

Guimarães, Portugal

Christopher Alexander has invested much time and effort to find a solution to this problem, but I think that the results are still not especially pleasing. A solution to the problem of the high energy costs of this material would also be welcome.

Too much of contemporary design is done simply because it is possible, not because it is sensible. Many structures from Dutch architects in the 1930s used brick in tension, and these buildings all too soon required major and very costly repairs. Lamentably, the root problem was not corrected during renovations.

a tiny flake off a Formica countertop and a completely different material is revealed. The surface cannot be reworked or repaired. Therefore, attempt to use homogeneous materials, particularly those that can be repaired if damaged. Wood is especially good in this regard. A high level of skill is required to make a good repair, which, while still visible, is never offensive.

Homogeneous materials are honest materials. They look like what they are. Although *faux* painting can be very artful, I find the deception unsettling. It makes me wonder what else about the building, including its structural elements, might also be fake. Reinforced concrete is not an honest material. It resembles stone but contains quite a lot of steel bar. Its structural properties are usually very good, and I do not doubt that we will be using a lot of it in the years ahead, but I have never liked it. It requires great care to make it look good as it comes out of the forms, and the slightest error in pouring leaves voids that, when patched, are ugly and also cause us to mistrust the workmanship. Although steel and concrete are relatively inexpensive materials, the required formwork is tiresome, expensive, and unforgiving. Mistakes are hard to correct and changes difficult to accommodate. Many have tried to make this material attractive, but few have succeeded. A practical and attractive substitute for this material would be a wonderful gift indeed.

Pay attention to the tactile qualities of materials. It is not necessary or even desirable that all materials be smooth to the touch, but those surfaces that we are likely to touch, particularly interior surfaces, should not be abrasive or gritty. Plaster trowelled to a smooth finish feels wonderful. It need not be painted.

Materials must be used with sympathy. They should never be asked to do something to which they are unsuited. Until recently, this was rarely a problem. Journeymen understood their materials and would balk if asked to do something inappropriate. No masonry is suited to tensile loads (even if it has some slight tensile strength), as over time it will almost invariably fail.

With steel or reinforced concrete, almost anything is possible, given enough money. This has permitted great arrogance on the part of many contemporary architects. Although their buildings rarely collapse, absurd masses of material are required to support them. I give as an example the CASA DA MÚSICA in Porto, with its vast, arbitrary cantilevers and strange sloping walls.

Buildings that have stood the test of time are reassuring. We trust them. By showing that they can stand the marks of use and weathering, they become old friends. Even the hardest stone will show the passage of millions of feet. Wood accumulates nicks and dings. It takes on a polish as hands caress it repeatedly. We are willing to take the time and trouble to maintain buildings made of these friendly materials. Time is not sympathetic to steel and glass. They show the passage of time in ways that are ugly or disturbing. Rusting steel is neither attractive nor reassuring. Glass, which has no real substitute, is essential.

THE MATTER OF STYLE

Style and fashion are not the same thing. A good style is timeless. Fashions are dated. Fashion has to do with clothing and hair cutting. Buildings have a style, and, if it is a good one, it lasts indefinitely. Even though it associates a building with a period, the building never looks dated. A style may become unfashionable and may even be temporarily hidden, but its merits may again be recognized and revealed.

Something went wrong with styles in the 20th century, when wide excursions from useful styles were made. The break began with Art Deco, a style that did not entirely lack antecedents or charm. Even some early Modern works had purity of form and a spare beauty. As the century wore on, the quality of design deteriorated steadily, which eventually gave rise to historic conservation efforts. In the USA, the New Urbanists reverted to traditional styles, sometimes imperfectly executed, but most

Technically, plastic sheeting can be used as glazing, but this material weathers and ages so quickly, and so badly, that I would not normally use it.

In the Netherlands in the 1950s, a Modernist rage led to the covering of lovely details in existing buildings. Today, slick plywood panels have been removed from doors to reveal their original fine moldings. Shame has sometimes led to the covering of Victorian gingerbread, but this modesty usually passes, and the gingerbread is once again to been seen and admired.

See Moe & Wilkie

new houses still lack real style. The street façades are intended to impress with their size and complexity, but the backs are often shockingly plain. The worst is Deconstructivism (which is really an anti-style). Its bizarre creations are varnished with a coat of fake intellectualism. This aberration will soon run its course, sparing us from more of these alienating buildings.

Styles come and go. Well into the 20th century, one historical style or another was usually enjoying a revival in the USA. The names alone tell the story: Greek revival, neo-Gothic, Tudor, and so forth. The original style is seldom reused in its literal form, but the references to the source are strong and clear. Architects caught up in the "originality trap" cannot abide these revivals, but ultimately all that can be done is to combine existing styles in new ways, or to break so far from previous styles as to venture into the absurd, in the way of Deconstructivism.

Styles have only a few basic sources. Pure geometry is one, and classical Greek and Roman buildings clearly express this, along with some structural treatments (such as dentils) they preserved during the transition from wood to stone. Living things are another source, often seen in Art Nouveau, whose lamp shades and metro entrances drew their inspiration from grasshoppers and vines. A style that lacks any antecedent is one to which we are unlikely to relate well; it is simply too alien.

Guimarães, Portugal

Styles & Design

Styles are a shorthand. If a single style predominates, builders know how to build it without detailed plans. Henry Glassie said:

> A man wants a house. He talks with a builder. Together they design the house out of their shared experience, their culture of what a house should be. There is no need for formal plans. Students of vernacular architecture search for plans, wish for plans, but should not be surprised that they

Venice

find none. The existence of plans on paper is an indicator of cultural weakening. The amount of detail in a plan is an exact measure of the degree of cultural disharmony; the more minimal the plan, the more completely the architectural idea abides in the separate minds of architect and client.

Brand, 132, quoting Glassie

Historically, few buildings were designed by architects. The practice of architecture requires a large expenditure of time by a highly-trained professional. We are never likely to be so rich that all buildings will be the subject of full architectural design. We need a cheaper solution that produces better results.

A partial exception is buildings that are designed by architects without a specific site or family in mind, such as those contained in the "plan books" sold by the million.

The Vernacular Solution

Local vernacular styles provide a ready solution. Everyone in a region knows these styles, which are the accumulated wisdom of buildings in harmony with local conditions and culture. They use relatively inexpensive local materials. Even within a region, local variations arise, which helps each town to develop a unique identity and sense of place. Almost any vernacular form yields buildings that are at worst satisfactory, which is good enough. The greatness of a vernacular style often lies not in individual buildings but in the ensemble. Despite their economy, the result surpasses most of what we build today.

Porto

Vernacular buildings are simple to arrange. The general arrangement, the number of floors, the number, size, and placement of windows and doors, and the basic form of the roof are part of the style. If the builders are true craftsmen, they may need no more plans than a few scratches in the dirt. As decisions come up, they will know intuitively what to do.

Vernacular styles are still widely used in the USA even today, but they are found in a jumble from coast to coast, often far from their origins. Manufacturing and transport systems supply the same framing lumber, plywood, roofing, and windows nation-

This engineering approach is widely used in the USA. Such codes enable ordinary people to design a safe building. The builders must understand both the practice and the underlying logic, but expensive professionals are only needed for a few hours if at all.

wide, and most housing built since 1945 has a dispiriting sameness. Transport costs will probably rise in the future, which will encourage greater reliance on local resources. In Europe, where freight rates remained at relatively high levels, styles were never universalized as in the USA. Europe still retains local vernacular styles, as in these recent VACATION HOUSES in Portugal's Algarve, which still express the regional style. Rubble walls covered by stucco have been replaced by earthquake-resistant buildings made from reinforced concrete. Still, the vernacular is the main source of form, as seen in this same development's CHIMNEYS.

Rising energy costs will encourage people to adopt designs that are better adapted to local conditions and use less energy. I expect that cities and towns will again take on distinctive styles as local conditions are expressed in local styles. Most people will welcome this change.

Building in the local vernacular style gives rise to coherence almost automatically. If a place lacks a well-developed vernacular style to draw on, one should be developed. A study of nearby regions will suggest ways to forge a sound local style.

Vernacular styles respond to the need for variety and for adaptive responses to the requirements of different families. Variety is interesting in and of itself, but we require it not just for its own sake but to ensure flexible responses to human needs and to the fact that people are *not* all the same.

We have ample evidence that ordinary people can design the objects used in their daily lives, including their houses. Most small buildings can simply be built in conformance with structural codes, as long as these codes are based on experience and sound engineering. Alexander proposed in *The Production of Houses* to develop standard structural details and construction methods for low-cost houses, without the need for case-specific engineering. This requires a few rules regarding permissible spans, wall thickness, and so forth, usually expressed in tables. Detailed plans are not strictly necessary.

Properties of Good Design

In *The Nature of Order*, Alexander postulated 15 fundamental properties of good design and explained them in detail. I will not delve into this beyond listing them (and elaborating on some of them in a few words):

- Levels of scale (detail both large and small)
- Strong centers
- Boundaries (to further define edges)
- Alternating repetition (with variations)
- Positive space (enclosure)
- Good shape
- Local symmetries
- Deep interlock and ambiguity (wrinkled edges)
- Contrast (of light and dark)
- Gradients (of scale)
- Roughness (geometric and manufacturing imperfections)
- Echoes
- The void (something empty near the middle)
- Simplicity and inner calm
- Not-separateness (integration of the parts)

These properties are clearly discussed and profusely illustrated, and it is easy to see how they might lead to better design.

Alexander is wrestling with the nature of design itself. He has attempted to define some general properties that, if respected, give rise to positive reactions within us. He then attempted to universalize these properties. I believe that he has overreached, but these properties probably do form a useful basis for any attempt at original design. Although I see opportunities for design using these methods on large and expensive projects, I do not think that we enjoy the luxury of a *tabula rasa* approach to designing ordinary houses and small buildings. Hence my proposal to rely instead on vernacular styles to reach pleasing and effective results at a cost that people can afford.

Valladolid

Alexander, TNO, I:143-242

Guimarães, Portugal

The Thirst for Detail

See the work of Nikos A. Salingaros

I believe that human beings have an innate thirst for objects that have some minimum level of detail, even though the acceptable range may be quite wide. Some florid Victorian designs verge on excessive detail, or go beyond. A far more common problem today is inadequate or incoherent detail. The WOLVENSTRAAT in Amsterdam gives a clear contrast. The building on the right is based on a style that is about 400 years old (the building itself may be newer). The impoverished building on the left is a complete break with the local style. The architect's sly attempt at humor (the misapplication of an arch) may amuse us briefly, but who wants to live with a parody as a neighbor? What really bothers me about this building, though, is the lack of scales from large to small and the lack of detail in the design. Where is the molding that gives real definition to the archway? Where are the windows? Only graffiti relieves the unadorned brick and tile.

Mathematical analysis reveals that elements in a satisfactory building are distributed across the spectrum of sizes, ranging from the very small up to the largest dimension of the building. Elements occur with high frequency at the small end of the range and only once or twice at the large end. There are no large gaps in the distribution. Modern and Deconstructivist buildings violate this dictum, but it is obeyed in virtually every older building. Buildings with large gaps are alien and disturbing. Be sure that all buildings, even the most humble, include enough detail at a wide enough range of scales to make them friendly.

Modernists complain that we can no longer afford detail in our buildings. (In fact, architect-designed Modern buildings are extremely expensive.) They contend that we must make do with machine-made parts. If we do not demand perfection in hand-made parts, they can be made quickly and economically, with detail. This COURTYARD ENTRANCE in Venice is full of imperfections that do it no harm.

COHERENT ARCHITECTURAL THEMES

Architectural themes help build a sense of place. Any element that is repeated in many buildings gives a boost. Consider these STONE DOORWAY ARCHES in Assisi. No two of them are alike, but anyone immediately notices the pattern. The simplicity is part of it. The arch in the middle is quite new but follows the pattern exactly, down to the pointed keystone. Details may evolve over time but must never deteriorate into a caricature.

Always consider which architectural themes characterize a region and express its history and values. Onion domes come in two forms. One creates an association with Russia and the other with Islam. The association is immediate and powerful. The Venetian arch, with its reverse curve, is an evocative symbol of that city. To ask a theme to be so powerful and unique is to ask a lot, but regional symbols are often there for the taking.

Coherence is difficult to define but easier to illustrate. Places that seem whole when we first see them and after long acquaintance are coherent. All truly good areas have it, although the degree of coherence ranges widely. Too much can be as bad as too little. The BEGIJNHOF in Amsterdam is surely coherent enough, but it might be judged to be at the lower end of the range. Notice that all of the buildings have gables facing the courtyard and that these gables are decorated in a similar manner, even though each is unique. Many recent areas are overly coherent, with hundreds of identical houses.

In fact, coherent does not mean consistent. A coherent skyline needs contrasting elements, as in the SKYLINE of Siena. Although the minor buildings are unique, they share a vernacular style, with similar roofs and rather plain façades, all built from similar materials. By contrast, the hilltop cathedral is built from different materials in a different style, which provides a point of emphasis, as does the church parapet and bells in the foreground. The total effect is coherent and highly satisfying.

Porto

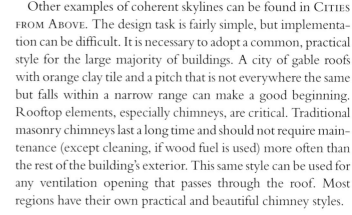

Other examples of coherent skylines can be found in CITIES FROM ABOVE. The design task is fairly simple, but implementation can be difficult. It is necessary to adopt a common, practical style for the large majority of buildings. A city of gable roofs with orange clay tile and a pitch that is not everywhere the same but falls within a narrow range can make a good beginning. Rooftop elements, especially chimneys, are critical. Traditional masonry chimneys last a long time and should not require maintenance (except cleaning, if wood fuel is used) more often than the rest of the building's exterior. This same style can be used for any ventilation opening that passes through the roof. Most regions have their own practical and beautiful chimney styles.

ROOF DETAILS

Modern roofs are often invisible from the street. Seen from the air, they are just great expanses of asphalt punctuated by air conditioners. They lack the slightest grace. Roofs should be visible from the street and ought to overhang the building, to keep water off the façade and reduce maintenance costs. Latitude and climate affect the required overhang. A moderate roof overhang is sufficient to shade top-floor windows from the noonday summer sun in most regions where heat is bothersome.

The street-facing gable is probably the most urbane façade for small buildings in dense areas. It is simple and cheap but can be extensively decorated if desired and may be executed in a wide range of designs, as in Amsterdam's BEGIJNHOF (just above).

To my eye, few things are more attractive than a city of orange TERRA-COTTA ROOFS, as in the case of Porto. This material has been in use since time out of mind and has proven its utility. When properly laid, these roofs stand long periods without any maintenance beyond replacing the occasional broken tile, which is simple. Their one disadvantage is that they are quite heavy and so increase structural loads during earthquakes; light-weight roofing materials are an advantage in earthquake zones. Thatch and wood shingles are beautiful, but the fire hazard precludes their use in cities.

Metal roofs come in a wide range of price and quality. They are often the most economical in the long run. Copper roofing is very dear and lasts indefinitely. It weathers to the familiar green, and a city with its highest roofs clad in copper is a beautiful sight. Zinc is fairly good. It solders well and bends easily into complicated shapes. Galvanized steel is usually corrugated to increase stiffness. It is the cheapest roofing material but also the ugliest, because it always rusts in the end.

Stone roofs are widely used in areas with plenty of slate or other clean-splitting rock, and MASSIVE STONE ROOFS can be beautiful, as here in Zermatt. They are heavy and expensive.

Composition and membrane roofing are used for flat roofs, except in some regions where concrete is used. The raw material is petroleum, and these materials will become expensive in the years ahead. These roofs are surprisingly heavy, and it is usual to tear off the old roof before applying a new one. They rarely last more than 25 years, which offsets their initial economy.

We will almost certainly see more solar collectors on roofs. Most contemporary installations look haphazard. Large-scale installation of photovoltaic roof collectors that also serve as the primary roofing membrane may occur in the near future. Their dark-blue cast might be fairly attractive if applied to most buildings in a district, although I prefer the warm color of tile.

Roofs must be fitted with gutters; water cannot be allowed to fall directly from a roof to splatter on the ground, because this wets passers-by, erodes paving, and damages walls. Cheap aluminum gutters are practical but quite ugly, whereas a high-quality gutter enhances a building. Downspouts should not run internally, as any blockage will likely flood the building.

A drip course is nothing more than a horizontal protrusion from an exterior wall, typically applied at the level of an upper

Salamanca

floor. They can be as simple as a course of bricks projecting a few centimeters (an inch) from the building and as complex as intricately carved marble. Expensive buildings often employ complex moldings, as with this CHURCH in Portimão, Portugal. Whatever their design, they cause rain that runs down the face of the building to fall clear, keeping the wall drier and reducing maintenance costs. Drip courses are rarely found in modern buildings. In older buildings they were a beautiful and practical addition to the façade. We should return to their use.

Floors

Braga, Portugal

Floors are troublesome, both the finished surfaces and the structures that support them. Every material and method has disadvantages. Local practice may point to the best compromise.

There is not much sense in building a masonry building and then installing wooden beams and flooring, as the fireproofing advantages of masonry are compromised. The risk may be accepted in small, single-family buildings with smoke detectors. Wood beams are easily managed on the building site and wood floors are comparatively quiet until they begin to squeak. We are probably going to have to make do with concrete floors. Poured-in-place concrete floors have excellent structural properties, even though they are fairly expensive to build and delay construction while they cure to a minimum safe strength.

Concrete floors have a large drawback: noise transmission. If a hard object is dropped on the floor above, the neighbors below will hear every bounce right up to the last just as loudly as whoever dropped it: the annoying "golf-ball effect." Concrete floors score poorly on noise transmission even when contact noise is not the concern. Work is being done to reduce this defect in what is otherwise a reasonably good floor system. Carpeting helps but is expensive and subject to mold and mildew.

A new flooring method is used in Spain. Precast reinforced

concrete I-beams are first set in place. Their top flange is a bit narrower than the bottom, allowing large, hollow terra-cotta blocks to be slipped into position, resting on the bottom flange. The top of the I-beam has steel loops that interlock it with a reinforced concrete floor poured on top of the initial structure, which serves as a form and becomes a part of the finished floor. These floors ought to transmit less noise between floors.

Concrete floors are cold to the feet. The use of in-floor radiant heating solves this problem and makes floors pleasant to walk on without shoes even in the coldest weather. Radiant heating also reduces energy consumption, as cooler air temperatures still feel comfortable if the body is exposed to radiating surfaces. This excellent method has been used since Roman times.

Braga, Portugal

Doors & Windows

If we like a building's windows and doors, we like the building; if not, we don't. They have an impact similar to the eyes and mouth of a human face.

Christopher Alexander has more to say about entrances than I will, and I suggest consulting *A Pattern Language* on this point. (See Patterns 102, 110, 112, 122, 125, 130, 158, 224, 242, and 243.) Many of his patterns really relate to larger buildings than we are considering here, but the principles remain valid.

This ARCHED ENTRANCE in Assisi is a fine example. The building stands flush with the edge of the narrow street. There is no mistaking this for a service entrance; clearly, this is the main entry. The arched form is pleasing and the double doors practical as well as attractive. A projecting roof shelters waiting visitors. The plantings are attractive and practical. The mailbox, added long after the original construction, is the only discordant element. This kind of quality may seem to have been priced out of existence today, but if the entrance is built out of local materials in a vernacular style familiar to craftsmen, few decisions are

required, and the work can be executed without plans. This brings the cost within reason; the materials are not expensive.

This RESIDENCE in Basel has a clearly defined main entrance in a beautiful style. The carved door, the iron filigree above, and the carved stone pediment capping the entrance would have been quite expensive, but this was money well spent. The remainder of the construction is fairly simple, but the lovely entrance carries the whole building and gives it an inviting appearance. The asymmetric plantings lend an informal air, as do the bicycles propped casually against the building. The windows, although not overly complex, are highly satisfactory and improved by the working shutters with which they are furnished.

Although the main entrance usually carries more weight than any one window, the total effect of the windows outweighs the entrance. Alexander has much to say about windows. Consult his patterns 192, 221, 222, 223, 231, 236, 238, and 239. We will consider windows primarily as seen from the outside, but remember that they exert a great influence on the interior. The impact of windows becomes apparent when a lovely old building is ruined by CRUDE NEW WINDOWS, as here in Budapest.

I agree with Alexander's "Small Panes" (Pattern 239), which calls for windows subdivided by mullions into small panes. The first glazed windows were made from palm-sized panes set in thin lead mullions. They are always beautiful. The modern practice of a mullion grill snapped into the interior side of the sash is obvious fakery. Divided lights reduce the problem of bird strikes, which kill huge numbers of birds.

Large-pane windows have, alas, become the norm, largely in response to the need for double glazing, which has better insulating properties than the attractive single-glazed windows seen here on the WOLVENSTRAAT in Amsterdam. Glass technology is evolving rapidly, and it is possible that we will soon have glass with good insulating properties that can economically be used in small, single panes. Modern double glazing makes small panes almost impossible to arrange, because the glazing is so thick that the mullions become heavy and clumsy, and the cost would be high. The only alternative is the old European practice of using two sets of double casement windows, one set opening out, the other opening in. This was used in the buildings fronting on the ALTER MARKT in Salzburg. It permits the use of small panes. The insulation is poorer if the two windows are not close to each other when shut; otherwise convection in the air space reduces the benefit. Shutters that can be closed at night reduce heat loss.

Alexander's "Windows Which Open Wide" (Pattern 236) is one to take to heart. Windows that slide, either horizontally or vertically, will not open more than half the area of the window frame. Double-hung windows are the most common sliding windows and can be opened from either the top or the bottom. They are sufficient in temperate climates. Only a hinged window can be fully opened. The DOUBLE CASEMENT WINDOW, seen here in Burano, is the best and most common hinged type. Two glazed frames are hinged on opposite sides of the opening and come together in a vertical line at the center. Air leaks around these windows were usual until about 50 years ago, when good seals were finally devised. Casements are the only windows that tolerate undivided lights reasonably well. They are the best and most practical choice now available, but pay attention to their proportions. They look good only when the panes have a strong vertical orientation. Single casements are useful when the frame is rather narrow. It is best if casement windows open inward because this simplifies cleaning, reduces weathering, and nearly eliminates the risk posed by a falling casement, if it is allowed to rot until it disintegrates.

Everyone loves bay windows. The prominent example in the foreground of the AUGUSTINERGASSE in Zürich is unusually fine. Bay windows relieve the face of a building and bring in lots of light. Bays are wonderful places to sit and read or chat, and in some cultures they are also observatories onto the street below.

Notice how the windows in these canal houses on the HERENGRACHT in Amsterdam get smaller as they go up. Alexander addresses this in "Natural Doors and Windows" (Pattern 221). He believes that smaller windows are more comfortable on upper stories, and that larger windows are needed on the ground floor to bring in enough light if the street is narrow. The tendency to reduce ceiling heights on the upper floors is also at work here (although it is sometimes the floor above the ground floor that has the highest ceilings). In this same pattern, Alexander calls for final window locations to be determined during construction, not during design. This approach works for small, isolated buildings, but imagine these buildings with irregular window placement—it simply wouldn't work.

Window sills must be high enough to prevent falls, unless bars or railings are fitted, which permits windows that go right to the floor. Anything less than 90cm (3') feels too low to me. Windows near ground level can have low sills, and French doors are perhaps the most beautiful windows of all.

To continue the analogy of windows and a door as a building's eyes and mouth, shutters are the eyelids, and nearly as important as the eyes. Like eyelids, they blink, as seen here on the PIAZZA IV NOVEMBRE in Perugia. Shutters are still routinely opened and closed throughout Italy. This constantly changes a building's appearance during the course of a day.

By no means all shutters are good—some destroy the appearance of a building. Hinged shutters, if provided with stops and latches to hold them firmly in the open and closed positions during strong winds, improve the appearance and comfort of a building. When louvered, they can allow fresh air into a room while providing visual privacy. They protect the glazing during storms and provide darkness for people who need to sleep late.

Roll-up shutters, however, are an abomination. At their worst, they ruin the appearance of a building, a fate that befell this OTHERWISE FINE BUILDING in Valladolid. I believe that their use should be prohibited in cities. They prevent break-ins, but good locks and high-strength glazing can achieve this objective. Often, they require the installation of HIDEOUS BOXES BELOW THE LINTEL into which the shutters roll when opened, which destroyed this otherwise inoffensive building in Évora.

Security can also be provided by iron bars or grilles over windows. Most such installations are ugly, but older ones, made of wrought iron, may be tolerable. In hot climates, this may be the only way to provide ventilation while maintaining security. Alas, grilles sometimes trap people inside during a fire.

When shop windows are left open and illuminated during the evening, they continue to sell for the store while improving the street environment. This will be regarded by shopkeepers as a riskier arrangement, but the damage done to the fabric of a neighborhood by roll-up shutters is severe and encourages the very crime that shopkeepers fear. Venice has not entirely banned roll-up shutters, but in the best areas, especially near San Marco, SHOP WINDOWS ARE LEFT UNCOVERED. This sheds a pleasing light on the street.

The hanging of laundry over the street is thought by many to blot the face of a city. Laundry can be hidden on rooftop drying racks or in courtyards, but I don't mind it too much. A compromise is to do laundry on Mondays, so that the streets are festooned only once a week. Best is probably not to worry.

SIGNS

Little details often have great impacts—an excellent place can be spoiled by small errors. Fortunately, these are usually easy to fix.

No detail has a greater effect than signage. Consider this STRIP MALL in Los Angeles. Although this area cannot easily be fixed, consider how much it would be improved simply by eliminating all of the signs, starting with the obnoxious monster in the foreground. Restrained signage gives a street a more civilized air, as

on the JUDENGASSE in Salzburg, in part because other values are expressed—the street is no longer a purely commercial undertaking that maximizes profits by screaming at all who pass by.

A good sign ordinance is essential. It should entirely forbid internally-illuminated signs and limit the size of a sign to, say, one-tenth the dimensions of the ground floor façade. Symbols are better than letters—the outline of a shoe announces clearly that the shop is either a shoe repair shop or a shoe store. Casual inspection will reveal which. When letters are used, there is considerable merit to signs made of sheet iron with the letters cut through the sheet. Brackets may be permitted, to support the sign so that it hangs over the street, as in Salzburg. These should be more than purely utilitarian fixtures.

Signs may be permitted on the face of a building, and they may be quite large without doing much harm, as in the case of this SHOPFRONT in Porto. Care was taken not only with the sign itself but the façade as a whole. In high-rent districts, the lettering will be in gold leaf, but good sign-painting is adequate. Machine-cut transfers do not look as good as signs hand-painted by an expert, which can be executed quickly and economically.

REGULATION OF DESIGN

Various schemes have been tried in an attempt to obtain coherent design, which has often been taken to be design in the same style. My own belief is that design in the same style is regimented and not necessary to achieving coherence. At the same time, some degree of commonality in style is at least useful in achieving coherence (although it does not by any means ensure either coherence or good design).

In the past, vernacular styles nearly always produced coherent designs even though each building was a unique variation on a common theme. I think this is the best approach when it can be attained, except perhaps for the most formal areas, where a

Praça 8 de Maio, Coimbra

consistent style may be desired. The use of vernacular styles may seem rather forced in most places today, as the underlying logic of their arrangement may largely be forgotten. As we move to more local arrangements, based on local sources of supply and local climatic and cultural requirements, I expect that updated vernacular styles will emerge, with a full understanding of their logic. If, then, it can be agreed to build a new neighborhood or district in this style, the need to regulate design should vanish. It may take some time before we can rely on this approach.

In many places in the USA during the past several decades, closed projects have employed design review boards. Anyone planning to build a house on a site in a given project must apply to the design review board for approval. Attempts have been made to codify these requirements, but it is surprisingly difficult to accomplish this in words, and the boards have sometimes been quite capricious in their interpretation of the design standards. The design review board is a rather crude instrument.

The New Urbanists have been making use of graphical codes. These have the advantage of concision and clarity; if a house meets the standards of the code, approval should be assured.

I would hope that the values clusters created by the formation of urban villages would make the task of selecting and approving architectural styles considerably simpler, although this remains to be seen. If necessary, architectural styles could be added as an axis for the purpose of village formation. (This would have to take account of the preferences of adjoining urban villages.)

BUILDING CODE ENFORCEMENT

Even with intense citizen participation, it will still be necessary to wrestle with building inspectors, unless inspection procedures are also changed. This, however, is not so difficult as it might seem. My own experience in a loft space in Emeryville, California, was that as long as I talked to the inspector about

Plaza Mayor, Madrid

For examples, see: Katz, 76-77, 110-116, 713, 196-197, 201; Duany, 36, 50-51, 72, 96-103; Urban Design Associates, 83-223.

Coimbra

what I wanted to do and asked him what problems might arise, I was able to proceed in a reasonable way. When the time came for the actual inspection, it was almost pro forma.

Building codes are generally quite clear about conventional practice, but they demand an engineered solution if any variation from standard practice is contemplated. This immediately becomes expensive. The codified solution proposed on page 492 is an effective one. It *is* an engineered solution, but the engineering has been done for the general case. Thus, tables of joist dimensions and spacing have been worked out carefully by engineers, so that the designer need only look it up in a table to have a solution that the inspector will approve. If a new building method is proposed for broad application on a site, a new code should be developed, with engineering review, and adopted for the site. Anyone building with the new method can simply look up the right way to do it, without the costs of custom engineering or any sleepless nights anticipating the inspector's arrival.

Salamanca

CASE EXAMPLES

I was able to make two tests of the methods proposed in this book. It must be admitted from the outset that these tests were at a much smaller scale than the district-level process I have proposed and involved only a few people, not the thousands who would participate in a full-scale application. Nonetheless, the experiences were useful and resulted in large changes to the text in this Part. Both trials are described here in some detail.

BUDAPEST, 2005: CLAY MAQUETTE

At the Towards Carfree Cities conference held in Budapest, 18-21 July 2005, some 30 conference participants built a maquette using potter's clay. The construction began on the second morning of the conference and was completed the same day. Discussions of city design, evaluation of the process, and assessment of the completed maquette occupied the next two days, at the conclusion of which the maquette was discarded.

The maquette we built depicted an area in the north of Budapest, on the western side of the Danube, which divides the city. It was hoped that this maquette might catalyze an effort to build an actual carfree district on the site, although it was never expected that the maquette would be built in literal form on the site, which was about half the size of the Reference District.

The construction of a clay maquette was, under the circumstances, the closest possible approach to a full-scale test of participatory design, but there were significant limitations, including the number of people able to work simultaneously on a maquette little larger than a card table. The lack of eye-level perspective at full scale was a serious limitation on the process. It is possible to use borescopes and miniature video cameras to give a street-level view of a scale model, but this view is far from duplicating the sense of space that would exist at full scale.

Maquette project, Budapest, July 2005

We were, however, able to test hypotheses regarding participatory design, physical (as opposed to paper-based) design, and the viability of medieval street arrangements. The process also verified the willingness and ability of citizens to design spaces that satisfy both the technical requirements of a carfree district and the aesthetic considerations that form the core of this book. We were also able to demonstrate that people with brief training can assist other citizens in the design of a carfree district.

Preparation

www.zofi.hu/english.shtml

The Hungarian Young Greens (Zöfi) sponsored the maquette project, and its members undertook the tedious preparations. I had anticipated that we would build the maquette on a hypothetical, featureless site. However, just a day before the start of maquette building, we identified two potential sites, and Zöfi members obtained photographs and MAPS AT A SCALE OF 1:500 for these areas. In a real design effort, urban planning would be essentially complete before the design of streets and buildings commenced, but this was obviously impossible in the time available. The exercise was able to proceed on an otherwise fairly realistic basis.

About ten members of Zöfi served as facilitators, along with seven urban design students from Istanbul, attending with their professor, Kevser Üstundag. They filled the role of assistants with a day's training. The day before building commenced, I met with them and explained the method and objectives. I asked them to help the others who would join us to understand the possible choices while still reaching sufficient density for a carfree district. I outlined my vision of participatory design and presented the Reference Design. I also explained what I see as the advantages of medieval city design. During the actual building, these assistants helped others and also did much of the work of designing and building the maquette.

First Steps

On the day of maquette construction, the first task was to select a site. Justin Hyatt, coordinating the Zöfi efforts, PRESENTED THE PHOTOGRAPHS AND OBSERVATIONS of the previous day's investigation of the two candidate sites.

The first site was readily accessible from the city center and had good public transport but was already fairly densely built. I suggested that this site was not a productive one to model, as it was unrealistic to propose demolishing the existing buildings. This suggestion was quickly accepted.

The second site was several kilometers north of the first. It was farther removed from the city center, but this was balanced by the crossing of two passenger rail lines. The southeast quadrant is a major archeological site and was promptly excluded from consideration. Tower blocks were built during the Communist era in the northeast quadrant, and we decided not to consider this sector either. We decided to build on the western half of the site, where the only major complications were the ruins of a Roman amphitheater and a large drainage canal running parallel to the east-west rail line, just to its north. This half of the site was otherwise in low-grade uses. It is very flat.

Preliminary Design & Site Assessment

We began by assessing the strengths and weaknesses of the site. The foremost weakness was that the two passenger rail lines crossed in the middle of the site without connecting. We quickly decided to build the missing interchange station at the crossing. That station then formed an ideal hub for a carfree district. The first actual feature was TWO BOARDING PLATFORMS (lower right). (Later in the process, a station was built, and the east-west tracks were raised above ground to reflect the actual condition.) A partial model of the amphitheater ruins is also visible.

An alternative approach would have been to change it into a creek with grassy slopes rather than vertical masonry walls, changing it from a central urban feature into a quiet creek. Such a change would have affected nearly every aspect of the design.

We next decided that the existing drainage canal presented both a problem and an opportunity. It is today an ugly concrete feature that runs right alongside the rail line. I pointed out that decisions regarding this canal would affect the whole design. I suggested that the water could be an asset if we rearranged the canal to BRING IT THROUGH THE NEIGHBORHOOD and gave it the form of an Amsterdam canal. I showed some photographs of this arrangement and discussed the quite considerable width that would be required.

The group decided that this would be a good improvement and that the canal should be wide enough to have tree-lined streets on both sides, in the manner of a MINOR CANAL in Amsterdam. I suggested that we assume that a simple weir would raise the water level of the canal and keep it full throughout the year. If, in fact, year-round flow is insufficient to maintain the water level, this feature would have had to be treated differently, unless an upstream reservoir could be established to supply water during dry periods. We had no idea of whether or not this would have been feasible in this case.

We decided to leave the canal crossing of the railroad unchanged, due to the cost of moving it. This meant that the canal had to converge on the new train station. I then raised the question of whether or not the canal should run straight to the station or should meander in its approach. I pointed out that in order to relocate the canal at all, we would have to introduce two reverse curves (one of them to the west of our site) into its present course but that we otherwise had a lot of freedom in the alignment. Several people then worked on possible courses for the canal, using scale buildings to mark the edges of the resulting street. This gave a good feeling for the proportions of the space. Once this was agreed, the canal was pencilled in. I think we might better have chosen a course with somewhat more curvature, as the actual design did not introduce full enclosure, although the arrangement is still attractive.

We did not immediately model and place all existing features of the site, and this proved to be a minor error. In particular, the amphitheater ruins, which could not be intruded upon, greatly affected the design of the area northwest of the station. In fact, the original design for a main square just north of the train station was entirely redone when it became apparent how greatly the amphitheater constrained the design. A LARGE SQUARE AND CHURCH (towards the bottom) had to be relocated to another site in the southwest quadrant. The area around the central station was the most constrained in its design and consumed more time and energy than any other part of the site.

Once the amphitheater had been completely modeled, a workable design for the MAIN SQUARE emerged fairly quickly. This square was a short distance from the new rail station, but it was thought that the distance was not great enough to impair its functioning. An arcade was built to link the triangular square with the canal. The amphitheater was connected directly to the square, bringing this historical feature back into daily use. The large bridge over the north-south rail line springs from just outside the edge of this square and is accessed through an archway in the base of a tower that carries four small domes.

MORPHOGENIC DEVELOPMENT

I was interested in testing the use of morphogenic sequences. These were not formally stated at the start of the project, but they guided my thinking throughout the process, and when it came time to make an important decision, the approaches I outlined to the group were guided by the principles established in DISTRICT LAYOUT and by the notion that all earlier elements will influence everything that comes later. In pure form, morphogenic sequences do not involve revisiting earlier decisions, but in this case, a few important decisions were revised when it was seen that they had led to problems that were difficult or

impossible to solve. The most important was the rearrangement of the main square after it became apparent that the influence of the amphitheater had not been sufficiently considered.

I was interested to see how readily people understood the need to work from large to small elements and to build away from the center of the district. Those constructing the maquette were continually influenced by what had gone before. The features of the site, even though limited in number, had a great influence. The gentle curve of the north-south rail line and the response to the amphitheater were particularly noteworthy. Everyone also understood that the east-west rail line was a barrier and that it was necessary to coordinate streets so that underpasses connecting the two sides coupled the two halves as closely as possible. I saw few actions that seemed to have been taken in the abstract, without reference to what was already built or without considering the impact of a given decision on the whole. Some people did feel the need to develop paper designs, upon which buildings were later constructed. In cases where the plans conflicted with other needs, the plans were ignored.

Assessment

The actual duration of maquette construction was only about four hours, the remainder of the time on that day having been spent on preparation and assessment. Better results would probably have been achieved with more deliberation, but the speed of the work adjusted itself to the time available. Certainly, when designing on-site, much greater precision is required and will arise of itself.

I was gratified by the unfolding of the process. The results achieved were considerably better than I had dared hope, especially given that the preparations had been made in haste. I was impressed by the energy, enthusiasm, and creativity that participants brought to the process. The clay maquette is worth

considering as part of any design exercise and may offer a useful training exercise prior to moving onto the site. Even if on-site design begins completely anew, as I think it should, maquette-building will reveal issues that must be dealt with and make clear the prejudices and desires of the participants. It also introduces people to the relationships between the various parts and their proportions.

In the two days following the building of the maquette, we discussed the process at length. I made a presentation of my work on this book only after the maquette was built. People believed that we had in fact employed many of these ideas in building the maquette. A detailed presentation of the theory plus illustrative examples *before* the start of construction would surely be a better sequence to follow.

I think the process demonstrated that citizens with little training in urban design can be drawn into the process. Conflicts, when they arose, were resolved in a friendly and cooperative manner. Much innovation was brought to the task.

Some participants seemed to avoid actual design work and instead made buildings for others to place on the maquette. This helped those doing the actual design, but the house-builders were not really full participants. This may simply be a case of people helping out in ways with which they are comfortable. Ideally, though, these people would be drawn into the design.

This one exercise convinced me that a single individual should probably never be asked or allowed to design an urban area without direct involvement by many others. Perhaps this involvement need not include large numbers of ordinary citizens, but I am certain that better design arises when many people work together to meet the challenges of a site.

One concern that I had with this process was the extent to which it was simply a reflection of my own ideas and opinions. I am known to many of the people who participated in the process, as was the nature of my work on this book. It was evident

to everyone that I was the principal facilitator, although several others played major roles. It could be argued that a different principal facilitator would lead to different results, perhaps very different. I know of no way to test this except to repeat this exercise with another facilitator and compare the results. I suspect, however, that I did influence the process. Perhaps that cannot be entirely avoided. I made a real effort to draw out the other participants, and quite a lot of what was done did not arise from my actions or suggestions. At the same time, not many things were done that seemed wrong to me.

Notes on Process & Technique

It became apparent that many participants lacked a clear idea of the scale at which we were working. Evidence of this can be seen in the trees and sculptures that were added to the courtyards, most of which were over-scaled. This problem arose despite a preliminary discussion of scale and the examples of urban density presented. However, rulers were frequently used to scale buildings, and many participants seem to have had a good grasp of the scale. People had strong urges to ornament the courtyards. Some ornaments had a humorous character, like the giant cat seen in the center of the photograph at the start of this chapter. This is harmless in the abstract, but most ornaments were so far out of scale that they confused the sense of scale. All elements should be at scale, thereby giving additional scale hints. The large church, with its four spires, was useful in this regard; it was a big building with appropriate detailing and gave accurate scale information.

In the future, I would prepare sample scale blocks with various types and sizes of buildings. Drawings and photographs like those in THE DENSITY QUESTION would be placed with these samples. This would help people to grasp the scale and to understand the implications of decisions regarding the size of

Examples can be found starting on page 118. Quite a good deal of additional material is available at: www.carfree.com/library.html

the elements. The desire for trees is so strong that a stock of scale trees should be available. They should be in a material that is clearly distinguishable from the clay.

I believe that the 1:500 scale is about right for this work. The size of the maquette is manageable, and people can reach any part of it without endangering buildings at the edge. The scale is large enough to show some detail and permits the larger buildings to be given some character. If a smaller area is under design, then a larger scale might be advantageous. The 1:500 scale is also convenient because scale conversions are so quick.

We used ordinary potter's clay (known in Hungary as "hobby clay"). Be sure to test a sample for workability; when it is fairly stiff, it is easy to work and not messy. We had 45kg (100 lbs) of clay. This cost about $35 in Hungary. We used about 40% of the supply to build half a standard district at a scale of 1:500. Clay has a relatively short working time. This can be extended overnight by lightly moistening the clay at the end of the day with a plant mister and draping the maquette in thin plastic sheeting. An alternative material is oil-based clay, often sold as "Plasticine." This clay remains workable for months. It is ten times as expensive as potter's clay but can be had in a wide range of colors.

The clay was easily cut using a fish-line cutter with two clothes pegs for handles. Ordinary, dull table knives were used to trim the clay (e.g., cutting the pitched roofs into a clay block).

Prague, 2006: Field Test of User Design

Following World Carfree Network's general meeting in Tábor, Czech Republic, a field test of user design was conducted on a large grassy field at Letnany, in northeastern Prague, on 28 May 2006. Thirteen people participated in this one-day test of in-the-field urban design using stakes and strings, not paper. The test came at a good moment, when the ideas in this Part had been well developed but while there was still time for significant

In customary units, use 40' to the inch, which is 1:480.

"Modeling clay" in the USA

I would like to thank all those who participated in the maquette-building process and especially the organizers and Zöfi. It was a great help to be able to test these ideas in this way.

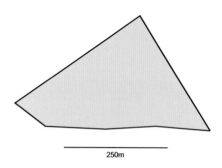

250m

rewriting, which did in fact occur on the basis of the experience gained on this day.

The site was a right triangle about 300m (1000') east–west and 200m (660') north–south at the east end. It was FLAT AND FEATURELESS, a small part of a grass airfield. All but a small part of the field had been recently mown. (Our stakes were too short to hold the string above the areas of uncut grass.) We assumed that the western point of the triangle was at the center of a carfree district and that the east end of the site would face permanent open space. The site was almost perfectly level and lacked any tree cover or other significant feature. I remarked during the exercise that the presence of even a single large tree would have led to calls for its preservation and so would have greatly influenced the design. The hypotenuse of the triangle was a low hedgerow that was assumed to represent a major radial street demarcating our neighborhood from another neighborhood to the south. The northern edge of the site was a graveled area and was assumed to represent another major radial street. We thus had a wedge to work on that was similar in size and shape to the neighborhoods defined on page 472.

We had originally hoped to have 50 people on the site, but bad weather and logistical difficulties limited attendance to 13, which proved sufficient to test many ideas but did not give a good sense of how the process would work at a neighborhood or district level, with hundreds or thousands of participants. Even so, several issues regarding in-the-field layout of large urban areas were revealed.

Preparations

I briefed many of the participants in Tábor a few days before the event. I explained the nature of the process and the questions I hoped to answer. This was followed by a walking tour of Tábor during which I pointed out some of the design features of this pleasant medieval town. (Principal among them was the siting of the tower of the main church on the highest point of land and the fact that this was a heavily fortified town whose walls remain substantially intact.) On arrival at the Letnany site, I handed participants several pages taken from THE DENSITY QUESTION, illustrating urban areas of densities and arrangements similar to those we sought to achieve during the exercise.

Few other preparations were required. We had cut 600 stakes from wire clothes hangers. These worked well enough except in areas of high grass, where, as noted, they were not long or stiff enough to stand above the grass. We purchased 4km (2.5mi) of string, most of it in a light blue color. It was fairly thick and not very stretchy, which is important.

I believe that the material was polypropylene but cannot be certain; low stretch is characteristic of this inexpensive artificial fiber.

I made the simple assumption that each person living on the site was entitled to 2m (6.6') of street frontage, which is a reasonable value. Upon arrival at the site, we began cutting strings of various lengths, ranging from 100m (330') to 170m (560'). This takes longer than might be expected, and it is no simple matter to keep the strings from tangling. We tied each string into a loop that was to represent the perimeter of a block of buildings and carried it out onto the site.

DESIGN OF BLOCKS

The use of perimeter strings seemed quite promising for entire blocks, but when attempting to design several blocks at once, we lacked sufficient numbers of people to represent more than just the corners of the blocks. With many more people on the site, I expect that as people from different groups approach each other, there would already begin to be negotiations regarding how to arrange things. The problem of where to start the various groups obviously requires early consideration; this was a significant finding and considerably influenced the development of the process that was ultimately proposed in this book.

Furthermore, it became apparent that each of the various urban villages will have to designate the approximate site that they seek and negotiate with other groups that may covet the same site. Provisions for location-specific preferences are thus required.

DESIGN OF STREETS & SQUARES

We tried several approaches to designing specific areas. When designing small areas, such as the one square that was designed in considerable detail, we had enough people to give a sense of scale in the space and to stand at the building façades, showing precisely how large the space would be. This part of the process went very well and the participants were deeply engaged. People were able to understand immediately how the buildings would fit together and the way in which the shapes and sizes of the spaces affected how they feel. We sat down and ate lunch in the square we made, and people agreed that they liked it. Participants even went so far as to decide where certain functions, such as the bakery, ought to be located.

Illustrated on page 140

Two things somewhat surprised me. First of all, people were willing and even eager to make very narrow streets, down to 2m (6.6') wide. Streets this narrow are common in old neighborhoods but are almost never laid out today. Car traffic has much to do with this, of course, but emergency access is a more stubborn problem. Japan has coped with this by devising fire engines of a size that can penetrate into the narrowest alleyways, and there really is no reason that this approach could not be more widely adopted. The strength of this yearning for narrow streets with non-parallel sides and complex geometry surprised and pleased me.

The second interesting point was that people were immediately willing to make passages into the interior courtyards that would make them open to the public. In Venice, such a passage is known as a "sottoportego" and is nothing more than a ground-level tunnel through a building into the space behind it. I have tended to assume that people would generally prefer to keep the courtyards closed and private, but in this group there was a ready willingness to open them up. (It should be noted that such arrangements are found in old parts of Prague.)

DIFFICULTIES

The site we used was rather remarkable for its almost total lack of features that would influence design. This was a significant impediment. Even a few small trees would have had considerable influence on the design as people sought ways to preserve them on the completed site.

Communication is very difficult during in-field design due to the rather large distances involved. If there is much wind, it is impossible to be heard over even fairly short distances. The use of mobile telephones or portable radios might help.

Even fairly thick, light-colored string quickly vanishes in the grass if on the ground. Dark string is nearly invisible.

Streets and large squares should be laid out before the start of the process. These features are subject to adjustment within some limits, however.

When strings are held at waist level by dozens of participants, reasonably good definition of a block is attained; this comes more from the people than the string, which only serves to constrain the size of the block.

Clarity of scale is essential, and distance is difficult to judge on a flat, empty site with just a few people scattered about. The presence of many people on the site would help, and certainly, during the design of small-scale elements, when each building was represented by one person, there was a much better sense of the scale of the area. Some people said they were more comfortable with the small design than when working at the block scale, which they found difficult to interpret.

I was concerned that it would be all too easy for the leaders to take control of the process, even inadvertently. This must be guarded against by both leaders and residents. In this case, strong winds made communication difficult, and at times I used hand signs to move people around. People were probably too ready to do as I suggested; be wary of the influence of "experts."

Conclusions

People like medieval areas. I have known this for some time, based simply on the fact that a remarkable number of popular tourist areas are in fact the oldest parts of their cities. Newer areas with wide, straight streets, dating mainly from the 17th century onwards, are rarely so popular a destination. People are quite ready to create more areas that resemble the medieval districts they like so much, and there seems to be an intrinsic understanding that small, intimate buildings, streets, and squares are essential to this process.

The use of a looped perimeter string was the most important discovery in this exercise. Decisions regarding the lengths of perimeter strings are critical, as they have a great influence on the actual design. Once again, the proper formation of urban villages and the negotiation of agreements regarding the total frontage of a block are deterministic for the process.

People need a better feel for how big the blocks would be. The approaches suggested on page 481 would help with this.

People enjoyed the process itself. They thought that it would initiate the building of social cohesion in a new neighborhood. The process was carried out in a spirit of cooperation, although some conflicts must be expected when the process is first applied to a real site, with real streets and buildings at stake.

The urban village must become the unit of user design. It is too much to expect a group of thousands of strangers to assemble into meaningful groups and lay out a carfree district the same day. Months of preparation will be required. Since the definition of blocks first requires an identification of their residents, it is difficult to see how on-site user design can proceed until people have grouped themselves into smaller social units. The block is the obvious unit for this. It seemed that some of the process of urban village formation should occur on the site itself, with people having the opportunity to get to know their prospective neighbors before getting down to actual design work.

The feasibility of on-site design at a scale smaller than a block was demonstrated by this exercise. People understood the issues immediately, and there were no difficulties regarding scope or scale. The process was seen as very direct. I was only concerned by the absence of a means of visualizing the completed space once comparatively tall buildings have been erected. People might then decide that they wanted their streets a little wider after all.

Oversight is much better with a maquette. When working on the site itself, it is practically impossible to see how the pieces fit together.

It is essential to give people good training and information. Clearly, the volunteers did not have enough, but in the case of people working on a real site, there would be weeks or months to prepare and to discuss their needs. Fairly detailed training in both the process and the urban planning issues that affect the site can be provided before on-site design begins.

Somewhat to my surprise, people were already aware of the desirable effects of enclosure in outdoor spaces. People were very interested in the process of defining squares and the surrounding buildings. The volunteers understood without my prompting that an enlargement of just two meters (yards) could have a significant impact on a street intersection and would, by itself, be nearly enough to cause a square to emerge. Corners were cut off to aid in the creation of a square. The occupancy of a square during its design by the people who will use it is

I would like to thank all those who participated in the field test. I am also very grateful to Jakub Sklenka and Jan Jelinek of CODECO Real Estate Development for making the site available and obtaining municipal permission for the exercise. I would also like to thank Randall Ghent of World Carfree Network for organizing the event. The trial had a large influence on this book.

important and helps them to see its scale. One square was designed in some detail and was remarkably small and intimate. Its shape was complex and subtle.

Participants were willing to accept smaller interior courtyards than I had foreseen. In fact, it appears to be possible to design areas that are only three stories high but which still reach a FAR of 1.5 or even somewhat higher, so long as the streets are kept very narrow and the courtyards of modest size.

More preliminary design is required than I had anticipated. In particular, questions regarding the routing of major streets and the approximate location and accessibility of main squares cannot be left entirely to field processes.

At the time of the exercise, I had envisioned the development of a morphogenic sequence to guide neighborhood design. However, this experience convinced me that the process can be appreciably more fluid than I had envisioned, and I abandoned the perhaps impossible task of developing a complete set of morphogenic sequences.

The size of blocks can be much more flexible than I had assumed. The use of Arab-style courtyard housing, U-shaped blocks with only a wall at one end, and so forth, makes possible the formation of urban villages of almost any desired size. At the upper end of the range, there can be sub-villages if the groups become too large for a single block.

POETRY

I only chose the rather odd title of this chapter after rejecting all other candidates. "Poetry" is what we are trying to create, using bricks and mortar. Like poetry created with pen and ink, the making of this kind of poetry is impossible to distill into rules. Yes, it is possible to give some guidelines that will help to avoid dreadful results, but glimmering spaces that will touch generations to come cannot be made by the application of what Oscar Wilde calls "dead rules." Just as with poetry, some expression of inner feeling must shine through before any magic can arise.

We cannot simply speak of aesthetics. There are too many urban styles to give rules for them all, and even when rules are given, they tend to lead to the chilly, lifeless results so typical of the architecture of Palladio, who slavishly followed the practices of the ancients. It is possible to build a "good" classical building by resorting to the rules of, say, the Ionic order. Correctly executed, there will be nothing "wrong" with the building, and it almost certainly will surpass any building in the Modern style, but it is likely to be lifeless and poorly adapted to its site. And how many buildings of this sort do you want in your city? Or can you afford? The trick is to build poetry using indigenous materials, labor, techniques, and styles. When done with feeling, the result can be surpassingly good.

To succeed, you must give of yourself. You and the neighbors with whom you will share the finished place must build your hopes and dreams into it. Even if there is but little hope that these dreams will come true, express them anyway. Simply putting them forth in concrete form brings them closer to reality. Build something that will cause those who wander through your streets centuries from now to say, "I *know* these people."

Perfection is not required, nor perhaps even desired. Great poetry is full of "mistakes." It is sometimes rough and ready, or at least it appears so. Yet there is something in it that speaks

Campo San Bartolomeo, Venice. One of the "talking plazas" where people gather to meet friends and chat. The beautiful surroundings and the silvery burble of voices on a Friday evening make this square one of the most inviting places in all Venice.

I am not opposed to the Baroque in principal. For me, the music of J.S. Bach surpasses that of any other composer. But composing music is a solitary task. Architecture is for everyone, by everyone, for all time. Unlike music, it is not an egotistical expression.

insistently, that strikes a chord, that paints an image, that gives rise to feelings that cannot really be voiced. I believe that I see this poetry more often in the places that came from many hands over the ages than in the brilliant perfection of some Baroque abstraction that sprang forth full bloom from one mind in a moment of dazzling inspiration late one night while hunched over a sheet of vellum, pen in hand.

Writing poetry is not a rational act. Rational faculties are necessary but insufficient. Just as the poet cannot always say why one couplet is perfect and the other not, I do not think we can always explain why once space fits like a glove and another pinches here and there. Both may substantially obey the rules of design, yet one lacks the spark that the other has.

Not all poems are successful. Some work only for the person who wrote them. Some work for a time and then seem stilted or dated. So it is with space. Not all spaces will come alive, even if that is our intention—we will fail often. However, unlike poetry, spaces are rewritten by those who come after us. If the armature we have created is good enough, then later generations will reuse it rather than rebuild. And when we have at last succeeded in creating a poetic space, we can hope that its message is so clear and perfect that people will simply leave it alone, cherishing and sustaining it. So, do not fear failure. Any attempt at poetry is likely to be better than any effort to create something using abstract, alien rules, like the CASA DA MÚSICA in Porto.

SOME GUIDELINES

So, what should you and your neighbors-to-be do when confronted with the daunting but wonderful task of building some poetry to live in? I will give some suggestions. Of some of them I am quite sure; others are only what I would do myself.

Begin by talking about your hopes and dreams. This may seem awkward at first, as it is something that often only children engage in (and do be sure to ask the children!). Get past the awkward phase. Take time with this, for it will govern all your decisions to come. Do you want quiet evenings under a tree in the gathering dusk with a bottle of wine? Or do you want loud block parties every Saturday evening that there's no frost on the ground? Do you want a lively mix of stores and workshops with apartments above or a quiet residential neighborhood? Do you want narrow streets and expansive courtyards, or are broader streets more to your liking? Will this be a neighborhood where kids go trick-or-treating and everybody puts a pumpkin on the stoop? Or will this be a more reserved neighborhood, where people tip their hats but leave one another lots of space?

I argue that you must answer these questions with clarity. Do not leave this process to some marketing guru who knows how to build condominiums that sell well to your "demographic." I argued in URBAN VILLAGES that groups of like-minded people should gather to form a new village in the city. If you can't reach agreement on the basic feel of the space you want to create and can't decide on some common elements of your lives that you want to share, even if at some distance, then your group is probably not a successful formation and you may want to try again.

So, once your group has achieved basic agreement regarding your goals for this place you are about to create, it is time to start thinking more concretely about the site. Get to know the place in all light and weather. Take a year over this if at all possible, so you know where the sun will rise and set in summer and winter, from whence the cold winds blow, where the snow drifts, when the birds return in spring. Visit the site at all times of the day, together with others if you can, alone if not. Get a feeling for the land, for the parts of it that are already beautiful as well as for the parts that seem somehow incomplete. I believe that only deep feeling for a site can inform a good design—flying over one afternoon in a helicopter and returning to the drafting board will at best yield a pretty drawing that is ill-suited to the site.

Tavira, Portugal

Madrid

Coimbra

As your group explores the site, you will notice that paths begin to form all by themselves. Some of these paths may lead around obstructing clumps of brush, and you may want to hack passages through them fairly early in the process. There will be muddy spots that might best be left unbuilt, or that at least require supplemental drainage. Throw a plank across the creek. Move it around until you like where it is. Notice which slopes are steep enough that they are a bother to climb.

Consider the wisdom of the local vernacular style. Ask if the traditional materials are still available in the required quantity and quality. Are the old skills still available? Are the old methods still regarded as sufficiently resistant to the hazards to which they will be exposed? In many places, the old ways are still practical and well adapted, and the necessary artisanship has been maintained. Think hard before deviating from the old practice. Some of these techniques may seem expensive today, but many of them will reduce maintenance costs. The old methods may be problematic. For example, if traditional buildings in your locale are built from heavy timbers, you may have to forego this due to a shortage of large-dimension lumber. Or perhaps the method can be reserved for a few special buildings. In Portugal, many recent buildings have been constructed using modern reinforced concrete but in the TRADITIONAL STYLE, as in this resort at Budens. These buildings look like they belong to the landscape, and, unlike traditional rubble-wall construction, their earthquake resistance is good. Traditional styles include both ornament and color, which can safely be adopted in new buildings.

Flesh out your ideas with friends. Pace off streets and buildings in the field. Set some provisional stakes. Show them to others, fiddle with them until they seem right. Imagine what the place will look like, how it would feel, who would use it, and when. Try always to minimize disturbances to the site.

Large spaces and big budgets no more make poetry than many pages and plenty of words. Poetry is economy—the distillation of meaning into a few well-chosen words or a modest number of well-placed stones. Many of the great cathedrals are truly poetic, as is the 90,000 lines of the Hindu *Ramayana,* but poetry is often better when it is spare. Be not afraid of small projects and tight budgets.

Do not forget the importance of the non-visual aspects of urban poetry. Remember that sounds, scents, and the feel of materials will all affect how a space feels. Imagine how outdoor cafés and restaurants will affect the smell of an area. Hear the children skirling through a street after school. Reflect on the temporal aspects of spaces—how their use and feel will change during the course of a day, a week, a year. Visualize how the changing light will affect the mood of the space and its users.

Lagos, Portugal

Above all, be aware of the details. Many once-poetic places have lost their poetry because small mistakes were made in their upkeep and management. Signage and windows have a much greater impact than people usually realize. Signs must be small, quiet, and tasteful unless you are trying to create a new Times Square. More good buildings have been spoiled by insensitive window treatment than any other cause. Get the details right.

The design of an urban area is an opportunity for people to leave their mark in history. Most people, given this chance, will attempt to leave something that expresses who they are and is of such high quality that generations to come will understand it and protect it. Poetic spaces are assured of longevity—people will rise to defend them against all threats.

HARMONY & RESONANCE

I think that the real foundation of poetic spaces lies in the achievement of harmony and resonance. Harmonious shapes are ones that fit together. Resonant shapes reinforce each other and further elaborate the harmony. Consider this ENTRANCE TO A MOSQUE in Fes-al-Bali, Morocco. The space is asymmetrical,

as a result of the intricately-detailed fountain on the right. It is, however, in balance. The harmony arises from the use of three arches based on the same horseshoe shape, with the largest of the three in the center. The detailing increases steadily from left to right; the left arch is quite plain, the center arch is highly detailed, and the right arch is astoundingly intricate (far more so than can be seen in this small photograph). The detail thus builds, reading from left to right, and the three forms ring like bells together. These three shapes, different as they are, belong together and strengthen one another.

Achieving harmony is not so easy as recognizing it. Harmonies have changed over the centuries, although most spaces that were ever regarded as poetic still are today. Just as with music, we may no longer compose in the style of Bach, but nearly everyone accustomed to Western harmonies can hear them in his music three centuries after it was written. We can seek harmony within the confining requirements of symmetry, or we can be bolder and base our harmonies on balanced compositions that may depart considerably from symmetry. There is no real right and wrong in this, there is only the question of what pleases us and our neighbors and can be hoped to please our progeny.

Madrid

COMPARATIVE POETRY

We now analyze pairs of spaces (and one quartet) on the measure of poetic expression. In some cases, the differences are subtle and people will not reach the same judgments. In other cases, I expect broad agreement. Merely considering these examples and discussing them with others will help to reach agreements on what is desirable and what can better be avoided.

The general framework will be order vs organization, with scale considered as nearly as important. Shapes, detailing, ornament, and color will also be considered. Not all aspects will be considered in every case.

Venice

We compare first a minor radial canal in Amsterdam, the REGULIERSGRACHT, with a small square in Guimarães, Portugal, the PRAÇA DE SANTIAGO. Neither is an especially grand location, and both are primarily residential. These two places are subject to considerably different requirements. The first is set in the cool, reserved culture of Holland, the second in the more extroverted culture of Portugal. The climates are also quite different. Guimarães has a hot and dry summer at a latitude 11° farther south. Amsterdam is seldom hot but often dark and cold in the winter, whereas Guimarães is warmer in winter and enjoys more sun. The effects of climate are large. In Amsterdam, it is desirable to bring as much light as possible into a building during nearly all of the year. In Guimarães, it will be necessary to shade the interiors from the sun during the summer. Brick is the usual material in Amsterdam, and stone in Guimarães.

Neither place is very orderly, and the lack of order runs nearly to chaos in Amsterdam, with great variance in the heights of the buildings and their style and general arrangement. In Guimarães, no two buildings are the same, but the range of variation is small and all buildings employ a similar arrangement. The pitched roofs in Amsterdam are arranged with the ridges running in the opposite direction from Guimarães. The roof overhang in Guimarães shades the top floor from hot summer sun. The different arrangements are well suited to local conditions.

The scale in both places is small and comfortable. The shapes in Amsterdam are excessively varied and not especially pleasing; the shapes in Guimarães are more satisfactory. The buildings in Amsterdam are nicely detailed, a characteristic of the local vernacular style. The detailing in Guimarães is entirely satisfactory but considerably simpler, and the corbelling of the upper stories out over the ground floor improves the overall appearance.

The buildings in Amsterdam are of a warm brick that is quite appealing. The stone ground floors in Guimarães are of a chilly grey stone offset by the bright white stucco of the upper floors.

We consider here two Portuguese squares of moderate size. The first, the LARGO DO POÇO in Coimbra, is a true rectangle and is hardly any longer than we see here. The second, the PRAÇA ALFONSO III in Faro's old walled quarter, flares open again behind the camera into a much larger square.

In plan view, the first square appears highly ordered, but is in reality less so, as the surrounding buildings are of a rather varied character. The second is quite ordered in terms of building style but not so much in terms of shape, which is quite complex. Both spaces are well organized and both see fairly heavy use. The scale of both places is moderate. No building exceeds four stories in either one. In the first, all buildings are narrower than they are tall. In the second, they are wider than they are tall.

The detailing of the first square is quite good; the lack of a consistent style does no great harm. The detailing of the second square is harmonious, even if the buildings are not exactly alike. The pavement in the first is rather plain by Portuguese standards and that of the second unusual for the absence of any design. The paving of the second is rather rough to walk on.

In both places, signage is restrained. The awnings in the first soften the space. The detailing of the three balcony railings in the second add a subtle but important richness. Good windows with stone trim have been used in both places, although in the first, the original ground-floor windows have given way to plate glass. In the second, beautiful cast iron brackets and detailed luminaires are attached to the buildings.

In the first square, colors are not especially well coordinated, but the contrast with the black and white stone pavement is pleasant. The buildings of the second take on delightful colors in the late afternoon sun and have a warm, inviting feel.

Both squares appear to function well. The first provides a good trade for the merchants. The second hosts several busy cafés. The second square is one to love, whereas the first is merely one to admire.

These two small squares, both in Lisbon's ALFAMA DISTRICT, are of similar size but exhibit quite different levels of order and organization. Both spaces are little larger than seen here.

The first space lacks both order and organization. This was a missed chance, as the stairway on the right (and the downgoing stairway just to its left) are in fact part of a fairly important pedestrian thoroughfare. Few people enter it except to make the turn onto the next flight of stairs. The varying height of the buildings appears random and serves no apparent purpose. The people passing through are not drawn into the space, nor does the square have a destination of its own. The second square also serves as a passageway, with one outlet visible beyond the tree and the other just out of sight in the left foreground. It is a quite highly ordered space, seemingly rectilinear. All of the buildings are of about the same height and exhibit a reasonable commonality of styles. This space also seems well organized, with benches providing places for people to linger. The lone tree is a fine addition that will grow into its own before too long.

The scale of both spaces is fairly small, but the first square feels too open and amorphous. The spaces seems to bleed away. The second square is intimate and nicely enclosed. Similarly, the first exhibits rather poor shape, whereas there is little or nothing to criticize in the second.

Once again it is the detailing that has an important effect on our perception of these two spaces. The first has nearly sufficient detail in the window and door moldings, but there is too little contrast in the color of the walls to make these heavy stone posts and lintels stand out. The second has similar levels of detail (although the windows are more attractively divided here), but the stone trim stands out more prominently in most of the buildings because of the color contrast. The building in the center would be more interesting with greater contrast between the window frames and the walls. The tile work in the building on the right gives it some distinction despite the poorly detailed door.

On this page and the next we look at four archways from different eras. The first is in the OLD WALLED QUARTER of Faro in southern Portugal and was part of a major defensive work. The photograph is taken from outside the wall. It appears that there was an inner gate, in the background, that gives way to two outer gates, one in the foreground and one on the right. There is a no-nonsense air about this gate. It lacks almost all ornament. The forms are pure, simple, practical, and easy to construct.

Its organization is interesting and functional. The elements are large because of their function, but not so large as to make us uncomfortable. This space exhibits a moderately high level of order, especially in the foreground, with the three matching circular arches at right angles to one another. The worn stucco in the foreground simply gives the place an old, used quality that I don't mind at all. The stonework in both the walls and the street is unpretentious and rugged. The warm color is pleasing. All that might be found to criticize here is the recent addition of boxy black floodlights at the spring of the first arch.

I know not how the gentle S-curve beyond the gate may have arisen, but the play of curves is pleasing. The relationship between the curves of the arch, the eaves of the buildings, and meandering curbs draw the eye through the gate.

The ARCO DA PORTA NOVA in Braga is an 18th-century addition to this ancient city. The ornamentation is considerable without being ostentatious, a rather restrained Baroque exposition. The genius of the space lies not so much in the gate itself as in its approaches. The space is highly organized but the order is imperfect; the buildings do not stand at exactly the same angle to the gate, but this actually improves the space by creating a distinct funnel towards the gate. The walls of the funnel are formed by buildings of a very pleasant character, built in the local style, with plenty of stone trim. The elements are of a good scale, and the large arch fits nicely. The colors are a bit cooler than in Faro but still agreeable.

This archway, also in the OLD WALLED QUARTER of Faro, was never a part of its defenses. It carries the second story of a rather large building across a street entering the Largo da Sé, the largest square in the old quarter. The arch thus provides additional space and connects two parts of a building while also helping to complete the enclosure of the square.

The perfect elliptical arch frames a distinctive roof line just beyond. Two pitched roofs, their gables facing the street, form a valley right under the center of the arch. Notice how the street approaches the arch at an angle, which further strengthens the enclosure on both sides. This is a simple, quiet design that gives a pleasing result. It is highly organized but not very orderly. The scale is intimate, and the warm colors are light and inviting.

The final archway is the BURCHTPOORT, once part of the city defenses in the Dutch town of Leiden. This, the only one of our four gates that is still operational, was built in 1658. It carries inscriptions, a coat of arms, and other insignia. Like most old structures in the Netherlands, it has settled unevenly, but this does no harm to its attractiveness.

This is an informal kind of poetry, more a saga passed along and changed slightly in each retelling. The place has a comfortable, grown-in feeling that invites further tinkering, although the gate itself is probably sacrosanct. The level of order is quite low, but the organization is attractive and functional. The scale is intimate. The bright white of the gate is an unusual but successful contrast with the dull red brick and blue stone surrounding it.

I arranged these four archways in declining level of order. All four are highly organized spaces. I find the example from Braga to be the most attractive, because it is surrounded by excellent buildings and is attractively ornamented. The last two examples would, however, be very well suited to a minor role, which the example from Braga is not. The three heavy arches in Faro are a bit forbidding but relieved by the intimate street beyond.

We compare here two streets with jogs in the lines of the buildings fronting the streets, both from Portugal. The first, the RUA DE SOBRE-RIPAS in the hilly part of old Coimbra, appears to have been maintained in substantially its original condition. The second, the RUA DOM PAIO PERES CORREIA in Tavira, appears to date from a later period. The second street has one unfortunate recent change in the foreground, the replacement of a wooden door with one of aluminum and glass. It lacks the physical relief that would almost certainly have characterized the original door. Because this door occupies such a prominent place in this view, this one minor change has a disproportionate impact on our appreciation of a street that is in many ways rather similar to the first. The ashlar stone in the first was very expensive and certainly adds to our appreciate of that street.

In both cases, the street is curved sufficiently to take it out of view a hundred paces farther on. In both cases, curbs have been added to the street, but in the case of the second, the walkway on the left is really too narrow except to stand on while waiting for a car to pass. The paving of the second is in perfect condition, which improves the street.

The façade of the jog is acceptable in both cases, although the overhanging plants in the first are especially attractive, as is the stone-framed doorway. In the second, the window on the ground floor is a little too small. The window on the second story is graced by a detailed ironwork railing of a type found throughout Portugal.

In the first street, the stone construction of the left-hand building is very attractive. The treatment of the large doorway is simple, but the varnished wood is pretty and lends a pleasing warm color. The windows and doors of the building on the right are of beautifully carved stone that is also of a warm hue. The solid stone members are practical and attractive. In the second street, all the buildings are of inexpensive painted stucco, which is characteristic of the region.

Compare these two narrow streets NEAR PIAZZA SAN MARCO in Venice. The first lies a few hundred paces to the east. The second is even closer to the great square, but to its west. Both places exhibit the relatively low order, irregularity, and gentle articulation that characterize streets in Venice. Both spaces are well organized, probably indirectly in response to the curving waterways of Venice, which tended to follow natural watercourses. It is probably no coincidence that the second street gives a view straight into the Piazza, allowing the majesty of the great square to build gradually. The "bead" (see page 435) in the second scene is a triumph, one of the finest small spaces in Venice. The first is no less good, merely quieter and less grand.

The scale of both places is intimate. These are both highly oversquare streets, with buildings that are much taller than the street is wide. The flat, floor-like paving of both spaces enhances the sensation of being in a hallway of great intricacy and interest.

I have generally been quite critical of plate-glass windows such as found in both of these places. Here they have been better handled than usual, in particular by the knee-high sill that is sufficient to keep people from walking into the glass. The quality of illumination is good in the first case but truly remarkable in the second. (These shops have no shutters, and the windows are illuminated all night, casting a warm glow onto the street (see page 531). The colorful rear-illuminated Venetian glass at the back of the ice cream shop is a delightful addition. Signage is, as nearly everywhere in Venice, tasteful and restrained.

Both spaces are well suited to their current uses. The first is home to modest bars, restaurants, and gelato vendors. The second is home to stores selling Italian high-fashion goods. I could not really say that one space is better than the other, only that each is perfect for what it is. I can wander endlessly through the narrow streets of San Marco, most of which are quite similar to these. They are at their best in the late afternoon and early evening, when the crowds are also at their peak.

Consider these two streets in Lisbon's ALFAMA DISTRICT. In the upper photograph, we see a narrow dead-end street that serves more as a courtyard than a street. The lower photograph is of a narrow street just around the corner from the first. I find rather little poetry in the first and a lot in the second. Superficially, they are similar—the streets are irregular and of comparable width, although the first one swells a good deal going away from the camera. The buildings are mainly four stories, with a few of three stories. Neither street is very orderly, but both exhibit fairly high levels of organization. The scale is in both cases small, but the range of scales in the second is more pleasing than in the first.

The first space feels overly enclosed, almost confined (there is little more space than we see here). This arises in part from the lack of a visible exit. The second is fully but comfortably enclosed; despite the narrowness of the street, it does not feel confining to me.

Both streets have small-block stone paving. The buildings are by no means sumptuous in either case. Both have stone-framed doors and windows. The foreground building in the second street has an attractive corner of massive stone blocks.

One could argue that the first shows a certain neglect, owing to the sloppy addition of laundry drying lines on both sides, with haphazard plastic sheeting sheltering the lines on the right. The second street also has a time-worn appearance, especially the weathered doors with torn posters pasted on them, but it escapes the feeling of neglect in the first example. These doors are nicely detailed and proportioned and remain attractive even after heavy wear. By contrast, the newer door in the foreground of the first street is crudely detailed. The pure white of all the buildings on the first street is boring, whereas the second street exhibits variations in color, tone, and texture. The first street also has many exposed utility access panels, and the two planters have been neglected.

Consider these two flights of steps, both from the BECO DE SANTA HELENA in Lisbon's Alfama, but separated by centuries in their conception. The first, near the Largo de Portas do Sol is Modern in its arrangement, consisting almost entirely of straight lines, excepting the arch. The second, at the intersection with Beco do Garcês, is pre-Renaissance in its conception if not in its construction. It meanders gently to and fro. The first stairway is highly ordered but not very well organized. It is too long and too steep. It fails to take advantage of the features of the site. It might just as easily have had two bends in it, allowing it to hug the walls and reducing both the steepness and the danger from a single, unbroken flight of stairs. The second, which shows a low level of order, is highly organized. It bends and swells to accommodate the site. It provides welcome breaks in the climb, which is nowhere too steep. It manages effectively the confluence of three flighted streets, in the foreground.

The shapes of the first I find almost brutal. It is only relieved by the church tower, the tree, and the one window. The second contains many attractive, interesting curves. The first is nearly devoid of detail; the second is rich with it, and these details are attractive, functional, and in keeping with local traditions.

The railings of the first are large and blocky. The elements in the second are small, with the exception of the long stone wall on the right, but its bulk is relieved by the overhanging trees, the texture of the stonework, and especially by the tiled artwork in the arched cove on the right. The absence of any detail framing the arch in the first stairway is a serious lapse. In the second, the elliptical arch is pleasingly framed in high-grade stone.

The first is paved with uniform, dark stone blocks. The second is paved in the traditional Portuguese manner. (The stone in the first gives good footing when wet, a point on which the second may be faulted.)

I find the first cold and forbidding. The second is warm and inviting. I think it will endure.

Salamanca

APPENDICES

RESOURCES AT CARFREE.COM

Via Volte, Ferrara

BIBLIOGRAPHY

The bibliography is not exhaustive; a few works are cited only in the one or two places where they are referenced.

Adam, Robert. *Classical Architecture: A Comprehensive Handbook to the Tradition of Classical Style.* New York: Harry N. Abrams, 1990.

Alberti, Leon Battista. *On the Art of Building in Ten Books.* Cambridge: MIT Press, 1988.

Alexander, Christopher. *The Nature of Order, Books I-IV* [referenced as "TNO"]. Berkeley: The Center for Environmental Structure, 2002-2005.

——. *The Timeless Way of Building.* New York: Oxford University Press, 1979.

—— et al. *A New Theory of Urban Design.* New York: Oxford University Press, 1987.

—— et al. *A Pattern Language: Towns, Buildings, Construction* [referenced as "APL"]. New York: Oxford University Press, 1977.

—— et al. *The Production of Houses.* New York: Oxford University Press, 1985.

Appleyard, Donald et al. *Livable Streets.* Berkeley: University of California Press, 1981.

Bacon, Edmund N. *Design of Cities.* New York: Penguin Books, revised edition, 1974.

Brand, Stewart. *How Buildings Learn: What Happens After They're Built.* New York: Penguin Books, 1994.

Calthorpe, Peter. *The Next American Metropolis: Ecology, Community, and the American Dream.* New York: Princeton Architectural Press, 1993.

Campoli, Julie, and Alex S. MacLean. *Visualizing Density.* Cambridge: Lincoln Institute of Land Policy, 2007.

Ching, Francis D.K. *Architecture: Form, Space and Order.* New York: Van Nostrand Reinhold, 1979.

——. *Building Construction Illustrated.* New York: Van Nostrand Reinhold, 1975.

Cole, Emily (ed). *The Grammar of Architecture.* Boston: Bullfinch Press/Little, Brown, 2002.

Crawford, J.H. *Carfree Cities.* Utrecht: International Books, 2000.

Delfante, Charles. *A Grande História da Cidade.* Lisbon: Instituto Piaget, 1997; trans. *Grande Histoire de la Ville.*

Dorling Kindersley. *Venice and the Veneto.* London: Dorling Kindersley, frequently revised.

Duany, Andrés, and Elizabeth Plater-Zyberk. *Towns and Town-Making Principles.* New York: Rizzoli, 1991.

Fathy, Hassan. *Architecture for the Poor: An Experiment in Rural Egypt.* Chicago: University of Chicago Press, 1973.

Fouchier, Vincent. *Les densités urbaines et le développement durable. Le cas de l'Île-de-France et des villes nouvelles.* Edition du SGVN, Secrétariat Général du Groupe Central des Villes Nouvelles, 1997.

——. "Mesuring [sic] the Density: But Which Density??" Paper presented at the Norwegian Ministry of Environment, Workshop on "Density and Green Structure," Oslo, 25-27 January 1996. The density figures given on page 10 of this paper were taken from *Dense Cité*, M.O.S. and I.N.S.E.E., 1990 or 1995 (dates conflict within the source and may refer to different editions).

Gatto, John Taylor. *Dumbing Us Down: The Hidden Curriculum of Compulsory Schooling.* Gabriola Island, B.C.: New Society Publishers, 1992.

Gehl, Jan, and Lars Gemzøe. *Public Spaces—Public Life.* Copenhagen: The Danish Architectural Press et al., 1996.

Goddard, Stephen B. *Getting There: The Epic Struggle between Road and Rail in the American Century.* New York: Basic Books, 1994.

Hale, Jonathan. *The Old Way of Seeing: How Architecture Lost Its Magic (And How To Get It Back).* Boston: Houghton Mifflin, 1994.

Hall, Peter. *Cities of Tomorrow: An Intellectual History of Urban Planning and Design in the Twentieth Century.* Oxford: Blackwell, 1988.

Institute for Community Economics. *The Community Land Trust Handbook.* Emmaus, Pennsylvania: Rodale Press, 1982.

Jacobs, Allan B. *Great Streets.* Cambridge: MIT Press, 1993, paperback edition.

———, Elizabeth Macdonald, and Yodan Rofé. *The Boulevard Book: History, Evolution, Design of Multiway Boulevards.* Cambridge: MIT Press, 2002.

Jacobs, Jane. *Cities and the Wealth of Nations: Principles of Economic Life.* New York: Vintage Books, 1985.

———. *The Death and Life of Great American Cities.* New York: Vintage Books, 1992, first pub. 1961.

Jackson, Kenneth T. *Crabgrass Frontier: The Suburbanization of the United States.* New York: Oxford University Press, 1985.

Katz, Peter. *The New Urbanism: Toward an Architecture of Community.* New York: McGraw-Hill, 1994.

Kay, Jane Holtz. *Asphalt Nation: How the Automobile Took Over America and How We Can Take It Back.* New York: Crown Press, 1997.

Kelbaugh, Doug (ed). *The Pedestrian Pocket Book.* New York: Princeton Architectural Press, 1989.

Knopf Guides. *Venice.* New York: Alfred A. Knopf, frequently revised.

Kostof, Spiro. *The City Assembled: The Elements of Urban Form Through History.* London: Thames and Hudson, 1992.

———. *The City Shaped: Urban Patterns and Meanings Through History.* London: Thames and Hudson, 1991.

Krier, Léon. *Architecture: Choice or Fate.* Windsor, UK: Andreas Papadakis, 1998.

Krier, Rob. *Town Spaces.* Basel: Birkhäuser, 2003.

———. *Urban Space.* New York: Rizzoli, 1979; first pub., London: Academy Editions, 1979.

Kunstler, James Howard. *The Geography of Nowhere: The Rise and Decline of America's Man-Made Landscape.* New York: Simon & Schuster, 1993.

———. *Home From Nowhere: Remaking Our Everyday World for the Twenty-First Century.* New York: Simon & Schuster, 1996.

Kushner, James A. *Comparative Urban Planning Law: An Introduction to Urban Land Development Law in the United States through the Lens of Comparing the Experience of Other Nations.* Durham, NC: Carolina Academic Press, 2003.

———. *The Post-Automobile City: Legal Mechanisms to Establish the Pedestrian-Friendly City.* Durham, NC: Carolina Academic Press, 2004.

Larkin, Jack. *Where We Lived: Discovering the Places We Once Called Home.* Newtown, CT: Taunton Press, 2006.

Lennard, Suzanne H. Crowhurst, Sven von Ungern-Sternberg, and Henry L. Lennard (eds.). *Making Cities Livable.* Carmel, CA: Gondolier Press, 1997.

Lynch, Kevin. *The Image of the City.* Cambridge: MIT Press, 1960.

———. *Managing the Sense of a Region.* Cambridge: MIT Press, 1976.

———, and Gary Hack. *Site Planning.* Cambridge: MIT Press, third edition, 1984.

Marshall, Stephen. *Streets and Patterns.* London: Spon Press, 2005.

McCamant, Kathryn, and Charles Durrett. *Cohousing: A Contemporary Approach to Housing Ourselves.* Berkeley: Habitat Press, 1988.

McShane, Clay. *Down the Asphalt Path: The Automobile and the American City.* New York: Columbia University Press, 1994.

Moe, Richard, and Carter Wilkie. *Changing Places: Rebuilding Community in the Age of Sprawl.* New York: Henry Holt, 1997.

Morris, A.E.J. *History of Urban Form: Prehistory to the Renaissance.* New York: John Wiley & Sons, 1972.

Moughtin, Cliff. *Urban Design: Street and Square.* Oxford: Architectural Press, third edition, 2003.

Oliver, Paul. *Dwellings: The Vernacular House World Wide.* London: Phaidon Press, 2003.

Olsen, Donald J. *The City as a Work of Art: London, Paris, Vienna.* New Haven: Yale University Press, 1986.

Pevsner, Nikolaus. *The Sources of Modern Architecture and Design.* London: Thames and Hudson, 1968.

Pirenne, Henri. *Medieval Cities: Their Origins and the Revival of Trade.* Princeton: Princeton University Press, 1925, paperback edition of 1969.

Pirsig, Robert M. *Zen and the Art of Motorcycle Maintenance: An Inquiry into Values.* (Page numbers refer to the 1984 Bantam revised mass-market paperback edition.)

Reid, Richard. *The Book of Buildings: Ancient, Medieval, Renaissance and Modern Architecture of North America and Europe.* New York: Van Nostrand Reinhold, 1983.

Rudofsky, Bernard. *Architecture Without Architects: A Short Introduction to Non-Pedigreed Architecture.* New York: Doubleday, 1964.

Safdie, Moshe with Wendy Kohn. *The City After the Automobile: An Architect's Vision.* New York: Basic Books, 1997.

Salingaros, Nikos A. *Anti-Architecture and Deconstruction.* Solingen: Umbau-Verlag, 2004.

——. "Complexity and Urban Coherence," in *Principles of Urban Structure.* Amsterdam: Techne, 2005.

——. "Connecting the Fractal City" (Keynote speech, 5th Biennial of towns and town planners in Europe, Barcelona, April 2003). PDF from: applied.math.utsa.edu/~salingar/connecting.html.

Sitte, Camillo. *City Planning According to Artistic Principles.* New York: Random House, 1965; first edition *Der Städtebau nach seinen künstlerischen Grundsätzen,* Vienna, 1889. Translated by George R. Collins and Christiane Crasemann Collins.

Southworth, Michael, and Eran Ben-Joseph. *Streets and the Shaping of Towns and Cities.* New York: McGraw-Hill, 1997.

Steen, Athena, Bill Steen, and Eiko Komatsu. *Built by Hand: Vernacular Buildings around the World.* Salt Lake City, UT: Gibbs Smith, 2003.

Taylor, John S. *Commonsense Architecture: A Cross-Cultural Survey of Practical Design Principles.* New York: W.W. Norton, 1983.

Unwin, Raymond. *Town Planning in Practice: An Introduction to the Art of Designing Cities and Suburbs.* London: T. Fisher Unwin, revised edition, 1911; page numbers refer to Princeton Architectural Press facsimile edition of 1994.

Urban Design Associates. *The Architectural Pattern Book: A Tool for Building Great Neighborhoods.* New York: W.W. Norton, 2004.

Van der Ryn, Sim, and Peter Calthorpe. *Sustainable Communities: A New Design Synthesis for Cities, Suburbs, and Towns.* San Francisco: Sierra Club Books, 1986.

Van Lengen, Johan. *The Barefoot Architect.* Bolinas, CA: Shelter Publications, 2008.

Watson, Donald, Alan Plattus, and Robert G. Shibley (eds). *Time-Saver Standards for Urban Design.* New York: McGraw-Hill, 2003.

Whittick, Arnold (ed). *Encyclopedia of Urban Planning.* New York: McGraw-Hill, 1974.

Whyte, William H. *City: Rediscovering the Center.* New York: Anchor Books, 1988.

——. *The Social Life of Small Urban Spaces.* Washington DC: The Conservation Foundation, 1980.

Wilde, Oscar. *De Profundis.* London: Penguin, 1973.

Wolfe, Tom. *From Bauhaus to Our House.* New York: Farrar Straus Giroux, 1981.

Wölfflin, Heinrich. *Renaissance and Baroque.* Ithaca, NY: Cornell University Press, 1966. Translated by Kathrin Simon.

Wycherley, R.E. *How the Greeks Built Cities.* New York: W.W. Norton, 1962, second edition, 1976.

Zucker, Paul. *Town and Square: From the Agora to the Village Green.* New York: Columbia University Press, 1959.

Zuckermann, Wolfgang. *End of the Road.* Post Mills, VT: Chelsea Green Publishing, 1991.

INTERNET RESOURCES

Internet sources may disappear or be relocated. URLs were current at press time. Carfree.com maintains a list of about 500 links, sorted into more than a dozen categories. As far as I have ever been aware, it is not necessary to type in the "http://" or "https://" at the beginning of a URL, so I have omitted this when giving URLs.

www.vtpi.org/	Victoria Transport Policy Institute
www.rudi.net/	RUDI (Resource for Urban Design Information)
www.pps.org/	Project for Public Spaces
www.intbau.org/	International Network for Traditional Building, Architecture & Urbanism
www.terrain.org/	Terrain: A Journal of the Built & Natural Environments
www.carfree.com/	Carfree.com
www.ecoplan.org/	EcoPlan International, host of The Commons, a sustainability workgroup
www.transact.org/	Transportation Action Network, source of the annual Mean Streets report
www.kunstler.com/	James Howard Kunstler
www.cyburbia.org/	Cyburbia: The Planning and Architecture Internet Resource Center
www.living-room.org/	The Living Room, see sprawl- and environment-related sections
www.worldwatch.org/	Worldwatch Institute
www.jhcrawford.com/	Home page of author J.H. Crawford
www.worldcarfree.net	World Carfree Network
www.carfree.com/cdm	Carfree Design Manual (site for this book)
www.newcolonist.com/	The New Colonist
www.preservenet.com/	The Preservation Institute
www.fhwa.dot.gov/tcsp/	Transportation, Community, and System Preservation Program
www.plannersweb.com/	Planning Commissioners Journal
www.istp.murdoch.edu.au/	The Institute for Science and Technology Policy (ISTP)
www.sierraclub.org/sprawl/	Highway and Sprawlbusters at the Sierra Club
www.patternlanguage.com/	Pattern Language on line
www.katarxis-publications.com/	Katarxis: On Contemporary Traditional Architecture and Urbanism

DRAWINGS

Some drawings were carried over from *Carfree Cities,* and these were originally prepared in Adobe Illustrator, most of them by Arin Verner and some by myself. Drawings that are new to this work were prepared by me, also in Illustrator.

PHOTOGRAPHS

The photographic techniques used in making the images in this book are described on Carfree.com at: www.carfree.com/cdm/photo.html

HISTORICAL PHOTOGRAPHS

The historical photographs were scanned from postcards printed around 1900 (with a few as late as 1930). In no case is the photographer known. Some damaged images were repaired in Photoshop. Some were cropped, but I did no other retouching.

Photographs have been retouched almost from the beginning of photography, and many of the postcards were retouched by their original producers. At that time, clouds were difficult to record on negatives, and they were often added later. Various other changes were sometimes made.

LIST OF PHOTOGRAPHS

My thanks to those who contributed photographs to this work. Locations and copyright information are given below. It may help to know, when searching for a city, that nearly all images are from Europe

2	Venice, Salizzada San Rocco	© 2005	J.Crawford
9	Basel, oversquare street	© 2002	J.Crawford
9	Valladolid, gallery	© 2005	J.Crawford
9	Bologna, arcade	© 1998	J.Crawford
11	Cascais, Alameda da Guia	© 2005	J.Crawford
11	Madrid, intersection	© 2005	J.Crawford
12	Venice, St. Mark's Basilica	© 1997	J.Crawford
13	Ravenna, Via Diaz	© 2002	J.Crawford
15	Ferrara, Via San Romano	© 2002	J.Crawford
16	Madrid, curved street	© 2005	J.Crawford
16	Spain, Ayamonte, main square	© 2005	J.Crawford
17	Portugal, Faro, forking streets	© 2005	J.Crawford
18	Livingston, NJ, New Urbanism	© 2007	J.Crawford
18	Portugal, Guimarães, small square	© 2005	J.Crawford
19	Portugal, Guimarães, narrow street	© 2005	J.Crawford
20	Madrid, street intersection	© 2005	J.Crawford
20	Salamanca, narrow main street	© 2005	J.Crawford
21	Valladolid, Plaza Mayor	© 2005	J.Crawford
21	Madrid, arched passageway	© 2005	J.Crawford
22	Lisbon, fountain	© 1998	J.Crawford
22	Paris, Boulevard Saint Martin	c. 1900	anon
23	Madrid, near Plaza Mayor	© 2005	J.Crawford
23	Salamanca, square	© 2005	J.Crawford
24	Ferrara, Piazza Trento e Trieste	© 2002	J.Crawford
25	Basel, Central Station	© 2002	J.Crawford
26	Salamanca, near Plaza Mayor	© 2005	J.Crawford
26	Venice, curved narrow street	© 2001	J.Crawford
27	Valladolid, major street	© 2005	J.Crawford
27	Salamanca, Calle de la Compañía	© 2005	J.Crawford
28	Ferrara, Via San Romano	© 2002	J.Crawford
29	Venice, near Piazza San Marco	© 2001	J.Crawford
29	Salamanca, Plaza de las Agustinas	© 2005	J.Crawford
31	Coimbra, street & arch	© 2005	J.Crawford
32	Madrid, restaurant	© 2005	J.Crawford
33	Trevi, church	© 2002	J.Crawford
34	Venice, social housing	© 2001	J.Crawford
37	Salamanca, Calle de las Velas	© 2005	J.Crawford
38	Athens, the Acropolis in 5 BC	© 2004	Gavin Zeno Watson
38	Venice, Lido congress hall	© 2005	J.Crawford
40	Madrid buildings	© 2005	J.Crawford
41	Fractal food		John Walker
41	Alfama, vernacular buildings	© 2005	J.Crawford
44	Coimbra, Praça 8 de Maio	© 2005	J.Crawford
45	Perugia, Piazza Lupattelli	© 2002	J.Crawford
47	Venice, hotel	© 2005	J.Crawford
48	Portugal, Faro, deep organization	© 2005	J.Crawford
49	Fes-al-Bali, Bab Boujeloud	© 2002	J.Crawford
49	Amsterdam, GWL project	© 1997	J.Crawford
50	Venice, Campo San Zulian	© 2001	J.Crawford
50	Houten, town square	© 1997	J.Crawford
50	Manhattan, intersection	© 1999	J.Crawford
51	Manhattan, West 57th Street	© 1999	J.Crawford
52	Venice, Campo San Rocco	© 2001	J.Crawford
52	Los Angeles, strip mall	© 1999	Richard Risemberg
53	Los Angeles, megastore	© 1999	Richard Risemberg
53	Amsterdam, high-rise	© 1999	J.Crawford
54	Los Angeles, Hollywood Boulevard	© 1999	Richard Risemberg
54	Lisbon, Alfama roofs	© 2005	J.Crawford
54	Porto, modern poverty	© 2005	J.Crawford
55	Cologne, cathedral interior	© 2002	J.Crawford
55	Amsterdam, Zuiderkerk	© 1999	J.Crawford
55	Lisbon, Alfama houses	© 2004	J.Crawford
56	Fes, doors	© 2002	J.Crawford
56	Lisbon, Art Nouveau portal	© 2003	J.Crawford
57	Cascais, repetitive building elements	© 2004	J.Crawford
57	Amsterdam, Begijnhof	© 1997	J.Crawford
58	Nancy, Hémicycle de la Carrière	c. 1900	anon
58	Parma, Strada Cavour	© 1998	J.Crawford
58	Los Angeles, Hollywood Freeway	© 1999	Jack Risemberg
59	Basel, Petersgasse	© 2002	J.Crawford
59	Amsterdam Zuidoost, straight street	© 2004	J.Crawford
59	Portugal, Braga, trees	© 2005	J.Crawford
60	Venice, Salizzada San Samuele	© 2001	J.Crawford
60	Óbidos, residential street	© 2006	J.Crawford
61	Amsterdam, ABN Bank	© 1999	J.Crawford
61	Groningen, ecohouses	© 1997	J.Crawford
61	Parma, Piazza della Pilotta	© 1998	J.Crawford
62	Venice, cathedral	© 2001	J.Crawford
62	Venice, Calle della Passione	© 2001	J.Crawford
62	Los Angeles, "sophisticated" office	c. 1990	anon
63	Amsterdam, Amstelplein	© 2003	J.Crawford
63	Strasbourg, Rue du Bain aux Plantes	© 1997	J.Crawford

The Author

J.H. Crawford was born and raised in North America. From the age of seven he lived within the orbit of New York City, except for two spells in the Town of Mount Royal, a railroad suburb of Montréal. As a youth, he traveled by train and bicycle through a Europe still relatively free of cars. He later traveled widely in North America, Asia, and Europe. He moved to Europe in 1990, dividing his time between Amsterdam and Lisbon. He was called home in 2006 to manage family problems caused by a car crash and finished this book while living in upstate New York.

His university education was in the liberal arts, although he delved into science, architecture, and engineering as a youth. After taking a few years off to sail and to photograph George McGovern's 1972 run for the US presidency, he went back to school for a master's degree in social work. For three years in the late 1970s, he provided child welfare services to families and children. During those years, he learned much about the poor and downtrodden. The grim reality of their lives made a lasting impression on him.

In 1979, as public transport ombudsman for the New Jersey Department of Transportation, a statewide bus and rail operator, he learned about most aspects of public transport operation during the course of investigating customer complaints.

In the early 1980s, he consulted with resorts in coastal South Carolina. Typical of these resorts is Sea Pines, on Hilton Head Island. This planned beachfront golfing community includes a mix of houses, apartment buildings, restaurants, stores, and activities. Harbour Town, a small, dense community built around a circular boat basin dredged out of the island, includes a carfree quayside promenade around the harbor, which is fronted by multi-story condominiums that are some of the most desirable housing on the island. In season and out, people gathered there, despite an entrance fee for nonresidents.

While working in South Carolina, he discovered Christopher Alexander's *A Pattern Language,* a work that provided the theoretical basis for understanding the popularity of communities with a carfree component, such as Harbour Town. He began thinking about the urban form in the context of Alexander's patterns and soon realized that high-quality urban life was impossible while cars still ruled the streets and occupied so much land. This eventually led to the development of his first sketches of carfree city forms.

Between 1983 and 1985, he managed projects for a robotics systems developer that specialized in the automated handling of standardized shipping containers. He saw that the universal adoption of a single standard for these containers had yielded an ideal method for shipping and storing freight.

Since 1985 he has taken assignments as a software developer, designer, planning consultant, university lecturer, public speaker, photographer, editor, and writer. *Carfree Cities,* his first book, appeared in 2000.

Ordering information for *Carfree Cities* and for *Carfree Design Manual* can be found on the Internet at: www.carfree.com